ADVANCE PRAISE FOR **Doing Democracy**

"In this era of neoliberal capitalism, democracy has been under siege. Used as a cover for imperialist policies and practices, and primed for the interests of the transnational capitalist class, the concept and exercise of democracy can no longer be taken for granted. A timely examination of the question of democracy has finally arrived in this outstanding new text by Darren E. Lund and Paul R. Carr. *Doing Democracy: Striving for Political Literacy and Social Justice* will prove to be an indispensable work for teachers, students, and cultural workers everywhere who are struggling for a deepening of democracy, and for freeing democracy from the chains of capital. This is an important examination of the question of democracy, a powerful and erudite new work that should be welcomed by progressive educators everywhere."

Peter McLaren, Professor, Graduate School of Education and Information Studies,
University of California, Los Angeles

"*Doing Democracy* is an essential resource for teacher educators, policymakers, pre-service and in-service teachers, administrators, and anyone concerned with rebuilding our educational institutions so that they serve as beacons for personal and social transformation, rather than function to produce compliant, docile citizens who passively adhere to the dominant ideologies and structures propagated to support the interests of the political and economic elite. ...Several provocative essays from leading scholars and educators...gauge the value of various forms of democracy espoused by educators, philosophers, and politicians alike. Other contributors configure innovative research designs, generate pedagogical initiatives, and tap theoretical insights in order to highlight the institutional barriers that must be subverted to ensure that political literacy and social justice resonate loudly across educational institutions, as well as in other social contexts, to provide effective strategies for doing democracy in...schools. This book will undoubtedly become a chief guidepost for future debates, research, and reflection on what steps must be taken to foster a shared vision of democracy in both formal and informal schooling structures, one that is capable of bringing people to work collectively to eliminate institutional forms of oppression and the myriad social problems breeding hate, hostility, and environmental degradation across the global landscape at today's historical juncture."

Brad J. Porfilio, Assistant Professor, Department of Educational Studies,
Saint Louis University

MORE ADVANCE PRAISE FOR *Doing Democracy*

"Darren E. Lund and Paul R. Carr, in concert with their contributors, have provided a rich synthesis drawn from a number of too-often disparate fields represented by democratic studies, critical pedagogy, teacher education, global studies, moral education, civic education, and social justice education. The result is a comprehensive and major contribution by which they have, with discernment and verve, managed two difficult tasks: A solid combination of depth with breadth and a reduction of the distance between theory and practice. I look forward to using *Doing Democracy* as a text in my democracy and education courses."

Tom Wilson, Director, Paulo Freire Democratic Project, Chapman University

Doing Democracy

Studies in the
Postmodern Theory of Education

Joe L. Kincheloe and Shirley R. Steinberg
General Editors

Vol. 322

PETER LANG
New York • Washington, D.C./Baltimore • Bern
Frankfurt am Main • Berlin • Brussels • Vienna • Oxford

Doing Democracy

Striving for Political Literacy and Social Justice

Edited by Darren E. Lund and Paul R. Carr

PETER LANG
New York • Washington, D.C./Baltimore • Bern
Frankfurt am Main • Berlin • Brussels • Vienna • Oxford

Library of Congress Cataloging-in-Publication Data

Doing democracy: striving for political literacy and social justice /
edited by Darren E. Lund, Paul R. Carr.
p. cm. — (Counterpoints: studies in the postmodern theory of education; v. 322)
Includes bibliographical references and index.
1. Citizenship—Study and teaching. 2. Democracy—Study and teaching.
3. Social justice. I. Lund, Darren E. II. Carr, Paul R.
LC1091.D65   370.11'5—dc22   2008003851
ISBN 978-1-4331-0343-8 (hardcover)
ISBN 978-0-8204-9745-7 (paperback)
ISSN 1058-1634

Bibliographic information published by **Die Deutsche Bibliothek**.
Die Deutsche Bibliothek lists this publication in the "Deutsche
Nationalbibliografie"; detailed bibliographic data is available
on the Internet at http://dnb.ddb.de/.

Cover photographs by Wim van Passel (*www.tijdlozemomenten.nl*)

The paper in this book meets the guidelines for permanence and durability
of the Committee on Production Guidelines for Book Longevity
of the Council of Library Resources.

© 2008 Peter Lang Publishing, Inc., New York
29 Broadway, 18th floor, New York, NY 10006
www.peterlang.com

Printed in the United States of America

TABLE OF CONTENTS

SECTION IV: TEACHING ABOUT AND FOR DEMOCRACY

SECTION V: AFTERWORD

ACKNOWLEDGMENTS

The experience of editing this book has proved to be rich and productive, both in terms of academic development and friendship. This is the second book we have co-edited, the first being *The Great White North? Exploring Whiteness, Privilege and Identity in Education*, published by Sense Publishers in 2007. A number of people have been influential and supportive throughout the conceptualization and writing of this book, and we would like to acknowledge the following people in particular: Joe Kincheloe and Shirley Steinberg, for their inspiration and guidance; James Banks and Daniel Schugurensky, for generously agreeing to write the Foreword and Afterword, respectively, and for their years of work within the area of democratic education; and George Sefa Dei, for his clarion ideas and humility, which have been indispensable in shaping the thoughts of both of the co-editors. The genesis of this project flows from the works of Paulo Freire and all those who continue to interrogate and extend a critical assessment of democracy.

Darren: I would like to acknowledge all of my supportive colleagues, staff and graduate students in the Faculty of Education at the University of Calgary. I especially acknowledge Dr. Ann Sherman, Vice-Dean, and Dr. Hans Smits, Associate Dean, for their solid and enthusiastic support. I am most grateful for a loving and understanding family, good friends, and a robust community of activists that continues to inspire me in this work. Not inconsequentially, I also enjoy the ongoing services of some amazing legal advisors—namely Robert, Ron, April, Linda, Megan and Sarah—without whose wisdom, encouragement and generosity of spirit I would not have withstood recent turbulence in my human rights work.

Paul: I would like to acknowledge the following persons: three of my colleagues at Youngstown State University—Rich Baringer, Chuck Vergon and Gunapala Edirisooriya—who have been extremely supportive of my research; the doctoral students at YSU, who have challenged me to think through numerous issues discussed in the book; Mike Bettross, assisted in the coordination of numerous aspects of this book; Carl James, of York University, for his support over the years; Marc Tardif, for being a wonderful friend, and a constant source of support; my family, especially my parents

(Chris and Bob), my Haitian family (Wes and Cleo), my daughters (Chelsea and Sarah), Nat and Tudor, and our wonderful Noah; and Gina, who has sparked a thousand fires, which have ignited my thinking around the meaning of social justice.

Pulling together the various components of the book, especially the chapters that form the core, has required the collaboration and support of all of the contributors, and we are grateful for their dedication to this project. Interacting with people on four continents, we are pleased that the editorial process functioned in such a positive and relatively seamless manner. We are grateful to our friend, Wim van Passel, photographer and humanitarian (see http://www.tijdlozemomenten.nl), who has graciously provided the photographic beauty for this book, as he did for our first book. We would like to thank the excellent staff at Peter Lang—especially Valerie Best, Sophie Appel and Chris Myers—who have provided insightful support throughout the project. Lastly, we are indebted to James Dittrich for meticulously formatting and aligning myriad details in order to turn the manuscript into a book.

James A. Banks

This book is designed to help educators conceptualize, design, and implement democratic education within the context of diversity and social justice in classrooms and schools. It is timely and needed because of the increasing racial, ethnic, cultural, linguistic, and religious diversity in nations around the world that is caused by international migration. Although migration and interaction among nations have existed since nations first came in contact through trade and exploration, never before in the history of the world has international migration been as extensive and continuous.

The number of people living outside their country of birth or citizenship grew from 120 million in 1990 to 160 million in 2000 (Martin & Widgren, 2002). There were nearly 20 million refugees and asylum seekers in the world in 2004 (Benhabib, 2004). International migration is not limited to movement from southern hemisphere nations to the wealthy nations in the northern hemisphere. Many migrants as well as most refugees settle within neighboring nations in the southern hemisphere.

The large number of people from diverse groups who are now living in the Western democratic nation states are challenging institutionalized notions of democracy, social justice, and citizenship. Historically in democratic nation states such as the United States, Canada, and Australia the goal of state schools was to create citizens who idealized the nation and its heroes and developed allegiance to the nation and its founding myths. Another goal of state schools was to assimilate children from diverse groups so that they would become culturally Anglo Saxons. In this process of becoming citizens of the nation-state, cultural, language, and ethnic minority students experienced self-alienation from their home and community cultures (Lomawaima & McCarty, 2006). Greenbaum (1974) states that in schools in the United States immigrant children learned shame and hope. They learned to be ashamed of their home and community cultures but were given hope that once they became culturally Anglo Saxons they would be able to attain social and economic mobility. This assimilationist idea was largely successful for most White immigrants to the United States (Jacobson, 1998). However, Americans of color remained structurally excluded even when they experienced high levels of cultural assimilation (Gordon, 1964).

Because of growing ethnic, cultural, racial, linguistic, and religious diversity throughout the world, citizenship education needs to be transformed so that it will prepare students to function effectively within their home and community cultures, their nation state, region, and within the world community. Students should not have to become alienated from or to surrender their home and community cultures and languages in order to participate fully in the national civic culture.

Democratic nation states should provide their citizens with cultural, language, and religious options, and diversity and unity should co-exist in a delicate balance. Unity without diversity results in cultural repression and hegemony. Diversity without unity leads to Balkanization and the fracturing of the nation-state (Banks, 2007). The attainment of the balance that is needed between diversity and unity is an ongoing process and ideal that is never fully attained. It is essential that both mainstream groups and groups on the margins of society participate in the formulation of societal goals related to diversity and unity. Both groups should also participate in action to attain these goals. Deliberation and the sharing of power by mainstream and marginalized groups are essential for the construction and perpetuation of a just, moral, and participatory democratic nation-state in a culturally diverse society.

Citizens in the 21st century need the knowledge, attitudes, and skills required to function in their cultural communities and beyond their cultural borders. They should also be able and willing to participate in the construction of a national civic culture that is a moral and just community. The national community of pluralistic nation states should embody democratic ideals and values, such as those articulated in the Universal Declaration of Human Rights, the Geneva Conventions, and the United States Constitution. Students also need to acquire the knowledge and skills required to become effective citizens in the global community.

While students need to acquire the knowledge, attitudes, and skills needed to become effective global citizens, nationalism is as strong as ever xiii

and poses serious challenges to educating citizens who have global
commitments and cosmopolitan values and behaviors. Both nationalism and
globalization are increasing and sometimes conflicting forces in the world.
The number of nations in the world is increasing rather than decreasing: The
number of United Nations member states increased from 51 in 1945 to 191 in
2002 (www.un.org).

The challenge for democratic citizenship education within multicultural
nation states is to help students develop balanced commitments to their
community, nation, region, and the global community. Nussbaum (2002)
believes that cosmopolitan citizens can maintain local identifications "which
can be a source of great richness life" (p. 9). Appiah (2006) also views local
identifications as an important anchor for cosmopolitan citizens.
Assimilationists worry that if students develop global commitments they will
have weak identifications with their nation states. However, because
identifications are interconnected, contextual, and complex, people are
capable of having thoughtful commitments to their cultural communities,
nation, and the global community.

To become effective citizens in a global world, students need to develop
decision-making skills as well as the skills needed to take action to make
their communities, the nation, and the world just and humane places in which
to live and work. To take thoughtful and effective civic action, students must
synthesize knowledge and values and take action that is consistent with
democratic values (Banks, 2006). A thoughtful and critical conception of
citizenship education can help to advance democracy and social justice in
classrooms and schools around the world.

References

Appiah, K. A. (2006). *Cosmopolitanism: Ethnics in a world of strangers*. New York: Norton.
Banks, J. A. (2006). *Race, culture, and education: The selected works of James A. Banks*.
    London & New York: Routledge.
Banks, J. A. (2007). *Educating citizens in a multicultural society (2nd ed.)*. New York: Teach-
    ers College Press.
Benhabib, S. (2004). *The rights of others: Aliens, residents and citizens*. New York: Cam-
    bridge University Press.

Gordon, M. M. (1964). *Assimilation in American life: The role of race, religion, and national origins*. New York: Oxford University Press.

Greenbaum, W. (1974). America in search of a new ideal: An essay on the rise of pluralism. *Harvard Educational Review, 44*, 411-440.

Jacobson, M. F. (1998). *Whiteness of a different color: European immigrants and the alchemy of race*. Cambridge: Harvard University Press.

Lomawaima, K. T., & McCarty, T. L. (2006). *"To remain an Indian:" Lessons in democracy from a century of Native American education*. New York: Teachers College Press.

Martin, P., & Widgren, J. (2002). International Migration: Facing the challenge. *Population Reference Bulletin, 57*, No. 1. Washington, DC: Population Reference Bureau.

Nussbaum, M. (2002). Patriotism and cosmopolitanism. In J. Cohen (Ed.), *For love of country* (pp. 2-17). Boston: Beacon Press.

INTRODUCTION: SCANNING DEMOCRACY

Darren E. Lund and Paul R. Carr

Democracy as More than Elections

A book about democracy that does not focus on elections? Could there be democracy without elections? Without political parties? Without the vociferously intense strain of the media spotlight, advertisements, and staged encounters with the candidates? Without all of the infrastructure that maintains the commonly accepted notion of legitimate, representative democracy via the electoral process?

The starting point for this book is that the democratic experience does, and must, surpass the obsession with the electoral politics that pervade the public psyche. We maintain that, for democracy to be meaningful and tangible, it must be connected to education as well as social justice (Chomsky, 2003; Dewey, 1964; Portelli & Solomon, 2001). A democracy that does not discourage (or is ambivalent about) racism, sexism, homophobia, homelessness, poverty, religious/linguistic/ethnic discrimination, and the torment of macro- and micro-level legislation or government polices that further marginalize individuals and groups must be taken to task (Banks et al., 2005). In other words, apart from the all-consuming electoral periods—which seem to stretch virtually from one election to the next—and which, inevitably, consume precious resources while diverting attention from serious problems, there need to be broad entry points in which average citizens can partake in the democratic experience (Demaine, 2004).

Paulo Freire (1973), in his seminal *Pedagogy of the Oppressed*, addresses the political nature of education and emphasizes the core elements of power and inequitable power relations that constitute a force in conceptualizing political literacy and transformational change in education. Although it may not be promoted on the nightly news or in mainstream media sources, students, workers, citizens, groups, associations, and myriad other groupings in society can, and must, engage themselves, to varying degrees, in politics, attempting to have their voices heard, to change society, and to present alternatives that may not be readily recognized as standard, "textbook" democracy. Through their collective efforts, which may not be synchronized with the formal, elite-centered democratic notion of freedom and equality, people are able to effect some measure of change in their lives. The passive acceptance of majority rule from above can also have the effect of constraining and pacifying the public. Since the lens of formal democracy is often focused on formal structures and events, it is questionable how education is, and should be, immersed in shaping the political, economic, and cultural life of society, especially in relation to democratic participation and engagement (Portelli & Solomon, 2001).

From our vantage point, elections constitute but a small part of democracy. For many, elections are about limited numbers of people, often elites with well-connected and sophisticated political machines, jockeying for power, submerged in what many consider to be questionable campaign practices, often cavorting with select special interests that support causes that effectively go against the interests of those without influence. Clearly, media coverage of candidates and parties, which is arguably extremely limited, biased, and programmed, is inadequate in relation to nourishing public debate (Herman & Chomsky, 2002). Democracy is about more than two sides of a coin, interlocked in a dual of talking heads, each aiming to denigrate the position of the other. While elections certainly have a place in democracy, this book challenges the commonly held assumption that they are the most fundamental part of the equation (Carr, 2007). We do, however, recognize that one of the driving concerns behind contemporary discussions about democracy in education, or democratic education, is hinged on the comparatively lower voter participation rates of young people in elections (Cook, 2004; Patterson, 2003), which raises questions about formal political engagement (Galston, 2003).

Framing the Focus of the Book

We approach this project with the firm belief that democracy needs to be cultivated, critiqued, demonstrated, and manifested throughout the educational experience (Dewey, 1964; Westheimer & Kahne, 2004). Our concern is principally with how we actually *do*, or *should do*, democracy in education. Do we know how to *do* democracy, how to talk about it, how to engage with it, and how to accept, as Schugurensky (2000) has argued, that it is more of a work in progress than a fixed object that we have achieved? Is democracy merely something that is isolated to a singular course or discipline, often bottled up within social studies or civics? Following Parker (2003), we argue that democracy needs to be infused in everything that happens at school, from the curriculum to the extracurricular activities, through the formal organization and structures, including interaction with parents and communities and also comprising the infinite number of issues that blend into the realms of decision making, participation, and shaping the identity, culture, and outcomes of the educational experience. At the theoretical level, Gandin and Apple (2005) have hypothesized that, building on the work of Barber (1984), there are *thick* and *thin* notions of democracy, and teaching about and for the latter generally avoids doing critical work and engagement destined to reinforce democracy. Our interpretation of democracy in education seeks to embrace the *thicker* elements of sociopolitical democratic engagement, participation, and educational experience.

Our project related to how to *do* democracy in education overlaps with the work of Kurth-Schai and Green (2006) who, in their book *Re-envisioning Education and Democracy*, present several pivotal questions:

- Given the importance afforded throughout our history to foundational concepts of "education" and "democracy," why does the gap between our aspirations and our achievement persist?

- Given the dimensions and dynamics of contemporary social and educational concerns, what, beyond rational problem solving, is necessary?

- Given the prevailing philosophic and pragmatic commitments to individualism, what is the meaning and purpose of social learning?

- Given the costs and consequences of failure, how can we responsibly risk innovation in an increasingly dangerous world?

Kurth-Schai and Green (2006) suggest that reenvisioning democracy involves a multitude of forces, considerations, creative forays, and ethical and aesthetic processes, which, together—given our insistence that democracy is an amalgam of factors, processes, structures, and phenomena, rendering it a philosophy, a culture, a way of thinking and living, and a political system that is flexible and responsive to the needs of a diverse society—point to a more complex, nuanced version of how students need to relate to their own implication, participation, and engagement with the society that they form (Darling-Hammond, French, & Garcia-Lopez, 2002).

The context for interrogating democracy in education is, as Shapiro (2005) effectively points out, the crisis-like situation characterizing schools in the United States and elsewhere:

> Issues such as the growing administrative control over teachers' lives, allegations about mediocrity of American schools, the crisis of funding, concern about what is called educational *excellence*, the impoverishment of increasing numbers of children and adolescents, the influence of the media on young lives, fears about moral degeneration, school violence, bitter contention over the nature of the curriculum and of school knowledge, and widening disparities in educational achievement among ethnic and racial groups must all be seen, at the same time, as both critical issues in American education and as metaphors for the larger human and societal situation. (p. ix)

When universal concerns, including the environment, racism, AIDS, war and military conflict, migration, and inequitable power relations in general, are added to the dynamic context characterizing pluralistic societies, it is easy to see how democracy, democratic values, and the democratic experience are as vulnerable as they are contested (Paehlke, 2003).

It is necessary to *do* democracy in education because to do otherwise will, ultimately, lead to apolitical, hyperpatriotic societies with only a limited understanding of what is becoming increasingly a multicultural citizenry (Kymlicka, 1995).

> Democratic habits and values must be taught and communicated through life of our society, our legal institutions, our press, our religious life, our private associations, and the many other agencies that allow citizens to interact with each other and to

have a sense of efficiency. The best protection for a democratic society is well-educated citizens. (Ravitch & Viteritti, 2001, p. 28)

Patrick (2003) argues that successful democratic education must include several interconnected components:

> Effective education for citizenship in a democracy dynamically connects the four components of civic knowledge, cognitive civic skills, participatory civic skills, and civic dispositions. Effective teaching and learning of civic knowledge, for example, require that it be connected to civic skills and dispositions of various kinds of activities. Elevation of one component over the other—for example, civic knowledge over skills or vice-versa—is a pedagogical flaw that impedes civic learning. Thus, teachers should combine core content and the processes by which students develop skills and dispositions. (p. 3)

Similarly, Laguardia and Pearl (2005) identify seven themes or attributes of a democratic classroom: "(1) persuasive and negotiable leadership; (2) inclusiveness; (3) knowledge made universally available and organized for important problem solving; (4) inalienable student and teacher rights; (5) universal participation in decisions that affect one's life; (6) the development of optimum learning conditions; and (7) equal encouragement" (p. 9).

Parker (2003), one of the leading scholars in the area of democratic education, further fleshes out the conceptualization of democratic education:

> First, democratic education is not a neutral project, but one that tries to predispose citizens to principled reasoning and just ways of being with one another. Second, educators need simultaneously to engage in multicultural education and citizenship education.... Third, the diversity that schools contain makes extraordinarily fertile soil for democratic education.... Fourth, this dialogue plays an essential and vital role in democratic education, moral development, and public policy.... Fifth, the access/inclusion problem that we (still) face today is one of extending democratic education to students who are not typically afforded it. (pp. xvi–xvii)

Parker (2003) elaborates on the seamless nature of citizenship, democracy, and diversity, and how teaching democracy must be synchronized with many of the same issues that are enmeshed in multicultural education. This interpretation of democracy is strongly aligned with the work of Dewey who believed in the notion of democratic education as enabling people to live together and also as a vehicle to resolve social problems (Simpson, Jackson, & Aycock, 2005).

Teaching, Learning, and Democracy

The fundamental core of democratic education at the classroom level is the teacher, which invariably places certain responsibilities on teacher education programs (Solomon, Portelli, Daniel, & Campbell, 2005). Teacher educators have encountered numerous challenges in inculcating democratic values in the curriculum and practical experiences. Simpson et al. (2005) illustrate how the teacher can play multiple roles in cultivating, nurturing, and engaging in what they call the "art of teaching," which can reinforce the democratic experience for students.

Carr (2006) has found that many teacher education students and teachers focus the majority of their attention on the electoral process in relation to their notion of teaching about democracy and, moreover, that most of the teacher education students and teachers in his study had only a limited democratic education experience while they were in elementary and secondary school. In particular, Carr (2007) emphasizes the following findings in his research (Figure 1):

Figure 1 – Carr's research and overview of literature in democratic education

1. A critical appreciation and analysis of democracy as a philosophy, ethos, political system, and cultural phenomenon is only thinly articulated by participants. There is little commentary on critical thinking, politics as a way of life, power sharing, decision-making processes, the role of the media, alternative systems, and social responsibility (Gandin & Apple, 2005).

2. Almost all of the participants focus on elections as the pivotal underpinning to democracy. Almost all participants—although extremely supportive of democracy in the US—are dissatisfied with a number of aspects associated with democracy (i.e., elections, issues raised, elected officials) (Patterson, 2003).

3. US democracy is often considered to be a model, far preferable to what exists in other systems/countries. However, there does not appear to be a strong understanding of what democracy looks like elsewhere (Holm & Farber, 2002).

4. The study reveals an excessive emphasis on presidential politics when talking about democracy, eclipsing local, regional and international issues.

5. There is extreme reticence about "politics" being part of education, with many participants mentioning a concern about "indoctrination" (Sears & Hughes, 2006).

6. Civic engagement is understood in very narrow terms, concentrated within a specific class/course or associated with elections (Galston, 2003).

7. The connection between education and democracy is a nebulous one, with many participants questioning the foundation of such a linkage (McLaren, 2007).

8. The critical area of social justice, especially in relation to race and poverty, is not fully supported as an integral part of the teaching about/for democracy (Portelli & Solomon, 2001).

9. The study underscored significant differences between African-American and White participants in relation to the place and significance of social justice in education (Carr & Lund, 2007).

Therefore, preparing those who will be teaching diverse students one day is a fundamental part of ensuring that democracy is cultivated in education (Simpson et al., 2005). Solomon, Portelli, Daniel, and Campbell (2005) have documented the limited understanding and engagement of White preservice teachers in relation to social justice, which underpins the need for a greater focus on White power and privilege in education at the policy, institutional, curriculum, and training levels (Carr & Lund, 2007). Further, as Lund (1998) has argued, creative ways must be found to engage all students in the struggle for social justice in schools, as a way of nurturing the kind of engaged and critical forms of democracy that can attend to equity concerns. Preparing the future teachers of these students to be open to engaging the next generation in new forms of activism has proven to be rewarding work, with tremendous potential for progressive social change (Lund, 2005).

The Impact of Neoliberalism on Democratic Education

As Osborne (2001), Karumanchery and Portelli (2005), and McLaren (2007) have argued, the notion of democracy cannot be disconnected from capitalism and neoliberalism. Hill (2003) has warned of the pervasive nature of neoliberalism in forcing a corporate, business agenda into the curriculum, the educational policy development and decision-making processes, and the myriad areas that shape the educational experience. The result is a mild, somewhat superficial, and *thin* exposure to critical democracy and engagement, especially in relation to social justice.

The neoliberal model of education involves a range of free-market principles—rationalization and cost cutting, declining investments, a limited selection of curricular options, privatization, the specter of school choice—the No Child Left Behind (NCLB) legislation in the United States is the best example—and a general assault on teachers in relation to effectiveness and efficiency levels (Carr, 2007; Hill, 2003; Torres, 2005). Similarly, a major focus of neoliberal education is the unwavering devotion to standardized testing, standards, and (supposed) accountability, all of which isolate and diminish the place of democracy and social justice in education (Sleeter, 2007).

The multiple tentacles masked in a foray of supposed prosperity, economic growth, freedom, and independence that are so skillfully articulated within the neoliberal discourse serve to undermine meaningful debate and engagement on democracy. With our focus on *doing* democracy in education, with specific attention paid to social justice, McLaren's (2007) analysis provides some context for the debate:

> Neo-liberal democracy, performing under the banner of diversity yet actually in the hidden service of capital accumulation, often reconfirms the racist stereotypes already prescribed by Euro-American national myths of supremacy—stereotypes that one would think democracy is ostensibly committed to challenge. In the pluralizing move to become a society of diverse voices, neo-liberal democracy has often succumbed to a recolonization of multiculturalism by failing to challenge ideological assumptions surrounding difference that are installed in its current anti-affirmative action and welfare "reform" initiatives. (p. 268)

Our inquiry is, therefore, biased toward a more active, and activist, role for educators and others involved in education in order to fully embrace the notion of critical engagement. As Freire (1973/2005) has suggested, education is a political enterprise, so it would, therefore, be necessary to understand, interrogate, and act upon political matters. Students are much more than the "empty vessels" of Freire's banking education critique, needing to be filled with knowledge; they need to be engaged with how power works (Delpit, 1996), as well as being positioned to challenge, reshape, and transform society (McLaren, 2007). As Westheimer (2006) has pointed out, this academic vacuum in which democracy and social justice can be quickly replaced with the suffocating scent of patriotism serves to homogenize thinking and dampen the plurality of opinion and experience that is required for a highly heterogeneous society, such as those that exist in North America and Europe.

Sleeter (2007) summarizes some of the confusion around how democracy is considered within the educational context, emphasizing that "where one stands on the relationship among individual rights, group claims and cultural identities, and shared common interest has implications for the extent to which one will view standardization of schooling and school curricula as a just and democratic means of promoting excellence for everyone" (p. 5). Sleeter (2007) also raises the significant concern of the "relationship between democracy as a governance structure and capitalism as an economic structure" (p. 5). Linking these issues has implications for educators and decision makers who can shape the texture and shape of democracy in education through their own understanding and experience with democracy. Here, the question of whether educators can *do* democracy if they do not have a belief in the importance of formalizing democratic education and experiences through critical engagement and the interrogation of controversial issues is pivotal (Carr, 2006).

Measuring Democracy in Education

Diamond and Morlino (2005) illustrate how difficult and problematic it is to assess the quality of democracy, introducing a range of concepts as measures and indicators, including the usual components related to voting, political parties, and alternative sources of media as well as an emphasis on procedure, content, and results. They continue to identify eight "dimensions on which democracies vary in quality": five procedural dimensions, including "the rule of law, participation, competition, and accountability, both vertical and horizontal"; two dimensions that are substantive in nature: respect for civil and political freedoms and the progressive implementation of greater political (and underlying it, social and economic) equality"; and the "last dimension, responsiveness, links the procedural dimensions to the substantive ones by measuring the extent to which public policies (including laws, institutions, and expenditures) correspond to citizen demands and preferences, as aggregated through the political process" (p. xii).

It is our contention that education must be a factor in assessing democracy, in how it is constructed, shaped, and lived, and, importantly, how it facilitates or restricts participation in the evolving processes that Diamond and Morlino (2005) present above. This book aims to highlight the multifaceted ways that democracy can be achieved in and through education, with particular emphasis on political literacy and social justice. In sum, it is important here to interrogate how education strives to achieve a nuanced, critical understanding of, and engagement with, democracy.

Banks et al. (2005), in their analysis of *Democracy and Diversity: Principles and Concepts for Educating Citizens*, have compiled a checklist to frame effectively the discussion around teaching for, and about, democracy (Fugure 2).

It is clear that, based on the comprehensive synthesis provided by Banks et al. (2005), democracy in education reposes on a strong theoretical, conceptual, and applied engagement with diversity, which is supported by the seminal antiracism work of George Dei (1996), James Banks (2008), Christine Sleeter (2007), Sonia Nieto (1999), and others. The above checklist also responds effectively to many of the findings in Torney-Purta's (Torney-Purta, Schwille, & Amadeo, 1999; Torney-Purta & Richardson, 2002) groundbreaking studies related to measuring civic attitudes internationally. This comparative work has demonstrated not only the need for greater political literacy and engagement in, and through, education but also, at the methodological level, the need for more research and the establishment of measures to determine and assess how and what students are learning about civic and citizenship education. We hope that this book will constructively add to the resources and thinking around how democracy should be conceptualized, cultivated, and applied within the educational context. One obvious shortcoming in the flood of neoliberal education reforms is the absence of a clear, critical focus on democratic education that includes attention to social justice, with the requisite resources being made available.

Democratic Education and Political Literacy

One of our central concerns within this book pertains to the notion of, and focus on, political literacy in education. Do schools aim for political literacy (Davies & Hogarth, 2004)? Do they formally and informally cultivate political literacy? Is there a place for political literacy within an educational

Figure 2 – Checklist for teaching for, and about, democracy

Principles

1. Are students taught about the complex relationships between unity and diversity in their local communities, the nation, and the world?

2. Do students learn about the ways in which people in their community, nation, and region are increasingly interdependent with other people around the world and are connected to the economic, political, cultural, environmental, and technological changes taking place across the planet?

3. Does the teaching of human rights underpin citizenship education courses and pro-grams?

4. Are students taught knowledge about democracy and democratic institutions and pro-vided opportunities to practice democracy?

Concepts

1. *Democracy*: Do students develop a deep understanding of the meaning of democracy and what it means to be a citizen in a democratic society?

2. *Diversity*: Is the diversity of cultures and groups within all multicultural societies ex-plicitly recognized in the formal and informal curriculum?

3. *Globalization*: Do students develop an understanding of globalization that encom-passes its history, the multiple dimensions and sites of globalization, as well as the complex outcomes of globalization?

4. *Sustainable Development*: Is the need for sustainable development an explicit part of the curriculum?

5. *Empire, Imperialism, and Power*: Are students grappling with how relationships among nations can be more democratic and equitable by discussing the concepts of imperialism and power?

6. *Prejudice, Discrimination, and Racism*: Does the curriculum help students to understand the nature of prejudice, discrimination, and racism, and how they operate at interpersonal, intergroup, and institutional levels?

7. *Migration*: Do students understand the history and the forces that cause the movement of people?

8. *Identity/Diversity*: Does the curriculum nurture an understanding of the multiplicity, fluidity, and contextuality of identity?

9. *Multiple Perspectives*: Are students exposed to a range of perspectives on varying issues?

10. *Patriotism and Cosmopolitanism*: Do students develop a rich and complex understanding of patriotism and cosmopolitanism?

milieu that has been submerged in the hazy clouds of neoliberalism (Schugurensky, 2000)? If we are not teaching about and for political literacy, what then is the mission of the school (Parker, 2003)? Is it to foster the skills and knowledge to prepare students for the world of work? Does it flow over to attitudes and behaviors so that students can live in harmony within a pluralistic society (Provenzo, 2005)? Are teachers trained, prepared, and able to be engaged in such a process (Fenimore-Smith, 2004)? Do curriculum policy documents nurture this order of thinking? What is inherently *critical* about the educational experience? Is the mantra of critical thinking embedded in the notion of schools being potential sites of transformational change, or is it simply loaded jargon to appease those who clamor for a more holistic educational experience?

As noted by Freire (2004), who crystallizes the notion of a socially just, politically literate society, in elaborating the conditions for a more decent society, democracy involves negotiating the limits of authority and freedom:

I am convinced that no education intending to be at the service of the beauty of the human presence in the world, at the service of seriousness and ethical rigor, of justice, of firmness of character, of respect for differences—no education intending to be engaged in the struggle for realizing the dream of solidarity—can fulfill itself in the absence of the dramatic relationship between authority and freedom. It is a tense and dramatic relationship in which both authority and freedom, while fully living out their limits and possibilities, learn, almost without respite, to take responsibility for themselves as authority and freedom. It is by living lucidly the tense relationship between authority and freedom that one discovers the two need not necessarily be in mutual antagonism. It is from the starting point of this learning that both authority and freedom become committed, within educational practice, to the democratic dream of an authority zealous in its limits interacting with a freedom equally diligent of its limits and possibilities. (p. 9)

Likewise, Giroux (1988) argues for "critical literacy as a precondition for self- and social-empowerment" and dissects the way that traditional forms of literacy, especially when imbued within the web of neoliberalism, serve to further marginalize the marginalized. He maintains that "the language of literacy is almost exclusively linked to popular forms of liberal and right-wing discourse that reduce it to either a functional perspective tied to narrowly coerced economic interests or to a logic designed to initiate the poor, the underprivileged, and minorities into the ideology of a unitary, dominant cultural tradition" (p. 61). Ultimately, in order to become engaged in democracy, there must be political literacy, the absence of which would make the prospect of meaningful social justice in society less likely.

Other authors have also emphasized the strong need for political literacy to enhance social justice. Tarcov (1996), for example, situates democratic education within the framework of popular political participation:

To think clearly about democratic education, we must reconsider the meaning and the goodness of democracy. It is sometimes said, and even believed, that democracy is the ultimate political criterion, good, or aspiration, and that all political evils should be attributed to the absence of full democracy and their cure sought in more democracy. That view is usually accompanied by an understanding of democracy that insists on the maximum of immediate and unlimited popular rule and the exclusion of any elements of other forms of government. Such a view sees democratic education as directed toward the propagation and actualization of such an understanding of democracy. (p. 1)

Davies and Hogarth (2004) argue that political literacy must be resituated as the focal point of citizenship education. Their vision of political literacy surpasses the "compound of knowledge, skills and procedural values" to also include "such areas as respect for truth and reasoning and toleration as opposed to substantive values which could mean that pupils would be told what to think about particular issues" (p. 182). They reject previous political literacy models, such as the "civics" model centered on "factual knowledge and a didactic teaching methodology" as the modus operandi (p. 182), and the "big issues" model in which adversarial political debates take place in class. For this latter approach, there is concern that issues will only be examined at a superficial level without serious follow up. Rather, they favor the "public discourse model," which "seeks to induct pupils into the language, concepts, forms of arguments and skills required to think and talk about life from a political point of view, emphasizing both process and product. Factual knowledge is important but is made subservient to other aspects that are centrally important to political literacy" (p. 183).

The Interplay, Symmetry, and Compatibility between Democracy and Citizenship

There has long been a robust debate, in both the public and academic domains, on the role that citizenship education can or should play in the fostering of democratic ideals. For example, according to the Corporation for National and Community Service (2005), effective citizenship education should prepare young people in three areas:

- Civic literacy—Fundamental knowledge of history and government, political and community organizations, and public affairs; skills for making informed judgments, engaging in democratic deliberation and decision making, influencing the political process, and organizing within a community.

- Civic virtues—Values, beliefs, and attitudes needed for constructive engagement in the political system and community affairs, such as tolerance, social trust, and a sense of responsibility for others.

- Civically-engaged behaviors—Habits of participating and contributing to civic and public life through voting, staying politically informed, and engaging in community service.

In a related vein, Santora (2006) examined why cooperative learning often failed to promote democratic behavior among culturally diverse students and found that students reacted to knowledge provided by the teacher in multiple ways, including finding avenues to dispute or complement such knowledge with that acquired in/from their families, the environment, and the media. Her study demonstrates how power, as it affects knowledge construction, is locally reproduced or reconstituted through classroom interaction.

The analysis above reflects Delpit's (1996) work on how minorities are systemically excluded from the decision-making process in the classroom, as well as in the broader society, through myriad processes that codify the implicit and explicit ways that power works. Within this context, we might ask the following questions: Why is there exclusion, who defines it, how do we measure it, and what can be done to remedy it? What are the implications of sustained marginalization? What formal and informal processes are in place to effectively bring together and to ensure constructive engagement between peoples from different races, social classes, ethnicities, religions, etc.? What is the responsibility of those who have access to power and decision making?

Gilmour (2006) raises a fundamental issue when considering the salience of citizenship education:

> Citizenship education has the potential to open up new and controversial areas of debate and, within the critical whole-school approach, can advance anti-racist developments. In Britain, however, the dominant tradition has been for citizenship education that reinforces the status quo by binding students to a superficial and sanitized version of pluralism that is long on duties and responsibilities, but short on popular struggles against race inequality. (p. 99)

In her work on citizenship and service learning, Waggener (2006) elaborates on this dichotomy between the political and social components of citizenship, and concludes that "more attention must be given to service learning projects that teach about the structure of governments and encourage students to engage in political action" (p. 4). Simon (2001) complements this research by effectively elucidating the dilemma of constructing meaningful democracy and citizenship:

> To be a citizen is not just to hold a legal status in relation to a particular nation state; rather it is to possess the capacities, and have access to the opportunities, to participate with others in the determination of one's society. This means being able to take into account the inter-related character of culture, politics, and economics. If we want people to be citizens, not subjects (i.e., those to whom economics, politics, and schooling simply happen), we will need to have young people think critically and be able to participate in society so as to transform inequities that impede full participation in democratic life. (p. 12)

Portelli and Solomon (2001) further tease out the:

> common elements such as critical thinking, dialogue and discussion, tolerance, free and reasoned choices, and public participation ... which are associated with equity, community, creativity, and taking difference seriously ... [a] conception [that] is contrasted with the notion of democracy that is minimalist, protectionist, and marginalist and hence promotes a narrow notion of individualism and spectacular citizenship. (p. 17)

Westheimer and Kahne (2003) have cogently argued that the emphasis on patriotism and community service in the post–September 11 era may effectively diminish the level and intensity of democracy in society, and may even be antidemocratic. They point to the formal, governmental push for volunteerism and charity as a potential lever that, despite creating the impression that society is becoming more democratic, does not achieve bona fide critical civic engagement. Friedland and Morimoto (2005), in their study of volunteerism, found that for "middle- and upper-middle-class high school students 'resume-padding' is one of the motivating factors driving the increase in volunteering," and it is "shaped by the perception that voluntary and civic activity is necessary to get into college; and the better the college (or, more precisely, the higher the perception of the college in the status system) the more volunteerism students believed was necessary" (p. 1). Therefore, as illustrated by Westheimer and Kahne (2004), there must be an authentic (and political) ring to the conceptualization and implementation of service learning for it to have any value for the students.

The absence of democratic citizenship (or rather the presence of an extremely nuanced approach to it) is evident when considering that only three U.S. states have specific standards for civic education, although almost half of them have addressed at least some components of civic education in their social studies curricula and standards (RMC Research Corporation, 2005, p. 7). Similarly, Galston (2003) has found that there is only limited civic knowledge among American students:

> The National Assessment of Educational Progress Civics Assessment has revealed major deficiencies in the overall results: For fourth-, eighth-, and (most relevant for our purposes) 12th-graders, about three-fourths were below the level of proficiency. Thirty-five percent of high school seniors tested below basic, indicating near-total civic ignorance. Another 39% were at the basic level, demonstrating less than the working knowledge that citizens need. (pp. 31–32)

O'Toole, Marsh, and Jones (2003) have found, despite the contention to the contrary, that young people are not apathetic, nor are they disinterested in politics, but they are discouraged from participating because of the way the current system seems to present issues; interestingly, they note that "politics is something that is done to them, not something they can influence," and "inequalities based on class, gender, ethnicity and age are crucial features of the lives of our respondents: they are not variables, they are lived experiences" (p. 359). In sum, the present neoliberal configuration of educational curricula, standards, expectations, and testing concurrently has a tendency to isolate political literacy and places a premium on a type of learning that can disenfranchise many students.

Synthesizing a Vision for the Book

Understanding and being able to participate in society in a critically engaged manner should not be a sidebar item on the educational agenda. Without question, students need to master certain skills and knowledge, they need to become literate in certain areas, and they also need to learn certain basic notions about society. However, as cultural capital (Delpit, 1996) plays a significant role in shaping the education experience of students, there is also the concern as to how educators understand difference and identity in doing democracy in education (McLaren, 2007). Missing out on focusing on validating and transcending boundaries, barriers and (lived) experiences can serve to further entrench injustice, inequity and antidemocratic thinking, values, and manifestations (Banks et al., 2005; Dei, Karumanchery, & Karumanchery-Luik, 2004; Parker, 2003).

Our contention that democracy is an ethos, an ideology, a set of values, a philosophy, a contested terrain of action and debate, and a complex, problematic, dynamic framework and terrain in which diverse forces, interests, and experiences intersect to develop relations and relationships that continue to evolve is the central theme binding the contents of this book. No singular or simplistic definitions of democracy exist, nor do we attempt to view democratic education in a *thin*, rigid manner (Shapiro & Purpel, 2005). Clearly, our interpretation includes, and focuses on, social justice and also involves an openly political commitment to advancing equity, the essence of democracy. We challenge those who hold that there is only one type of democracy, or that democracy is a unique political system, or that democracy is principally consumed with elections.

We are concerned that if we do not *do* democracy in education there will be clear and obvious consequences for society as a result. Is there a connection between a high degree of political literacy and a lower level of patriotism, for example, or at least a more critical vantage point concerning monumental decisions that lock societies into generations of ill-will and decline because of weak engagement and understanding of politics? Are people less likely to be manipulated if they have higher levels of political literacy? Would people likely be more critical of the media, and of democracy for that matter, if they were more fully engaged in the critiquing, experiencing, and fostering of democracy in schools? The contributors to this book collectively seek to answer affirmatively that education can and must be a vehicle for advancing a more critical engagement in democracy, one that effectively advances social justice and political literacy for the good of all citizens.

Overview of the Book

Although there is a range of theoretical, conceptual, and methodological approaches adopted and advocated by the contributors to this book, they all follow the same thread of articulating a version and vision of democracy in education. An explicit attempt to offer a critical assessment of democracy forms the cornerstone of this volume. Similarly, all of the contributors have sought to underscore the importance of social justice in their analysis of democracy in education. The theme of *doing* democracy is, therefore, illustrated through diverse strands and examples, coalescing around a framework of teaching and learning that encourages critical thinking and engagement. Each chapter concludes with five questions for further reflection that can help facilitate dialogue on the applicability of various conceptualizations of democracy in diverse education systems.

The first section of the book frames the notion of democracy and democratic education, and includes five chapters. Dave Hill, from Great Britain, has the first chapter, in which he argues for a new type of education in/on democracy, one that resists neoliberal global capitalism. In elaborating a framework that critically analyzes the political and ideological orientation of neoliberalism, Hill points out how it has become increasingly difficult and problematic to integrate social justice into the formal curriculum and educational experience. He also provides evidence of the "growth of undemocratic (un)accountability," which has served to further drive a wedge between the social classes while reinforcing racism and marginalization. Hill concludes with three potential arenas of resistance: within the education and media apparatuses; working outside of the classroom; and mass action as part of a broader movement for economic and social justice.

Michael O'Sullivan, from Canada, continues the discussion with a critique of critical pedagogies and global citizenship education in the era of globalization, interrogating the meaning of democracy in education as well as its positioning within the school experience. Underpinning his analysis with Dewey's (at the time) revolutionary notion of education being the lever for collective, participatory, and emancipatory action, O'Sullivan stresses how much neoliberalism is a "dominant anti-democratic ideology" and proposes a framework for introducing ideas, concepts, and experiences aimed at critical democratic work through, and under the auspices of, global citizenship education, which can be found in the formal curriculum. He is rightly concerned with the numerous obstacles and barriers limiting critical pedagogical work in schools and advocates for a more systemic approach to raising issues and building support, especially in the area of preservice teaching.

Jennifer Tupper, from Canada, interrogates citizenship and democracy in education, seeking to examine the implications for disrupting universal values. She questions the essentialist notions of universal citizenship that are infused into what students learn in, and through, formal education. In elaborating on the concept of "commonsense," Tupper challenges the beliefs/stories of those in power or who have privilege in society, which are considered "cultural truths" and are simply seen to "just make sense"; she writes, "the uncritical acceptance of commonsense (embodied in curriculum) shifts down possible alternative visions for what society might look like by consistently reifying a dominant vision." By using critical race and feminist theory as a means to deconstruct commonsense, Tupper argues for a broader, more critical and meaningful place for democracy in education, especially in teacher education programs where teachers need to become engaged with social justice and democracy in authentic ways.

The next chapter, by Ali Sammel and Gregory Martin, from Australia, is entitled "'Other-ed' pedagogy: The praxis of critical democratic education," and builds on some of the themes identified by Hill, namely the application of neoliberal reforms in education, especially the impact at the classroom level. Sammel and Martin focus on notions of White privilege among teachers, and draw conclusions, based on their study in Australia, that have implications for teaching and learning in relation to democracy. Their analysis focuses on the social construction of the role of the teacher within the context of the prevailing standards movement, which can constrain the quest for democratic debate and action. Interrogating Whiteness, especially when the vast majority of teachers in developed countries are White, is a necessary step in deconstructing how social justice can be advanced in classrooms.

Rounding out this section is a chapter by Reinaldo Matias Fleuri, from Brazil, who discusses the notion of rebelliousness in relation to democracy and raises important concerns about the role of power within the educational context. Using a conceptual framework based on the work of Michel Foucault to understand discipline and transgressive behaviors, Fleuri also builds on the work of Paulo Freire and Célestin Freinet to help explain the pedagogical context and experience as well as the potential for democratic experience. He introduces how discipline is structured in a school context in which exams are used as an arbiter of progress, which involve sanctioning and surveillance from above. Fleuri then presents the notion of resistance and rebelliousness to discipline in an attempt to analyze the impact and relationships that are created, and which ultimately affect the texture of, and potential for, democracy in education.

The second section of the book, entitled "Reflections on democratic dissonance and dissidence," contains five chapters that present alternative perspectives for democratic education. From an Aboriginal point of view, Jason M. C. Price, from Canada, has the lead chapter, and writes about "Educators' conceptions of democracy," underscoring "educators' understanding of democracy [that] influences their pedagogical and curricular decisions, and ... [how] the daily life of teachers is culturally, economically, environmentally and politically meaningful." He identifies four interconnected and interdependent core qualities of democracy in education (voice; critical thinking, reflection, and action; community, cooperation, and consensus; and nondiscrimination and nonoppression), explored in conjunction with the backdrop of Red Democracy. Price concludes by stating that "rather than equating democracy with process-related practices (votes, political parties and elite representation), the educators [in his study] emphasized the core qualities of democracy as being related to values, attitudes, approaches to decision making and the importance of generalized, empowered and active discursive participation by all community members."

Alexandra Fidyk, a Canadian teaching at an American university, writes a chapter entitled "Democracy and difference in education: Interconnectedness, identity, and social justice pedagogy." Fidyk emphasizes that "attending responsibly to democracy and difference in education requires a shift (ontologically) in the way we perceive, interpret, and respond to events." In what might seem to be an atypical approach to understanding democracy, Fidyk relies on a conceptual framework incorporating "Buddhist and Jungian thought, Vedic philosophy, and quantum physics ... to offer an integrative perspective of our deep interconnectedness as an alternative to the subject." She explores how heightened consciousness and love can be translated into meaningful action in the classroom. Fidyk's approach to democratic education calls for an intensive process of conscientization, one that may lead to the peaceful resolution of numerous conflicts that occur in pluralistic societies.

Lisa Karen Taylor, from Canada, discusses "Beyond 'open-mindedness': Cultivating critical, reflexive approaches to democratic dialogue" and illustrates how students can become engaged through critical pedagogy. Her starting point reflects one of the major premises of this book: "Within Liberal and neo-liberal conceptions of democratic societies, therefore, citizens are imagined as either unfettered by difference (being of dominant, unmarked gender, class, ethnoracial affiliation, ability, etc.) or as needing to overcome and set aside their difference from normative dominant identities through presumed neutral, universal forms of reasoning." Through classroom activities with preservice teachers, Taylor unravels some of the anxiety, mystery, and reticence about heteronormative values and, importantly, how students can start to critically deconstruct and act through reflective dialogue aimed at enhancing democracy.

Alireza Asgharzadeh, a Canadian of Iranian origin, presents a chapter entitled "Secular humanism and education: Re-imagining democratic possibilities in a Middle Eastern context." He raises a number of pivotal questions about how problematic it is to achieve democratic education in contexts that reject secular humanism. Asgharzadeh emphasizes that "schools can play a major role to this end by educating young people to be open-minded, to think critically, and to respect universal values, such as human rights, peace, difference and diversity." Tackling the issue of fundamentalist thinking raises a number of related questions about normative values and power relations, thus extending the study and existence of democracy. The debate over religion in education is not restricted to the Middle East but, as is increasingly evident, there are numerous manifestations, proposals, and conflicts over the place of religion within the curriculum, in school conduct codes, and the institutional culture of education in diverse contexts across the globe.

The last chapter in this section is by Glenda Tibe Bonifacio, a Canadian of Filipino origin, who writes about "Doing democracy and feminism in the classroom: Challenging hegemonic practices." After having examined the salience of race, language, and religion in relation to the potential for democratic education, this chapter shines a light on how gender is an integral part of how we understand democracy and social justice. Arguing that "teaching feminism in the classroom is inherently doing democracy" and, moreover, that it "constructively builds on citizenship practice, and grounds democratic values and processes in education," Bonifacio argues that identity is an indispensable component to any interrogation of the value of democracy. In discussing how feminist education has the potential to be transformative, Bonifacio outlines various strategies for promoting feminist approaches that overlap basic concepts comprised in democratic education.

The third section of the book presents four case studies that further raise questions about how to understand and *do* democracy in education. Njoke Nathani Wane, a Canadian of Ghanian origin, leads off with a chapter dealing with primary education for girls in Kenya and stresses the impact of colonialism in shaping the present context, something that is a significant factor in influencing the education of hundreds of millions of students in developing countries. In elaborating on the notion of democracy, Wane explores the salience of indigenous African education, highlighting the barriers for the education of girls. In repositioning democracy from the typical North American vantage point, Wane concludes by arguing that "there is a powerful correlation between low enrolment, poor retention and unsatisfactory learning outcomes, and this requires nothing less than the integration of gender, class, regional and outcomes into the design and implementation of relevant inter-sector policies and strategies."

Sarah E. Barrett and Martina Nieswandt, of Canadian and German origin, respectively, and who both teach in Canada, explore the role of science education in fostering democracy. They critically assess the potential for science educators to be engaged in teaching and learning, emphasizing social justice, ethical responsibility, the implications for scientific research, and the possibility of empowering students. They raise pivotal questions about how teachers should approach controversial issues, such as global warming, nuclear weapons, nuclear power, and the exploitation of nonreusable resources including oil. Barrett and Nieswandt conclude by suggesting that teachers need to explore cognitive, activist, and critical approaches to teaching science education in their teacher education programs, with the objective of assisting them to be able to more effectively support a democratic education for their students.

Mary Frances Agnello and Thomas A. Lucey, from the United States, explore the notion of critical economic literacy, which is compatible with political literacy. As was the case with Barrett's and Nieswandt's chapter, this one makes the case for a more democratic and multicultural approach to teaching economics, arguing that an uncritical pedagogy reinforces hegemonic forces that do not serve the interests of society. Here, again, the curriculum and, especially, teacher preparation and engagement are considered key. Agnello and Lucey emphasize how the propensity for testing has limited the scope and critical nature of economics in schools. They also point out that the array of standards blanketing education in the United States does not adequately address the study of economics, which further diminishes the possibility for meaningful and contextualized learning in the field. Last, they provide evidence of only an extremely limited reference to social class issues in history, geography, and economics textbooks used in U.S. schools.

Karim A. Remtulla, from Canada, discusses the pedagogical paradoxes of online activism, highlighting the potential for social justice through electronic networks and technology. Underscoring how the integration of electronic media has created a "digital divide," and is far from being neutral in nature, Remtulla elucidates some of the issues for democracy in the classroom related to critical pedagogy and civic engagement. He introduces various angles of the problematic, including the implications for race, gender, and subjectivity, as well as for citizenship, community development, and participation. This chapter further fleshes out the concern for how we actually *do* democracy in education, with a particular emphasis on ethical responsibilities for those in schools in relation to the Internet.

The fourth section addresses teaching about and for democracy, starting with a chapter by Suzanne Vincent and Jacques Désautels, from Quebec, Canada, entitled "Teaching and learning democracy in education: Articulating democratic citizenship in/through the curriculum." They clearly situate the role of the school within contemporary education: "the School's work of 'providing an education' can be considered to be a sociopolitical project or agenda in that it evinces the intentions underlying not only a given society's preferred model of development but also the type of citizen that this same society aspires to produce." Vincent and Désautels then proceed to diagnose critically the role of citizenship education within the framework of the broader mission of the school. They conclude with an analysis on the importance of addressing the hierarchy of the subject-disciplines in education, intertwined with the role of power in diminishing the impact of education on diverse groups in society, particularly if the school is not attuned to the need to achieve greater conscientization among the students.

Patrick Solomon and Beverly-Jean Daniel, from Canada, focus on the challenges of democratic engagement while reporting on a study of preservice teachers during their field-based experiences. Distinguishing between theorized and actualized democracy they find that the former affects the latter; teacher "candidates' theoretical notions of democratic education provide them with an effective lens for critiquing educational practices within varied contexts, including their teacher education program, their practicum school, and community placements." Solomon and Daniel make a strong case for a more explicit pedagogy and experience in the preservice teaching program in relation to democracy, including taking advantage of antidemocratic predispositions and actions in students' field-based sites. The theme of approaching political issues from a politically sensitive vantage point is clearly framed by these writers.

Georg Lind, from Germany, writes about "Teaching students to speak up and to listen to others: Fostering moral-democratic competencies," emphasizing the importance of cultivating skills, comportments, and experiences to be able to discuss issues with a view to resolving conflicts peacefully. Building on the work of Lawrence Kohlberg and Jurgen Habermas, Lind stresses that "to be effective, democratic competencies must be rooted in an unconscious cognitive structure." He further elaborates on three strategies or principles for ensuring that effective discussion takes place in school—the constructivist principle of learning, the principle of maintaining an optimal level of arousal through alternating phases of support and challenge, and the principle of mutual respect and free moral discourse in the classroom—which makes the task of engaging students in democracy attainable as well as meaningful.

Heidi Huse, from the United States, tackles the issue of fostering democratic literacy, arguing that apathy, combined with a reluctance to *do* democracy in education, has imperiled the political debate and prospects for critical engagement at several levels. Huse starts with an overview of how little university students, in general, know about democracy and social justice, all the while stressing that they seem to be intonating, according to the title of her text, "Don't teach me what I don't want to know." She emphasizes how student resistance to democratic literacy is twofold, encompassing simple disinterest and outright hostility, and she presents strategies to engage students in writing and thinking about democracy. As is the case in several other chapters, Huse argues for more creative teaching approaches and a more explicitly democratic curriculum as a means to help encourage democratic engagement among students.

Shazia Shujah, from Canada, elaborates on "A pedagogy for social justice: Critical teaching that goes against the grain," making the case for social justice in a multicultural society, such as Canada, and also exploring what *doing* democracy in schools looks like. Situating the analysis on the curriculum in Ontario, Shujah advocates for a more thorough examination of lived identities in order to develop critical democratic literacy, especially since the formal requirements laid out by the government are largely silent on the issue of engaged citizenship. While highlighting the role of educators in the process of democratizing education, she states that democratic education "must commence with premise that race, class, gender, sexuality, ablism—among other social markers—are all factors that continue to influence education." Thus, as is echoed throughout this book, Shujah concludes with a call for a *thick* or broader conceptualization of democracy, one that incorporates and validates multiples voices and lived experience.

Each of the provocative and insightful chapters in this volume concludes with a set of questions for consideration by readers; we hope these add richly to this volume's use in classrooms and to its contribution to the ongoing debates and discussions around what kind of democracy we want, and how we might best use educational settings and institutions to bring it about. Far from providing a straightforward roadmap on this journey toward social justice, we have gathered these original contributions from leading and emerging scholars from around the globe to serve you as a helpful guide along your own path. As editors, we are in admiration of the dedication to excellence and the creative and thoughtful research and reasoning of these amazing colleagues.

References

Banks, J., McGee Banks, C. A., Cortés, C. E., Hahn, C. L., Merryfield, M. M., Moodley, K. A., et al. (2005). *Democracy and diversity: Principles and concepts for educating citizens in a global age.* Seattle, WA: Center for Multicultural Education.

Banks, J. A. (2008). *An introduction to multicultural education* (4th ed.). Boston: Pearson Education.

Barber, B. R. (1984). *Strong democracy: Participatory politics for a new age.* Berkeley, CA: University of California Press.

Carr, P. R. (2006). Democracy in the classroom? *Academic Exchange Quarterly, 10*(2), 7–12.

_____. (2007). Experiencing democracy through neo-liberalism: The role of social justice in education. *Journal of Critical Education Policy Studies, 5*(2). Retrieved December 1, 2007, from http://www.jceps.com/index.php?pageID=article&articleID=104

Carr, P. R., & Lund, D. E. (Eds.) (2007). *The great white north? Exploring whiteness, privilege and identity in education.* Rotterdam: Sense.

Chomsky, N. (2003). *Chomsky on democracy and education.* New York: RoutledgeFalmer.

Cook, S. A. (2004). Learning to be a full Canadian citizen: Youth, elections and ignorance. *Canadian Issues Magazine*, pp.17–20.

Darling-Hammond, L., French, J., & Garcia-Lopez, S. P. (2002). *Learning to teach for social justice.* New York: Teachers College, Columbia University.

Davies, I., & Hogarth, S. (2004). Political literacy: Issues for teachers and learners. In J. Demaine (Ed.), *Citizenship and political education today* (pp. 181–199). Hampshire, UK: Palgrave Macmillan.

Dei, G. J. S. (1996). *Anti-racism education: Theory and practice.* Black Point, Nova Scotia: Fernwood.

Dei, G. J. S., Karumanchery, L., & Karumanchery-Luik, N. (2004). *Playing the race card: Exposing white power and privilege.* New York: Peter Lang.

Delpit, L. (1996). *Other people's children: Cultural conflict in the classroom.* New York: New Press.

Demaine, J. (2004) *Citizenship and political education today.* Hampshire, UK: Palgrave Macmillan.

Dewey, J. (1964). *Democracy and education.* New York: Macmillan.

Diamond, L., & Morlino, L. (2005). *Assessing the quality of democracy.* Baltimore, MD: Johns Hopkins University Press.

Fenimore-Smith, J. K. (2004). Democratic practices and dialogic frameworks: Efforts toward transcending the cultural myths of teaching. *Journal of Teacher Education, 55*(3), 227–239.

Freire, P. (1973/2005). *Pedagogy of the oppressed.* New York: Continuum.

———. (2004). *Pedagogy of indignation.* Boulder, CO: Paradigm.

Galston, W. (2003). Civic education and political participation. *Phi Delta Kappan, 85*(1), 29–33.

Gandin, L. A., & Apple, M. (2002). Challenging neo-liberalism, building democracy: Creating the citizen school in Porto Alegre, Brazil. *Journal of Education Policy, 17*(2), 259–279.

Giroux, H. (1988). Literacy and the pedagogy of voice and political empowerment. *Educational Theory, 38*(1), 61–75.

Herman, E., & Chomsky, N. (2002). *Manufacturing consent: The political economy of the mass media.* New York: Pantheon.

Hill, D. (2003). Global neo-liberalism, the deformation of education and resistance. *Journal for Critical Education Policy Studies, 1*(1), 1–30.

Holm, G., & Farber, P. (2002). Teaching in the dark: The geopolitical knowledge and global awareness of the next generation of American teachers. *International Studies in Sociology of Education, 12*(2), 129–144.

Kurth-Schai, R., & Green, C. (2006). *Re-envisioning education and democracy.* Greenwich, CT: Information Age.

Lund, D. E. (1998). Nurturing democracy in the schools: Engaging youth in social justice activism. *Multiculturalism/Interculturalisme, 17*(2), 26–31.

———. (2005). Addressing multicultural and antiracist practice and theory with Canadian teacher activists. In B. J. McMahon & D. E. Armstrong (Eds.), *Inclusion in urban educational environments: Addressing issues of diversity, equity, and social justice* (pp. 255–274). Greenwich, CT: Information Age.

McLaren, P. (2007). *Life in schools: An introduction to critical pedagogy and the foundations of education.* Boston: Allyn & Bacon.

Nieto, S. (1999). *The light in their eyes: Creating multicultural learning communities.* New York: Teachers College Press.

O'Toole, T., Marsh, D., & Jones, S. (2003). Political literacy cuts both ways: The politics of non-participation among young people. *Political Quarterly, 74*(3), 349–360.

Parker, W. (2003). *Teaching democracy: Unity and diversity in public life.* New York: Teachers College Press.

Patrick, J. (2003). *Teaching democracy (ERIC Digest).* Bloomington, IN: ERIC Clearinghouse for Social Studies/Social Science Education.

Pearl, A., & Pryor, A. (2005). *Democratic practices in education: Implications for teacher education.* Lanham, MD: Rowman & Littlefield.

Portelli, J., & Solomon, R. P. (2001). *The erosion of democracy in education: From critique to possibilities.* Calgary, AB: Detselig.

Provenzo, E. (2005). *Critical literacy: What every American ought to know.* Boulder, CO: Paradigm.

Ravitch, D., & Viteritti, J. P. (2001). *Making good citizens: Education and civil society* New Haven, CT: Yale University Press.

Schugurensky, D. (2000). Citizenship learning and democratic engagement: Political capital revisited. *Proceedings of the 2000 Adult Education Research Conference,* Vancouver, BC. Retrieved September 5, 2007, from http://www.edst.educ.ubc.ca/aerc/2000/schugurenskyd1-web.htm

Sears, A., & Hughes, A. (2006). Citizenship: Education or indoctrination? *Citizenship and Teacher Education, 2*(1), 3–17.

Simpson, D., Jackson, M., & Aycock, J. (2005). *John Dewey and the art of teaching: Toward reflective and imaginative practice.* Thousand Oaks, CA: Sage.

Sleeter, C. E. (Ed.). (2007). *Facing accountability in education.* New York: Teachers College Press.

Solomon, R. P., Portelli, J. P., Daniel, B.-J., & Campbell, A. (2005). The discourse of denial: How white teacher candidates construct race, racism and "white privilege." *Race, Ethnicity and Education, 8*(2), 147–169.

Torney-Purta, J., Schwille, J., & Amadeo, J. (1999). *Civic education across countries: Twenty-four national studies from the IEA civic education project.* Christchurch, New Zealand: Eburon.

Torney-Purta, J., & Richardson, W. K. (2002). *Sources of civic behavior and knowledge: School related experiences and organizational membership among adolescents in a 28-country comparative study.* Unpublished manuscript. McGill University, Montreal, PQ, Canada.

Torres, C. (2005). No Child Left Behind: A brainchild of neoliberalism and American politics. *NewPolitics, 10,* 2. Retrieved September 27, 2007, from http://www.wpunj.edu/newpol/issue38/torres38.htm

Westheimer, J. (2006). Patriotism and education: An introduction. *Phi Delta Kappan, 87*(8), 569–572.

Westheimer, J., & Kahne, J. (2004). What kind of citizen? The politics of educating for democracy. *American Educational Research Journal, 41*(2), 237–269.

SECTION I

FRAMING THE NOTION OF DEMOCRACY AND DEMOCRATIC EDUCATION

1

RESISTING NEO-LIBERAL GLOBAL CAPITALISM AND ITS DEPREDATIONS: EDUCATION FOR A NEW DEMOCRACY

Dave Hill

Introduction

In this chapter I set out the major impacts of neo-liberal global capitalism and its accompanying neo-conservatism on society and education, focusing on (1) the obscene and widening economic, social, and educational inequalities both within states and globally; (2) the de-theorisation of education and the regulating of critical thought and activists through the ideological and repressive state apparatuses; and (3) the limitation and regulation of democracy and democratic accountability at national and local educational levels.

Capitalist Agendas, Education, and Resistance

In the face of capitalist agendas in and for education, this chapter calls for contestation of, and critical engagement with, the Radical Right in its neo-liberal, neo-conservative, and revised social democratic manifestations, such as those of Blair's and Clinton's and Schroeder's "Third Way." Writing from a Marxist perspective, it is necessary to challenge ideological and cultural fashions within the media and the academy fashions such as post-modernism, social democracy/left revisionism that, ultimately, serve the function of "naturalising" neo-liberal capital as the dominating hegemonic "common sense." Post-modernists and social democrats do this, as much as neo-liberals and neo-conservatives. They ignore, or deride, Marxist-derived/related concepts of social class, class conflict, and socialism. Such academic fashions and governmental policies that laud hierarchical and increasing difference as inevitable, desirable, and productive, ideologies such as post-modernism and left revisionism, debilitate and displace viable solidaristic counter-hegemonic struggles of the sort the transnational capitalist class and its governmental stooges and acolytes thought had been dumped in the dustbin of history with the overthrow of the Soviet Stalinist regimes of Eastern Europe.

This chapter asks what role can we, as critical transformative and revolutionary educators and cultural/media workers, play in ensuring that capitalism, with its omnipresent class-based apartheid, most brutally evident in the capital's urban centres, is replaced by an economic and social system more economically and socially just as well as environmentally sustainable than state capitalist, social democratic, and (secular or religious) traditionalist alternatives?

Neo-liberal Global Capital and Its Effects

Neo-liberal policies globally have resulted in a loss of equity and economic and social justice for citizens and for workers, a loss of democracy, democratic control and democratic accountability, and a loss of critical thought and space.

Global capital, in its current neo-liberal form, in particular, leads to human degradation, inhumanity, and increased social class inequalities within states and globally. These effects are increasing (racialised and gendered) social class inequality within states and between states. The degradation and capitalisation of humanity, including the environmental degradation impact, manifest themselves primarily in a social class related manner. Those who can afford to buy clean water do not die of thirst or diarrhoea. In many states across the globe, those who can afford school or university fees end up without formal education or in grossly inferior provision (see Greaves, Hill, & Maisuria, 2007, for a discussion of immiseration under capitalism). Wealth inequality has reached grotesque levels.

In Britain, the increasing inequalities, the impoverishment, and creation of a substantial underclass has also been well documented (Dorling et al., 2007). According to the Office for National Statistics, the life expectancy gap between the richest and poorest parts of the country is at an all-time high. Women living in Kensington and Chelsea can expect, on average, to live 12 years longer than their counterparts in Glasgow city, while men born in Glasgow city face a worse life expectancy level than those in developing nations such as Algeria or Vietnam (Conway, 2005).

Harris (2007) notes, in a discussion of the separate economy of the super-rich, "Richistan," the growth of such a large, super-rich class, coupled with a deepening poverty in many communities, is starting to tear at the fabric of society. Inequalities within states have widened partly because of the generalised attack on workers' rights and trade unions, with restrictive laws hamstringing trade union actions (Rosskam, 2006; see also Hill, 2005a; Hill, 2006) and lowering corporation taxes as well as taxes on the rich over the past 20 years.

The Growth of Educational Inequality

There is a considerable amount of data globally on how, within marketised or quasi-marketised education systems, poor schools have, by and large, become poorer, in terms of relative education results and in terms of total income, and how rich schools in the same terms have become richer. Whitty, Power, and Halpin (1998) examined the effects of the introduction of quasi-markets into education systems in the United States, Sweden, England, Wales, Australia, and New Zealand. Their conclusion is that one of the results of marketising education is that increasing "parental choice" of schools, and/or setting up new types of schools, in effect, increases the likelihood of schools choosing parents and their children. This sets up or exacerbates racialised school hierarchies (see also Gillborn & Youdell, 2000; Hill, 2008a; Hill & Rosskam, 2008). Indeed,

> poor parents have fewer resources to support the education of their children, and they have less financial, cultural, and social capital to transmit. Only policies that explicitly address inequality, with a major redistributive purpose, therefore, could make education an equalizing force in social opportunity. (Reimers, 2000, p. 55)

Hirtt (2004) comments on the apparently contradictory education policies of capital "to adapt education to the needs of business and at the same time reduce state expenditure on education" (p. 446). He suggests that this contradiction is resolved by the polarisation of the labour market, that, for neo-liberal capital, from an economic point of view, it is not necessary to provide high level education and of general knowledge, to all future workers: "It is now possible and even highly recommendable to have a more polarized education system ... education should not try to transmit a broad common culture to the majority of future workers, but instead it should teach them some basic, general skills" (Hirrt, 2004, p. 446).

The Growth of Undemocratic (Un)accountability

Within education and other public services, business values and interests are increasingly substituted for democratic accountability and the collective voice. Private companies—national or transnational—variously build, own, run, and govern state schools and other sections or sectors of local government educational services in different countries. Is it right to allow transnational or national private providers of educational services in India, Brazil, or Britain, for example? Where is the local democratic accountability? In the event of abuse or corruption or simply pulling out and closing down operations, where and how would those guilty be held to account?

This anti-democratisation applies at the national levels as well. As Barry Coates, discussing the General Agreement on Trade in Services (GATS), the World Bank agreement whereby services such as education are "liberalised," or placed on the open buyers and sellers' markets, has pointed out, "GATS locks countries into a system of rules that means it is effectively impossible for governments to change policy, or for voters to elect a new government that has different policies" (2001, p. 28; see also Hill, 2006; Rikowski, 2001a, 2003).

De-theorised Education and the Loss of Critical Thought

The increasing subordination and commodification of education, including at the university level, have been well documented (see, e.g., Giroux, 2002, 2007; Giroux & Giroux, 2004; Levidow, 2002). In my own work (e.g., Hill, 2001, 2004, 2005b, 2007a), I have examined how the British government has, in effect, expelled most potentially critical aspects of education, such as sociological and political examination of schooling and education, and questions of social class, "race," and gender, from the national curriculum for what is now, in England and Wales, termed "teacher training," which was formerly called "teacher education."

In teacher education in England and Wales, "how to" has replaced "why to" in a technicist curriculum based on "delivery" of a quietist and overwhelmingly conservative set of "standards" for student teachers.

Social Class Exploitation: What Is the Current Project of Global Capitalism?

The development of ("raced" and gendered) social class-based "labour-power" and the subsequent extraction of "surplus value" is the fundamental characteristic of capitalism. It is the primary explanation for economic, political, cultural, and ideological change.

The fundamental principle of capitalism is the sanctification of private (or corporate) profit based on the extraction of surplus labour (unpaid labour time) as surplus value from the labour power of workers. It is a creed and practice of (racialised and gendered) class exploitation, exploitation by the capitalist class of those who provide the profits through their labour, the working class.

The State and Education: Labour Power, Surplus Value, and Profit

In Britain and elsewhere, both Conservative and New Labour governments have attempted to "conform" both the *existing* teacher workforce and the *future* teacher workforce (i.e., student teachers) and *their* teachers, and importantly the reproducers of teachers, the teacher educators. Why conform the teachers and the teacher educators at all? Like poets, teachers are potentially dangerous. But poets are largely invisible, and reading poetry is voluntary. Schooling is not. Teachers' work is *the production and reproduction of knowledge, attitudes, and ideology.*

Glenn Rikowski's work[1] develops a Marxist analysis based on an analysis of "labour power" (the capacity to labour). With respect to education, he suggests that teachers are the most dangerous of workers because they have a special role in shaping, developing, and forcing the single commodity on which the whole capitalist system rests: labour power.

In the capitalist labour process, labour power is transformed into value-creating *labour,* and, at a certain point, *surplus value*—that is, value over and above that represented in the worker's wage—is created. *Surplus value* is the first form of the existence of capital. It is the *lifeblood of capital.*

The state needs to control the social production of labour processes for two reasons. First, it must try to ensure that this occurs. Second, it must try to ensure that modes of pedagogy that are antithetical to labour power production do not and cannot exist. In particular, it becomes clear, on this analysis, that the capitalist state will seek to destroy any forms of pedagogy that attempt to educate students regarding their real predicament: to create an awareness of themselves as future labour powers, and to underpin this awareness with critical insight that seeks to undermine the smooth running of the social production of labour power. This fear entails strict control of teacher education, of the curriculum, and of educational research.

The Salience and Essential Nature of Social Class Exploitation

Social class is the inevitable and defining feature of capitalist exploitation, whereas the various other forms of oppression are not *essential* to its nature and continuation, however much they are commonly functional to this, and however obviously racialised and gendered capitalist oppression is in most countries. "Left revisionist" analyses that pose an equality, or parallelism, between different forms of structural oppression, for example, "race" or gender (such as, e.g., in the work of Michael Apple, 2001, 2006), or those who argue that "race" inequality or gender equality are the primary forms of structural oppression, occlude the essential and primary nature of social class oppression in capitalist economies today.[2]

The face of poverty staring out from post-Katrina New Orleans was overwhelmingly black. It was also overwhelmingly black working class. It was also poor white working class. Richer black and white car owners drove away. Within educational curricula and pedagogy, and within the media (and, indeed, wherever resistant teachers and other cultural workers can find spaces), the existence of various and multiple forms of oppression and the similarity of their effects on individuals and communities should not disguise, nor weaken, a class analysis that recognises the structural centrality of social class exploitation and conflict. In capitalist society this has consequences for political and social strategy, for mobilisation and for action.

Marxist, Post-modernist, and Left Revisionist Analyses of Social Class

Outside the Marxist tradition, it is clear that many critics of class analysis confound class consciousness with the fact of class, and tend to deduce the non-existence of the latter from the "absence" of the former or, if not an absence, then the decline in salience in advanced capitalist countries. The collapse of many traditional signifiers of "working-classness" has led many to pronounce the demise of class. Beverley Skeggs (1991) observes, "class inequality exists beyond its theoretical representation" (p. 6).

Marx took great pains to stress that social class is distinct from economic class, and necessarily includes a political dimension, which, in the broadest sense, is "culturally" rather than "economically" determined. Class consciousness, a cultural phenomenon, does not follow automatically or inevitably from the fact of (economic) class position. In *The Poverty of Philosophy*, Marx [1847] (in Tucker, 1978) distinguishes a "class-in-itself" (class position) and a "class-for itself" (class consciousness) and, in *The Communist Manifesto* (Marx & Engels [1848], in Tucker, 1978), explicitly identified the "formation of the proletariat into a class" as *the* key political task facing the communists. In *The Eighteenth Brumaire of Louis Napoleon*, Marx (1852) observes:

> In so far as millions of families live under economic conditions of existence that divide their mode of life, their interests and their cultural formation from those of the other classes and bring them into conflict with those classes, they form a class. (Marx [1852], in Tucker, 1978, p. 608)

The recognition by Marx that class consciousness is not necessarily or directly produced from the material and objective fact of class position enables neo-Marxists to acknowledge the wide range of contemporary influences that may (or may not) inform the subjective consciousness of identity, but in doing so, to retain the crucial reference to the basic economic determinant of social experience.

The notion of an essential, unitary self was rejected, over a century and a half ago, by Marx in his *Sixth Thesis on Feuerbach* (1845), where he stated, "but the human essence is no abstraction inherent in each single individual. In its reality it is the ensemble of the social relations" (Marx [1845], in Tucker, 1978, p. 45). Furthermore, in some specific contexts, "resistance postmodernism" can have/has had some progressive appeal and effects, for example, in recognising/allowing official recognition of, for example, gay/lesbian sexuality and feminist/women's rights, in states emerging from religious, Stalinist, or fascist/quasi-fascist authoritarian dictatorships.

The overall criticism of post-modernism, however, remains. The absence of class in post-modern theory actively contributes to the ideological disarmament of the working-class movement.[3] The local, specific, and partial analyses that mark the limitations of post-modernism all either lack or oppose social-class strategy or policy.

The Education and Media Ideological State Apparatuses

Education and the media are the dominant ideological state apparatuses (ISAs), though, from the United States to Iran and Israel and elsewhere, religion is also assuming a more salient role. Each ISA contains disciplinary repressive moments and effects. One of its greatest achievements is that capital presents itself as natural, free, and democratic, and that any attack on free-market, neo-liberal capitalism is damned as anti-democratic. Any attack on capitalism becomes characterised as an attack on world freedom and democracy itself.

The most powerful restraint on capital (and the political parties funded and influenced by capitalists in their bountiful donations) is that it needs to persuade the people that neo-liberalism—competition, privatisation, poorer standards of public services, greater inequalities between rich and poor—is legitimate. It may also be seen as in the pocket of the international and/or national ruling classes and their local and national state weaponry.

To minimise this de-legitimation, to ensure that the majority of the population considers the government and the economic system of private monopoly ownership as legitimate, the state uses ISAs, such as schools, colleges, and the media, to "naturalise" capitalism to make the existing status quo seem "only natural." If and when this doesn't work, the repressive state apparatuses kick in, sometimes literally, with steel-capped military boots.

The term "state apparatus" does not refer solely to apparatuses such as ministries and various levels of government. It applies to those societal apparatuses, institutions, and agencies that operate on behalf of, and maintain the existing economic and social relations of, production. The school or university is no hiding place. In other words, these are the apparatuses that sustain capital, capitalism, and capitalists. Educators and cultural workers are implicated in the process of economic, cultural, and ideological reproduction, of training for capital, and of instilling individualistic, consumerist, capitalist common-sense.

Ideological and Repressive State Apparatuses

Althusser argues that the ideological dominance of the ruling class is, like its political dominance, secured in and through definite institutional forms and practices: the ideological apparatuses of the state. As Althusser suggests, *every ideological state apparatus is also in part a repressive state apparatus* (see Althusser, 1971; Hill, 2001, 2005b), punishing those who dissent.

ISAs have internal "coercive" practices (e.g., the forms of punishment, non-promotion, displacement, being "out-of-favour" experienced by socialists and trade union activists/militants historically and currently across numerous countries). Similarly, *repressive state apparatuses* attempt to secure significant internal unity and wider social authority through ideology (e.g., through their ideologies of patriotism and national integrity and religion). Every *repressive state apparatus,* therefore, has an ideological moment, propagating a version of common sense and attempting to legitimate it under threat of sanction.

Governments, and the ruling classes in whose interests they act, prefer to use the second form of state apparatuses, the ISAs. Changing the school and initial teacher education curriculum, abandoning "general studies" and "liberal studies," and horizon broadening in the United Kingdom for working-class "trade" and skilled worker students/apprentices in "Further Education" (vocational) colleges, is less messy than sending the troops onto the streets or visored, baton-wielding police into strike-bound mining villages, or protests by the landless. It is also deemed more legitimate by the population in general.

Capitalist Agendas and Education

The Agenda of Capital for/in Education, it is argued, comprises the following:

- a reduction in public expenditure on public education services;

- a Capitalist Agenda *for* Schooling and Education;

- a Capitalist Agenda *in* Schooling and Education;

- a new public managerialism mode of organisation, surveillance, and control of workers;

- a Capitalist Agenda for Education Business, including British and the United States (and other leading local capitalist states) based corporations in the vanguard of international privatisation and profit taking.

The Contexts of Educational Change and the Neo-liberal Project

The restructuring of schooling and education systems across the world needs to be placed within the ideological and policy context of the links between capital, neo-liberalism—with its combination of privatisation and competitive markets in education characterised by selection and exclusion— and the rampant growth of national and international inequalities. The current crisis of capital accumulation—the declining rate of profit, particularly within the turn of the millennium U.S. economy—has given an added urgency to the neo-liberal project for education globally.

Cutting Public Expenditure

Not only do education and the media have the function of creating and reproducing a labour force fit for capitalism, but capital also requires cutting public spending and the social wage (i.e., the cost and value of the state pensions, health, and education services), and reducing the "tax-take" as a proportion of gross domestic product. These are all subject to the variegations of short-term policy and local political considerations, such as upcoming elections or mass demonstrations, the balance of class forces—the objective and subjective current labour–capital relation (i.e., the relationship between the capitalist class and the working class and their relative cohesiveness, organisation, leadership, and will).

Capital and the Business of Education

The capitalist state has a Capitalist Agenda *for* Education as well as a Business Plan *in* Education. It also has a Capitalist Agenda *for Education Business*. The Capitalist Agenda *for* Education centres on socially producing labour power (people's capacity to labour) for capitalist enterprises. The Capitalist Agenda *in* Education focuses on setting business "free" in education for profit making.

The first aim is to ensure that schooling and education engage in ideological and economic reproduction. National state education and training policies in the Capitalist Agenda *for* Education are of increasing importance for national capital. In an era of global capital, this is one of the few remaining areas for national state intervention. It is the site, suggests Hatcher (2001), where a state can make a difference. Thus, capital first requires an education fit for business, in order to make schooling and further higher education geared to produce the personality, ideological, and economic requirements of capital.

Second, capital wants to make profits from education and other privatised public services such as water supply and health care. The aim here is for private enterprise, private capitalists, to make money out of it, to make private profit out of it, to control it, whether by outright control through private chains of schools/universities, by selling services to state-funded schools and education systems, or by "voucher" systems through which taxpayers subsidise the owners of private schools.

Thus, business makes education fit for business, rendering schooling, including higher education, subordinate to the ideological and economic requirements of capital, ensuring that schools produce compliant, ideologically indoctrinated, pro-capitalist, effective workers.

The third education Business Plan for capital, the Capitalist Agenda *for Education Business,* is to "bring the bucks back home," for governments in globally dominant economic positions (e.g., the United Kingdom, the United States), or in locally dominant economic positions (e.g., Australia, New Zealand, Brazil), to support locally based corporations (or, much more commonly, locally based transnational corporations) in profit taking from the privatisation and neo-liberalisation of education services globally (Hill, 2003, 2004, 2005a, 2006).

Arenas for Resistance and Critical Engagement

Critical education for economic and social justice can play a role in resisting the depredations and the "common sense" of global neo-liberal capital, and play a role in developing class consciousness and an egalitarian sustainable future. Critical education for economic and social justice is where teachers and other cultural workers act as critical transformative and public intellectuals within and outside of sites of economic, ideological, and cultural reproduction. Such activity is both deconstructive and reconstructive, offering a *utopian politics of anger, analysis, and hope* based on a materialised critical pedagogy that recognises, yet challenges, the strength of the structures and apparatuses of capital. Such activity encompasses activity within different arenas of resistant and revolutionary activity.

Arena 1: Within the Education and Media Apparatuses

The first arena is within the sites of education and the media themselves. Critical educators can indeed recognise that education has the potential to fuel the flames of resistance to global capitalism as well as the passion for socialist transformation.

Educators and cultural workers should develop "critical reflection" and a commitment to critical action and to moral/ethical egalitarian action. Teachers without the capacity to stimulate critical enquiry leave education always on the edge of indoctrination and quiescence, which is the antithesis of democratic education.

School and teacher education courses, as well as film and other media, need to present data on equality issues: on racism, sexism, social class inequality, homophobia, and discrimination/prejudice regarding disability and special needs. Many teachers and students are simply not aware of the existence of such data in education and society or the impact of individual labelling, and of structural discriminations on the lives and education of the children in their classes, schools, and society.

Critical pedagogy, Freirean pedagogy, socialist pedagogy, and revolutionary critical pedagogy (McLaren, 2005; McLaren & Farahmandpur, 2005; McLaren & Jaramillo, 2007) are important theoretical and theory-inspired practices that both present and theorise, such inequalities, the ways schooling for conformity is continued, and education for emancipation can be effected and be effective. I have, elsewhere (e.g., Hill, 2002, 2005c; Hill & Boxley, 2007), suggested a set of more detailed principles and proposals—first, for the education system, and, second, for teacher education. Together, with co-writers in the *Hillcole Group of Radical Left Educators* in Britain (Hillcole Group, 1991, 1997), we have suggested principles and policy in and for a socialist education system and society. However, divorced from other arenas of progressive struggle, the success of critical pedagogy and intervention will be limited.

Arena 2: Working Outside of the Classroom! Local Action[4]

Using schools and educational sites as arenas of cultural struggle, and education, in general, as a vehicle for social transformation, is premised upon a clear commitment to work with communities (see Martin, 2005), parents, and students, and with the trade unions and workers within those institutions. This is the second arena of resistance, working outside of the classroom on issues relating to education and its role in reproducing inequality and oppression.

Working "with" means "knowing" the daily, material existence of the exploited class strata and groups. Ideally, it means fulfilling the role of the organic intellectual, organically linked to and part of those groups. This also infers working with communities in developing the perception that schools and education themselves are sites of social, economic, and ideological contestation, not "neutral" or "fair" or "inevitable," but sites of economic, cultural, and ideological "class" domination. It is, thereby, important to develop awareness of the role of education in capital reproduction as well as in the reproduction of class relations.

Arena 3: Mass Action as Part of a Broader Movement for Economic and Social Justice

Globally and nationally, societies are developing to a greater or lesser degree, critical educators, community activists, organic intellectuals, students and teachers whose feelings of outrage at economic, social class, racial and gender, and other forms of oppression lead them/us into activism. Thus, the *third arena* for resistance is action across a broader agenda, linking issues and experience within different economic and social sectors, connecting different struggles.

Ideological intervention in classrooms and in other cultural sites can have dramatic effect, not least on some individuals and groups who are "hailed" or, in Althusser's (1971) terminology, "interpellated" by resistant ideology. Through well-organised and focused non-sectarian campaigns organised around class and anti-capitalist issues, those committed to economic and social equality and justice and environmental sustainability can work towards local, national, and international campaigns, towards an understanding that we are part of a massive force—the force of the international—and growing working class. Harman (2002) suggests that

> what matters now is for this [new] generation [of activists] to connect with the great mass of ordinary workers who as well as suffering under the system have the collective strength to fight it. (p. 40)

Questions for Reflection

1. What are some examples of the ideological and the repressive education state apparatuses?

2. According to the author, what are the aims of capital with respect to education?

3. What is a Marxist critique of post-modernism and of "Left Revisionist" analysis in education?

4. What are the impacts of capital, in its current neo-liberal and neo-conservative form, on education?

5. What are the forms and arenas of resistance to neo-liberal/neo-conservative capital open

to and used by education workers and students?

Notes

1. See Rikowski (2001a, 2001b), and his web site at

    http://www.flowideas.co.uk/?page=about&sub=Glenn%20Rikowski

2. For a Marxist discussion of the salience within capitalism of social class exploitation, that is "raced" and gendered social class exploitation, see, for example, Cole, Hill, McLaren, and Rikowski (2001); Kelsh and Hill (2006).

3. For Marxist critiques of post-modernism in education, see, for example, Cole (2008); Cole, Hill, and Rikowski (1997); Cole et al. (2001); Hill, McLaren, Cole, and Rikowski (2002).

4. For instances of resistant counter-hegemonic actions, see Bircham and Charlton (2001) and Hill (2008b). Discussion of these three arenas for action and the role of socialist/critical educators can be found in Hill (2007b).

References

Althusser, L. (1971). Ideology and state apparatuses. In *Lenin and Philosophy and Other Essays* (pp. 85–116). London: New Left Books.

Apple, M. (2001). *Educating the "right" way: Markets, standards, God, and inequality.* New York and London: RoutledgeFalmer.

———. (2006). Review essay: Rhetoric and reality in critical educational studies in the United States. *British Journal of Sociology of Education, 27*(5), 679–687.

Bircham, E., &. Charlton, J. (2001). *Anti-capitalism: A guide to the movement.* London: Bookmarks.

Coates, B. (2001). GATS. In E. Bircham and J. Charlton (Eds.), *Anti-capitalism: A guide to the movement* (pp. 27–42). London: Bookmarks.

Cole, M. (2008). *Marxism and educational theory: Origins and issues.* London: Routledge.

Cole, M., Hill, D., McLaren, P., & Rikowski, G. (2001). *Red chalk: On schooling, capitalism and politics.* Brighton, UK: Institute for Education Policy Studies.

Cole, M., Hill, D., & Rikowski, G. (1997). Between postmodernism and nowhere: The predicament of the postmodernist. *British Journal of Education Studies, 45*(2), 187–200.

Conway, E. (2005, November 25). Where to live if you want a healthy old age. *Daily Telegraph.* Retrieved September 20, 2007, from http://www.telegraph.co.uk/news/main.jhtml?xml=/news/2006/11/22/nhealth22.xml

Dorling, D., Rigby, J., Wheeler, B., Ballas, B., Thomas, B., Fahmy, E., et al. (2007). *Poverty, wealth and place in Britain 1968–2005.* York, UK: Joseph Rowntree Foundation. Retrieved September 20, 2007, from http://www.jrf.org.uk/bookshop/eBooks/2019-poverty-wealth-place.pdf

Gillborn, D., & Youdell, D. (2000). *Rationing education: Policy, practice, reform and equity.* Buckingham, UK: Open University Press.

Giroux, H. (2002). The corporate war against higher education. *Workplace: A journal of academic labour,* 5(1). Retrieved September 20, 2007, from http://www.louisville.edu/journal/workplace/issue5p1/giroux.html

———. (2007). *The university in chains: Confronting the military-industrial-academic complex.* Boulder, CO: Paradigm.

Giroux, H., & Giroux, S. (2004). *Take back higher education: Race, youth, and the crisis of democracy in the post-civil rights era.* London: Palgrave Macmillan.

Greaves, N., Hill, D., & Maisuria, A. (2007). Embourgeoisment, immiseration, commodification—Marxism revisited: A critique of education in capitalist systems. *Journal for Critical education Policy Studies,* 5(1). Retrieved September 20, 2007, from http://www.jceps.com/index.php?pageID=article&articleID=83

Harman, C. (2002). The workers of the world. *International Socialism, 96,* 3–45.

Harris, R. (2007, July 22). Welcome to Richistan, USA. *The Observer.* Retrieved September 20, 2007, from http://observer.guardian.co.uk/world/story/0,,2131974,00.html

Hatcher, R. (2001). Getting down to the business: Schooling in the globalised economy. *Education and Social Justice, 3*(2), 45-59.

Hill, D. (2001). State theory and the neo-liberal reconstruction of teacher education: A structuralist neo-Marxist critique of postmodernist, quasi-postmodernist, and culturalist neo-Marxist theory. *British Journal of Sociology of Education, 22*(1), 137–157.

———. (2002). The radical left and education policy: Education for economic and social justice. *Education and Social Justice, 4*(3), 41–51.

———. (2003). Global neoliberalism, the deformation of education and resistance. *Journal for Critical Education Policy Studies, 1*(1). Retrieved September 20, 2007, from http://www.jceps.com/index.php?pageID=articleandarticleID=7

———. (2004). Books, banks and bullets: Controlling our minds—the global project of imperialistic and militaristic neo-liberalism and its effect on education policy. *Policy Futures in Education, 2,* 3–4. Retrieved September 20, 2007, from http://www.wwwords.co.uk/pfie/content/pdfs/2/issue2_3.asp

———. (2005a). Globalisation and its educational discontents: Neoliberalisation and its impacts on education workers' rights, pay, and conditions. *International Studies in the Sociology of Education, 15*(3), 257–288.

———. (2005b). State theory and the neoliberal reconstruction of schooling and teacher education. In G. Fischman, P. McLaren, H. Sünker, & C. Lankshear (Eds.), *Critical theories, radical pedagogies and global conflicts* (pp. 23–51). Lanham, MD: Rowman & Littlefield.

———. (2005c). Critical education for economic and social justice. In M. Pruyn and L. Huerta-Charles (Eds.), *Teaching Peter McLaren: Paths of dissent* (pp. 146–185). New York: Peter Lang.

———. (2006). Education services liberalization. In E. Rosskam (Ed.), *Winners or Losers? Liberalizing public services* (pp. 3–54). Geneva: International Labour Organisation.

———. (2007a). Critical teacher education, new labour in Britain, and the global project of neoliberal capital. *Policy Futures, 5*(2). Retrieved September 20, 2007, from http://www.wwwords.co.uk/pfie/content/pdfs/5/issue5_2.asp

———. (2007b). Socialist educators and capitalist education. *Socialist Outlook, 13.* Retrieved September 20, 2007, from http://www.isg-fi.org.uk/spip.php?article576

———. (Ed.) (2008a). *The rich world and the impoverishment of education: Diminishing democracy, equity and workers' rights.* New York: Routledge.

———. (Ed.) (2008b). *Contesting neoliberal education: Public resistance and collective advance.* New York: Routledge.

Hill, D., & Boxley, S. (2007). Critical teacher education for economic, environmental and social justice: An ecosocialist manifesto. *Journal for Critical Education Policy Studies*, *5*(2). Retrieved September 20, 2007, from http://www.jceps.com/index.php?pageID=article&articleID=96

Hill, D., McLaren, P., Cole, M., & Rikowski, G. (Eds.) (2002). *Marxism against postmodernism in educational theory*. Lanham, MD: Lexington Press.

Hill, D., & Rosskam, E. (Eds.) (2008). *The developing world and state education: Neoliberal depredation and egalitarian alternatives*. New York: Routledge.

Hillcole Group. (1991). *Changing the future: Redprint for education*. London: Tufnell.

———. (1997). *Rethinking education and democracy: A socialist alternative for the twenty-first century*. London: Tufnell.

Hirtt, N. (2004). Three axes of merchandisation. *European Educational Research Journal*, *3*(2), 442–453. Retrieved September 20, 2007, from http://www.wwwords.co.uk/eerj

Kelsh, D., & Hill, D. (2006). The culturalization of class and the occluding of class consciousness: The knowledge industry in/of education. *Journal for Critical Education Policy Studies*, *4*(1). Retrieved September 20, 2007, from http://www.jceps.com/index.php?pageID=article&articleID=59

Levidow, L. (2002). Marketizing higher education: Neo-liberal and counter-strategies. *Education and Social Justice*, *3*(2), 12–23. Retrieved September 20, 2007, from http://www.commoner.org.uk/03levidow.pdf

Martin, G. (2005). You can't be neutral on a moving bus: Critical pedagogy as community praxis. *Journal for Critical Education Policy Studies*, *3*(2). Retrieved on September 20, 2007, from http://www.jceps.com/index.php?pageID=article&articleID=47

McLaren, P. (2005). *Capitalists and conquerors: A critical pedagogy against empire*. Lanham, MD: Rowman & Littlefield.

McLaren, P., & Farahmandpur, R. (2005). *Teaching against global capitalism and the new imperialism*. Lanham, MD: Rowman & Littlefield.

McLaren, P., & Jaramillo, N. (2007). *Pedagogy and praxis in the age of empire*. Rotterdam, Netherlands: Sense.

Reimers, F. (2000). *Unequal schools, unequal chances: The challenges to equal opportunity in the Americas*. Cambridge, MA: Harvard University Press.

Rikowski, G. (2001a). *The battle in Seattle*. London: Tufnell.

———. (2001b). Fuel for the living fire: Labour-power! In A. Dinerstein & M. Neary (Eds.), *The labour debate: An investigation into the theory and reality of Capitalist work* (pp. 179–202). Aldershot, UK: Ashgate.

———. (2003). Schools and the GATS enigma. *Journal for Critical Education Policy Studies*, *1*(1). Retrieved September 20, 2007, from http://www.jceps.com/index.php?pageID=article&articleID=8

Rosskam, E. (Ed.). (2006). *Winners or losers? Liberalizing public services*. Geneva: International Labour Organisation.

Skeggs, B. (1991). Post-modernism: What is all the fuss about? *British Journal of Sociology of Education*, *12*(2), 255–267.

Tucker, R. (Ed.) (1978). *The Marx-Engels reader*. New York: W. W. Norton.

Whitty, G., Power, S., & Halpin, D. (1998). *Devolution and choice in education: The school, the state and the market*. Buckingham, UK: Open University Press.

CHAPTER

2

FROM THE MARGINS TO THE MAINSTREAM:
GLOBAL EDUCATION AND THE RESPONSE TO
THE DEMOCRATIC DEFICIT IN AMERICA

Michael O'Sullivan

Introduction

It is the central thesis of this chapter that there is a direct link between the crisis of American democracy and that of public education. I also argue that critical-democratic educators, that is, those educators who work to infuse critical pedagogies with a view to contributing to an authentically participatory (or deliberative) democracy, are strategically placed to contribute to a solution to both of these crises. However, because their social and pedagogical perspectives lie outside of the mainstream of educational thinking, critical-democratic educators frequently find themselves at odds even with some of their fellow teachers who are, in the words of one researcher, consigned to "the periphery of the concerns of the profession" (Schweifurth, 2006, p. 49). Despite this marginalization, their role in promoting schools as sites of social change is far from peripheral. Forming part of a growing "globalization from below" social movement (Apple, Kenway, & Singh, 2005), critical-democratic educators are involved in two central aspects of far-reaching transformational educational reform. The first of these is the infusion, classroom by classroom, of a critical-democratic pedagogy into the curriculum. The second is a dialogue with their mainstream colleagues who teach within the framework of the dominant neoliberal ideology, the objective of which is to encourage them to feel increasingly comfortable moving their classroom practice in more critical directions.

The goal of this radical-democratic professional practice is to nurture the growth of critically thinking, globally minded young citizens who have both the political will and the intellectual skills to participate in a *deliberative* democracy, a concept central to John Dewey's thinking on the relationship between democracy and educational reform (Dewey, 1939/1963; Kadlec, 2007). The practice of deliberative democracy, be it in the classroom or in our communities, involves shifting and enriching our understanding of democracy from one that effectively reduces public political participation to the act of voting to one that sees democracy as an ongoing process where an informed and motivated citizenry engages in public debate and political engagement at the local, national, and, increasingly, the global level (Benhabib, 1996; Habermas, 1996; Kadlec, 2007).

Transforming American education to put it at the service of deliberative democracy is a formidable task, especially in a society where the primary role of citizens has shifted from one of political participation to that of being a consumer (Ladson-Billings, 2005; Spring, 2006). Michael Walzer (2002) argues for democratic equality, by which he means devoting the "money, talent, and energy … necessary to lift … our students into full political, economic, and cultural literacy" (p. 75). Failure to do so, he states, "will put our democracy at risk" (p. 75). I go one step further than Walzer; I argue that American democracy has been so trivialized and depoliticized that, in order for it to be viable, it must be reconstituted. For this to happen, teachers, and the public at large, must be won over both to a transformatory democratizing educational project and a parallel political project. To begin thinking about this, contemporary critical-democratic educators can draw upon the reflections of critical pedagogues and social thinkers including Dewey and those who followed him.

What is at the heart of critical-democratic pedagogy is a concern with power and empowerment (Freire, 1970, 1985, 1993; Giroux, 1988, 1995, 1997, 2003). No pedagogy that avoids the central issue of who exercises power, on whose behalf it is exercised, and the adequacy or inadequacy of our democratic institutions and practices, has any claim to being considered critical.

Many compelling critical-democratic pedagogies have emerged over the years that contribute to our ability as educators to teach from a critical perspective. However, it is my contention that the school of thought known as global education, or more recently global citizenship education (GCE), constitutes the most promising and inclusive framework for critical-democratic educators in our elementary, secondary, and postsecondary institutions.[1] Global education and GCE is a world-minded and student-centered pedagogy that contains the three essential elements that characterize all good curricular practice, namely, thinking/feeling/doing (Miller, 2007). Global education has, as its central concern, understanding the interconnectedness of events with issues of race, class, gender, war and peace, the environment, and so forth, from a critical-democratic perspective. Selby's *Global Education as Transformative Education* (2004) offers a succinct and compelling analysis of the transformational potential of global education.

Recently, however, a process of mainstreaming aspects of the critical-democratic pedagogies is occurring in much the same way that many of Dewey's progressive methods were, in their day, inserted into the official, or mainstream, curriculum. Such mainstreaming, while it undeniably serves to blunt the critical edge of transformative pedagogical strategies, nonetheless creates an opportunity for critical-democratic practitioners to emerge from the periphery and influence, through a dialogic process with their colleagues, how these mainstreamed but potentially critical curricular themes might be incorporated into classroom practice. This can be viewed as a political-pedagogical strategy at the school level, which combines two components: teaching and mentoring. I argue that, as the broader struggle mentioned by Walzer (2002) for institutional reform unfolds, there exist openings that allow for such a strategy. In fact, a process of infusion, classroom by classroom, of critical-democratic pedagogy from a global perspective has been underway in many classrooms for years.

The Crisis of American Democracy: A Century-old Story

The observation that American democracy is in crisis is hardly new. John Dewey (2000/1916, 1997/1938) was deeply worried about a *democratic deficit* in the early decades of the twentieth century (Carr & Hartlett, 1996). He argued, in opposition to his conservative critics (most famously Walter Lippmann, 1999/1922), that the solution to the crisis of democracy was not to limit popular political participation to occasional voting, leaving the serious business of public life to professional politicians, but rather, he favored the reform of the system of public education such that the majority of citizens possessed the intellectual tools and the motivation to participate in a process of *deliberative democracy* (Kadlec, 2007; Westbrook, 1991). Dewey's thoughts on democracy and education are relevant to us today because, despite the passage of time, his era was characterized by many of the debates about schooling, democracy, and America's role in the world that parallel the issues that we face today (Kadlec, 2007; Walzer, 2002). At the beginning of the twentieth century, much of the world was experiencing monumental social, political, and economic changes. In the United States, industrialization, urbanization, and the growth of American influence on the world stage created a sense of optimism and the belief that America offered unlimited possibility. Today, the changes being forged by the forces of neoliberal globalization are arguably of even greater significance than those of a century ago (McGrew, 2005). The United States, like Great Britain before it, is experiencing a vigorous challenge to its economic and political hegemony in an increasing multipolar world. Rather than coming to terms with this evolving realignment in the global balance of power, neoconservatives have sought to reassert declining U.S. influence through military means (Dyer, 2007), the export of neoliberal capitalism (Klein, 2007), and limited neoliberal "packaged democracy" (Talbert, 2005). That such an approach is completely counterproductive is increasingly evident to a wide range of American public opinion (see, e.g., Schwenninger, 2004). Despite the traumatic lessons of Vietnam and the almost unanimous global opposition to the invasion of Iraq, American neoconservatives faced little domestic opposition as they manipulated public reaction to, and anger about, the events of September 11, 2001, and built popular and bipartisan political support for the Iraq invasion. The Iraq quagmire and the subsequent successful efforts at imposing neoliberal economics globally (Klein, 2007) constitute telling evidence of a crisis in both American democracy and in American education.

Noam Chomsky (2006) analyzes in some detail the trivialization and depoliticization of American politics through his critique of the electoral process. He argues that the fundamental issues facing America, and the world, hardly appear on the U.S. popular political agenda (p. 209). Even during elections, candidates for the most powerful office in America are not judged by their record in dealing creatively with the many complex issues that impact people's lives. Rather, the media, owned and controlled as it is by the very corporate interests that profit from this neoliberal expansion (Cohen, 2005) and, unfortunately, much of the electorate, focuses on secondary considerations such as the candidates' demeanor (and their misdemeanors), a gaffe caught on an open microphone, or the acceptability (or otherwise) of their religious beliefs. The life and death issues for which these politicians, once elected, will be responsible are largely ignored during the one occasion when it might be presumed that the electorate would be listening intently with a view to holding the candidates accountable.

Despite his critique of the functioning of American democracy, Chomsky, like Dewey before him, demonstrates great faith in the potential of that democracy. To realize this optimism, schools will have to be transformed, as Dewey suggested decades ago, with a view to providing students the political skills and habits of mind required for effective participation in democratic society. In addition to infusing critical pedagogies into classrooms, the main point taken up in this chapter, the social context has to be created whereby socially disadvantaged students are able to take advantage of critical-democratic curricular reforms. This involves building up *communal* social capital as conceived by Carnoy (2007). Social capital is usually thought of as resulting from "family and community cohesiveness, supportiveness, and networking [that] help students that are part of these families and communities to learn more in school and have higher expectations for themselves" (p. 11). Carnoy argues that where families and/or communities are not able to provide such support, through the institution of schools states can generate just as potent a form of social capital in promoting educational achievement as families can, and that state generated social capital is essential to improving educational achievement for low-income groups—those that have the least cultural capital and most difficulty in acquiring and accumulating capital on their own. (p. 12)

Viewed in this way, social capital is not simply an "asset" accumulated by individuals as it is now, but is communal. All students, and thus the community as a whole, have their social capital elevated. Space limitations do not permit further inquiry into this important aspect of school reform.

Global and Global Citizenship Education: A Way Forward

Building on a rich history of progressive and critical-democratic educational thinkers, contemporary educators are constructing pedagogies that respond to the growing awareness of the interconnectedness of world events (Banks, 2004; Noddings, 2005; Openshaw & White, 2005; Selby, 2004). Not only are corporations thinking globally as they extend their reach to new markets (Bartlett & Ghoshal, 2000; Rosenau, 2003), but social movements, which include significant teacher involvement, are themselves going global (e.g., the Global Social Forum). In so doing, they form part of a "globalization from below" movement of social change (Apple et al., 2005).

Given this growth of global perspectives on the part of critically democratic teachers, it is quite understandable that global education has emerged as a promising pedagogy for these educators. The global education movement started with Hanvey's groundbreaking article "An attainable global perspective" (1982). Despite its undeniably cognitive bias, Hanvey's work was an important starting point for an alternative global pedagogical vision, developed further by Graham Pike and David Selby in their influential work *Global Teacher, Global Learner* (1988). Pike and Selby, in this and subsequent contributions (Pike, 1996, 2000; Selby, 2004), encouraged educators not only to teach about global issues (the cognitive domain) but also to privilege empathy (the affective domain) and social engagement. The literature (and practice) of global education grew quickly. Educators in America and elsewhere contributed to the evolution of the global education literature[2] and positioned it as a social justice–oriented critical pedagogy capable, in the hands of thoughtful and well-prepared practitioners, of infusing a democratically deliberative perspective into the curriculum. Importantly, the more recent literature stressed that global education can't be thought of as simply focusing on what is happening *out in the world*, but rather, to be relevant to students, it must include an important element of the interconnectedness of global trends with what is happening at home. This refocusing constitutes an important corrective to a miscomprehension of global education—it must include a strong recognition of the local as an integral part of the global (Noddings, 2005). In so doing, it opens the door to teaching what are usually thought of as local issues through a global lens.

Recently, a new literature focusing on GCE has emerged.[3] Originating primarily in England, critical-democratic GCE has challenged and enriched global education as defined by Hanvey and his successors. This body of work promotes and frequently problematizes GCE as the most appropriate pedagogy for infusing critical-democratic values and expanded notions of multicultural citizenship education in the era of globalization. This work, and the urgency it communicates about the precarious state of the planet and all of us who live on it, invites a citizen-initiated response to aggressive economic neoliberalism and militarized political neoconservatism.

Within the field of global education, and arguably also within the field of GCE, no single definition of what it means to be a global (citizenship) educator has emerged. Pike (1996) argued that there is a broad consensus that involves concepts such as connectedness, student global awareness, and an opening up of ourselves to others. These orientations, Pike noted, are "expressed in various ways with a host of different emphasis" (p. 8).

Pike (1996) views this ambiguity as being "both inconvenient—is its tendency to undermine a clear-cut, marketable definition—and convenient in its propensity to harbor a diversity of educational initiatives" (p. 9). In fact, this ambiguity is precisely what allows a wide range of global educators to dialogue with their mainstream colleagues as they struggle to "bring the world into the classroom" (p. 8). This situation expands the space available to critical-democratic educators who seek to challenge neoliberal curricular interpretations and nudge their colleagues in a more critical direction.

Recently, Pike (in press), in response to the rise of GCE, argues that there exist "exciting possibilities for the development of an ethos of global citizenship in our schools." He identifies six dimensions of such an ethos:

1. an expansion of the concept of loyalty, including multiple loyalties, coexistent loyalties, and shifting loyalties;

2. a critical appraisal of both nationalism and globalism and their presumed benefits;

3. the development of global thinking, including relational thinking and the deepening of our understanding of the concept of sustainability;

4. understanding citizenship as "doing," not just "being" or "knowing";

5. accepting the moral responsibilities of global citizenship, including an understanding of the negative consequences of imperialism and the impact of affluent minority lifestyles on the poor; and

6. an understanding of citizens' roles in determining the future of the planet (Pike, in press).

It is important to note that global education, GCE, or, for that matter, any of the other "educations" (e.g., multicultural, antiracist, antisexist, environmental, peace, etc.) are not inherently critical-democratic pedagogies. Each of these can be, and frequently are, taught by teachers who use mainstream pedagogies that do not touch upon issues of power or empowerment, the touchstones of criticality, nor do they examine the root causes of social, political, or economic phenomena. It is for this reason that, as they infuse critical pedagogies into their own classrooms, these critical-democratic educators need to support and mentor their colleagues into feeling comfortable with, understanding, and incorporating greater degrees of criticality into their classroom practices. This is the opportunity that accompanies the process of mainstreaming critical-democratic pedagogies.

Mainstreaming Critical Pedagogy

Mainstreaming is the process by which ideas with a progressive or critical-democratic intent are adapted for use in regular classrooms (Ibrahim, 2005). Consequently, pedagogies intended to challenge the status quo are infused into classrooms whose purpose is to do the opposite: play a central role in social reproduction, thereby maintaining or strengthening the prevailing social order (Bourdieu, 2006; Giroux, 1997). The process of mainstreaming critical ideas has a long history. Many elements of Dewey's progressive thought were incorporated into the curriculum. This resulted in these pedagogies losing their radical edge, a situation that Dewey himself recognized as he reflected on his legacy in his later years (Tanner & Tanner, 1995). This *domestication* of the criticality of socially transformational pedagogies occurs because, in mainstream classrooms, curriculum is taught by teachers who, for the most part, have been imbued since childhood with the dominant ideology. Understandably, they interpret everything they teach through the lens of this dominant perspective that fails to query issues of power and social inequity (Glass, 2000).

The possibility that, if left to their own devices, mainstream teachers would "neoliberalize" such curriculum is underscored by the fact that in a recent survey in Ontario, Canada, 71 percent of the teacher-respondents felt that certain issues that they identified as "controversial" were "too political" (Larsen & Faden, in press). The teachers surveyed had volunteered to pilot a new global education unit. It would be safe to presume that such volunteers, as a group, might well be more open to alternative pedagogies than many of their colleagues. By the end of the pilot stage, during which they had been mentored by experienced global educators, these same teachers were speaking very favorably of teaching issues that they had been recently nervous about.

Another element of the challenges provided by mainstreaming is that it simultaneously gives de facto *permission* to classroom teachers to teach critical-democratic pedagogies, although, of course, that is not the intention of the curriculum developers who appropriate alternative pedagogies. Indeed, the intention is quite the opposite—to dilute the critical component and neoliberalize the content.

What does it mean to say permission is granted to teach from a critical-democratic perspective? An example from Ohio gives us some insight. The September 2007 issue of the Department of Education's (DOE) newsletter, *Ohio Social Studies Signal*, is a promising source of critical-democratic potential. Curricular content that is suggested in that newsletter includes "Project Citizen," which encourages students to learn "how to monitor and

influence public policy" (p. 3), while "Youth for Justice" provides for teams
of students to "research problems of injustice in their schools or communities
and work ... to implement their solutions" (p. 3). Permission to deal with
controversial local and national issues could not be more clearly articulated.
Furthermore, from a more explicitly global perspective, the same edition of
the newsletter invites Ohio teachers to pilot a unit developed by UNICEF
based on the 2006 *State of the World's Children Report*, which documents
and analyzes the extent of child poverty around the world and the resulting
death of 9.7 million children a year (pp. 3–4). All of these initiatives have the
potential to be turned into powerful "critical-democratic teachable
opportunities," during which all three elements of critical pedagogy—
thinking, feeling, engaging—could occur. Of course, all of these examples,
and others mentioned in the newsletter, can be (and usually are) taught from
a mainstream perspective that reinforces widely held assumptions about life
in America. This, it is safe to presume, was the intention of the Ohio DOE
curriculum planners. Whatever their intentions, however, such assignments
constitute an invitation to challenge conventional assumptions and encourage
students to think broadly about alternatives.

Of course, not all teachers will welcome this opportunity to teach
controversial issues. The literature is clear on this: practitioners often shy
away from teaching controversial topics because they feel inadequately
prepared to teach such topics and they quite understandably fear lack of
support from colleagues and administrators should they attempt it and
controversy results (Davies, 2006, pp. 14–16). This is where the mentoring of
mainstream teachers by their critical-democratic colleagues can contribute to
overcoming such resistances.

Another largely unacknowledged impediment to teaching critically is the
issue of encouraging student social engagement. Anxiety about turning
schools into centers of student activism results in critical pedagogies, when
practiced, being frequently treated as purely academic exercises. No
opportunity is provided for meaningful student engagement with the
important social issues that these approaches inevitably raise. If critical
pedagogies are, as Street (1995) suggests, "a social practice," then space
must be provided for student *empowerment* vis-à-vis the social issues that

will emerge in class. Courts (1991) affirms that a *call to action* is central to critical thinking.

When teachers provide students with the opportunity to develop a critical perspective on a range of issues but do not provide them with the means to engage with these issues, the value of the exercise is badly compromised. In our controversy-adverse school systems, *creative* thinking (in contrast with authentic *critical* thinking) is encouraged; employers, after all, increasingly recognize the need for students to think "outside of the box." However, the "call for social action" rarely occurs. Anything that can be remotely considered activist is discouraged because it is the *activist* aspect that concerns parents, frightens teachers, and terrifies administrators, trustees, and senior government officials. There is evidence, however, that this is changing. Larsen and Faden (in press) report that mainstream teachers who have been in-serviced on GCE accept the importance of *activist-based pedagogy*.

This perspective respects the fact that students, no matter how young, are citizens. Citizenship implies that they have rights and responsibilities that are *commensurate with their age and level of maturity* (Howe, 2005). Students are not merely future citizens; they are current citizens with the right and responsibility to learn about, and intervene in, public issues of concern to them. Action on these issues can vary widely. Even very young students can engage in research on public issues and write letters to officials about their concerns. They can post research results on a class web site for parents, fellow students, and community members to read. Classroom debate about how to, or whether to, respond to a particular issue is a critical educative process in itself.

All of these factors—the opposition of the powerful to schools being converted into centers of potential resistances, the influence of the dominant ideology on teachers, the ill-preparedness and lack of support felt by teachers who are inclined to teach critically, the constraints upon any social action that exceeds the bounds of making charitable donations, and the fact that the globalization from below movement is just in its very early stages— contribute to the marginalization of critical pedagogies and those who teach them in our schools, despite the mainstreaming of some of these issues.

Exemplary Global Classroom Practice: One Teacher's Experience

Undeniably, there are impediments placed in the way of teachers who want to teach from a critical-democratic perspective. While it is important to understand those impediments, with a view to getting around them, it is also important to recognize the opportunities available to teach critically and progressively. A particularly illustrative example of taking the *permission* granted to teach critically, whether in the form of documents like the Ohio DOE newsletter or in curricular documents, comes from the Canadian province of Ontario. Schweifurth (2006), in her study of the classroom practices of graduates of the University of Toronto's Community and Global Education cohort, demonstrated that a creative interpretation of the province's existing curriculum provides ample space to infuse critical global content into the classroom while meeting current curricular standards (p. 41), at the same time pointing out that these particular new teachers were activist oriented.

Though little research exists on the actual implementation of global or GCE (Gaudelli, 2003), a recent study examines the practice of N.C., an elementary teacher in Ontario (O'Sullivan & Vetter, 2007). N.C. not only engages in exemplary critical-democratic and global classroom practice but she also does so within a highly collaborative context where a critical mass of her colleagues are engaged in similar practice—in short, she teaches and she mentors. N.C. is, along the lines suggested by Nel Noddings (1992, 2002, 2005), a caring and nurturing teacher who wants her students to be similarly caring, nurturing, and self-directed. She also wants them to become, in her words, "letter writers" to let authority know when something needs attention. N.C. teaches in a small-town school north of Toronto. One of the many units that she teaches from a global perspective involves the use of the novel *The Heaven Shop* (Ellis, 2004), a text approved by the Ontario Ministry of Education, in her Grade 7 class. This novel deals with the story of three siblings in Botswana who are orphaned by AIDS. During this novel study she covers curricular expectations relating to

- language arts (the novel study itself, creative writing, journaling, expository writing);

- math (creating charts and graphs, interpreting data on the incidence of global HIV/AIDS using data from the World Health Organization web site);

- geography (locating the countries and the regions from which the data is taken, examining basic socioeconomic indicators);

- critical thinking (examining why life expectancy for HIV-positive people is greater in the North than in Africa, and why the incidence of HIV/AIDS is much higher in the lesser developed countries); and

- research skills (finding and interpreting data) (O'Sullivan & Vetter, 2007).

Prior to formally teaching the unit, N.C. does a "feelings" check with her students. They record their beliefs and attitudes about HIV/AIDS patients and at the end of the novel study she asks them to revisit this work and write a short piece on whether or not they still feel the same way. They are asked to reflect upon and explain any changes in their views.

Another end-of-unit activity that N.C. assigns is to encourage the students to write government officials raising questions about the limited extent of Canadian overseas development assistance in support of the efforts of anti-AIDS work in Africa. With this activity she engages her students, albeit in a modest way, in civic action. By the time they complete this cross-curricular novel study, N.C.'s students have a heightened knowledge of a range of issues they are beginning to understand through a social justice and global perspective lens. This includes sensitivity to the devastating consequences of the HIV/AIDS epidemic and its impact on children. They have been encouraged to engage in a safe and age-appropriate political intervention (e.g., the letter writing) around these issues. From a practical point of view, N.C. can check off dozens of established, mandatory, cross-curricular expectations. Furthermore, should anyone question the content of her classroom instruction, everything she is doing can be justified in the curriculum (O'Sullivan & Vetter, 2007).

N.C. is fortunate in that the global perspective that permeates her school emerged from a teacher-based initiative that quickly gained the support of an exceptionally sympathetic principal (O'Sullivan & Vetter, 2007). That principal, as the result of a promotion, was transferred out of the school about four years into the program. Given that the new principal's priorities lie elsewhere, this means that global education initiatives at the school now depend very much on the efforts of individual teachers. Clearly, such initiatives benefit greatly from a sympathetic administration; however, important work can be done at the classroom level even in environments where the teachers are left to their own devices.

Some Concluding Observations

I have argued that there is a direct link between the crisis of American democracy and that of public education, and that critical-democratic educators are central to the solution to both of these crises. The agency assigned to these educators is based on the acceptance of several critical assumptions that run counter to the dominant ideology that constitutes the "worldview" and "common sense" of most Americans, including most teachers. These assumptions include

- U.S. democracy has, for all intents and purposes, failed to provide Americans with the opportunity to develop their full democratic potential. Democratic practice in America has been reduced to providing a framework in which an ever-decreasing percentage of the electorate takes the opportunity to vote from time to time and then, in effect, withdraws from the political process until the next election;

- this situation leaves the important business of running the country to the politicians and appointed officials, who then make what often prove to be disastrous public policy decisions affecting vital domestic and foreign issues including military and aggressive "diplomatic" interventions abroad. The public, sensing that they do not have the information or analytical skills to process these complex issues, respond in a variety of ways including cynicism and political passivity; and

- the responsibility for this political "disarming" of the American people is closely related to the failure of the educational system to teach authentic democratic values and practice. It is not teachers, however, who are to be blamed for the shortcomings of public education. They are, after all, products of that same system and are expected to teach curriculum established by others. Responsibility rests with timid policy makers and curriculum developers who avoid infusing the necessary democratic values and practices essential to prepare students for civic engagement into the curriculum. This is consistent with the school's assigned role as the agency most responsible for producing citizen-consumers who accept the prevailing logic.

Given that permission can be found, implicitly or explicitly, to teach controversial and critical-democratic issues, it can be concluded that the limitations on teaching from a critical-democratic perspective are not so much a question of what is found in, or absent from, the official curricular documents. Rather, the limitations lie with the willingness, preparedness, and predisposition of educators to take up the critical-democratic challenge. There certainly are teachers who do teach critically, even at the cost of finding themselves working on the margins (Schweifurth, 2006). It is essential that the efforts of these teachers be supported and their impact extended as part of a coherent and explicit critical-democratic strategy to reconfigure the authentically democratic traditions of the United States, much of which depends upon a deep process of educational reform.

In the final analysis, moving forward on the issue of democratic reform or school reform from a critical-democratic/global perspective means successfully challenging the dominant ideology, the worldview we know as neoliberalism. If we are going to find solutions that counter the logic of the ideas that sustain the belief in radical free market capitalism it is essential that, in the worlds of Marginson (2006), we understand that "neoliberalism is by no means invincible" (p. 218). An idea for which there seems to be no alternative is, of course, an idea that will persist. Former British Prime Minister Margaret Thatcher successfully achieved the neoliberal transformation of Great Britain by convincing people that "there is no alternative" (Marginson, 2006, p. 218). George W. Bush made "that grim and gritty neocon promise of certainty-in-an-uncertain-world," a promise "which received another lease of life after 9/11" (p. 218). What critical-democratic teachers and their allies outside of schools need to recall, and promote, is Marginson's optimism that "when there is an alternative, the political landscape will look very different" (p. 218).

Questions for Reflection

1. Can faculties of education develop new, more effective ways of encouraging critical classroom practices that have a greater impact than has arguably been the case to date?

2. Should certain core undergraduate subjects be considered essential for aspiring teachers regardless of their subject specialization so as to ensure they have a satisfactory grasp of global literacy?

3. Are preservice programs attracting teacher candidates whose ethnic, racial, class backgrounds, and life experiences reflect those of the students who will most likely be sitting in their classrooms? If not, what can be done to ensure that the profile of student teachers who are recruited to these programs is more representative of the ever-changing student population?

4. How can teachers who embrace the need to teach critically, but are perplexed about how to do so, be more effectively supported in their efforts to bring the world to their classroom in meaningful ways? What supports need to be put into place to encourage teachers to deepen the critical components of their classroom practice?

5. Critical-democratic pedagogy will get into mainstream classes in a significant way only when there are effective demands from beyond the school system to ensure that it happens. How can teachers and teacher-educators become part of broader globalization from below social movements that make such demands on educational authorities?

Notes

1. Global education and GCE are two closely related but distinct pedagogies. Some work has been done on defining the distinctions between the two (Davies, Evans, & Reid, 2005); however, Pike (in press), among others, argues for finding commonalities rather than constructing barriers between these two global pedagogies.

2. Authors too numerous to name but including Bigelow and Peterson (2002), Holden (2000), Hurley (2004), Merryfield (1997), Noddings (2005), and Tye (1999) were among the many contributors.

3. Contributors to the GCE literature include Apple et al. (2005), Banks (2004), Davies et al. (2005), Davies and Issitt (2005), L. Davies (2005, 2006), Howe (2005), Ibrahim (2005), Noddings (2005), and Torres (1998).

References

Apple, M. W., Kenway, J., & Singh, M. (Eds.). (2005). *Globalizing education: Policies, pedagogies, and politics*. New York: Peter Lang.
Banks, J. A. (Ed.). (2004). *Diversity and citizenship education: Global perspectives*. San Francisco: Jossey-Bass.
Bartlett, C. A., & Ghoshal, S. (2000). Going global: Lessons from late movers. *Harvard Business Review, 78*(3), 132–142.
Benhabib, S. (1996). *Democracy and difference: Contesting boundaries of the political*. Princeton, NJ: Princeton University Press.

Bigelow, B., & Peterson, B. (Eds.). (2002). *Rethinking globalization: Teaching for justice in an unjust world*. Milwaukee, WI: Rethinking Schools.

Bourdieu, P. (2006). The forms of capital. In H. Lauder, P. Brown, J.-A. Dillabough, & A. H. Halsey (Eds.), *Education, globalization and social change* (pp. 105–118). Oxford, UK: Oxford University Press.

Carnoy, M. (2007). *Cuba's academic advantage: Why students in Cuba do better in school*. Stanford, CA: Stanford University Press.

Carr, W., & Hartlett, A. (1996). *Education and the struggle for democracy: The politics educational ideas*. Buckingham, UK: Open University Press.

Chomsky, N. (2006). *Failed states: The abuse of power and the assault on democracy*. New York: Metropolitan Books.

Cohen, E. (2005). *News incorporated: Corporate media ownership and its threat to democracy*. Amherst, NY: Prometheus Books.

Cohen, P. (2007, July 23). Journalist chosen to lead a public policy institute. *New York Times*. Retrieved August 1, 2007, from http://www.nytimes.com/07/23/arts

Courts, P. L. (1991). *Literacy and empowerment: The meaning makers*. New York: Bergin & Garvey.

Davies, I., Evans, M., & Reid, A. (2005). Globalizing citizenship education? A critique of "global education" and "citizenship education." *British Journal of Educational Studies, 53*(1), 66–89.

Davies, I., & Issitt, J. (2005). Reflections on citizenship education in Australia, Canada and England. *Comparative Education, 41*(4), 389–410.

Davies, L. (2005). Teaching about conflict through citizenship education. *International Journal of Citizenship and Teacher Education, 1*(2), 17–34.

———. (2006). Global citizenship: Abstraction or framework for action? *Educational Review, 58*(1), 5–25.

Dewey, J. (1963/1939). *Freedom and culture*. New York: Capricorn Books. (Original work published 1939.)

———. (1997/1938). *Experience and education*. New York: Touchstone. (Original work published 1938.)

———. (2000/1916). *Democracy and education: An introduction to the philosophy of education*. Lanham, MD: Rowman & Littlefield. (Original work published 1916.)

Dyer, G. (2007). *The mess they made: The Middle East after Iraq*. Toronto, ON: McClelland & Stewart.

Ellis, D. (2004). *The heaven shop*. Toronto, ON: Fitzhenry & Whiteside.

Freire, P. (1970). *The pedagogy of the oppressed*. New York: Seabury.

———. (1985). *The politics of education: Culture, power and liberation*. South Hadley, MA: Bergin & Garvey.

———. (1993). *Pedagogy of the city*. New York: Continuum.

Gaudelli, W. (2003). *World class: Teaching and learning in global times*. Mahwah, NJ: Lawrence Erlbaum.

Giroux, H. A. (1988). *Teachers as intellectuals: Toward a critical pedagogy of learning*. Granby, MA: Bergin & Garvey.

———. (1995). *Academics as public intellectuals: Rethinking global politics*. New York: Routledge.

———. (1997). *Pedagogy and the politics of hope: Theory, culture, and schooling*. Boulder, CO: Westview.

———. (2003). *The abandoned generation: Democracy beyond the culture of fear*. New York: Palgrave Macmillan.

Glass, R. D. (2000). Education and the ethics of democratic citizenship. *Studies in Philosophy of Education, 19*, 275–296.

Habermas, J. (1996). *Between facts and norms: Contributions to discourse theory of law and democracy.* Cambridge, MA: MIT Press.

Hanvey, R. G. (1982). *An attainable global perspective.* New York: Global Perspectives in Education. (Original work published 1976.)

Holden, C. (2000). Learning for democracy: From world studies to global citizenship. *Theory into Practice, 39*(2), 74–80.

Howe, B. (2005). Citizenship education for child citizens. *Canadian and International Education, 34*(1), 42–49.

Hurley, N. P. (2004). Once bitten, twice shy: Teachers' attitudes towards educational change in Canada. In P. Poppleton & J. Williamson (Eds.), *New realities of secondary teachers' work lives* (pp. 57–72). Oxford, UK: Symposium Books.

Ibrahim, T. (2005). Global citizenship education: Mainstreaming the curriculum? *Cambridge Journal of Education, 35*(2), 177–194.

Kadlec, A. (2007). *Dewey's critical pragmatism.* New York: Rowman & Littlefield.

Klein, N. (2007). *The shock doctrine: The rise of disaster capitalism.* Toronto, ON: McClelland & Stewart.

Ladson-Billings, G. (2005). *Differing concepts of citizenship: Schools and communities as sites of civic development.* New York: Teachers College Press.

Larsen, M., & Faden, L. (in press). Supporting the growth of global citizenship educators. *Brock Education.*

Lippmann, W. (1999). *Public opinion.* Oxford, UK: Oxford University Press. (Original work published 1922.)

Marginson, S. (2006). Engaging democratic education in the neoliberal age. *Educational Theory, 56*(2), 205–219.

McGrew, A. (2005). *The logic of globalization.* Oxford, UK: Oxford University Press.

Merryfield, M. M. (1997). A framework for teacher education in global perspectives. In M. M. Merryfield, E. Jarchow, & S. Pickert (Eds.), *Preparing teachers to teach global perspectives: A handbook for teachers* (pp. 1–24). Thousand Oaks, CA: Corwin.

Miller, J. P. (2007). *The holistic curriculum.* Toronto: University of Toronto Press.

Noddings, N. (1992). *The challenge to care in schools: An alternative approach to education.* New York: Teachers College Press.

———. (2002). *Educating moral people: A caring alternative to character education.* New York: Teachers College Press.

———. (2005). *Educating citizens for global awareness.* New York: Teachers College Press.

Ohio Department of Education. (2007). *Ohio social studies signal* [newsletter]. Retrieved September 10, 2007, from http://www.ode.state.oh.us

Openshaw, R., & White, C. (2005). Democracy at the crossroads. In C. White & R. Openshaw (Eds.), *Democracy at the crossroads: International perspectives on critical global citizenship education* (pp. 3–11). Lanham, MD: Lexington Books.

O'Sullivan, M., & Vetter, D. (2007). Teacher-initiated, student-centered global education in a K to 8 school. *Journal of Teaching and Learning, 4*(2), 13–28.

Pike, G. (1996). Perceptions of global education in Canada. *Orbit, 27*(2), 7–11.

———. (2000). A tapestry in the making: The strands of global education. In T. Goldstein & D. Selby (Eds.), *Weaving connections: Educating for peace, social and environmental justice* (pp. 218–241). Toronto: Sumach Press.

———. (in press). Citizenship education in global context. *Brock Education.*

Pike, G., & Selby, D. (1988). *Global teacher, global learner.* London: Houghton & Stoughton.

Rosenau, J. N. (2003). *Distant proximities: Dynamics beyond globalization*. Princeton, NJ: Princeton University Press.

Schweifurth, M. (2006). Education for global citizenship: Teacher agency and curricular structure in Ontario schools. *Educational Review, 58*(1), 41–50.

Schwenninger, S. R. (2004). *Beyond dominance*. New America Foundation. Retrieved on June 27, 2007, from http://www.newamerica.net/publications/policy/ beyond_dominance

Selby, D. (2004). *Global education as transformative education*. Retrieved July 5, 2007, from http://www.citizens4change.lrg/global/intro/global_introduce.htm

Spring, J. H. (2006). *The politics of globalization: The rise of the educational security state*. Mahwah, NJ: Lawrence Erlbaum Associates.

Street, D. V. (1995). *Social literacies: Critical approaches to literacy in development, ethnography, and education*. New York: Longman.

Talbert, T. L. (2005). Freedom or French fries: Packaged democracy for world consumption. In C. White & R. Openshaw (Eds.), *Democracy at the crossroads: International perspectives on critical global citizenship education* (pp. 31–54). Lanham, MD: Lexington Books.

Tanner, D., & Tanner, L. (1995). *Curriculum development: Theory into practice* (3rd ed.). Englewood Cliffs, NJ: Prentice Hall.

Torres, C. A. (1998). Democracy, education and multiculturalism: Dilemmas of citizenship in a global world. *Comparative Education Review, 42*(4), 421–447.

Tye, K. (1999). *Global education: A worldwide movement*. Orange, CA: Interdependence.

UNICEF. (2006). *State of the world's children report*. Retrieved September 15, 2007, from http://www.unicef.org

Walzer, M. (2002). Spheres of affection. In J. Cohen (Ed.), *For love of country?* (pp. 125–127). Boston: Beacon.

Westbrook, R. B. (1991). *John Dewey and American democracy*. Ithaca, NY: Cornell University Press.

3

INTERROGATING CITIZENSHIP AND DEMOCRACY IN EDUCATION: THE IMPLICATIONS FOR DISRUPTING UNIVERSAL VALUES

Jennifer A. Tupper

> Anyone's injustice is everyone's injustice.
> —Walter C. Parker

Introduction

In North America, a fundamental means of supporting and sustaining democracy is through the education of young people as citizens. John Dewey discussed this in his 1916 manuscript *Democracy and Education*, arguing that the job of public schools is to "create a democratic public" capable of preserving democratic communities (as cited in Carson, 2006). As students represent the future members of democratic communities, schools function as important sites of citizenship education, with educators acting as "the primary stewards of democracy" (Parker, 2003, p. xv).

Parker (2003) suggests that teachers "must do what no else in society has to do: intentionally specify the democratic ideal sufficiently to make it a reasonably distinct curriculum target" (p. xvii). Having stated that, it is important to consider what is meant by the democratic ideal. Does this ideal involve actively working for equity and justice? Does it require an ongoing interrogation of the values associated with citizenship and the experiences of citizenship? It is equally important, within the context of education, to consider carefully the ways in which various subjects, curriculum documents, pedagogical practices, classroom engagement, and individual experiences advance or undermine democratic principles and ideals of universal citizenship. We might ask the question To what extent does education tell a particular story of democracy, one in which democracy is presented as an accomplishment? We might also consider the degree to which a discourse of universality permeates citizenship education (Miller, 2000). If, indeed, the story of democracy is one of accomplishment, progress, and universal citizenship, then what of individuals whose experiences suggest otherwise?

Social Studies, perhaps more than any other subject, has become the site for educating about citizenship and the ideals of democracy, and, in some cases, educating for citizenship and for democratic practices (Adler, 2004; Avery, 2004). Social Studies education is regularly "framed in relation to citizenship education and particularly the preparation of individuals to participate in a democratic society" (Ross, 2000, p. 54). However, I believe that educating *about* rather than *for* citizenship and democracy dominates Social Studies education, despite (and perhaps because of) persistent calls by the public for the education of democratic citizens (Tupper, in press).

In this chapter, I have two objectives. First, through feminist sociopolitical theory and critical race theory, I attempt to dispel the veracity of citizenship as universal (essentialist notions of universal citizenship) that seems to permeate education and more specifically, the curriculum of Social Studies (Tupper, 2005, 2006, in press). Second, I advance the notion of *(un)usual narrative* (Tupper & Cappello, in press) by using Amnesty International's (2004) *Stolen Sisters Report* to disrupt the discourse of universal citizenship and democracy that students encounter through officially sanctioned curriculum. These stories can be understood as the commonsense (discussed in more detail later in this chapter), as dominant/usual narratives serving to reify power and dominance. *(Un)usual narratives* describe the potential of *Stolen Sisters* to disrupt the commonsense, operating as both productive and interrogative, helping students and teachers to see "new" stories, and make new sense of democracy and citizenship.

Citizenship and the Commonsense

The notion of commonsense comes from the work of Antonio Gramsci (1975), who theorized that ideologies become part of the unconscious as they permeate culture and politics. Once part of the unconscious, these ideologies engender "sedimentation of common sense" (Gramsci, 1975, p. 173), a collective understanding that the way society is structured and how it works has innate reason. Commonsense may be found in the collective stories we tell ourselves about the world. In North America, these stories tell us that: we live in a democracy; that universal citizenship exists; that as citizens of a democracy, we enjoy the same rights and freedoms; and significantly, that we are equal. In this narrative, citizenship is separate from our racialized or gendered selves. These beliefs/stories make sense to those of us occupying more privileged social locations and, in our acceptance of them, we avoid having to account for our privilege or take responsibility for social injustice.

Curricular commonsense is an extension of this concept. The way the curriculum is structured, the content that students are to learn, the literature they will study "just makes sense." The commonsense of the curriculum is thus caught up in the (re)production of society's "cultural truths" through the stories students are invited to learn and the identities they are invited to accept (McCarthy, 1998). In Canada, for example, students are expected to know certain historical information, including the year that Canada became a country, its first prime minister, and when the Canadian Pacific Railway was completed. Knowledge of these "facts" has become a marker of citizenship. When the public perceives students to be ignorant of such facts (played out in the media yearly, usually in conjunction with Canada Day, on July 1), they express concern, even alarm. However, no parallel distress seems to exist around students' ignorance of the numbered treaties (signed between First Nations people and the government) or of the Indian Act (a policy implemented in 1870 by the federal government to exercise more "parental" control over First Nations people). Thus, particular knowledge becomes commonsense, associated with public narratives about citizenship values and responsibilities in a democracy.

The uncritical acceptance of commonsense (embodied in curriculum) shuts down possible alternative visions for what society might look like by consistently reifying a dominant vision (Tupper & Cappello, in press). Social Studies curriculum is implicated in the production and perpetuation of commonsense meanings, particularly as these are manifest in teaching *about* citizenship and democracy (Tupper, in press) through the inclusion of particular content. Though this content may, at first glance, seem neutral, it is anything but, for the story being told is reflective of the lives, values, and experiences of a dominant group. In turn, this privileged (White) group comes to realize that it is "the inclusive kind of human… the norm and the ideal" (Greene, 1993, p. 215).

The Story of Universal Citizenship: Feminist Perspectives

In her book *The Disorder of Women: Democracy, Feminism and Political Theory,* Carol Pateman (1989) challenges democracy as accomplishment, arguing that women have never experienced democracy the way it was intended, that "women have never been and still are not admitted as full and equal members and citizens in any country known as a 'democracy'" (p. 210). She is critical of what she perceives as the failure of political theorists to dispute the assumption that the political world is sexually neutral or universal and that democracies are inclusive of all citizens regardless of difference. Pateman argues:

> Political theorists present the familiar account of the creation of civil society as a universal realm that (at least potentially) includes everyone … there is a silence about the part of the story, which reveals that the social contract is a fraternal pact that constitutes civil society as a patriarchal or masculine order. (p. 33)

Pateman is critical of political theory for advancing the commonsense of universal citizenship as gender neutral.

Similarly, Anne Phillips (2000) suggests that "one of the problems of citizenship is that it divides people into those who belong and those who do not" (p. 36), despite advancing a narrative whereby gender disappears from individuals' experiences as citizens. Arnot and Dillabough (2000) argue that "the social relations of power which shape … identities tend to be masked by the abstractness, rationality and principles of universality which define citizenship in modern Western European nations" (pp. 3–4). The privileging of rationality or reason as integral to good citizenship is challenged by Lynch, Lyons, and Cantillon (2007), who argue that "the model citizen at the heart of liberal education … is being prepared for economic, political and cultural life in the public sphere" rather than for "relational life as an interdependent, caring and other-centred human being" (p. 2). Thus, in considering citizenship education, particularly what constitutes "good" citizenship, students are encouraged to "see" or accept this story of citizenship, the commonsense of universality and its corresponding values of rationality and individuality.

In curriculum documents, students are invited to explore the ways in which they may become "good" or "responsible" citizens through the exercise of reasoned judgment or rational thought (Tupper, 2006). Although there is an obvious commitment to citizenship education, these documents rarely encourage students or teachers to explore citizenship as a gendered concept. Feminist sociopolitical theory offers spaces to begin interrogating the historical construction of citizenship as masculine (Lister, 1997), and to consider carefully the role that Social Studies education continues to play in this construction.

The Story of Universal Citizenship: Critical Race Theory

Finding its origins in American legal studies, critical race theory "acknowledges racialized structures that are limited by a dominant construction of reality that perpetuates racial oppression" (Tyson, 2003, p. 22). These structures, argues Tyson (2003, p. 22), "create a reality and relationship to what it means to be a citizen and participate in ... democracy." An individual's ability to engage as a citizen and enjoy the rights and freedoms offered in a so-called democracy is, to a large extent, shaped by race. The telling of counterstories features prominently in critical race theory, whether they are being used to reveal the racist underpinnings of the legal system or education. Delgado (1989) states that

> stories and counterstories can serve an equally important destructive function. They can show that what we believe is ridiculous, self-serving, or cruel. They can show us the way out of the trap of unjustified exclusion. They can help us understand when it is time to reallocate power. They are the other half—the destructive half—of the creative dialectic. (p. 2415)

Like feminist sociopolitical theory, critical race theory offers a means of challenging the commonsense of universal citizenship, through the telling of "new" stories. Ladson-Billings (2003) suggests that, in Social Studies, critical race theory be used as an analytical tool to "explain the systematic omissions, distortions, and lies that plague the field" (p. 9). These shape stories students learn of what it means to be good and effective citizens, so often framed in the absence of race and racism. Marshall (2003) advocates that consideration be given to the ways in which policy documents, and the curriculum they inform, "persistently promote a deracialized agenda for citizenship education which is both monotonous and impotent" (p. 72). Owing to this, racism (and ideology and hegemony) must be rooted within the commonsense, within what is culturally and officially sanctioned, but that remains unexamined in school curriculum (Tupper & Cappello, in press). For example, in the Grade 12 Saskatchewan Social Studies curriculum, students learn about the "road to democracy" of nineteenth-century Canada, along with democratic structures and principles that shaped the creation of government in the new Confederation (Saskatchewan Learning, 1997). Nowhere in the written objectives are students asked to consider the relationship between racism and Canada's birth as a "democratic" nation. It is as if racism never existed in this country.

Rather than accepting that racism is unconscious, and that dominant society remains unaware of its racialized past and present, it is helpful to draw on King's (1991) notion of dysconsciousness: "an uncritical habit of mind (including perceptions, attitudes, assumptions, and beliefs) that justifies inequity and exploitation by accepting the existing order of things as given" (p. 135). Whereas Gramsci (1975) roots the commonsense in society's unconscious, King (1991) suggests a willingness to remain ignorant of inequity and/or be complicit in its perpetuation. Dysconsciousness, therefore, is a way of maintaining power and privilege, rather than being accountable for it. This uncritical acceptance of the existing order is encouraged by and through curricula and schools where the racial realities of society struggle to enter as objects of study (Tupper & Cappello, in press).

Part of the project of teaching for democracy and social justice is to foster in students a critical disposition as they (re)read curriculum content. Although Social Studies curriculum documents advance critical thinking as an important skill objective, it is important to explicate key differences between critical thinking and critical disposition. Briefly, critical thinking has been described as "essentially a matter of judging the reasonableness of alternatives" (Case & Wright, 1999, pp. 181–183). Teachers can facilitate this sort of thinking in students without ever having them challenge curriculum content, without ever requiring a critical habit of mind. A critical disposition, or what Giddens (2000) refers to as "a critical spirit," may be understood as "a critical engagement with one's own position in society and an awareness of the wider forces to which all of us as individuals are responding" (p. 25). It is in direct contrast to the ignorance of dysconscious racism. Education for the critical spirit thus attempts to counter the dangers of dysconsciousness, particularly as these further entrench the commonsense.

(Un)Usual Narratives: Disrupting the Commonsense

As a means of critically challenging the curricular commonsense, I draw on (un)usual narratives, a notion Cappello and I have advanced in earlier work (see Tupper & Cappello, in press). We describe (un)usual narratives as follows:

> [The] telling of a different story—enabling students to wrestle with the "dysconscious" roots of racism in society, instead of merely believing the usual story that racism just is (or is not)—reveals to students how racism is supported, what it looks like in society through the conscious choices that people have made throughout history … (Un)usual narratives function in at least two significant ways. First, they function as corrective to dominant stories: *(Un)usual narrative as productive.* They work to fill in the blanks left by dominant narratives, nuancing those privileged stories, raising questions about the claims to veracity and the tacit consent of an impartial approach to knowledge. Second, they function to question that dominance: *(Un)usual narrative as interrogative.* They question dominance by making the privileging of the dominant narrative part of the inquiry, part of the story itself. Why and how did these stories come to be representative? (Tupper & Cappello, in press)

In the context of this discussion, (un)usual narratives permit students (and teachers) to wrestle with the patriarchal and racist roots of society, offering stories detailing the mechanisms through which dominance is enacted, privilege secured, and marginalization produced. To illustrate this, and the potential of (un)usual narratives to disrupt the commonsense, I draw on the 2004 Amnesty International Report *Stolen Sisters: A Human Rights Response to Discrimination and Violence Against Indigenous Women in Canada* (Amnesty International, 2004). The report is a condemnation of Canada's complicity in the ongoing disappearances and murders of Aboriginal women in this country. It is suggestive of how gender and race shape the degree to which individuals are able to experience the rights and freedoms associated with being a citizen in a democracy and it is a useful pedagogical tool to assist students in interrogating citizenship and democracy.

The report (2004) argues that if the missing and murdered women (and they are many) were not Aboriginal, then greater resources would be directed toward finding them, their killers, or both. Given the right of Canadians to security of person, it would seem reasonable, even "rational" to expect this to be the case. Further, the report highlights how a history of racism toward Aboriginal peoples in Canada is entrenched in government policies that "have torn apart indigenous families and communities" as well as pushing "a disproportionate number of Indigenous women into dangerous situations including poverty, homelessness and prostitution" (p. 2). These policies stand in stark contrast to the democratic principles advanced through such official documents as the Canadian Charter of Rights and Freedoms (1982). Thus, *Stolen Sisters* (2004), as an (un)usual narrative, provides spaces for the interrogation of democracy and citizenship through the lenses of race and gender. For further discussions of the relationship between race and experiences of democracy, see also Tyson's work on slave narratives in the United States (Tyson, 2003).

Stolen Sisters as Productive: Filling in the Blanks

> Helen Betty Osborne was a 19-year-old Cree student from northern Manitoba who dreamed of becoming a teacher. On November 12, 1971, she was abducted by four white men in the town of The Pas and then sexually assaulted and brutally murdered. A provincial inquiry subsequently concluded that Canadian authorities had failed Helen Betty Osborne. The inquiry criticized the sloppy and racially biased police investigation that took more than 15 years to bring one of the four men to justice. Most disturbingly, the inquiry concluded that police had long been aware of white men sexually preying on Indigenous women and girls in The Pas but "did not feel that the practice necessitated any particular vigilance." (Amnesty International, 2004, p. 1)

As I have argued earlier (see Tupper, in press), the life experiences of many Aboriginal women in this country are expressions of the way citizenship is experienced. Helen Betty Osborne, and Aboriginal women in general, become second-class citizens through the racializing and gendering of their identities. The act of assaulting and killing is an expression of dominance and power but so, too, is the egregious failure of the justice system (and policing) in this instance. Given the complexities of human relations, it is unrealistic to expect that we should all always be immune from harm. However, it is realistic to expect that the principles of justice be applied in cases where we are not free from harm. Even though a provincial inquiry was conducted in the case of Helen Betty Osborne, it was long after the crime had been committed and did little to address systemic problems that allow for discrimination against Aboriginal people (Amnesty International, 2004).

Helen Betty Osborne's story offers a productive site for student learning, an (un)usual narrative as productive, corrective to the dominant story, for it tells another story of "universal citizenship," provides another way of looking at the justice system and policing through the lenses of gender and race. Similarly, the story of Pamela Jean George challenges the veracity of universal rights in Canada (Amnesty International, 2004). Her story is of particular significance to me, as Pamela Jean George was murdered in Regina, and the two men convicted of manslaughter were both students at the university. Pamela's body was found severely beaten, lying face down in the mud, outside the city limits. Initially, the police investigation focused on "Indigenous people and people living on the street" (Amnesty International, 2004, p. 46). It was not until the police received a tip from a woman "who said one of the killers had confided in a friend of hers" that two White men, Steven Tyler Kummerfield and Alexander Dennis Ternowetsky, were arrested. The case was tried before an all-White judge and jury, who were asked to consider Pamela Jean George's life as a prostitute. The two men were convicted of manslaughter and sentenced to 6 years in prison (Amnesty International, 2004).

Stories such as these offer a perspective largely lacking in curriculum. By focusing attention on the women who have disappeared or been murdered, and on the official response to the violence perpetrated on these women, the relationship between universal citizenship as status and practice is recast. These stories produce new knowledge for students, not only of harrowing situations faced by many Aboriginal women in Canada, but also of the inequitable experiences of citizenship (the granting of full rights and privileges) when considered through the lens of race and racism as well as the lens of gender and sexism.

Stolen Sisters as Interrogative: Questioning Dominance

> Violence against women, and certainly violence against Indigenous women, is rarely understood as a human rights issue. To the extent that governments, media and the general public do consider concerns about violence against women, it is more frequent for it to be described as a criminal concern or a social issue. It is both of those things of course. But it is also very much a human rights issue … When a woman is targeted for violence because of her gender or because of her Indigenous identity, her fundamental rights have been abused. And when she is not offered an adequate level of protection by state authorities because of her gender or because of her Indigenous identity, those rights have been violated. (Amnesty International, 2004, pp. 2–3)

In considering *Stolen Sisters* as a vehicle for teaching about (and for) democracy, and in considering what is revealed about the patriarchal and racialized nature of citizenship, it is clear that the report can be read as an (un)usual narrative. Citizenship as universal, and the values we associate with universal citizenship, fall apart in light of the stories contained in the report. Notions of democracy as accomplishment also come undone when placed in sharp contrast to the stories detailed throughout the report. These women have never experienced the ideals of democracy nor the corresponding rights accorded citizens. *Stolen Sisters* as interrogative enables the questioning of racism and sexism, creating a space where the production of racialized and gendered identities can be interrogated.

If, however, we read this report and accept uncritically that the fates these women encountered were because of the lifestyles they "chose" (as the judge suggested to the jury in the case of Pamela Jean George), then we are indeed embodying King's (1991) dysconscious racism. In many respects, it is easier to accept such a belief because it requires no interrogation of race or racism, no interrogation of privilege or power. These things happened simply because the women lived high-risk lifestyles. Within the context of common-sense, it is rational; it is a natural consequence. Thus, the responsibility for tragedy lies not with the perpetrators of the violence or a social system that does little to prevent such violence, but with the women themselves, women who were not safe, nor free from violence. This is the dominant story challenged by the report:

> These cases also represent two critical aspects of the reality of violence and discrimination against Indigenous women. In some instances the violence itself is racist and sexist. In other cases it may be the response from the police, other authorities, the media and the general public that is racist and sexist. In yet other cases it is both. (Amnesty International, 2004, p. 38)

(Un)usual narratives as interrogative attempt to question dominance by making the privileging of the dominant narrative part of the inquiry, part of the story itself. In tidy, mandated units on government that students encounter in Social Studies, the commonsense story of universal citizenship, free from sexism and racism, is reinforced. Studying, even celebrating the Charter of Rights and Freedoms, without carefully and critically considering how the charter has not been realized for all citizens contributes to the curricular commonsense. What teachers and students need to begin asking is why and how did these stories come to be representative in official curricula? Who benefits from the telling of these stories? What happens when we begin to interrogate the story through the lens of race and gender? Rational citizenship falls apart in consideration of the harrowing stories contained in the report. *Stolen Sisters*, therefore, as an (un)usual narrative, traces stories detailing the mechanisms through which dominance is enacted, privilege secured, and marginalization produced.

Conclusion

Amnesty International has found Canada complicit in the ongoing disappearances and murders of Aboriginal women. These individuals, because they are women and because they are Aboriginal, are not considered citizens nor are they able to experience the rights of citizenship in the same way as members of the dominant group. Yet, citizenship education, as it is currently mandated in curriculum, does little to question the veracity of universal citizenship (Tupper, in press). Howard (2003) suggests "the effects of racial injustice are subject to multiple interpretations, however; most concerning is the fact that many of the conceptions of Social Studies theory have not posed examinations of race within historical or contemporary contexts" (p. 33). This critique must also be levied at examinations of gender within historical or contemporary contexts, particularly as these pertain to the ideals of democracy and claims of universal citizenship. Education has long been complicit in reifying power and dominance with serious consequences for the attainment of democratic ideals. Both feminist sociopolitical theory and critical race theory reveal this to us.

The presence of only dominant stories that reinforce commonsense understandings produces students/citizens "who are less able to understand the complexities of the world they inhabit, less able to integrate those experiences into a growing 'making sense' of that world" (Tupper & Cappello, in press). To create a curriculum that disguises or distorts the realities of racism and sexism is to yet again privilege the vantage point of dominant (White) students who rarely experience racial discrimination, who can remain unaware of the privilege they carry. *Stolen Sisters* as an (un)usual narrative provides a tangible way to begin interrogating the commonsense, the discourse of democracy as accomplishment, the values of rationality and individuality, and citizenship as universal. The report represents an opportunity for dismantling the dominant narrative, for recognizing the story that students have learned about democracy and citizenship is incomplete, and for revealing how power and privilege (and Whiteness) operate to create hierarchies of citizenship in a country that claims democracy as an accomplishment.

Stolen Sisters is but one of many (un)usual narratives that might be used in classrooms to foster critical dispositions in students. In Canada, for example, the case of Neil Stonechild and the Kashechewan water crisis all represent (un)usual narratives. They tell different stories of democracy and citizenship. They create opportunities for the unmaking of dominant stories of what it means to be a citizen in a democratic society. These narratives represent a new place for students to stand, allowing them to begin making new sense of the world. In order to do democracy, it is imperative that educators contextualize and critically examine problematic and contentious cases that illustrate social injustice.

Questions for Reflection

1. How do I understand the ideals of democracy?

2. To what extent does education tell a particular story of democracy and citizenship?

3. To what extent do school subjects, curriculum documents, pedagogical practices, classroom engagements, and individual experiences advance or undermine democratic principles and ideals of universal citizenship?

4. How can we work to unmake the dominant narrative, disrupting the curricular commonsense within our own personal and professional contexts?

5. Why might there be resistance to (un)usual narratives?

References

Adler, S. (Ed). (2004). *Critical issues in social studies teacher education*. Greenwich, CT: Information Age.

Amnesty International (2004). *Stolen sisters: A human rights response to the discrimination and violence against indigenous women in Canada*. Retrieved March 3, 2007, from www.amnesty.ca/campaigns/resources/amr2000304.pdf

Arnot, M., & Dillabough, J. (Eds.) (2000). *Challenging democracy: International perspectives on gender, education and citizenship*. London: RoutledgeFalmer.

Avery, P. (2004). Social studies teacher education in an era of globalization. In S. Adler (Ed.), *Critical issues in social studies teacher education* (pp. 37-58). Greenwich, CT: Information Age.

Carson, T. (2006). The lonely citizen: Democracy, curriculum, and the crisis of belonging. In G. H. Richardson, & D. W. Blades (Eds.), *Troubling the canon of citizenship education* (pp. 25–30). New York: Peter Lang.

Case, R., & Wright, I. (1999). Taking seriously the teaching of critical thinking. In R. Case & P. Clark (Eds.), *The Canadian anthology of social studies* (pp. 179–193). Vancouver, BC: Pacific Educational Press.

Delgado, R. (1989). Storytelling for oppositionists and others: A plea for narrative. *Michigan Law Review, 87,* 2411–2441.

Giddens, A. (2000). Citizenship in the global era. In N. Pearce & J. Hallgarten (Eds.), *Tomorrow's citizens: Critical debates in citizenship and education* (pp. 19–25). London: Institute for Public Policy Research.

Gramsci, A. (1975). *Prison notebooks: Volume 1* (J. A. Buttigieg & A. Collari, Trans.). New York: Columbia University Press.

Greene, M. (1993). Diversity and inclusion: Toward a curriculum for human beings. *Teachers College Record, 95,* 211–221.

Howard, T. (2003). The dis(g)race of the social studies: The need for racial dialogue in the social studies. In G. Ladson-Billings (Ed.), *Critical race theory perspectives on social studies* (pp. 27–43). Greenwich, CT: Information Age.

King, J. E. (1991). Dysconscious racism: Ideology, identity, and the miseducation of teachers. *Journal of Negro Education, 60*(2), 133–146.

Ladson-Billings, G. (Ed.). (2003). *Critical race theory perspectives on social studies.* Greenwich, CT: Information Age.

Lister, R. (1997). *Citizenship: Feminist perspectives.* New York: New York University Press.

Lynch, K., Lyons, M., & Cantillon, S. (2007). Breaking silence: Educating citizens for love, care and solidarity. *International Studies in Sociology of Education, 17*(1), 1–19.

Marshall, P. L. (2003). The persistent deracialization of the agenda for democratic citizenship education: Twenty years of rhetoric and unreality in social studies position statements. In G. Ladson-Billings (Ed.), *Critical race theory perspectives on social studies* (pp. 71–97). Greenwich, CT: Information Age.

McCarthy, C. (1998). *The uses of culture: Education and the limits of ethnic affiliation.* New York: Routledge.

Miller, D. (2000). Citizenship: What does it mean and why is it important? In N. Pearce & J. Hallgarten (Eds.), *Tomorrow's citizens: Critical debates in citizenship and education* (pp. 26–35). London: Institute for Public Policy Research.

Parker, W. C. (2003). *Teaching democracy: Unity and diversity in public life.* New York: Teachers College Press.

Pateman, C. (1989). *The disorder of women: Democracy, feminism and political theory.* Stanford, CA: Stanford University Press.

Phillips, A. (2000). Second class citizenship. In N. Pearce & J. Hallgarten (Eds.), *Tomorrow's citizens: Critical debates in citizenship and education* (pp. 36–42). London: Institute for Public Policy Research.

Ross, W. (2000). Social studies teachers and curriculum. In W. Ross (Ed.) *The Social Studies Curriculum: Purposes, Problems and Possibilities* (3-18). Albany, NY: State University of New York Press.

Saskatchewan Learning. (1997). *Social Studies 30 curriculum guide.* Regina, SK: Government of Saskatchewan.

Tupper, J. (2005). *Searching citizenship: Social studies and the tensions of teaching.* Unpublished doctoral dissertation, University of Alberta, Edmonton, AB.

————. (2006). Education and the (im)possibilities of citizenship. In G. H. Richardson & D. W. Blades (Eds.), *Troubling the canon of citizenship education* (pp. 45–54). New York: Peter Lang.

————. (in press). Unsafe water, stolen sisters, and social studies: Troubling democracy and the meta-narrative of universal citizenship. *Teacher Education Quarterly.*

Tupper, J., & Cappello, M. (in press). Teaching treaties as (un)usual narratives: Disrupting the curricular commonsense. *Curriculum Inquiry.*

Tyson, C. A. (2003). A bridge over troubled water: Social studies, civic education, and critical race theory. In G. Ladson-Billings (Ed.), *Critical race theory perspectives on social studies* (pp. 15–25). Greenwich, CT: Information Age.

CHAPTER

4

"OTHER-ED" PEDAGOGY: THE PRAXIS OF CRITICAL DEMOCRATIC EDUCATION

Ali Sammel and Gregory Martin

Introduction

This chapter reflects on the social construction of teacher identity, professional knowledge, and pedagogical practice in teacher education programs in Queensland, Australia. We are particularly interested in the effects of the implementation of new standards for teacher accreditation and professional praxis in Queensland and their potential impacts on antiracist and critical multicultural pedagogy. We reflect on the pressures that neoliberal educational policy conjoined with a pernicious form of neoconservative thinking has on what it means to value diversity in education within a liberal democracy. We focus on the Professional Standards for Queensland Teachers and what these might mean for future pedagogical practice in schools. Unpacking this social imaginary that fixes or stabilizes a performative ideal or "standard," we argue that the new standards might only produce a cursory interest in liberal multicultural pedagogy as a necessary component of professional accreditation. This "tick-the-box" mentality does not interrogate the ways in which White privilege is preformed through educational institutions and practices. If the educational profession is going to "value diversity" as the Professional Standards for Queensland Teachers mandates, then teacher educators will need to engage in praxis around antiracist pedagogies as well as listening to how students make sense of their preservice courses.

Australia's Political and Educational Frames

In the aftermath of 9/11, and the Bali, London, and Madrid bombings, the forces of imperialism launched an open-ended and permanent "war on terrorism" aimed at frightening the public and driving a further wedge into class relations as workers compete against each other for fewer jobs and lower wages at the end of a period of prolonged economic growth (McLaren & Martin, 2004). In Australia, the Howard government has sought to use Aboriginals, refugees, and Muslims as blanket targets to justify its heavy-handed actions on the "home front" (see, e.g., WorkChoices, the "Pacific Solution," Northern Territory intervention, border controls; Cameron, 2006; Pilger, 2005, 2007).[1] Deploying the Australian Dream as a key social imaginary to mobilize traditional values such as "mateship," "a fair go," and English language skill acquisition, the Howard government has initiated a campaign to promote an aspirational Australian identity aimed at bolstering social integration through patriotism and national unity (i.e., Anglo-European supremacy).

As part of a wider culture war, the Howard government has launched a wide range of policy initiatives with schools and universities in the frontlines. With a focus on shaping student identity and the boundaries of civic engagement in Australian democracy, schools are required to fly the national flag (to compete for their share of federal government funding) and to provide a program of study in "values education" consistent with the National Framework for Values Education in Australian schools (Guerrera, 2004; National Framework for Values, 2005). To help educate students to participate in civic engagement and embrace democratic citizenship, the current Education Minister Julie Bishop recently announced a federally funded pilot program in schools in Muslim areas in Western Sydney. Lapsing into a deficit discourse hidden in the politically neutral language of meritocracy, she announced, "It is important to help all Australian schools educate our children about values which support our democratic way of life and our capacity to live in harmony with each other, regardless of individuals' circumstances, backgrounds or beliefs" (Hart, 2006). Here, the government has created a smoke screen to disguise the deep social cleavages and animosities that are building beneath the surface of Australian public life.

Under such circumstances, the "illusionary community" of liberal bourgeois democracy (i.e., civil society and/or the public sphere) operates as a mask for capitalist domination (Marx, 1978, p. 197; see also Brosio, 2005; Meiksins-Wood, 1995).

Having defined what is good and achievable, Howard has rallied the right with his Australian values crusade constructing public schools as a pivotal battleground with fierce attacks on alleged left-wing bias in the school curriculum and university teacher training programs. In 2004, the former minister for Education Brendan Nelson created a sense of national crisis and "moral panic" when he announced an inquiry into the preparation of teachers at Australian higher education institutions. Blinded by dogmatism and a belief that most teachers at all levels are "politically correct" liberals who are engaged in an insidious left-wing social engineering and multicultural brainwashing project, the former minister for Education, Science, and Training, Brendan Nelson (2005) loudly opined that "teacher training" had degenerated into simply being "a quasi sociology programme" (see also Maiden, 2005).

Against the backdrop of neoliberalism and a belief in free-market solutions, Howard insists there is no underlying malice in his tough-love approach to achievement, standards, and accountability, something that has become a politically fashionable strategy in dealing with the problem of state failure. Having opened the window to the cold winds of ideological change that have swept through the publicly funded higher education system, the government has ensured that teacher education programs are reduced to little more than cost-efficient assembly lines for producing compliant teachers who are judged to meet the required performance standards. Within these governing discourses of professionalism and legitimation, critical education becomes a marginal enterprise in the identity processes of teachers (Freire, 1993; Kincheloe, 2004; Kincheloe & Steinberg, 1998; McLaren, 2007).

Australian Multiculturalism and "After"

Against a growing "backlash" to defend a perceived loss of traditional authority and values, recent events in Australian political and public culture, including the recent outburst of violence in Sydney with the Cronulla riots in

2005, have once again cemented the idea that race is central to state formations of identity and citizenship (Langton, 1999). Manifesting as a form of reactionary popularism that has exceptionally long roots in Australia, such expressions of race and racism have historically flickered in and out of visibility on the national scene—as they are anchored firmly in White normativity—which has remained a relatively stable category in relation to successive waves of highly politicized and racialized "others" who have been held up for political and cultural scrutiny. Previous incarnations of "liberal" multiculturalism in Australia have attempted to purge our institutions of this ugly side of racism (i.e., "White Australia"), opting instead for a program of inclusiveness that expresses neutrality between its members. Since the 1970s, multicultural education, or inclusive education, has been a key site for engaging students in multiple social practices that promote a shared understanding of civic identity in order to bring marginalized cultural identities into the mainstream. Breathing life into an idealized version of the "imagined community" in Australia (Anderson, 1983), liberal multiculturalism seeks to value diversity, as long as that "diversity" does not unsettle borders and sits within the comfortable parameters of the status quo (Sleeter & McLaren, 1995; Sleeter, 1996).

Operating as we are now in the "after" of liberal multiculturalism, it is more than ironic that we might feel nostalgic for something many critical educators spent a great deal of ink critiquing throughout the 1980s and the 1990s. Indeed, multiculturalism has always been a highly contested concept in the field of citizenship education (for different typologies of political standpoints within multicultural education, see May, 1999; McLaren, 1995; Sleeter, 1996), and has been criticized for promising far more at the level of rhetoric and policy than it has been able to deliver in terms of practical and durable outcomes (May, 1999; see also Dei, 2000; Dei & Calliste, 2000). Given the tarnished image of multiculturalism, which has been subject to the criticisms of both the radical left and the neoconservative right, these real and substantive challenges need to be acknowledged and not whitewashed or ignored. Like Dei (2000), McLaren (1997), Singh (1997), and others, we are highly critical of multicultural policies, strategies, and pedagogies that are not antiracist, and we believe that the ideological mystifications within its more liberal variants ought to be exposed. However, we also recognize that under the current conservative "corrections" to national education policy there is an acute need to defend the social gains of multicultural liberal democracy (e.g., the extension of core aspects of liberal citizenship such as the electoral franchise, as well as the legal protection of certain civil rights to free speech and public assembly) that are in danger of being erased altogether. It is on this difficult pedagogical terrain of social relations that teacher education programs in Australia now operate. They are caught between the proverbial rock (the production of a subject "outside" of and free from the entrappings of "race") and a hard place (the need to develop antiracist pedagogies that meaningfully develop a critique of neocolonialism and that acknowledge difference).

Queensland's Educational Context: Teacher Education and "Symbolic Control"

While a preservice teacher's previous career and experiences have a powerful influence on his or her epistemological world view (Ball & Goodson, 1985; Johnson, 2002; Olsen & Kirtman, 2002), research has also demonstrated the influence of preservice teacher education on beginning teachers' burgeoning philosophies of teaching and learning as well as their future professional practice (Ballantyne, 2002). Unfortunately, all too often, teachers working in schools today are required to adjust their personal teaching styles to take into account the external context of the learning environment rather than draw upon emerging epistemological ideas and values that inform content and process choices (Sung, 2007). With regard to the development of activist models of teacher professional identity that are committed to struggles for social justice through democratic civic engagement (Gale & Densmore, 2003; Sachs, 2003), this process is compounded by the thwarting of what Freire (1998) calls a capacity for "epistemological curiosity" (p. 32). Here, the development and exercise of "epistemological curiosity" that is "critical, bold, and adventurous" is a direct challenge to "common sense"—in both Gramsci's and Freire's understanding of how largely unconscious ways of perceiving the world are the product of ideological hegemony—and inculcated within institutions such as universities and schools (p. 38).

Without a sense of nostalgia for some romantic past in civil society, the challenge is to use that common sense as the basis to enlarge the foundations for what Gramsci (1971) termed "good sense," which he defined as an oppositional epistemology or counterhegemonic impulse to critique bourgeois institutions and ideology.

Generally speaking, globalization and its attendant effects on immigration and emigration as well as the restructuring of national economies and labor markets has driven a need to promote internal cultural and linguistic diversity as a foundation of "social integration," "labor market opportunity," and "national building." However, teacher education programs have been slow to explore new teaching strategies or adapt their curriculum materials to demographic change and have addressed the challenge of multiculturalism or cultural difference in an ad hoc way with a "quick fix," "feel good," and "add-on" approach (Ballantyne, 2002; Darling-Hammond,1998; Olsen & Kirtman, 2002; Mills, 2006). Vulnerable to top-down initiatives and faddish solutions and commitments, such a limited and superficial approach has produced mixed results, in part because legislation and policy also vary across the states and territories (Mills, 2006). In the grip of a moral panic about the decline of teacher education, traditional values and English language, numeracy and literacy (Kostogriz, 2006), initial teacher education preparation in Australia has fallen victim to a highly choreographed, publicized, and politicized campaign to "get tough" on results and standards, particularly as it relates to attacks on "political correctness," whole language methods of reading instruction, and micromanaging Aboriginal and Torres Strait Islander education (Devine, 2007; Gannon & Sawyer, 2007).

Against this backdrop, the concept of the "teacher as professional" is closely aligned with language of "outcomes," "standards," and "control." Although a great deal of diversity exists in the design and implementation of teacher education programs in Australia, a recent trend of neoliberal reforms has been toward a new version of the social efficiency model that dominated in the early part of the last century (Ballantyne, 2004; Zeichner & Liston, 1990). With its current emphasis on improving technical efficiency based on the promotion and application of an "evidence-based" decision-making framework for teachers and researchers, the neoliberal education reform agenda has legitimated tactical cost reductions connected to the consolidation and streamlining of operating systems and programs as well as the provision of practical knowledge on behalf of the hegemonic social order. Here, market-driven reform measures based on managerial definitions of quality, productivity, and efficiency are also closely tied to the government's attempt to reclaim professional development as a form of human capital.

Within the context of globalization and the emergence of a knowledge-based economy, the activities of knowledge-based service providers are increasingly important to ensuring the productive quality of labor power within the social universe of capital. Elaborating upon Marx, Rikowski (2002) defines labor power as the individual's capacity to labor in the form of epistemological paradigms, skills, language codes, attitudes, and dispositions. Here, identity is not a "free-floating" concept or purely discursive formation but is rather constantly made and remade (realized) through language, discourse, and everyday praxis, including how the "Other" is addressed. Without privileging a textual over a materialist analysis, identity here is understood as being individually and collectively performed and enacted within a definitive set of concrete historical social relations.

With regard to ensuring the legitimacy of teacher identity and "professional knowledge," the concept of life-long learning promoted by policy makers, academics, and practitioners alike ensures that teachers are "hailed" or interpolated throughout their careers into an appropriate ideological identity that is perpetually responsive to the ever-changing needs of the market, for example, under the auspices of professional development (Althusser, 1971). The construction of professional identity is relatively unstable and changes over time. Within the dominant discourse of teacher professionalism, however, Sachs (1997) defines a professional as a person who has the ability to "continue learning throughout [their] career, deepening knowledge, skill judgment, staying abreast of important developments in the field and experimenting with innovations that promise improvements in practice" (p. 266).

These developments, particularly changes in teachers' identity formation as reflected in changes in teacher training, are reflected in Queensland that promotes the philosophy and practice of outcomes-based education in state schools and the notion of continuous professional development in documents such as the Queensland College of Teachers' (QCT, the organization that controls the accreditation of all teacher education courses in Queensland) *Professional Standards for Queensland Teachers* and Education Queensland's *Professional Standards for Teachers* (Education Queensland, 2006). With a relatively weak conception of teacher autonomy and control, the framework of professional standards sets out the observable skills, dispositions, and competencies expected of beginning teachers. Equally significant, the ideology built into the institutional culture of teacher education programs reinforces the internalization of performance norms that are often difficult to monitor or measure. Undermining the idea of teacher education as democratic practice, these Professional Standards, now compulsory in teacher education courses, have been developed to reflect the market-driven "real world" needs of teachers (Education Queensland, 2006).

Professional Standards for Queensland Teachers

Professional standards are political. They have been applied in countries such as the United Kingdom, the United States, and Australia by governments and used as regulatory frameworks and certification procedures (Sachs, 2003). The QCT standards provide the minimum levels of achievement that a Queensland teacher must demonstrate in relation to various teaching practices to be granted registration. Aligned closely with government bodies, and less with professional associations and other community stakeholders, the standards do not put forward a neutral "quality" framework. What is put forward in the standards reflects the shared common values, beliefs, and goals of the hegemonic culture. These values are not reflective of all communities, for as Louden (1999) comments, the nature of how Australian standards are developed (in relatively little time and with few resources), and the nature of who developed them (their political intent) are reflective of government agendas. As a form of neoliberal governance, the new Professional Standards for Queensland Teachers constitutes a hegemonic device, a way of both introducing and legitimating changes, for the social construction of teacher identity, professional knowledge, and practice. At the most practical level, it serves a legal mechanism for legitimating teachers to work in formal educational institutions by requiring them to hold provisional or full registration with the QCT. This process also requires documenting how teachers meet the new "standards." The standards, as they have come to be known, were finalized in 2007, and consist of 10 overarching standards that "teachers will possess in order to provide high-quality instruction and support improved student learning" (QCT, 2007, p. 6). Functioning as both a social practice and an ideological vehicle for knowledge and identity, these standards will do more than simply provide a list outlining successful teaching practices; they will also play a significant role in the social construction of what it means to be a teacher in Queensland. As the Professional Standards lie at the heart of the formal teacher registration process and university approval procedures, this has implications for what agendas are constructed as politically and ethically important in the praxis of future teachers. The QCT (2007) states that:

> These standards provide benchmarks for the full registration of teachers and will be used to inform the development of policies and practices including … approval of preservice teacher education programs, to manag[ing] the provisional registration of graduates from Queensland higher education institutions; consideration of registration for applicants who have not attained the prescribed qualifications and experience for registration; renewal of teacher registration. (p. 4)

The QCT has the political power and resources to ensure that these standards constitute the official institutional infrastructure for the future Queensland teacher. Understanding how such policies and commitments might practicably work in future classroom pedagogy is of course difficult to anticipate. However, what the standards represent is a powerful site for the identity formation of teachers and for the construction of professional knowledge. This nexus of power/identity/knowledge unfolds along two important trajectories. The first trajectory involves the accreditation processes that effectively ensure all preservice education programs align their courses and programs with the standards if they want their graduates to be qualified to teach in Queensland. All education courses in universities across Queensland have changed, or are in the process or changing, to align with these standards. Acting as official curricula, these 10 standards are given prominence in tertiary education policy and protocols. Educational values, agendas, and theories not specified within these 10 standards are deemed to become marginalized even if they are emphasized in national and international educational research agendas. Along the second trajectory, the standards act as a key ideological and performative site for the enactment of the "model" teacher. Only those teachers who provide sufficient evidence of meeting these standards can gain formal registration to teach in Queensland.

Maintaining and legitimating an imaginary identity fit for consumption that is difficult to erase, teachers are now spending precious time understanding and demonstrating these values, rather than values that are accountable to and "rooted in a community-guided, antiracist value system" (Freeman & Johnson, 2003). Over time, administrators, teacher-educators, preservice students, and teachers will view these particular standards as the values that have cultural currency, and others will be silenced or marginalized as somehow "less relevant," "not appropriate," or even "deviant" for Queensland teachers to learn. This is already occurring within grant applications in Queensland, for if you can focus your grant to one of the "new" standards, it is understood as being more "relevant" to the "needs of Queensland," and, therefore, more worthy of accessing funding. This has a significant impact on which educational aspects are investigated—and hopefully, better understood—and which are ignored.

Closer inspection of the standards reveals that within each standard there are interrelating practice, knowledge, and values statements. The QCT (2007) describes the practice statements as focusing on "how teachers apply their understandings about learners, the curriculum and teaching and learning in working with students, their families and colleagues" (p. 6). Further, the QCT (2007) suggests the knowledge statements "identify the body of knowledge that underpins effective practice and the values statements describe the behaviours that communicate the qualities valued by teachers and schools" (p. 6). However, it is in the values statements that the reader can see that a teacher needs to develop not only "the knowledge and practice of, but also acknowledge, the importance of appropriate values and dispositions for teaching" (p. 13).

The implementation of Professional Standards should not be viewed as a magic bullet for addressing any perceived "crisis" in education, as they cannot address inherent problems of inequity and dysfunction that underlie school systems and curricula (Darling-Hammond, 1998; Sachs, 2003). However, this point is not emphasized within the standards themselves.

Gazing on the Standards: Exploring Diversity

These standards must be judged for their ability to construct the identities of teachers and shape the teaching profession to meet the current needs of the diversity of students they serve and the ever growing complexity of their communities, as well as for their ability to be flexible enough to serve the needs of the future. Australia is an increasing multicultural society, but the demographics of preservice education students are yet to reflect this trend. Therefore, as teacher educators, we believe it is important to explore what the formal government discourse on diversity and ethnicity education expects of teachers in Queensland. For this reason, we would like to offer a brief glimpse into the only stand that addresses diversity, Standard 4, which states, "design and implement learning experiences that value diversity" (p. 13). The QCT (2007) outlines the minimum requirements that graduates of approved preservice teacher education programs and beginning teachers must be able to achieve (see Figure 1).

In seeking clarification to understand for what purpose and within what ideological frame the QCT seeks teachers to "value diversity" within their classroom, we turned to the details of Standard 4. Here, we find clues, such as "establish learning environments in which individual and group differences are valued and respected and all students are treated equitably" (p. 13). This is a noble sentiment, and certainly something to aim for, but as a standard for which teachers must demonstrate evidence that they are meeting, we argue that it is written without naming or recognizing the complexity of personal and infrastructural power relations, the historical implications of the social constructions of the "Other," the role of colonialism, and the creation of a national identity. Further, the QCT does not take into account how the above impact an individual's pedagogic understandings and duties.

Another example can be explored in relation to the mandate that teachers must demonstrate knowledge of "individual learning needs and know how to apply strategies for teaching students with particular learning needs including students with disabilities and learning difficulties, and gifted students" (p. 13). Embedded within this aspect is the assumption of an outcome of learning. Strategies are, therefore, needed to help students with "particular needs" to reach a certain standard, or norm. Again, students who may fall outside of the historically established "norm," for whom the system was set up to teach, are now to be assisted in order to help them achieve the content that was also established to support the hegemony of White privilege. The focus is on the technical or process aspects of teaching rather than on content investigation or individual or infrastructural deconstruction of how diversity is constructed, internalized, played out, resisted, and needed in all

Figure 1 - Standard 4: Design and implement learning experiences that value diversity (QCT, 2007, p. 13)

Practice

1. Identify and develop understanding of the diverse backgrounds and characteristics of the students they teach
2. Plan and implement individual and group learning activities that take account of the backgrounds, characteristics, and learning styles of students
3. Establish learning environments in which individual and group differences are valued and respected and all students are treated equitably
4. Identify individual learning needs and know how to apply strategies for teaching students with particular learning needs including students with disabilities and learning difficulties, and gifted students
5. Identify and use strategies that result in high levels of expectations and achievement by all students across all learning areas
6. Apply Information and Communication Technologies (ICT) to empower students with diverse backgrounds, characteristics, and abilities and enable their learning
7. Identify and know how to apply strategies for working and communicating with parents and caregivers to support individual student learning
8. Review their personal skills in responding to diversity and identify ways of developing this aspect of professional practice

Knowledge

In order to meet these minimum expectations, graduates of approved preservice teacher education programs will have a sound fundamental knowledge of:

1. Contemporary evidence-informed theories and research on teaching and learning factors such as socioeconomic circumstances, gender, ethnicity, language, religious beliefs, and special needs and their impact on the world view of individuals
2. Australian Indigenous culture and history
3. School and employing authority policies on diversity
4. Individual learning needs, including the particular needs of students with disabilities or learning
5. Difficulties and gifted students, and support services for such students
6. Pedagogical approaches that result in high levels of expectation and achievement by Indigenous students
7. How to use ICT to increase opportunities for learning and address the individual learning needs of students
8. The negative impact of bias, prejudice, and discrimination on students, families, and communities
9. Cross-cultural sensitivities and perspectives

Values
The development of elements of knowledge and practice through the preservice program should acknowledge the importance of appropriate values and dispositions for teaching.

aspects of the educational endeavor in Queensland. This standard, which is reflective of the other nine, gives voice to Bourdieu's (1977a) statement that

> the action of the school, whose effect is unequal among children from different classes, and whose success varies considerably among those upon whom it has an effect, tends to reinforce and to consecrate by its sanctions the initial inequities. (p. 493)

As such, the disciplinary and normalizing agenda of education perpetuates difference as a form of "symbolic violence" but with a more liberal "multicultural" rather than a color-blind stance (Bourdieu, 1977b, pp. 191–192). Standard 4 focuses on the individual teacher's role and silences the institutional effects that construct, constrain, and insist that certain students remain labeled (with all the associated implications) as "diverse" within the system. Masquerading as common sense, albeit with an element of sound pedagogy, the complexity of issues such as diversity are simplified and reduced down to liberal interpretations akin to calls for tolerance. These approaches are politically attractive as they offer possibilities within liberal

socially acceptable parameters and are ambiguous in their meaning and intent
to deflect most superficial criticism. To address issues that move beyond the
superficial would move the standards into new and highly charged political
territory.

The standards encourage superficial understandings of diversity by
focusing on those deemed to be "Others," and ignoring the social
constructions of the Australian culture, the preservice students' own identity
construction and the implications these complex dimensions have on
pedagogy. It asks students to "design and implement learning experiences
that value diversity" (p. 13) that, at best, maintain and perpetuate the racist
status quo. Hence, they provide examples of how White privilege shapes
policies and practices in Australia, and in turn, impacts teacher subjectivities.

(No) Conclusion

After a period of "benign neglect" over the past decade in Australia (Jasmin,
2002), recent moves toward state and institutional accreditation and
regulation of initial teacher education to ensure "minimum standards" must
be understood within the current context of Howard's conservative
neoliberalism. Here, the normalization of performance expectations ensures
that no one subjected to professional standards is left unjudged or
unmeasured. Thus, the challenge is to redefine the concept of teacher
professional, particularly within a neoliberal Eurocentric imagination, which
holds that difference and social exclusion are shaped by cultural beliefs and
values at the micro-level of the individual, and that "integration" into the
utopia of the free market is the only solution.

Given that our identities are constituted in and through historical forms
of work within hierarchical organizations, we argue that educators committed
to substantive social change need to move beyond the narrow confines of
professionalism that set the limits of the knowing and acting subject (Maxey,
2004). Challenging and transforming dominant structures within the sphere
of production requires that we connect the often intensely individual,
internal, and imagined quest to renegotiate a new identity to the collective
struggles and material interests of oppressed and exploited groups, strata, and
classes in society. For if we do not engage our students in reflecting on the

individual and infrastructural complexities associated with teaching about the "Other" or the reflection of the "ethnic self" within the backdrop of the hegemony of White privilege in Queensland, then they will not understand the complexities of teaching in this century.

Questions for Reflection

1. In what ways can those bound by liberal standards speak back to those forms of professionalism shaping their identities?

2. Who has the right or responsibility to define the teaching profession in Queensland and elsewhere?

3. What are some alternative ways to think about teachers' professional identity beyond standards while providing a road map to navigate antiracist teaching?

4. How do we teach for a reconciliation of a critical ideology toward diversity in this prevailing hegemonic liberal ideology?

5. How can university programs prepare activist teachers to engage in critical multicultural and antiracist pedagogy for a democratic society?

Notes

1. The 2002 Bali bombings were a defining moment in the construction of the Australian national imaginary that brought the global war-on-terror "home." More Australian citizens were killed and injured in the terrorist attack than any other nationals. On December 11, 2005, approximately 5,000 people of Anglo-Saxon background gathered at Cronulla Beach to protest so-called Lebanese gangs that had been accused the prior week of harassing beach-goers (Kelly, 2005). Swathing themselves in the Australian flag and singing "Waltzing Matilda" as well as the national anthem, a number of people in the crowd decided to "reclaim" the beach by chanting racist and nationalist slogans. Elements within the crowd also verbally abused and physically attacked anyone who was Middle Eastern or Muslim. The racist violence, which spilled into neighboring suburbs, made headlines around the world (Kennedy, Murphy, Brown, & Colquhou, 2005).

References

Althusser, L. (1971). *Lenin and philosophy and other essays by Louis Althusser*. New York: Monthly Review Press.

Anderson, B. (1983). *Imagined communities: Reflections on the origin and spread of nationalism*. New York: Verso.

Ball, S., & Goodson, L. (1985). Understanding teachers' concepts and contexts. In S. Ball & L. Gordon (Eds.), *Teachers' lives and careers* (pp. 1–26). London: Falmer.

Ballantyne, J. (2002). *Current trends in teacher education: Some implications.* Retrieved October 21, 2007, from http://www.aare.edu.au/03pap/bal03226.pdf

———. (2004). An analysis of current reform agendas in preservice teacher education. In S. Danby, E. McWilliam, & J. Knight (Eds.), *Performing research: Theories, methods and practices* (pp. 265–276). Flaxton, Queensland: Post Pressed.

Bourdieu, P. (1977a). Cultural reproduction and social reproduction. In J. Karabel & A. H. Halsey (Eds.), *Power and ideology in education* (pp. 487–511). Oxford, UK: Oxford University Press.

———. (1977b). *Outline of a theory of practice.* Cambridge, UK: Cambridge University Press.

Brosio, R. (2005). Civil society: Concepts and critique from a radical democratic perspective. *Cultural Logic.* Retrieved October 10, 2007, from http://clogic.eserver.org/2005/brosio.html

Cameron, M. (2006). Racism: Who's stirring it up? *Green Left Weekly.* Retrieved October 9, 2007, from http://www.greenleft.org.au/2006/653/7630

Darling-Hammond, L. (1998). Policy and change: Getting beyond bureaucracy. In A. Hargreaves, A. Lieberman, M. Fullan, & D. Hopkins (Eds.), *International handbook of education change* (pp. 642–667). Amsterdam: Kluwer.

Dei, G. (2000). Towards an antiracism discursive framework. In G. Dei & A. Calliste (Eds.), *Power, knowledge and anti-racism education* (pp. 23–40). Halifax, Nova Scotia: Fernwood.

Dei, G., & Calliste, A. (2000). Mapping the terrain: Power, knowledge and anti-racism education. In G. Dei & A. Calliste (Eds.), *Power, knowledge and anti-racism education* (pp. 11–23). Halifax, Nov Scotia: Fernwood.

Devine, M. (2007). New chapter: The class revolution. Retrieved October 21, 2007, from http://www.smh.com.au/text/articles/2007/10/17/1192300857454.html

Education Queensland. (2006). *Professional standards for teachers: Guidelines for professional practice.* Retrieved October 31, 2007, from http://education.qld.gov.au/staff/development/standards/standards.html

Freeman, M., & Johnson, L. (2003, February). Yes! A literacy program's antiracist journey. *Focus on basics: Connecting research and practice, 6.* Retrieved September 28, 2007, from http://www.ncsall.net/?id=209

Freire, P. (1993). *Pedagogy of the oppressed.* New York: Continuum. (Original work published 1970.)

———. (1998). *Pedagogy of freedom: Ethics, democracy and civic courage.* Lanham, MD: Rowman & Littlefield.

Gale, T., & Densmore, K. (2003). *Engaging teachers: Towards a radical democratic agenda for schooling.* Berkshire, UK: Open University Press.

Gannon, S., & Sawyer, W. (2007). "Whole language" and moral panic in Australia. *International Journal of Progressive Education, 3*(2), 30–51. Retrieved October 21, 2007, from http://www.inased.org/v3n2/gannonsawyer.html

Gramsci, A. (1971). *Selections from the prison notebooks of Antonio Gramsci* (Q. Hoare & G. N. Smith, Trans.). New York: International.

Guerrera, O. (2004). Schools told to fly flag or lose cash. *The Age.* Retrieved October 9, 2007, from http://www.theage.com.au/articles/2004/06/22/1087844937754.html

Hart, C. (2006, December 28). Schools eye Muslim dress. *The Australian.* Retrieved September 15, 2007, from http://www.theaustralian.news.com.au/story/0,20867,20980453-2702,00.html

Jasmin, A. (2002, February). *Initial teacher education: Changing curriculum, pedagogies and assessment.* Paper presented at "Challenging futures: Changing agendas in teacher education" conference, Armidale. Retrieved October 31, 2007, from http://scs.une.edu.au/CF/Papers/pdf/jasman1.pdf

Johnson, L. (2002). "My eyes have been opened:": White teachers and racial awareness. *Journal of Teacher Education, 53*(2), 153–-167.

Kelly, R. (2005, December 12). Government and media provocations spark racist violence on Sydney beaches. *World Socialist Web Site.* Retrieved October 10, 2007, from http://www.wsws.org/articles/2005/dec2005/riot-d12.shtml

Kennedy, L., Murphy, D., Brown, M., & Colquhou, T. (2005). Race riots spread to suburbs. *Sydney Morning Herald.* Retrieved October 10, 2007, from http://www.smh.com.au/news/national/race-riots-spread-to suburbs/2005/12/11/1134235951313.html

Kincheloe, J. (2004). *Critical pedagogy primer.* New York: Peter Lang.

Kincheloe, J., & Steinberg, S. (1998). *Unauthorized methods: Strategies for critical teaching.* New York: Routledge.

Kostogriz, A. (2006). *On strangers, "moral panics" and the neo-liberalization of teacher education.* Retrieved October 21, 2007, from http://www.aare.edu.au/06pap/kos06253.pdf

Langton, M. (1999). Why "race" is a central idea in Australia's construction of the idea of a nation. *Australian Cultural History, 18*, 22–-37.

Louden, W. (1999, January). *Standards for standards: An Australian perspective on the development and assessment of professional standards.* Paper presented to the "New professionalism in teaching, teacher education and teacher development in a changing world" conference, Hong Kong.

Maiden, S. (2005, February 28). Step up teacher training: Nelson. *The Australian, 28*, p. 4.

Marx, K. (1978). The German ideology. In R. Tucker (Ed.), *The Marx-Engels reader* (2nd ed., pp. 146–200). New York: W. W. Norton. (Original work published 1972.)

Maxey, L. (2004). Moving beyond from within: Reflective activism and critical geographies. In D. Fuller & R. Kitchin (Eds.), *Radical theory/critical praxis: Making difference beyond the academy* (pp. 157–171). Vancouver, BC: University of British Columbia & Praxis Press. Retrieved October 24, 2004, from http://www.praxis-epress.org

May, S. (Ed.) (1999). *Critical multiculturalism: Rethinking multicultural and antiracist education.* London: Falmer.

McLaren, P. (1995). White terror and oppositional agency: Towards a critical multiculturalism. In C. Sleeter & P. McLaren (Eds.), *Multicultural education, critical pedagogy and the politics of difference* (pp. 33–70). Albany, NY: State University of New York Press.

———. (1997). *Revolutionary multiculturalism: Pedagogies of dissent for the new millennium.* Boulder, CO: Westview.

———. (2007). *Life in schools: An introduction to critical pedagogy in the foundations of education* (5th ed.). Boston: Pearson/Allyn & Bacon.

McLaren, P., & Martin, G. (2004). The legend of the Bush gang: Imperialism, war and propaganda. Cultural *Studies/Critical Methodologies, 4*(3), 281–303.

Meiksins-Wood, E. (1995). *Democracy against capitalism: Renewing historical materialism.* Cambridge, UK: Cambridge University Press.

Mills, C. (2006). Pre-service teacher education and the development of socially just dispositions: A review of the literature. Retrieved October 21, 2007, from http://www.aare.edu.au/06pap/mil06221.pdf

National Framework for Values Education in Australian Schools. (2005). Department of Education, Science and Training. Retrieved October 9, 2007, from

http://www.valueseducation.edu.au/verve/_resources/Framework_PDF_version_for_
    the_web.pdf
Nelson, B. (2005, August 10). *National Press Club address*. Canberra. Retrieved September
    15,   2007,   from
    http://www.dest.gov.au/Ministers/Media/Nelson/2005/08/trans300805.asp
Olsen, B., & Kirtman, L. (2002). Teacher as mediator of reform: An examination of teacher
    practice in 36 California restructuring schools. *Teachers College Record*. Retrieved
    October 21, 2007, from http://www.tcrecord.org/Content.asp?ContentId=10829
Pilger, J. (2005, February 7). *Fear and silence in the "lucky" country*. Retrieved October 9,
    2007, from http://www.johnpilger.com/page.asp?partid=326
———. (2007, January 19). *Cruelty and xenophobia shame and stir the lucky country*.
    Retrieved October 9, 2007, from http://www.johnpilger.com/page.asp?partid=424
Queensland Teachers College (QCT) (2007). *Program approval guidelines*. Retrieved
    September   15,   2007,   from   http://www.qct.edu.au/teacher-
    education/stds_guidelines_te1.aspx
Rikowski, G. (2002, March). *Methods for researching the social production of labour power
    in capitalism*. Presented at the School of Education research seminar, University
    College   Northampton.   Retrieved   October   31,   2007,   from
    http://www.ieps.org.uk.cwc.net/rikowski2002b.pdf
Sachs, J. (1997). Reclaiming the agenda for teacher professionalism: An Australian
    experience. *Journal of Education for Teaching, 23*(3), 264.
———. (2003). *The activist teaching profession*. Philadelphia: Open University Press.
Singh, M. (1997). Education for anti-racism in a multi-racist, multicultural society. *Australian
    Educational Researcher, 23*(2), 125–132.
Sleeter, C. (1996). *Multicultural education as social activism*. Albany: State University of
    New York Press.
Sleeter, C., & McLaren, P. (Eds.) (1995). *Multicultural education, critical pedagogy, and the
    politics of difference*. New York: State University of New York Press.
Sung, Y. (2007). Are pre-service teacher constructivists in the constructivist teacher education
    program? *KJEP, 4*(1), 9–24.
Zeichner, K., & Liston, D. (1990). Theme: Restructuring teacher education. *Journal of
    Teacher Education, 41*(2), 3–20.

C H A P T E R
5

CAN REBELLIOUSNESS BEAR DEMOCRACY?

Reinaldo Matias Fleuri

Introduction

The struggle against authoritarianism to build democratic processes in the school environment has been one of the main goals of my pedagogic practice (Fleuri, 2001). However, on many occasions, I have realized that the attempts to promote the active participation of students in the planning, execution, and evaluation of the educational work within the school context has resulted in reconfigured schemas of subjugation and exclusion strategies among students. From 1990 on, I researched how and why such subjection mechanisms are constituted. It was necessary to deconstruct these mechanisms so as to support democratization initiatives at the pedagogical level. I found in Michel Foucault the necessary theoretical underpinning to understand how the disciplinary power at school works, and this allowed me to envision the possibilities for resistance that are sometimes articulated in acts of individual or collective rebelliousness. In particular, I tried to understand how some of the transgression practices perpetrated by students at school are traditionally transformed into delinquency, and this becomes the focus of the authorities to be banned or eliminated. On the other hand, I also intended to understand how these initiatives, paradoxically identified as "indiscipline," can be rearticulated as factors for emancipation in terms of democracy at and within school.

I understood that, for an educator who is able to problematize and engage in dialogue, the rebelliousness of the instigators may be one of the fundamental challenges for the ongoing pedagogical struggle to articulate the personal and collective interests, usually denied by the educational system, in a creative, pleasurable, and meaningful way. In the school ambit, these transgression practices may also reveal their revolutionary potential, constituting the bases for the educational processes that can overcome the disciplinary knowledge-power relationships, as they are collectively (consolidating reciprocity and solidarity relations) and actively assumed (cultivating initiative and interactions diversity). To empower the dynamic solidarity networks, including the creativity, freedom, and democratic organization cultivated at the school level, it is necessary to disentangle it from the transgression and delinquency that is forced upon it by surveillance and punishment, developing problematized dialogue, and cooperation mechanisms among the participants of the educational process.

This chapter, therefore, concisely adapts Michel Foucault's (1977, 1988) theory of the disciplinary actions of power to indicate how the processes of violence are configured, ambivalently, as delinquency or rebelliousness, and as subjugated consolidation or contestation. This demonstrates the disciplinary devices employed in a unidirectional, monofocal, unidimensional, and monocultural perspective that characterizes interpersonal interactions. It also enunciates the need to understand the complexity and the interculturality of educational relations in order to construct and develop democracy at school. This eventually reveals elements of the pedagogical framework espoused by Paulo Freire (1974) and Céléstin Freinet (1973), which point to the overcoming of these disciplinary devices. These writers promote the recognition and potential for a relationship among the different subjects and their respective contexts, favoring the development of infinite and fluid singularities; these ultimately produce the multiple and ambivalent meanings that intertwine with the existence of democratic processes at school.

Disciplinary Relations of Power

Michel Foucault (1977) characterizes "discipline" as methods that permit the accurate control of the body's operations and the constant subjugation of its activities. However, they are not repressive methods because rather than reducing the strength and impairing individual capacity, discipline facilitates one's energy and enhances one's abilities, turning them into useful and productive skills. The discipline trains the individuals, articulating two characteristics in one's capacities: docility and productivity.

The set of these social control strategies that frame people's bodies configures "disciplinary power." This reconstitutes itself insofar as it distributes the individuals in space, establishes mechanisms of activity control, programs the evolutionary processes, and articulates collectively individual activities. To achieve this, it uses coercive resources such as surveillance, punishment, and examinations.

Discipline distributes individuals in this space. The delimitation and organization of the spaces within the institution allow for the control of the location and movement of individuals. The disciplinary space is "analytical" because it is subdivided into compartments, with predefined functions. This allows the "analysis" and "automatic" control of the activities individuals carry out. The determination of location responds to the need to not only survey but also break dangerous communications and create a space where the individuals' work can be better used and controlled. The subdivision of the space allows two types of control simultaneously. On the one hand, it makes possible the control of each individual's activities. On the other hand, the space ordination permits the control of a group of individuals, establishing a general correlation, which is key among the people who act in the same place simultaneously.

The space organization in *cells,* places, and ranks assumes a real and, at the same time, ideal dimension. On the one hand, the position of buildings, rooms, and furniture is determined. On the other hand, this architecture determines a hierarchy between people and objects. This was named "tableaux vivants" (see Foucault, 1977, pp. 135–169), in which the table is a knowledge process where it permits the classification and verification of relationships; it is a power mechanism because it allows controlling a group of individuals.

The control of the activities of individuals in a disciplinary institution is also done through time conditioning. With the collective and obligatory rhythm imposed from outside by cultural time conventions, discipline carries out a temporal elaboration of the individual act that aims to make human activity increasingly more efficient. Discipline requires effort from the individual as to embody precise procedures. This does not mean, however, that the disciplinary learning process is repressive or violent. It is not violent because it respects the objective and natural conditions of the body. Equally, it is not repressive because, on the contrary, it optimizes the individual potential for development. The elaboration of these acts is based on the accurate study of the body, as well as on various tools that are manipulated, so as to establish an optimal correlation between body and object. Its goal is, therefore, to obtain the best result with the least amount amount of waste, thus highlighting the efficiency of discipline.

Such mechanisms, which guarantee the continual shaping of differentiated individuals, constitute the exercise. This is understood as the technique by which one imposes on the body tasks that are both repetitive and different but always graduated (Foucault, 1979, pp. 160–161). The exercise—characteristic of military and religious practices—is assimilated into educational practice through the educational program, which frames the formal schooling experience for the child/student from year to year with activities of increasing complexity (Foucault, 1979, p. 161).

Both in the army and in the factory, collective action results from the cooperation between the elementary forces of the individuals involved. It is a machine in which the individual becomes an element that can move and project onto others. In the same way, this chronological series characterizing education should be adjusted to other people's time so that individual forces can be fully useful and combined to achieve an optimal result.

Thus, discipline is constituted in a set of power mechanisms. Through the precise construction of the physical environment, a table identifying and classifying the individuals is presented. It establishes movements, imposing a mandatory, collective rhythm, codifying a series of individual acts. It also institutes exercises that induce students to a progressive apprenticeship and an everlasting characterization of the individual. Further, it develops tactics that meticulously combine the individual forces so as to improve collective results. Such procedures construct the individual, articulating his/her identity and reality on the collective experience. The control of individuals in an institution is undertaken through disciplinary measures while being constantly observed. This spatial organization should provide the constant vigilance monitoring of the subaltern by their superiors.

Vigilance, however, is not carried out only through the force of the architecture setting. It is concretized through a hierarchical network of relations. The organizational chart at school, for example, resembles a pyramid: principal, supervisor, teachers, and students, with a range of administrative, pedagogical, and maintenance assistants added to the mix. The surveillance system establishes relations of reciprocal control among all individuals who belong to a disciplinary institution. This system of multilateral censorship obliges all to adapt to the norms through the hierarchical application of punishment.

Thus, disciplinary systems function based on a subliminal mechanism that qualifies and represses behaviors that escape the larger systems concerned with major punishment. The punishment purpose in this disciplinary relation is mainly to decrease deviation and perceived unacceptable behavior. Punishment, therefore, is privileged in an exercise-like format. However, the disciplinary sanction works as a double system of reward and punishment. The rewards stimulate the persistent quest to follow established norms, with the fear of punishment reinforcing the behavior of those who have been recalcitrant.

This mechanism qualifies performances between two opposed poles, good and evil. At school, all behaviors are, ultimately, reduced to good or bad grades. These sanctions institute a subtle and graduated game of promotion or failure. The graduation system also rewards students with the possibility to move on to higher degrees and can also punish students by failing them. This produces a performance classification for students, activating processes that are enmeshed in a game of power among individuals, forcing comparisons as well as the exclusion of those who do not adhere to the established norms. In sum, this normalizing process of sanctioning combined with a hierarchical surveillance materializes in one of the key mechanisms of disciplinary and bureaucratic institutions: the exam.

The exam involves a combination of techniques, including hierarchical surveillance and a process of sanctioning in a perceptibly "normal" way. It is a ritual that encourages the qualification, classification, and punishment of individuals. It also configures a relationship of knowledge and power at the same time, *knowledge* because it makes it possible for the evaluators of exams to know and to classify students and *power* because it demands that subalterns follow prescribed norms. The superiors, thus, control (observe and determine) the subaltern behavior and, at the same time, induce it to adapt to norms through a system of classificatory sanction.

The exam or examination articulates and mobilizes the different constitutive mechanisms of the relations inherent in disciplinary power and knowledge. Through the systematic application of these control mechanisms, it is possible to define the characterization of each student as well as the composition of a classificatory table that establishes a hierarchy of individual performances in each group, in each series, and in each grade of the school unit which, ultimately, subjects everyone automatically to a complete and impersonal control (constitutive of knowledge and power).

Power and Resistance

When we see structural characteristics from centuries ago in contemporary schools, we need to ask ourselves why the school continues to reproduce the same mechanisms from year to year in spite of all the reform efforts. It seems that the results of the vast restructuring processes eventually reinforce the same problems that motivated them, echoing the notion of a vicious circle. Would the supposed failure of the school along with its reforms—as Foucault questions (1977, p. 239) about prisons—not be related to the way that the school functions?

Several studies on education view the problem as one of reproduction in the larger system, constituted by politicoeconomic contexts, particularly the state, even when resistance processes are identified (Althusser, 1970; Giroux, 1983, among others). Foucault (1988) however, considers power as a strategy connected to power correlations, constituted of the unstable and ambivalent interaction of multiple agents that constantly sustain and threaten the general formula of domination (p. 90). The same correlations of power in schools result in processes that shape attitudes of docility and utility as well as creativity and rebelliousness.

How is it, then, that this conflict between discipline and rebelliousness manifests itself in the educational life? School routine seems, paradoxically, to reproduce the power and resistance mechanisms whose logic is reconstituted insofar as their strategies and manifestations are reconfigured in different contexts. School architecture and routine, under different forms, then embody norms and procedures strewn together in successive attempts to restructure the educational system, even within the context of deep social revolutions. However ambivalently, in the cracks of the walls and in the opportunities that convulse within school routines, real and differentiated relationships emerge and can also take revenge at any time.

The classroom space can be seen as a "class cell" (Fleuri, 1990, p. 2) and is differentially occupied by students according to informal criteria and relationships. The desks placed at the front, in general, are considered more dedicated; at the back, they are viewed as the transgressors. It is an almost spontaneous habit that, although sometimes it becomes a rule, reflects an invisible relationship network, conflicting with the strategies of educational discipline. Brandão (1986, pp. 107–122) indicates that, despite the spatial division and imposition of daily routines, real life in classroom processes are perceived as a conflict between the establishment of norms and the development of individual or collective transgression strategies. The relationships created and recreated through the classroom routine reveals resistance principles and strategies related to the disciplinary mechanisms existing in the educational system.

This relationship network appears clandestinely and continuously, and spreads transgression throughout the institutional rules and disciplinary mechanisms. It trespasses onto the physical-spatial limits and barriers. It establishes collective rhythms and actions invisible to observers. It develops conflicting processes that interfere with the formation of youths' personalities. It articulates agreements and complicity, which are subversive or parallel to the bureaucratic hierarchy. It attempts to escape vigilance or invert it, and challenges punishment mechanisms. Last, it cheats the formal examination protocol.

Clandestinity and Rebelliousness

To Foucault (1988, pp. 91–92), the strategic codification of resistance trespasses social stratification, making individual unity a necessary precursor for revolution. The main challenge for those who dare to promote autonomous initiatives and movements in the school is facing the control of the normalizing system. How, then, can we liberate the transgression potential in education and articulate it in transformative processes?

The construction of a world of delinquents in the school ambit becomes pertinent to the discussion around the maintenance of disciplinary order. Not only because it segregates and systematically excludes every person that presents divergent behavior, submitting it to a constant vigilance and exemplary punishment, but, above all, because it prevents the appearance of ample and open rebellious forms, deviating initiatives and movements of contestation in controllable forms of transgression. Thus, the maintenance of a disciplinary milieu within the school structure becomes an antidote to the development of democratic processes. The construction of democratic processes implies, therefore, the deconstruction of the disciplinary mechanisms of power.

Deconstructing Subjection

To deconstruct the disciplinary forms of pedagogical relation that facilitate the construction of democratic and cooperative, emancipatory processes, it is necessary to know beforehand why relationships tend to configure subjugation in the disciplinary organizations.

From Foucault's point of view, the *regard* sustains the strength of the power that is exercised on individuals. It is the regard that is carried out as vigilance, a regard that, through the analysis and observation of the object, segments it into individual and comparable parts in a manner that reduces them to a classification table. This analytical classification serves as a perception filter to the "other," one that conditions the attitudes and behaviors of the observer in the sense that he/she exercises domination in relation to the observed subject. At the same time, the classificatory analysis becomes a censorship mechanism in relation to the knowledge. It tends to determine the ambit and type of answers allowed to the other, excluding all forms of reaction that do not coincide with the established parameters. Similarly, concerning the exercise of power, it shapes coercive instruments, which reinforce certain behaviors (by rewarding) and discourage others (by punishing).

These mechanisms converge in the examination regard, a relationship strategy that materializes in multiple institutional situations. Vigilance, sanction, and examinations are resources for good training; that is, to induce the individuals to align themselves to disciplinary relations (individual, classificatory, and hierarchical ones) in which the productive but docile individuals form their identities. The disciplinary regard becomes a relation of unidirectional control permitting it consider the other only as an object. But it does not permit to be observed by the other. The type of regard that establishes the disciplinary relationship excludes not just the reciprocity of the regard. An objectivistic kind of visual perception is privileged so that other possible meanings of it are reduced or excluded, such as in relation to curiosity, reception, seduction, or valorization of the other. In addition, hierarchical vigilance is a control system based mainly on the visual sense. In this way it constitutes a power and knowledge structure unable to embody the diverse dimensions of human interactions, constituted by the language of hearing, tasting, smelling, and touching, favoring a kind of *unisensorial* relation.

The analogy of the disciplinary power-knowledge (hierarchical, formal, and positive) dynamic as a kind of *unidirectional, unisensorial,* and *unifocal* regard constitutes itself on an interpretative basis, from which it is possible to foresee the problematic of educational disciplinary relations.

First, such reconfiguration of the educational process implies constituting relations of reciprocity between educated-educator subjects in the knowledge process. Overcoming the unidirectionality of the hierarchical relation, or of the "banking education" concept (Freire, 1974), means honoring the reciprocity of dialogical and cooperative relations among people. At the same time, a person teaches to, and also learns from, another. Similarly, when a subject observes, he/she is also observed by the other, influencing and being influenced in his affective, intellectual, active, interactive, and communicative processes. In the educational process, insofar as people constitute mutual relationships of knowledge and power, they develop the potential for critical and creative interactions, overcoming the subjugation produced by disciplinary mechanisms.

Second, this dialogical reciprocity only constitutes itself insofar as the multiple dimensions of human communication permit their existence. This human interaction is not reduced to visual communication. The interaction is constituted in the communicative dimension when it develops simultaneously the reciprocity of the multiple forms and languages of verbal and bodily communication. In the emotional and mental dimensions, when welcoming and being welcomed, and when understanding and being understood, the reciprocity becomes evident. Since different languages are used in a simultaneous way, the reciprocity in communication between different people becomes a reality. Speaking and listening may seem to be a unidirectional relation between an active and a passive subject, if you consider only the aural-oral communicative dimension. However, taking into consideration the multiples languages and communicational dimensions, we realize that, as they are developed, the different interlocutors participate actively and reciprocally in relation to the sustenance of the communicative context. Concerning the multidimensional and complex, communication is essentially dialogical.

Third, the overcoming of the disciplinary mechanism in the unidirectional regard implies the overthrow of the unifocal character. The teacher, when examining the student's performance, focuses on and values only aspects related to certain preestablished goals, ignoring all other components that form his/her context. The dialogical relation, on the contrary, implores us to consider the constitutive contexts of the multiple meanings developed by people's actions and interactions. Thus, it becomes necessary to develop the capacity for perception and comprehension of the context (Severi & Zanelli, 1990) and their transformative processes. It is from the social, subjective, historical, cultural, and environmental contexts that actions are constituted and acquire meaning; "without a context, words or actions have no meaning" (Bateson, 1986, p. 23). The apprehension of the context requires a logical jump, so as to identify not only the objects but also, simultaneously, their interrelations.

The recognition of the multiplicity of (subjective interpersonal, social, cultural, economic, political, and ecologic) contexts, developed through the interaction of different subjects in the relations and educational processes implies perceiving and guiding them according to a logic (or epistemological paradigm) capable of understanding the relationship of the unity of the group with the diversity of elements that constitute it. Thus, the transformation of the disciplinary mechanisms of knowledge-power and the institution of educational processes of dialogical character—such as the ones proposed by Paulo Freire and Céléstin Freinet (Fleuri, 1996)—constitutes a second learning field, insofar as it implies the development of educational contexts that permit the articulation between different subjective, social, and cultural contexts. This translates into understanding and building educational processes in which the distinct subjects constitute their identity, elaborating autonomy and critical consciousness. It also means establishing reciprocal (cooperative and conflicting) relationships with other subjects, creating, supporting, and modifying significant contexts that interact dynamically with other contexts which, consequently, create, support, and modify communicative metacontexts.

The educator, in this sense, is properly situated as a subject that is inserted in an educational process, one that interacts with other subjects, dedicating particular attention to the relationships and contexts that are being created. This contributes to the explanation and elaboration of the senses (perception, meaning, and direction) that allows subjects to construct and reconstruct relationships. In these contexts, the curriculum and the didactic programs, more than a logic character, have an ecological function. The educational processes are constituted, thus, simultaneously, within the perspective of singular subjects, as relationships among people mediated by the world, according to Paulo Freire. At the same time, the people who interact dialogically can mediate cultural, social, and environmental relationships.

Perspectives on the Construction of Democracy in the Educational Process

The construction of democratic processes in school implies the development of dialogical educational mechanisms that overcome disciplinary mechanisms. There are two educators who, although contemporary, have evolved in very diverse social contexts, namely France and Brazil. Freinet was mainly concerned with the education of children up to 14 years of age.

Paulo Freire was initially concerned with adults who were not full participants in formal, traditional education. But their proposals present points in common. Both understand that education is not politically impartial; both refuse the manipulation of human beings; both believe that pedagogical action, despite all its conditioning, is fundamental for human liberation and social transformation.

Both also gave voice to people to speak about their lives as a crucial step in the hope of achieving autonomy, and to be able to engage in world transformation. "Free expression" was Freinet's great discovery that provided a voice for the child. Through this experience and the possibility to recount their own lives, children develop their autonomy, their critical judgment, and their responsibility. Yet, for Paulo Freire, to understand the word is to transform the world, as in people consciously construct their own ways through words (Ribeiro, 1977, pp. 74–75). Both Freinet and Freire defend the dialogue and the cooperation among subjects to problematize, understand, and transform reality. Freire focuses primarily on the educational work linked to sociopolitical action and the organization of the adult world. Freinet underscores the transformation of the educational environment by developing active methods, cooperative organization, and communicative channels within the natural and social milieus.

Freinet's and Freire's pedagogical proposals complement each other. Freire, in his initial elaboration of "consciousness," developed the thematic investigation, codification, and decodification method (Freire, 1975, pp. 89–141). However, he has warned against the dangers of the tendency to mystify methods and techniques. Thus, he emphasized the necessity to develop dialogue and the interaction between educators and the educated to problematize and transform the world. Complementarily, Freinet realized that many politically active teachers adopted, in the classroom, domination methods and techniques diametrically opposed to their ideological relation to freedom and solidarity, underscoring the importance of the technical and pedagogical organization. In this sense, the preoccupation with the political clarity of the educational process ends, so emphasized by Freire, joining the techniques proposed by Freinet in relation to the possibilities for mediation within the practice of school education.

The disciplinary organization within the educational space of the school identifies itself to the auditorium-scriptorium of the traditional school. Against this functional school model, Freinet proposes that the school become a workshop that is both communitarian and specialized, thus demanding a new architectural structure. Here, within the natural milieu, the buildings are considered a priority. In the primary school a basic architectural module comprised of a common room is proposed, where children can gather for collective work with internal and external specialized workshops (i.e., vegetable gardens, orchards, play areas, and livestock). In this school space, activities tend to be taken over by student groups, according to their interests and plans, subverting the hierarchical mechanism.

Thus, the theme discussed in the pedagogical context is called a *generator theme* by Freire (1975), since the approach to such a theme generates a discussion of other correlated themes. However, "'the generator theme' ... can be only understood in man-world relations" (p. 115). It is important, therefore, that the explanation of the generator theme focuses the dialogue, thought, and action of the people on their specific reality. Thus, the thematic investigation needs to be accomplished by subjects in dialogue through which they can manifest their action-reflection on the situation in which they live.

In Freire's and Freinet's pedagogical proposals we can identify the confrontation with the disciplinary mechanisms in an attempt to promote creative and productive school education processes. However, such proposals are not reduced to a mere set of techniques or *innovative* pedagogical methods to be applied at school. It would be important to *adopt* Freinet's pedagogical proposals to construct or adapt school buildings and spaces, including classrooms and specialized workshops (interior and exterior), or adapting schedules, methods, and programs to become more creative and participatory. In the same way, the problematizing dialogue around the key themes, proposed by Freire, is executed neither in a spontaneous nor in a mechanical way. Since these methodologies can be easily assimilated to a disciplinary structure that places individuals in a hierarchy, then the personal options and the correlation of forces in a certain context favor the hierarchization and subjugation in the institutional relations. In a disciplinary institution, paradoxically, resistance relations and options develop that point of the other form of organization, instigating structural changes.

The most important component in the work of constructing democracy at school is to creatively engage in human relations, bravely facing the game of power in which students, teachers, and others participate, creating and recreating critically, step by step, the means that support relations aimed at autonomy and reciprocity and, at the same time, neutralizing the ones that produce loneliness and submission.

Questions for Reflection

1. Why might the disciplinary mechanisms of space, time, and collective processes promote a political passivity in people?

2. How does the exam process with its supervision and sanctioning model induce people to be subjugated?

3. What epistemological changes are necessary to overcome the disciplinary mechanisms inherent in knowledge and power in educational practice?

4. How should education and the role of the educator be conceived in a complex perspective?

5. What methodological indicators can we find in and through Paulo Freire and Céléstin Freinet to develop democracy in the pedagogical practice?

References

Althuser, L. (1970). *Ideologia e aparelhos ideológicos do Estado*. Lisboa: Editorial Presença.
Bateson, G. (1986). *Mente e natureza: A unidade necessária*. Rio de Janeiro: Francisco Alves.
Brandão, C. R. (1986). A turma de trás. In Regis Morais, Regis (Ed.), *Sala de aula: que espaço é esse?* (pp. 105–122). Campinas, SP: Papirus.
Fleuri, R. M. (1990, June). A cela de aula. *Jornal da APUFSC, 10*, 2-20.
———. (1996). Freinet: Confronto com o poder disciplinar. In Elias, Maria del Cioppo Elias (Ed.), *Pedagogia Freinet: Teoria e prática* (pp. 195–207). Campinas, SP: Papirus.
———. (2001). *Educar, para quê? Contra o autoritarismo da relação pedagógica na escola*. São Paulo: Cortez.
Foucault, M. (1977). *Vigiar e punir: História da violência nas prisões*. Petrópolis: Vozes.
———. (1988). *História da sexualidade I: A vontade de saber*. Rio de Janeiro: Graal.
Freinet, C. (1973). *Para uma escola do povo*. Lisboa: Editorial Presença.
Freire, P. (1974). *Educação como prática da liberdade*. Rio de Janeiro: Paz e Terra.
———. (1975). *Pedagogia do oprimido*. Rio de Janeiro: Paz e Terra.

Giroux, H. (1983). *Pedagogia radical: Subsídios*. Tradução de Dagmar M. L. Zibas. São Paulo: Cortez/Autores Associados.

Ribeiro, S. A. de Oliveira. (1977). *Em busca de uma metodologia para uma educação libertadora*. Inéditos dissertação de Mestrado, São Paulo, PUCSP.

Severi, V., & Zanelli, P. (1990). *Educazione, complessità e autonomia dei bambini*. Firenze: Nuova Italia.

SECTION II

REFLECTIONS ON DEMOCRATIC DISSONANCE AND DISSIDENCE

CHAPTER

6

EDUCATORS' CONCEPTIONS OF DEMOCRACY

Jason M. C. Price

Introduction

The basis of this chapter is the belief that, first, educators' understanding of democracy influences their pedagogical and curricular decisions, and second, that these daily decisions made by educators are culturally, economically, environmentally, and politically meaningful. As with research, education is never politically neutral. This political chapter is inspired by the teachings of indigenous knowledge keepers or Elders in North America, who struggle daily to live democracy (Red Democracy).[1] Oral cultures depend on memory and the power of the spoken word to pass on knowledge. This chapter intentionally privileges the voices of self-described democratic educators. In contrast, the Western education system, and the discourse around education, relies on a written tradition usually formed by elite. In a sense, one could refer to this chapter as an *iterature* rather than *literature* review.

The gap between democratic theory and practice in education is observed by a wide range of educators, academics, theorists, policy makers, and citizens. This chapter examines the democratic viewpoint of 10 educator-participants working in diverse urban schools in Canada. Four of the educators are experienced urban public K-12 school administrators. The chapter describes how the experienced educators, who identified themselves as "democratic educators," define the core qualities of democracy. Aboriginal Elders and some seminal scholars have long argued that beliefs and values motivate and guide expectations and actions.[2] Nurturing a critical understanding of democratic beliefs requires the clear articulation of these beliefs.

As mentioned above, the decisions made by educators are culturally, socially, economically, and politically saturated, ripe with implications. The pedagogical and organizational decisions made by teachers can arguably greatly influence the way students perceive democracy, are prepared for participation in democracy, as well as the kind of democracy they may choose to believe in or practice. Democratic teachers' stories (or culture stories) add new points of view to the discourse on democracy and education. The research-participant views described in this chapter are ideals worth striving for in schools; ideals of democracy stressing content as well as process. They describe democracy as a trinity comprised of *participation, protection*, and *provision*.

In this chapter I attempt to fill three "gaps" in the literature of education and democracy identified by Beyer (1996) in his book *Creating Democratic Classrooms: The Struggle to Integrate Theory and Practice,* namely

> 1) the commitments of progressive educational scholars; 2) the informed hope of creating alternative educational and social possibilities; and 3) descriptions of the actual practices that will give expression to concrete actions and value commitments. (p. 20)

Why Paddle the Backwaters of Democracy in Public Schools?

The dearth of studies on the philosophy of educators, classrooms, and schools is disturbing. Schools are widely accepted as political, economic, cultural, and social terrain in which democratic transformation must be developed. The discussion of educators' philosophy of democracy, and claims to pedagogical practice, regrettably, has been a neglected backwater.

The significance of educator theories and knowledge of democracy is supported by an eclectic group of researchers. Covell and Howe's (1999) research suggested a strong relationship between educators' knowledge of human rights and their practice. Solomon and Levine-Rasky (1996) argued that a strong relationship exists between educators' knowledge of anti-racism and their practice, although they recognized a problematic gap between knowledge and action. From their qualitative research with practising public-school teachers, Biggs (1999) and O'Brien (2001) argued that most teachers are not prepared to help students make connections between important concepts and discourses in democratic education. These concepts include social, ecological, and economic justice, equity, equality, rights, and democracy as a way of life. These findings are disturbing, given that "teacher translation" of "philosophic concepts" provides the scaffolding that "enables students to engage concepts and issues thoroughly" (Biggs, 1999; Moar & Taylor, as cited in O'Brien, 2001). Evidence indicates that "political practice" in schools depends largely on the leadership of the principal, and that facilitative leadership correlates with "strong democracy" in schools (Rollow & Bryk, 1995).

Finally, the significance of this chapter is that the educators' stories of democracy may assist readers in examining their own concept of the "indigenous" or core qualities of democracy, and their approach to educating students in democracy.

Backwaters Run Deep and Are Worth Paddling

Little is known about educators' political philosophy or knowledge of theories of democracy. Unfortunately, the popular view often defines *democracy* narrowly in terms of representative democracy, political parties, votes, and decision making by law-making elite representatives, usually jurists (Price, 2004, in press) and free-market capitalism. The participants in this study were asked to reflect upon (a) which interests are served by the popular view of democracy; (b) their own concept and practice of democracy and pedagogy; and (c) their influence on the education of our collective future, their students.

Methodology

The philosophy of hope and possibility, guiding the research examined in this chapter, springs from the discursive and redemptive moral and intellectual power of indigenous wisdom, practices, and institutions. In short, the spirit of indigenous resistance animates my theoretical framework and methodology. This chapter waves a red flag in the face of the continuing degradation of democracy in education. The aim is to realize a participatory democracy, or Red Democracy, in education.[3] The insights from the Four Sacred Directions and Four Sacred Colours of the diverse *subjects* that participated in this study are the power behind the thrust.

Participants and the Study

The 10 educator-participants were passionate and articulate during our intensive semi-structured discussions. They often alternated between questions and ideas when trying to make connections between their theory of democracy and their teaching practice. I had the impression that this was an important exercise for them. Most participants spoke about being energized by our discussion. My own experience working in schools on four continents is that conversations about democracy are rare in schools. I believe that some of the educators were being asked to think about democracy and schools for the first time. The others were prompted to think in new ways about democracy and their practice of educating students in democracy. For the first time, they made connections between what they *want* in democracy and their classroom, and what they actually *do* as educators to realize this objective.

Although educators are asked to evaluate their objectives in lessons or units of study, they are rarely asked to look at the totality of experiences and opportunities, the obvious curriculum, and the hidden curriculum of their classroom and school. This study asked the participants to evaluate how their pedagogy and curriculum influenced their role and responsibility to prepare critical, active, informed, and generative citizens. It is important to note that, although most of the participants had to think about their responses, it did not mean they were not being honest and genuine. The follow-up interviews suggested that the participants were expanding their notion of democracy and the perception of their practice. This process is a good argument for broad conceptual discussions between public educators and academics. For example, what they may have considered pedagogy in support of "equity-related goals" or "citizenship" changed during the interview and became (constructed by the participants) democratic practice. Is this a case of the demeaning of democracy in popular or education-related discourse, or simply a case of semantics? I would like to think it was a natural growth in the understanding of democracy as a way of life, stressing *content* as much as *process*.

The Rough Map for Our Backwater Journey

The following question was provided in written form to each of the educator-participants at the beginning of our semi-structured discussion. *What are the core qualities and values of your understanding of democracy?* It focused but did not limit our discussions.

Four Core Qualities of Democracy: Main Beams for a Democratic Longhouse?

Four core qualities of democracy emerged from the interviews; they were noted by all participants. The participants emphasized some qualities over others; the qualities described later are not presented in any particular order. A list is useful for the reader or researcher but may create a false impression because the whole (in democracy) is greater than the sum of its parts. Many ingredients of democracy must be blended to achieve the ideal. Each ingredient is both dependent upon and inter-dependent of the others. The four main inter-connected and inter-dependent core qualities of democracy in education, identified by the educators in this study, were

1. voice;
2. critical thinking, reflection, and action;
3. community, cooperation, and consensus; and
4. non-discrimination and non-oppression.

Voice

All participants said that *talk* is the foundation of their concept of democracy. They defined it as both the content and process of democracy and stated that the "voices of all" must be heard. Pauline[4] stated that, "in a democracy, all voices must be greeted by everyone carefully listening." Most participants suggested that a special effort must be made to ensure that marginalized voices are heard, including this statement:

> Democracy is about making sure spaces are created and maintained, where the voices of all segment no matter how disjointed or disconnected their input maybe. In a democracy, the voices of the people who are not often listened to are heard, and I think this is essential in what I would consider a genuine democracy.... In a

democracy, everyone must know that a person who is poor, an Aboriginal, or other member of a marginalised group has the same voice as the Bay Street person; there can be no difference in the power that those people yield. (Moneca)

Some participants agreed on the importance of *listening* as a democratic skill that is essential for "all citizens to learn and practise in all areas of the society" (Melissa). Pauline emphasized *listening* as a skill to be taught and said that listening demands evidence:

> If there is no listening, there is no voice. If we don't learn to listen to one another with our ears and eyes, how can we ever expect to learn? The old ones teach us this with the stories. We must watch them carefully to see the feelings, the expressions. They are subtle but important.... That is why dance can say so much, and song can create visions with sound. Listening is one of the roots of democracy. Beside the voice of everyone, it is song to dance. You have to watch the listener to see what the words mean. What they are trying to say is found in the body, the tone, the expression. You have to ask yourself questions about what they are saying while they are talking or telling. You must show your interest with your face and eyes to show respect to the speaker.... When they finish you honour them with smart questions about things that went unsaid in words, but that you may have heard only in echo.

Gloria noted the importance of this deep, "emphatic listening" or watchful hearing as a core quality of democracy. She contrasted *listening* in democracy and *hearing*, which she characterized as non-critical, reactionary, and judgemental. Listening contained *questioning for clarification*:

> We hear but we don't listen. They are not the same. I hear politicians and people say all kinds of things about democracy, but when you listen to them, they are not saying anything with meaning. We need to listen to one another, give them a chance to be heard, to voice their thoughts before challenging them, but we have to listen carefully to make sure they are really saying something first. If not, we can hear all kinds of things we want to hear that are not there, or that we want to be there, but they never said. And the next part of listening is to clarify things with thoughtful questions. (Gloria)

Listening is a complex skill that empowers voice, giving it meaning and substance in democracy. *Active listening* is a form of engagement between a speaker and a listener that empowers both. The participants described *watchful listening* as both a procedure and the content of democracy.

Catherine referred to the problem of "asymmetrical power relations" in the public space. Most participants agreed; several noted the importance of "democratic authority" in encouraging many voices. Some participants emphasized providing opportunities for children and marginalized groups to express their viewpoint in a public forum outside school. The participants noted the importance of "all citizens" taking a stand and defending them in the public space. "If everyone does not get a chance to speak and be heard it is not a democracy, is it?" (Rosa).

> There is lots of talk by all the same people in our so-called democracy. Talk does not make it democracy—that depends on who talks, who gets heard, who speaks for whom and who listens. We seldom hear from the people that need to be heard, should be heard. Who listens to the kids and the poor and others who don't have the social power or money to get heard, or has the confidence or skills to negotiate a way to get heard, or to respond to all the things said for them by others so different from them? (Catherine)

Others participants elaborated on this notion of democracy giving voice where now there is silence in our schools and communities. As "people of colour," Rosa, a self-described "Black" educator, and Tamina, a self-described "visible Muslim" woman educator, speak directly to the connection between lack of voice in school and in our "democratic" community:

> My community does not get a chance to speak or defend themselves. Once in a while, they have someone or another to speak for some community group, but not in the editorials, or in the places with real power that people listen up to. The kids in these communities never get a chance to speak so they can be heard. I have to pry it out of them. We have to make times and places for the kids and the community to be heard directly. I can do it in class and the school, where we can sit face to face, but unless there is a killing or something, we don't get a chance to sit face to face with the people that make the decisions, and then they usually do the talking and explaining about why they can't listen. (Rosa)

As Rosa noted, spaces for voices to be heard and amplified by power and setting are essential to a democracy. These opportunities or spaces for input into discussions and decision making arguably must begin, or at least be supported in schools.

Tamina raised the question of who gets to speak for whom and who controls the delivery and dissemination of news and information. As Tamina constructed democracy, the need for new technologies, spaces, and opportunities for direct communication between groups and individuals will be the main beam of a democratic longhouse:

> Look at the words they have put in our mouths. Do we get a chance as people of colour and difference to defend ourselves so that ordinary people can hear the good things? Sure, some get through but it can't be heard because of all of the other things that are being said about us. There have to be more opportunities for people to talk directly to each other. (Tamina)

The participants were aware of the potential for "noise" when spaces are created for open dialogue. They realized that a democracy constructed upon voice and talk is "messy and noisy" (Moneca). However, *voice* is the dynamic that animates their vision of democracy. *Voice* is not simply a utilitarian concept connected with deliberation, consensus building, and decision making. They described it as a life force, as essential to the healthy democratic body as breathing is to the human body: democratic inspiration through oral inhalation within the body social, cultural, economic, and political. It is a form of collective thinking, reflecting and deciding aloud. It is a method of getting individuals and the community morally and intellectually vibrant.

For the participants, *talk* is democratic. By encouraging and engaging in discussion, the community is practising democracy. Talk, as many Elders have taught me, is a metaphysical act capable of binding together people and revealing previously unknown human connections. The educators clearly construct *talk* in democracy as an integral process that is both critical and creative; *"voice* is the main quality in a democracy" (Tamina).

> Voice, pure and simple is the basis of a democracy. How else do we know what the other is saying and thinking, or wants? If we don't ask and listen we don't know or learn. We end the possibilities for our community with silence. It's loud and messy, but it is essential. We have to talk and explain, and we have to learn it by doing it. Getting things straight together. It takes time but it is worth it. (Moneca)

Voice is, as Moneca explained, not just about communicating, but by its very nature an act of thought:

> You have to let everyone have a chance to speak or it isn't right. If they don't have a chance to talk they don't know what they are thinking or what it even means because they don't get a reaction or have to explain what they are thinking and why. For me it is the point of it all, to get everyone talking and listening to each other. (Curtis)

As Curtis stated, one of the rationales for education and democracy has to be to get people communicating with one another. Voice is then both an end and a means:

> There is a saying my grandfather used to say, that pretty much ... well it means, "Talk heals everything in time." He was right, you know. Most of the hurts that people carry with them are because no one listens to them seriously or gives them the chance to explain themselves. I see this everyday in my office. When the kids come in and talk and I listen to them they leave feeling better, like they have been made stronger. It is respect to listen and let others speak. It is what makes us human, that builds our identities as peoples and communities. Some people, especially kids, never get a chance to talk, and that means to talk and be listened to. (Rocco)

Rocco reinforces the importance of the curative power of talk—talk that is, of course, heard. The importance of talk being truly listened to is an important distinction that each of the participants noted at some point in their interviews. Sadly, they all suggest that students are not often heard during the few opportunities they get to speak to power.

According to the educators, another essential quality or dynamic of democracy is *creativity*. Creativity is one of the riches mined from the deep veins of democratic talk in all parts of the community. For the educators, democratic creativity implies risk taking. The educators portray *risk* as important in maintaining democracy. Like a grain of sand in an oyster, the creative individual, group, community, idea, or work of art creates possibilities for transformation in a democracy:

> Risk is important. It is what gets us talking to each other and doing things. Somebody has to be the first to put themself *[sic]* on the line, to challenge things that are accepted by everyone else or the majority. Without risk, you have conformity and that is not compatible with democracy—that has to be open. I have

taken risks in my career and they can hurt you, but you have to take them, and I encourage all the teachers I have worked with to do the same. (Moneca)

If creativity implies risk, Moneca makes an important connection between risk and sacrifice. The participants all shared asides or direct testimony to the personal and professional "costs" of being a democratic educator. Pauline made the important connection between risk and change and the important role that leaders can play as members of a community:

If we had not taken risks, we would not have survived. We had to trust one another in order to defend what we had in common or they would have swallowed us up and we would have nothing left. But it took a few brave people to begin the talking to get people to see new possibilities, new futures and what was at stake if we did not take some chances. I mean the Peacemaker risked everything. Leaders in our community risk their lives all the time to get heard or protest an injustice. It is the right way. (Pauline)

The participants believed that democracy must always be open to the possibilities generated by human creativity. Creativity is the product of democratic talk and liberation from oppression, colonization, and discrimination. Importantly, creativity is presented by some educators as a feature of a community that revels in diversity rather than tolerating it.

Creativity ... ideas ... in my school with 750 kids, 15 languages being spoken, a concentration of Asian languages and Aboriginal students, you bet. There were always learning opportunities for everyone ... and possibilities being revealed. When we lifted the lid of oppression, fear ... and communicated, we soared as a community together. All the talk fed more cooperation, and more cooperation produced more possibilities. (Gloria)

Critical Thinking, Questions, and Reflection

The participants said there are no "inappropriate" questions in a democracy. They believed that "a democracy must make room for all questions and strive to reflect upon and provide substantive responses to all questions" (Jasmin). Likewise, "in a democracy all questions are welcomed, and responses to all questions should be forthcoming and thorough" (Melissa).

The educators declared that democracies are "open" and "demystify" political, economic, and social processes and positions (Moneca, Rocco).

Most of the educators noted the importance of *questions* in developing "new ways of thinking about old and new problems" (Mina). Differences of opinion are not ignored in a democracy; instead, they become "the basis for further discussion and reflections" (Melissa). The participants noted the importance of *critical thinking, reflection, awareness,* and *action* as the core qualities of a democracy. They agreed that individuals and groups are expected to raise educative, substantive questions, respond to them thoughtfully, and act upon their positions.

The participants stressed critical reflection. In a democracy "members" must be given "opportunities and encouragement to think about the problems challenging the community" (Rosa). Several noted the importance of providing "alternative sources of information" (Rosa) and giving community members access to "all of the details needed to have informed discussion and deliberations." They believed that democracies must tolerate differences of opinion: "Democracies don't sweep differences under the table" (Jasmin). Catherine spoke about the need to "unpack ideas" and "question things" in a democracy, and the difficulty of doing this in schools despite the "neoconservative reforms and climate in education."

> We are in a position now where schools may be the last place available to create a model of what democracy can look like ... it is a difficult thing to do, and I don't want to make it sound like there is some simple answer to it at all. What you have to keep doing is keeping questions open. I mean there are things that you cannot practically do unless you are willing to give up your job, which has been a serious consideration on my part more than once, but the least that you have to do is not let people get so used to making decisions based on taken-for-granted assumptions. (Catherine)

Community, Cooperation, and Consensus

Community was defined as a group of people living and working together in a space undefined by geographic, political, or ecological considerations. Most said that people cooperate in a democratic community.

> The community and democracy are places where people communicate and care for each other. They really look at each other and respond to each other as people and neighbours even if separated by differences. They are not competing with each other and they know this and embody it. (Catherine)

Like Catherine and Rosa, below, the participants to a greater or lesser degree stressed a notion of community care in democracy, which seems to be defined by non-competition, sharing of resources and skills, cooperative problem solving, and working across differences:

> The community cares for one another and supports one another. I mean, when someone needs something, they find a way to get it for them. No one goes without because someone has it all. When they have a problem, they find a shared solution; this is the democratic thing about community. (Rosa)

The participants believed that in democratic communities, people valued one another; all people have inherent value and must be treated well. Democratic communities are "egalitarian" places where "institutions, policies and people are sensitive to the needs of all members" (Mina).

> There are other core qualities of democracy ... awareness of others and sensitivity to the needs of all the people in a group or community. To do that you have to be particularly diligent in trying to find out and be sensitive to the needs of peoples on the margins as they are not as likely to be as forthcoming in expressing their needs. It is more difficult for them to express their needs ... you have to seek it out; you have to be deliberate. You have to put more into finding out about the needs of people who might not be well served. (Catherine)

Most participants stated that children have a special place in democratic communities, so they must consider "the impact on children and the future when making decisions" (Curtis).

The participants believed that democracy "stresses," is "based upon," and "recognizes the importance of" community. The terms *democracy* and *community* were inextricably linked for the educators. They described *democracy* as being dependent upon community and *community* as being dependent upon democracy. Some participants believed a democratic community is achieved only when members experience "true brother- and sisterhood" (Gloria). Most participants said that a democratic community is "community in balance" (Pauline), a space where economic needs are balanced with the social, intellectual, and spiritual needs of community members. Some participants distinguished between *community* and *conformity*. The participants' democratic community would not only "tolerate differences" but would nurture them as "important to revealing possibility" and a "celebration of democratic values" (Gloria).

The participants believed that democracy helps to build community. Most of them contrasted the *community basis* of their understanding of democracy with the *individualistic nature* of "Western democracies." They saw democratic communities as "cooperative not competitive" (Pauline). Moneca stated, "Capitalism is not compatible with democracy or community." Pauline believed that "greed and selfishness are obstacles to democracy." Catherine described the discordant note that competition can ring in a community struggling towards democracy:

> Competition is not a democratic concept, period. For if you are being competitive you want to and are setting yourself above the group or the community, you are wanting to set yourself apart, as better than the rest. Competition is the antithesis of the democratic way. (Catherine)

A democratic community is a place where all members "share a sense of responsibility for each other and the community as a whole" (Mina). Two participants added that they should also "share a sense of responsibility for the health of the environment." (Rosa, Pauline). Melissa stated, "Democracy is built upon the foundation of community or is in a sense a natural extension or product of community." Several participants said that democracy (as a concept and practice) should be defined by the community.

The participants believed that democratic communities needed to "make decisions and set goals collectively" (Gloria). Like Pauline, several educators specified that democratic communities "must make decisions based on consensus." Unfortunately, they provided few details about organizing the forums for making community-wide decisions by consensus. Moneca summed up the participants' awareness of the obstacles to (and possibilities of) consensus-based decision making: "Consensus is not an easy process," and "deliberation takes time and massive effort." Catherine gave an example of consensus making as an educator in a First Nations community:

> Democracy takes time. So that notion of everybody having a say, it never felt like it was controlled by the front. It began from the front but then people would get up and have their say, and of course there was that wonderful way of answering a question

in a circuitous way, I don't mean trying to avoid the question but by using analogy
and metaphor. By the time the story was ended, it was crystal clear.... My point in
bringing this up is that democracy is often not efficient. (Catherine)

Most of the participants spoke of the need for leadership "consistent with the
core qualities of democracy" (Rosa) "to see that decisions get made, and
decisions get applied" (Gloria). Without exception, the participants agreed
that even in democratic communities, "the exercise of authority is sometimes
required" (Moneca) to ensure that core qualities are upheld by the
community. The participants reiterated this theme when speaking about
democracy in education.

Non-discrimination and Non-oppression

The participants passionately agreed that *non-discrimination* and *non-
oppression* are core qualities of democracy. Most participants specified that
in a democracy there must be "equal access" and "treatment and opportunity"
(Gloria, Rocco) for all members. To achieve this goal, they described
democracy as developing beyond the indifference of tolerance and the often-
empty celebration of diversity, and concentrating on "nurturing difference"
(Rosa). The participants used phrases such as "unity in diversity" and
"difference is a source of strength" (Gloria) to describe their positive,
proactive interpretation of diversity in a democracy and the importance of
non-discrimination and non-oppression in establishing the social and
intellectual climate required for a democracy.

Most of the participants used the term *equity* when discussing diversity
and democracy. Although not everyone discussed the concepts of *equality*
and *equity*, it was evident that they believed both concepts were compatible
at different times and in different ways:

I think equity extends beyond voice, because we talk in schools about equity of
opportunity, but not equity of outcome. So, treating people the same is not treating
people equitably. And that is something we must struggle with in a democracy.
(Moneca)

Conclusion

The democracy stories told by the educators in this study relate to critical, caring, cooperative, and creative communities rooted in a democracy defined by four core qualities: (a) voice; (b) critical thinking and reflection; (c) community and cooperation; and (d) non-discrimination and non-oppression. These qualities are dramatically different from the popular discourse on democracy. The participants exhibited indignation and even moral outrage in the face of this "demeaning" of democracy. Rather than equating democracy with process-related practices (votes, political parties, and elite representation), the educators emphasized the core qualities of democracy as being related to values, attitudes, approaches to decision making, and the importance of generalized, empowered, and active discursive participation by all community members. The participants said they believed that by rooting democracy in the voice of all community members, it can foster an approach to problem solving that is both critical and reflective. The result will be a "Great Tree" of community and cooperation, which creates democratic shade, a shade that first and foremost provides and protects. One must ask what are the human, social, and environmental costs of having an elite and process-based "democracy" that does not encourage participation and meaningful engagement? What would be possible in a democracy that reflected the visions, ideals, beliefs, and practices of all "citizens"?

The democracy stories related in this chapter encourage the creation of discursive spaces for educators and students. Time should be allocated at all levels of teacher education and professional development to discuss the question of *ideals* in society and schools as well as, significantly, the specific question of the *gap between the rhetoric and the practice of democracy* in education, communities, and nations.

Questions for Reflection

1. What is your working conception of the core qualities of democracy?

2. How do you attempt to realize your conception of democracy in your teaching or admin-istrative practice?

3. What constraints and obstacles do you face in actualizing your concept of democracy in your work as an educator? How might you overcome some of these constraints and clear

the obstacles in your path?

4. What opportunities do you have to discuss your living philosophy of democracy and democracy in education? How might you open more opportunities for these important discussions with your colleagues or staff?

5. Which single action can you take in your educational practice that will enable you and your students to live Red Democracy in your school or community?

Notes

1. My notion of Red Democracy stresses content over process and includes cooperation, non-oppression, and non-discrimination, generalized participation at the point of decision making, and the love of all life forms and beings (see Price, in press).

2. Teachings I have received from Aboriginal and Indigenous Elders from the Haudenosaunee, Ojibway, and Kuna Yala of Turtle Island to the Semai of Malaysia have made this crucial connection. Most organized Western and Eastern religions stress the mediation of belief and action. Dewey (1933) and Bandura (1986) have made this point.

3. See Sandy Grande's notion of Red Pedagogy, and Price (2004) where I construct the main poles of Longschoolhouse.

4. All names are pseudonyms.

References

Bandura, A. (1986). *Social foundations of thoughts and action: A social cognitive theory.* Englewood Cliffs, NJ: Prentice Hall.

Beyer, L. (1996). *Creating democratic classrooms: The struggle to integrate theory and practice.* New York: Teachers College Press.

Biggs, J. B. (1999). *Teaching for quality learning at university.* Philadelphia: Society for Research into Higher Education & Open University Press.

Covell, K., & Howe, R. B. (1999). The impact of children's rights education: A Canadian study. *International Journal of Children's Rights, 7,* 171–183.

Dewey, J. (1933). *How we think.* Boston: D. C. Heath

O'Brien, M. (2001). Forming a more perfect union: Reconceptualizing civics and citizenship education in Australia. Retrieved September 15, 2007, from http://www.towson.edu/internationalassembly/files/2001%20IA%20Meeting/2001-4.pdf

Price, J. M. C. (2004). *Reclaiming democracy for the Longschoolhouse.* Unpublished doctoral dissertation, OISE, University of Toronto.

———. (in press). Red democracy. *Journal of Thought.*

Rollow, S. G., & Bryk, A. S. (1995). Catalyzing professional community in a school reform left behind. In K. S. Louis, S. D. Kruse, & Associates (Eds.), *Professionalism and community: Perspectives on reforming urban schools* (pp. 105–132). Thousand Oaks, CA: Corwin.

Solomon, R., & Levine-Rasky, C. (1996). When principle meets practice: Teachers' contradictory responses to antiracist education. *Alberta Journal of Educational Research, 42*(1), 19–33.

C H A P T E R

7

DEMOCRACY AND DIFFERENCE IN EDUCATION: INTERCONNECTEDNESS, IDENTITY, AND SOCIAL JUSTICE PEDAGOGY

Alexandra Fidyk

Introduction

Recent educational literature (Kincheloe & Steinberg, 1997; McCarthy, 1993; Sleeter & McLaren, 1995) indicates increasing support for critical theory as a theoretical framework for school reform aimed at social justice. The curricular work by teacher educator Kevin Kumashiro (2004) supports teachers in negotiating the challenges related to anti-oppressive teaching. Theorists, such as Amy Gutmann (1987), have written convincingly about empowering students for democratic participation; however, they have been unable to initiate lasting challenges to existing structural inequities in contemporary education. Critical theory has provided progressive scholars with a rich framework for theorizing about the transformative goals of education, related to issues of sexism, homophobia, racism, and other social justice concerns. However, understanding "engaged pedagogy" as a way of transforming consciousness, to provide educators and students with ways of knowing that enable them to know themselves better, to know "difference," and to live in the world in a more engaged manner seems a necessary step for democracy and social justice in education.

Attending responsibly to democracy and difference in education requires a shift (ontologically) in the way we perceive, interpret, and respond to events. Growing attention has been given to school-based activist programmes and collaborative research with students, activists, and practitioners (Lund, 2006). However, my recent research considers reconceptualizing ethical relations by drawing from traditions not typically considered in social justice research.

Influenced by Buddhist, Vedic, Jungian thought, and quantum physics, I offer an integrative perspective of our deep inter-connectedness as an alternative to the subject–object dualism that not only dominates our classrooms but also underlies much thinking and theorizing about "otherness." Here, several themes are considered, including inter-connectedness, consciousness, and their relationship to love as they relate to social justice education. Parallels are drawn among these fields and between ideas rooted in contemporary Eastern and Western thinking. The ideas of inter-connectedness and inter-relatedness challenge previously held beliefs about power and privilege and are proposed as a way to enliven our pedagogical and activist work. The ontological positioning of such ideas is crucial for any discussion about democracy and social justice in education.

Engaged pedagogy implies that teachers must be actively committed to a process of individuation[1] if they are to teach in a manner that empowers students. Teachers, in turn, are empowered by being receptive in the classroom, and by being present in mind, body, and spirit. Given that engaged pedagogy seeks to transform consciousness, to provide students with ways of knowing that enable them to know themselves better and to live in the world more fully, and more ethically, to some extent it must rely on the presence of care, and even love, in the classroom. Smith (1999) suggests that our most serious need in educational reform may be for adults to simply be "present" to children, to attend to the "deep attunement to the valence between genuine intimacy and detachment" (p. 88). Conversely, those of us who teach the same old subjects in the same old ways are often inwardly bored, lacking imagination, and unable to rekindle the care that we may have once felt.

If, as Merton (1967) suggests, the purpose of education is to show students how to define themselves "authentically and spontaneously in relation" (p. 3) to the world, then teachers can best teach if we are in touch with the fertile ground of consciousness. Merton (1967) reminds us that "the original and authentic 'paradise' idea ... implied not simply a celestial store of theoretic ideas ... but the inner self of the student" who would discover the ground of her being in relation to herself, to higher powers, and to community (p. 9). The "fruit of education ... was in the activation of that utmost center" (p. 9). To restore meaning to our educative experience, teachers must find again the locus of care within ourselves.

Such a view extends Banks' (2002) argument for conceptualizing the school as a "unit of change," and for "restructuring the culture and organization of the school so that students from diverse racial, ethnic, and social-class groups will experience educational equality and empowerment" (p. 17). Here, through an on-going process of deep inner address, teachers and students become change agents, both locally and globally, where they understand and respect democracy and diversity on multiple levels.

Interconnectedness, Engaged Pedagogy, and Love

> Man [sic] has the capacity to love, not just his own species, but life in all its shapes and form. This empathy with the interknit web of life is the highest spiritual expression I know of. (Eiseley, as cited in Lorimer, 1990, p. 72)

Perhaps love and empathy exist not only between humans but between other entities as well. If so, the inter-knit of life extends further, and is more immediate, present, and prescient than we commonly imagine. What might become of our senses of being if we made this connectedness a basis for our lives and for our pedagogical practices? Certainly it would shift the very nature of what we now call ethical relations. If we acknowledged our connection to all things at the most subtle and expansive levels, our actions would unfold as care for our trees, water, and selves. Any uncaring thoughts or actions would knowingly harm oneself and every other. In this way, love and ethics arise from relational consciousness which form the basis of social justice.

All curricula overlap, flow into one another, and aim at greater awareness and understanding of self and the world. Teaching literature can become an occasion for philosophy, history, quantum physics, art, math, narrative, geography, spirituality, biology, and so on. Teaching physics may be an occasion for studying Shakespeare. We impose artificial divisions between subjects only for convenience and organization. Those boundaries are arbitrary.

Our Inter-connected Existence

Inter-connectedness is an unavoidable idea in our time. In Buddhism, the Jewelled Net of Indra offers a vision of reality where each being, each gem at each node of the net, is illumined by all the others and reflected in them. As part of this integral world, one contains the whole, where all that has preceded this moment is carried forth within that gem or individual entity. Breaking open a seed to reveal its life-giving kernel, the sage in the *Upanishads* tells his student: *"Tat tvam asi*—That art thou." He explains: the tree that will grow from the seed, that art thou; the water that will nourish the seed, that art thou; the sun light that will warm the seed, that art thou.

Kumashiro (2004) also points to Buddhist thought as offering a different representation of reality, one that challenges knowledge centred on binaries such as "self and other, inner and outer, us and them, means and ends, win or lose" (p. 41). Not only do the binaries reinforce hierarchies of one over the other, but also exclude third spaces as when male and female make sense only because other, inter-sexed genders have been excluded. Buddhism problematizes knowledge produced about the world that leads people to believe that things are permanent (unchanging) and independent (unconnected to other things). Both the context and the meaning of a thing can change its very nature. From a Buddhist view, all things are related with one another and cannot be known in isolation.

A similar view was recently echoed by South African Jungian analyst and wilderness guide Ian McCallum, who eloquently reminded us of our molecular origins, to our geology, to those first cellular membranes, and to the eventual expression of a species capable of reflecting upon itself. The relationship of principal cations (the electropositive elements) of the blood serum of all animals and human beings is constant ("calcium : sodium : potassium = 5 : 10 : 160") (McCallum, 2005, p. 64). This measurement is a close representation of their respective proportions in seawater, differing only by a greater content of magnesium in the oceans of today. He further writes:

The animals, then, are in us and with us; we share their genes and their juices. Made up of countless molecules, cells and complex organs, each one of us is the carrier not only of the pattern of embryonic gill slits and tails, but the entire history of life also. It would appear that the aboriginal "water of life" still circulates in the blood of every animal, including us. (p. 65)

The image of Indra's Net applies not only to our species but to the elements and creatures that came before and continue to evolve along with and through us. So then, how can an attitude that is both purposeful and democratic, one that reaches out with the intention not only of bringing out the best in the other, but also of learning from that other, not include the molecular and chemical origins of this planet?

The various and overlapping views of inter-connectedness suggest that there is no separateness. Yet, as with our academic subjects and curriculum planning, we divide our experience and our understanding into exclusive systems, such as physics, philosophy, and poetry, or self and other. Here, I treat these parts as the jewels on Indra's net, all connected in a system or design of which we may not be aware. The flow-through of matter, energy, and information that is transformed by one's own experiences and intentions is, I propose, love. Buddhist Joanna Macy (1991) writes: "as lovers seek for union, we are apt, when we fall in love with our world, to fall into oneness with it as well" (p. 11). Similarly, bell hooks (2003) whose work draws from Buddhist monk Thich Nhat Hanh, advocates for engaged pedagogy where love unfolds among students and teachers: "Love in the classroom prepares teachers and students to open our minds and hearts. It is the foundation on which every learning community can be created" (p. 137). Yet, we cannot come to such love without a radical shift in the way that we perceive ourselves in relation to other—elemental or tribal.

All of Earth's life is inescapably connected at a quantum mechanical level: atmosphere, water, or matter. We are co-dependently arising. With such inter-connection, our full *self* (which includes multiple selves and seeing other as self) extends beyond the boundaries of our skin. In such a collective, individuals may be more attentive to, and less violent towards, others (human, animal, plant, and systems). Inter-connectedness does not exclude individuality. The "one" is not subsumed by the collective as formations are unique, separate, yet fluid, continuously degenerating and regenerating, and not containing or restricting new relationships or formations.

Humanity, perhaps democracy, is not defined by human fellowship but by the subtle and essential inter-dependency with animals and landscape. The web is inclusive not only of our immediate surroundings, our geology and biology, but also of space and time. Within this field the basic elements of the physical world, including electrons and photons, behave in some situations like waves and in other situations like particles. Paradoxically, they are both. To use analogous thinking, is it not conceivable then that we have both particle-like individuality and a wave-like, shared being-ness and inter-connectedness? While we all have personal narratives, we are also part of a larger, communal history.

An Image of Consciousness

In what follows, I presuppose that we are inter-connected, fluid, and boundless, both at the physical level and at the level of consciousness. Consciousness, conceived of as a field of energy and likened to love, is the phenomenon from which all else arises.

Perhaps Bell's theorem provides the most dramatic demonstration of inter-connectedness in the micro-world of quantum physics. Briefly, in 1964, Bell showed that quantum theory predicted that any two particles that originated from a single source (such as two electrons born out of an energetic collision) would later behave as if they maintained some kind of on-going, non-local connection. In other words, there is an elemental oneness to the universe, where particles operate and influence each other within a field. This connection can be revealed by measuring some property of each particle, such as the spin of each electron. It is instantaneous and unaffected by time or distance. According to Bell, these measurements should be more highly correlated than if the two particles were truly separate. The implications of this finding are profound, particularly if one believes that all matter comes from a single source. Thus, Bell's theorem implies at a quantum level that the physical world is an inseparable whole.

This physical inter-connectedness is based on widely accepted science, and it does not interfere with the core sense of individuality. But when inter-connectedness is considered at the level of consciousness, both these characteristics change. In Jungian psychology (Jung, 1963), the coinciding of events and happenings occurs in synchronous time where there is acausal, non-local inter-relatedness. For example, we have all had the experience of thinking of someone when the telephone rings, and it is that person. We all have stories, incidents, or coincidences when we think that we just happened to be at the right place at the right time, but from many perspectives, it seems to be a palpable meeting between mind (psyche) and substance. The feeling is one of being immersed in a field of actions, interactions, intention, and attention; it is as if we have touched upon a potential that has been lost, one that illustrates that everything in the universe is connected. This reference to Jungian psychology functions here to locate similar beliefs in different disciplines, metaphorical junctures in the jewelled net. What is striking for social justice and democracy in education is the way that radical inter-connectedness promotes a sense of continuity, narrows the gap between our inner and our outer lives, and connects subject and object, or self and other.

In the emerging image of consciousness, it can be understood as a collective consciousness among people, which forms a field of non-local intelligence wherein we all dwell. It extends beyond the individual and is spaceless and timeless. Consciousness is an ordering principle that can insert information into disorganized systems and create higher degrees of order. Consciousness is not the same as awareness. The ordering power of consciousness can occur completely outside awareness, such as in dreams or at the unconscious level. Both individual and group consciousness can insert and withdraw order or information from the world. Coherence among individuals, expressed as love, empathy, caring, oneness, and connectedness, is important in the ordering power of consciousness. Consciousness affects humans and non-humans alike, for our pets and forests "resonate" with, and respond to, human consciousness (Radin, Rebman, & Cross, 1996).

To take on this responsibility is to consider what it means to think with intention. To illustrate, Lopez (as cited in McCallum, 2005) describes the imminent death of a moose in an encounter with a wolf, as engaged in a conversation of death: "The moose, standing quite still, its eyes fixed on the grey hunter, knows what is going to happen next. It is an ancient contract" (p.

150). Similarly, the Kalahari Bushmen understand and honour this contract for there is no hunt unless it is filled with "intention, continuity, and connection. There is no hunt unless the prey and the prayer from the hunter become the same thing" (McCallum, 2005, p. 150). Here, to pray unceasingly is to be continually mindful of the patterns of connections between all things, vigilant to one's participation in a field of life. It means that fear of otherness, as thought or feeling, even unexpressed in action, carries potency. As McCallum (2005) states,

> To pray unceasingly is to think molecular. It is to see the small things, including oneself, in the bigger picture. It means being able to look at a green leaf differently, to see the science and the poetry in it, to be aware that you and the leaf are linked.... It is to hold one's breath and then to give it back again in the realisation that the chlorophyll and haemoglobin molecules are almost identical. What makes them different is the presence of a single trace element in each molecule. (2005, p. 150)

To live from this awareness challenges the democratic principle that human rights are necessary, or, its assumption that human beings are in need of protection. While majority rule is a means of organizing government and deciding public issues, it is uncommon that radically different ontologies are welcome in public schools where both knowing and doing unfold in various ways. Oppression occurs through exclusion, repression, and the silencing of a minority group, an individual or an ontology. In this way, democracy in education, while initially challenged, may lead to a reconceptualization of what it means to know about and live with the other.

If we imagine consciousness not as some emergent property of life, as mechanistic science and our education typically suppose, but as a primary quality of the universe, then it becomes at least as fundamental as space, time, and matter. With this image of reality our understanding of the physical world would not be altered significantly, but our understanding of mind would be transformed with a fuller realization of this inter-connectivity. Our world view would shift from the intrinsically materialist to the intrinsically inter-connected one, and so affect what it means to teach and learn.

In this inter-connectedness the strands of the web run both horizontally and vertically. Think of the horizontal in terms of groups, tribes, communities, and collectives, crossing provincial and national boundaries, and the vertical in terms of the individual (human and non-human). Likewise, we live with both non-local and local consciousness simultaneously. Although we can speak of consciousness in many different ways, I turn here to consciousness as the capacity for inner experience, whatever its nature or degree. The faculty of consciousness is common among us, but the content of our consciousness varies widely. This content is our personal or individual reality. Most of the time, we forget that this is only our personal reality, and think that we are experiencing physical reality directly. This reality is "real" or actual, but we would be less limited experientially if we balanced this perspective with other views.

Shifting Consciousness for Learning

How can students experience the intersections of a universe that "happens" without our doing (which implies not doing, or not leading with the ego), if they are continuously busy, moving from one task to another or if they know self only in relationship to externals that appear independent and separate? For that possibility they need to pause and become present to a more complex understanding of life. Further, belonging together is an awareness perceived as something already known theoretically. It is perceived, not simply "known." Whatever the activity, one focuses her awareness on the individual self or personal ego. Precisely because one is identified with the self-contradiction to the exclusion of everything else, one cannot "know" her own inter-connectedness. One has to be so "involved" in the event that the self is forgotten, such as during those moments in the classroom when something "happens," which is not something to (always) be named or identified, but to be referred to in silent recognition and then perhaps pursued. In forgetting the self and opening to the other, we "generate both awakening and empowering, freeing students to act responsibly in a relational world" (Kaza, 1996, p. 149).

As we reach deeper or higher states of consciousness, also considered as relational, removing boundaries is a lofty goal, not only for the monastic but also for kindergarten through graduate levels. Gaining awareness and growing in consciousness would escape the dualistic-symbolic mind, a way for teachers and students alike to become open to a fresh source of generative energy.

A critic might dismiss these experiences as dreamy mysticism and warn that they will lead to a withdrawal from the practical side of life. But the opposite may well be more likely. The experience of deeper consciousness, according to Vedic, Buddhist, and Jungian thought as well as some activists, poets, and artists, leads to a greater compassion and a deep abiding sense of love (love implying more of a "whole" experience of other, rather than a lopsided emotion of infatuation), which may provoke more active and socially just participation in the world. If true, unless one learns to quiet the mind and understand that she is not just her ego, she will continue to be object directed, relating externally to a world brought forth only through sensory perception. However, if one recognizes that she is not just her ego (though it is a significant part of her individuality) and meditates on the present by being inner directed, she becomes open to possibilities beyond those usually suggested by the traditional view of learning—through sensory perception and others' knowledge. By turning inward and partaking in activities that honour and call forth silence, there is the possibility that images, ideas, and rhythms can arise that inform in a different way. This meditative or contemplative process opens this space for learning, where one is not borrowing from the past, re-shaping, re-forming, and re-arranging. Rather, it turns away from backward and forward visions to a disciplined practice of living in the present. This notion of "freeing oneself" acts as a tool of social change. Such practices in education could, like Dewey (1916) believed, lead the way to a more just and free society, a society in which the ultimate aim is not the production of goods, but the production of free human beings in relation to one another in terms of equality.

Rather than look for a quick "fix" or solution, one attends to the present where the ordinariness and simplicity of life are valued, and the demanding challenges of life are always perceptible, everywhere, and mediated in the here and now. In some way, silence, as embodied in living in the moment, unifies present, past, and future. Time aligns vertically rather than running horizontally. Love, for instance, expresses itself by silence more than by speech, as those who love each other are moved to a space beyond the merely temporal (Picard, 1948). "The purpose of meditation," according to Trungpa Rinpoche, "is not to get higher, but to be present" (as cited in Smith, 1999, p. 87). The purpose of silence in meditation, ultimately, is to aid one in being present.

The Buddhist, Vedic, and Jungian practice of looking within helps us understand that the consciousness of the universe (spirit) is the same as one's individual consciousness (soul). This consciousness transcends duality, and it includes all simultaneously while deeply grounded in relationships with the Earth, animals, and neighbouring communities. Through the practice of attending to the present as in meditation, teaching, or karate, the "within" becomes the "beyond." Such moments live in our practices when the teacher loses herself with the students to the possibilities of a topic that might otherwise be closed by a prescriptive approach to education.

A Pattern that Connects

The paradox, again, is that every individual atom, each narrative and self is singular and unique and, at the same time, an integral part of the tightly woven fabric of being. The quantum shift in the psyche's identity takes place as one realizes that the self, as light,[2] is simultaneously a particle and a wave, is both one and unique, and yet embraces the entire world.

In Buddhist and Vedic traditions, an awareness dominated by the subject–object dualism cannot perceive reality as it is, the non-local reality as unity of consciousness, when there is no sense of separate self. The isolated subject "in here" may perceive a sense of lack or fragmentation because it does not recognize its relatedness with the rest of the universe. Suffering then is not something that happens to the separate self, but is inherent in the separate self. In Buddhism, suffering is a necessary experience in order to transform consciousness and living. As Gautama Buddha put it, to end suffering you must end the self as they rise and fall together. I am not suggesting death to the ego for a healthy ego is necessary for development, but it needs to be balanced by a more encompassing, inter-connected view. Here arises the wisdom of "The Four Noble Truths"[3] and "The Eightfold Path."[4] Suffering, however, is not to be feared or avoided because without suffering, we cannot evolve. It is important to note that teachers who have undertaken their own processes of individuation become models for students. Suffering, as with learning to withdraw projections and accept one's shadow,[5] is no easy task and, without engagement to learn from other's perspectives and experience, some may struggle endlessly. Indeed, what we often refer to as "unreal," that which "breaks through" in times of trauma, tragedy, or unexplainable events, comes from a much deeper source that demands attention.

In Einstein's theory of general relativity, space and time are not separate, but are connected and part of a larger whole (the space–time continuum). Similarly, Bohm (1985) adds that *everything* in the universe is part of a continuum. Despite the apparent separateness of things at the explicate level, everything is an extension of everything else, where the implicate (the "enfolded" or unseen) and explicate (unfolded or seen) orders blend into each other. So difference is and is not (but an illusion). In other words, the visible world contains the invisible world, and the invisible world spreads out into space which is actually super-connected because it is all energy. Indeed, this "space" may be conceived of as a vacuum, overflowing with information and energy, a quantum sea of possibility, a profound energy waiting to be discovered, explored, and tapped. Like the Buddhist notion of "void," this space is not "empty space" but rather "creative unformed energy." It makes sense, then, as contemporary quantum physics suggests, that living energy systems have relative locality, beginning in a specific place and extending out into space in all directions, and non-locality, being "everywhere." However, the logic will not be local versus non-local as in the reductionistic vision (Schwartz & Russek, 1999), rather *both and* as in local, non-local, and creative unformed energy. Just as our individual, local mind is real, so, too, is its complement, our universal, non-local consciousness. Our limitless, non-local mind, which may be sensed in deep contemplative acts, silence and love, does not destroy or reduce our individuality. The two co-exist, as do wave and particle; both are required in describing what it is like to be conscious, to have a mind.

Love as Purpose and Action

What allows a person to shift from a self-oriented way of experiencing the world to one in which there are fewer boundaries between ourselves, or in which boundaries become avenues of exchange between one and others rather than lines to be defended? What might assist us in attaining a perspective that balances, even momentarily, inter-connectedness and separateness; the individual and collective; and the inner and outer experience, without diminishing either in a re-forming of democracy in education?

I believe the necessary ingredient in shifting our being and doing is love, an active condition of caring and compassion that is so deep and genuine, the barriers we erect around the self are dissolved or transcended. Love, invisibly present in our work, may dissolve frustrations that prevent us from attending deeply to our students, our research, and our writing.

Proposing love as a way of being and proceeding may be problematic because the concept has become, for some, *passé*. However, considering love to be trite suggests that there is something of significance to love. Love has become overly romanticized, conditional, and bound to a sense of choice, where choice is interpreted as a desire located solely within an individual. Love as a companion to silence is without mere romance, without condition, without choice, and without self. To love is to see—differently. The lover's condition inspires others (and that part of the self that nurses old injuries and fears, takes pride in autonomy and harbours the illusion of self-sufficiency) to move beyond, to transcend singular concerns into recognition of their deeper, true being (non-ego self), and their extended allegiance. Unconditional love comes not from ego's choice but from our unchanging nature, self. For many people, the notion of love is difficult for it has been used as a weapon of control by the state, the church, and our culture. Truth in this way is seen as having moral value, not as a presence or an *ethos* that imbues all things and guides ethical relations.

Closely related to love is empathy, which involves seeing oneself as other, and feeling a resonance with what he feels. In order for cooperative work with our students and colleagues to flow between us, and for it to yield a response or action, the teacher must be capable of both love and empathy—

the willingness to become someone else—to hold close the other's experiences as our own. This means that in order to be a "good" teacher (or student), a teacher must be willing to become non-local, to transcend her personal boundaries. If she is too hesitant, proper, professional, guarded, too local to emphatically become her student, she will be limited in her experience. Yet, this is the most common expectation of a good teacher. A teacher who reaches out to "experience" a student emphatically gives new meaning to "being present."

Although hooks (1994) speaks directly to boundaries of identity, culture, gender, and race, these cannot be transgressed without attention to the inner condition. Influenced by Freire and Thich Nhat Hanh, she has created strategies for what Freire (1992) called "conscientization" in the classroom—translated to critical awareness and engagement. Similarly, the focus for all three is on "praxis"—action and reflection onto the world in order to transform it through personal and social evolution.

Knowing how to proceed or even why to proceed requires, in some cases, a non-local mind so that the teacher and student can become interchangeable polarities of each other's many selves. We need to adjust our "seeing" and perceptions of students beyond local time and space. This approach considers the influence of culture, history, gender, race, emotions, and so on. Students also play a role in this approach, even if only through willingness to engage with the teacher. When we are attentive to the other, seeing self in other, we can hear words, messages, and lessons from one another that would have previously been ignored. This state may well be experienced in teaching when the topic under exploration draws both student and teacher into its richness as the individuality of those involved is lessened.

In order to hear the student one needs to be quiet, inwardly as well as outwardly; one needs to cultivate silence (which is part of the process of individuation). Being quiet, alert, and attuned enables one to listen with such care that a bodily felt understanding unfolds. To do so, one's own judgements, prejudices, and desires are suspended; indeed, one's entire sense of self disappears. We have all been in dialogue with another but often present only to our own mind chatter. How often do we fail to hear the other person because we are sure in advance of what he is about to say and so do not listen? Or when we cannot hear because what the other is saying is too threatening and might even make us defend our views or behaviour?

There comes a different kind of freedom when we can suspend the consciousness of self and truly hear the other. This ability has been referred to as "listening with the third ear" (Keen, 1992, p. 181). It is in these moments that we can "feel really close to, fully in touch with, another person" (Rogers, 1969, p. 222). Rogers writes in *Freedom to Learn* (1969):

> When I can really hear someone, it puts me in touch with him. It enriches my life.... When I really hear someone, it is like listening to the music of the spheres, because, beyond the immediate message of the person, no matter what that might be, there is the universal, the general. (p. 222)

To hear deeply, one does not impose one's own expectations on the speaker, but stills the ego-self so that the other can be heard. Being willing and able to listen to a student at all levels may enable him to articulate what is most central to him. Being present and listening deeply may release knots within a student. His speech comes not from a desire for the listener to be responsible for what is said, but to be heard as deeply as he can. Such hearing requires that the teacher resonate to him at all levels so as not to disrupt the unfolding possibilities—all the levels at which he was endeavouring to communicate. This kind of "hearing" has consequences. When one does truly hear a person, hearing not simply his words, but him, many things can happen, even corresponding depth. The more deeply one can hear the person the more may emerge.

In listening to others, we begin to "love them" in their irreducible difference; we help them to listen to themselves, to heed the speech of their own body of experience. Moreover, by listening well to ourselves and to others, we deepen our own capacities to know ourselves. Doing so essentially can be a political act. The ability to listen deeply is a condition of informed political action, action that emanates from the deeply considered need to feel connected to communities and partake in work that will sustain and enhance them.

Buddhists believe that seeing the truth of our inter-connectedness leads to the state of *metta* or loving kindness that characterizes the *bodhisattva*, one who commits to the path of enlightenment for the sake of others. With loving kindness we become the ally of all beings everywhere. We recognize that our own liberation is intertwined with the liberation of others, without exception. It means that, rather than seeing other beings as adversaries, we must see them as colleagues in this endeavour to freedom. Indeed, it adds complexity and contradiction to the democratic belief in human rights and, further, that for a free people to govern themselves, they must be free to express themselves—openly, publicly, and repeatedly. This endeavour is central to engaged pedagogy. Such freedom is not a final, attainable state but the process of working towards fewer restrictions, and for the incremental gains made along the way. Rather than viewing others with fear or contempt, which arises from a belief in separation, we see them as part of who we ourselves are.

It may seem impossible to genuinely care about all beings everywhere. But the heart of loving kindness can be developed without straining, pretending, being a saviour, or glossing ourselves with positive sentiment. Loving kindness is a capacity we all have. We do, however, need to choose (within the complexities of choosing, choice, and the chooser) to be open to know from other perspectives, particularly our inter-connectedness.

If we make time to be quiet, to attend within, we begin to see the interplay of conditions which is the force of life itself, as it comes together to co-create each moment. When we look and hear deeply, and when we attune ourselves to the present, we see constant change: impermanence, insubstantiality, repetition. If we re-vision our world and our relationships to it so that we are not trying to control but to connect to things as they are, then we see through that insubstantiality to our fundamental inter-connectedness which is at the heart of re-visioning political and educational action. Being fully connected to the ways we interpret and respond in body to our own experience guides us to our connectedness with all beings. Understanding this relatedness is the root of compassion and loving kindness and a new form of democracy in education.

Conclusion

My brief approach to Buddhist, Vedic, Jungian thought, and quantum physics points to a limitless unbounded field of energy and information that informs, governs, and brings forth our space–time reality. This implicate experience is known in physics as light and, in this context as well as to mystics and poets, it is known experientially as love. Expansion into this possibility is at the core of this consideration of democracy and difference in education, that is, for an engaged pedagogy. By placing our classroom experiences against an unlimited expansion, we promote the well-being of self and other, and teach to empower and to enlighten.

Questions for Reflection

1. How can an ethical or socially just (egalitarian) attitude include learning from children, forests, and animals?

2. What possibilities might arise from a more inclusive and integral imagining of the universe?

3. What pedagogical practices might assist us in attaining a perspective that balances, even momentarily, separateness and inter-connectedness without diminishing either?

4. How might the notions of "freedom" and "right" challenge and extend the principles underlying democracy?

5. If our intentions, beliefs, and thoughts can affect the outcome of distant events, what might this presently mean for ourselves and the world? How does this affect the ways that we interpret and respond to events now? What does it mean for the way we think about students, curriculum, and assessment?

Notes

1. Individuation implies the process of psychic (inner) development that leads to the conscious awareness of wholeness. Not to be confused with individualism.

2. Any exchange of energy between any two atoms in the universe involves the exchange of photons. Each interaction in the physical world is mediated by light. Consciousness is often spoken of as the inner light. Those awakened to the reality–actuality paradox are often call illumined and frequently describe their experiences in terms of light. This inner light is spoken of and experienced as love.

3. "The Four Noble Truths" are the Buddha's most insightful teachings. First, life is suffering. Second, desire and attachment are the roots of suffering. Third, we need to recognize and acknowledge the presence of attachment to a preferred form so that we can refrain from doing the things that make us suffer. The Fourth is the path that leads to refraining

from doing the things that cause us to suffer. In order to know how to do so, one follows "The Eightfold Path."

4. "The Eightfold Path" consists of Eight Right Practices: Right View, Right Thinking, Right Speech, Right Action, Right Livelihood, Right Diligence, Right Mindfulness, and Right Concentration. Right is meant "in the right way," "straight" not bent or crooked—beneficial to the collective which extends from love and compassion, not in the promotion of ego self.

5. The shadow comprises of the rejected and unaccepted aspects of personality that are repressed and form a compensatory structure to the ego's self ideals and to the persona.

References

Banks, J. A. (2002). *An introduction to multicultural education* (3rd ed.). Boston, MA: Allyn & Bacon.
Bohm, D. (1985). *Unfolding meaning: A weekend of dialogue*. London: Routledge.
Dewey, J. (1916). *Democracy and education*. New York: Macmillan.
Freire, P. (1992). *Pedagogy of the oppressed*. New York: Continuum.
Gutmann, A. (1987). *Democratic education*. Princeton, NJ: Princeton University Press.
hooks, b. (1994). *Teaching to transgress: Education as the practice of freedom*. New York: Routledge.
———. (2003). *Teaching community: A pedagogy of hope*. New York: Routledge.
Jung, C. G. (1963). *Collected works* (Trans. R. F. C. Hull). In H. Read, M. Fordham, G. Adler, & W. McGuire (Eds.). Bollingen Series 17. Princeton, NJ: Princeton University Press.
Kaza, S. (1996). *The attentive heart: Conversations with trees*. Boston: Shambhala Press.
Keen, S. (1992). *The passionate life: Stages of loving*. New York: HarperCollins.
Kincheloe, J. L., & Steinberg, S. R. (1997). *Changing multiculturalism*. Philadelphia: Open University Press.
Kumashiro, K. (2004). *Against common sense: Teaching and learning toward social justice*. New York: RoutledgeFalmer.
Lorimer, D. (1990). *Whole in one*. London: Arkana.
Lund, D. E. (2006). Rocking the racism boat: School-based activists speak out on denial and avoidance. *Race, Ethnicity and Education, 9*(2), 203-221.
Macy, J. (1991). *World as lover, world as self*. Berkeley, CA: Parallax.
McCallum, I. (2005). *Ecological intelligence: Rediscovering ourselves in nature*. Cape Town, ZA: Africa Geographic.
McCarthy, C. (1993). After the canon: Knowledge and ideological representation in the multicultural discourse on curriculum reform. In C. McCarthy & W. Crichlow (Eds.), *Race, identity, and representation in education* (pp. 289–305). New York: Routledge.
Merton, T. (1967). *Love and living*. Orlando, FL: Harcourt Brace.
Picard, M. (1948). *The world of silence* (Trans. S. Godman). London: Harville.
Radin, D. I., Rebman, J. M., & Cross, M. P. (1996). Anomalous organization of random events by group consciousness: Two exploratory experiments. *Journal of Scientific Exploration, 10*(1), 143–168.
Rogers, C. (1969). *Freedom to learn*. Columbus, OH: Charles E. Merrill.

Schwartz, G., & Russek, L. (1999). *The living energy universe: A fundamental discovery that transforms science and medicine*. Charlottesville, VA: Hampton Roads.

Sleeter, C. E., & McLaren, P. L. (Eds.). (1995). *Multicultural education, critical pedagogy, and the politics of difference*. Albany, NY: State University of New York Press.

Smith, D. (1999). *Pedagon: Interdisciplinary essays in the human sciences, pedagogy and culture*. New York: Peter Lang.

8

BEYOND "OPEN-MINDEDNESS": CULTIVATING CRITICAL, REFLEXIVE APPROACHES TO DEMOCRATIC DIALOGUE

Lisa Karen Taylor

Introduction

> Democracy is best learned in a democratic setting where participation is encouraged, where views can be expressed openly and discussed, where there is freedom of expression for pupils and teachers, and where there is fairness and justice. (Banks, 2004, p. 13)

In the statement above, cited in Banks' (2004) introduction to an international anthology on democratic education and social diversity, openness and freedom are touchstones of democratic processes and learning. Particularly in an age of increasingly violent empires and clashing fundamentalisms (Ali, 2003), openness toward different ways of being and thinking as well as freedom of expression and participation are, indeed, increasingly under siege, and their absolute necessity becomes particularly clear in their absence. At the same time, these are slippery terms with tremendous baggage. Within prevalent approaches to education for democracy, the goals of open and free dialogue are most commonly framed within neoliberal ideologies, which posit a model of society as a level playing field of free-willed, rational, transparent, and autonomous individuals. In this chapter I argue that education for democracy must be articulated with a social justice perspective that cultivates in students a critically reflexive capacity for dialogic deliberation of societal issues structured through collective forms of power, privilege, oppression, and difference.

*"All Speech Is Not Free"[1]: Democratic Dialogue Beyond Liberal
Egalitarianism*

Goldberg (1993) has traced the ways liberalism as a political philosophy and
discourse renders considerations of systemic discrimination or collective
belonging irrelevant and unthinkable:

> Basic to modernity's self-conception, then, is a notion not of social subjects but of a
> Subject that is abstract and atomistic, general and universal, divorced from the
> contingencies of historicity as it is from the particularities of social and political
> relations and identities. This abstracted, universal Subject commanded only by
> Reason, precisely because of its purported impartiality, is supposed to mediate the
> differences and tensions between particular social subjects. (p. 4)

In a sense, the liberal subject transcends collective identities, which are
represented as compromising liberty and rational civic conduct.

Within liberal and neoliberal conceptions of democratic societies,
therefore, citizens are imagined as either unfettered by difference (i.e., being
of dominant, unmarked gender, class, ethnoracial affiliation, ability, etc.) or
as needing to overcome and set aside their difference from normative
dominant identities through presumed neutral, universal forms of reasoning
(Razack, 1998). Goldberg (2002) refers to this as "state racelessness"; when
the citizen is imagined as raceless (or White[2]), the impact of racism can
neither be recognized nor redressed, and ethnoracial collective identities are
silenced (p. 222). The cost of such narrow definitions of normative identity
are most often borne silently by those deviating from this norm as they are
reduced to, and stigmatized by, their difference. This drastically
impoverishes the forms of experience and knowledge that might be
articulated and heard within public spaces of dialogue or debate. For
example, despite my efforts to establish a classroom environment inclusive of
all socioeconomic class backgrounds, I know that ideological and
institutional discrimination have the effect of rendering mid- and upper-class
subjectivities and experiences the dominant norm in undergraduate university
cultures, silencing working-class subjects. The minority of working class and
struggling single parent students in my classes rarely speak from this
collective identity; rather, they tend to approach challenges they face on an

individual, ad hoc, and private basis. Razack (1998) argues that liberal ideologies "isolate[s] the individual from his or her group to the point that one could no longer see how group membership alter[s] or constrain[s] individual choices and opportunities" (p. 26).

Liberal notions of democratic dialogue ultimately presume a negotiation of competing goals defined in individual terms carried out within a supposedly common and universal logic of self-interest and rationalism (as defined by European Enlightenment epistemes). Entire societies are likewise presumed to be engaged in a larger historical process of rational progress and enlightenment as collective affiliations or commitments, portrayed as irrational and premodern, are progressively evacuated (Goldberg, 1993). When democratic processes are framed within these individualist and rationalist terms, the "openness" and "freedom" of the liberal civic subject are predicated upon his transcendence of the particular demands and claims of collective identities.

The liberal individualism, egalitarianism, and rationalism described above can be discerned as underpinning many of my students' reflections on the ways they hope to create spaces of engagement and participation as teachers. They suggest that democratic dialogue in the classroom is best created through "open" whole-class discussions and free votes, or formal debates allowing "both sides of the story" to be heard.[3] Foucauldian (1980) notions of power, however, remind critical observers that discursive fields are never neutral but constituted through formations of power and knowledge that selectively admit, recognize, and authorize particular viewpoints and bounded imaginaries while silencing others. Each time I articulate experiential knowledge, I *speak as* a particular identity constituted within particular narratives and taxonomies of identities; in particular, when speaking on issues from a dominant identity (e.g., speaking about global or class inequality as a First World middle-class citizen), my assertion of authority and agency can invoke an exclusionary hierarchy of identities (Alcoff, 1995; Boler, 2004, pp. 7–9; Ellsworth, 1997).

A growing body of scholarship on education for democracy argues that educators must not confuse the horizon with the ground underfoot; Boler (2004), Parker (2006), Junn (2004), Mayo (2004), and others warn that in preparing students or teachers for democratic process of dialogue and deliberation, presuming a level playing field amongst autonomous speakers can exacerbate systemic inequalities, mount new regimes of selective silencing, and potentially fuel "parasitic appetite … in a dominant group fantasy or romance about access to and unity with the other" (Burbules, 2004, p. xviii). Articulating social justice and democratic education, therefore, necessarily involves developing an analysis of the ways the space for dialogue is always already structured in exclusionary terms proscribing *who* can speak and *how* they are heard (Spivak, 1988) in order to develop strategies to work against these power dynamics.[4] Even more challenging for identities differentially structured through privilege, social justice approaches to civic education imply developing differently positioned students' facility in "pulling the rug from under oneself while standing on it" (Schick & St. Denis, 2005); that is, the capacity to listen to embodied forms of knowing and being upon whose occlusion one's self-image as a neutral, rational, and open-minded individual depends.

I am proposing that this critical reflexivity is fundamental to the intellectual skills of democratic citizenship: citizens need to be able to think "critically about conditions of political and civic life" (Patrick, 2006, p. 2), particularly about conditions of inequality (Boler, 2004) and one's implication in these. Junn (2004) and Mayo (2004) argue that, when democratic education does not cultivate this critical analysis of inequitable institutional, epistemic and social relations, it risks exacerbating these very inequities amongst students because of the selective forms of recognition upon which liberal notions of democratic dialogue depend. Pursuing democratic dialogue, not as an abstract and presumed neutral space of interaction, but as a counterhegemonic project in which our speaking bodies and collective affiliations are profoundly embedded, is just such a critical faculty I am proposing.

I argue later for a social justice approach to *learning democracy* through reference to a case study of student learning within a teacher education course focused on social justice education. Specifically, I examine the forms of embodied reflexivity and critical interventions into liberalist dialogue that emerge when teacher candidates are asked to design and facilitate small group discussions of a series of films focused on different forms of systemic discrimination and resistance.

Methodology and Research Site

This qualitative case study examines samples of student work and classroom observations from three sections of a mandatory undergraduate course on social justice and education in a 2-year period, 2005–2006. In the assignment that is the focus of this case study, groups of 6–9 students are expected to preview and design a series of questions to guide their facilitation of small-group discussions after screening one of five films viewed in the course. Each film or documentary focuses on a particular form of systemic group-based discrimination. Excerpts are cited below from field notes on whole-class discussions, discussion questions written by film facilitation groups, and individual student facilitators' reflections on the tensions and dynamics in small-group discussions they had led. While the data set includes written material from 122 participants in the form of individual reflections or group discussion questions, the analysis below cites the individual work of 4 students and the collectively produced work of 47. Even though these excerpts reflect patterns that emerged across the data set, they have been selected to illustrate possible forms of reflexive deliberation amongst students that grapple with collective and systemic forms of inequality within democratic processes.

As a White, Anglophone, Canadian-born academic, I recognize the forms of structural privilege that authorize and position me as "objective" or "neutral" in the analyses I model and encourage (Schick & St. Denis, 2005). It is also important to contextualize this course within the pre-service program of the small English-language liberal arts university in Quebec, Canada. The majority of the almost 250 students in this 4-year B.Ed. program is White, Canadian-born Anglophones aged 19–24 hailing from ethnically homogeneous rural communities.[5] The sample in this study is thus largely consistent with the predominance of Euro-Canadian middle-class candidates in teacher education programs across the country (Levine-Rasky, 1998). Confirming much antiracism research (e.g., Levine-Rasky, 2002; Sleeter, 2001), my documentation of this course suggests that Canadian-born, White-identified preservice students tend to bring a poverty of cross-cultural experiences or analysis of structural discrimination and privilege. Egalitarian ideologies of North American society as an immigrant meritocracy figure prominently in many students' conception of multicultural education as a fairly straightforward program of liberal color-blindness, "open-mindedness," and occasional additions to the mainstream curriculum.

From Open-mindedness to Critical Reflexivity in Classroom Dialogue

Broaching analyses of systemic inequity implies making visible the ontological and epistemic distinctions and hierarchies that underpin the positions we each stake out in democratic debate. The course introduces students to conceptual frameworks from antiracism and Whiteness studies, feminist, postcolonial, and queer theory (Hall, 1997) in order to shift liberal multicultural discourses of the plight/problem of the essentialized Other to a critical focus on the politics of representation: "who has the power to define whom, when and how" (McCarthy & Crichlow, 1993, p. xvi). Course assignments are designed to explore the ways students' very conceptualization of democratic dialogue guiding their deliberations can fortify the very hegemonic practices of dominance they both deny and invest in. Here, Levine-Rasky's analysis (2002) of the contradictory practices of White dominance is instructive:

> The ideological shibboleths of liberal democracy—freedom, equality, individualism—are contingent upon their reflection in the oppositional other who is constrained, unequal, nondescript. Critical whiteness studies delineate the symbolic and material interdependence of white and other. In the political economy of racism, whites obtain a normalized identity, status, rewards, dominance, and invisibility contingent upon situating those who are different relative to these characteristics. (p. 18)

The course, therefore, begins with exercises in analyzing intersecting discourses of racialized, gendered, classed, sexualized, nationalist, ability- and faith-based identity that populate the social imaginary and circulate through our consumption/production in popular and mass culture. Using examples from popular and mass media and culture, we analyze the ways in which, within cultural processes of representation, dominant identities are constructed through binary oppositions that reduce subordinate identities to essentialized foils (Morrison, 1992; Said, 1978). For example, examining the portrayal of First Nation peoples in mass media, we identify the ways White and "Indian" are divided into polarized identities, how Aboriginals are reduced to static traits projected by White settler anxieties such that the figure of the "Indian" shores up a naturalized White modern Canadian identity (Chow, 1994; Crosby, 1991; Francis, 1992; Morrison, 1992) (see Figure 1). We also explore the ways we have witnessed and participated in White hegemony in which ethnically diverse non-natives identify with and invest in the White settler paradigm of citizenship and Canadian national identity. For example, one student explored how her self-image as belonging to the "right side of town," despite her family's working-class status, was enabled in some ways by the very presence of First Nation children at her school, children who clearly symbolized the "wrong side."

Admittedly, this conceptual model risks reproducing the very object of its critique, that is, essentialized binary dichotomies of identity. Pedagogically, it is vital to explore its limits and contradictions through discussion of concrete examples from our own personal experiences, and an insistence on an intersectional analysis of how "Othering" relations of race, gender, sexuality, class, ethnicity, faith, ability, accent, and national origin, among others, converge differently on specific bodies depending on the particular context. Nevertheless, this model does act to push our discussions beyond a power-blind, reductive diversity paradigm to examining how difference is contained, pathologized, and disenfranchised (Bhabha, 1994, p. 208).

Drawing from this framework, student groups are expected to research and analyze particular forms of systemic discrimination in the Canadian context in order to design and facilitate small-group postscreening discussions of five films that employ a range of counterdiscursive educational strategies. Their challenge is to bring a critical social justice perspective to the processes of collective analysis ("How are we implicated?") and pedagogy ("How now do we teach?").[6] The two documentaries that are the focus of student work analyzed in this chapter— *Under one sky: Arab women in North America talk about the hijab* (Kawaja,

1999) and *It's elementary: Talking about gay issues in school* (Chasnoff & Cohen, 1996)—address, in the first case, Orientalism and Islamophobia through interviews and analyses of Arab feminists and, in the second case, homophobia and heteronormativity through interviews with elementary teachers and students engaged in antihomophobia education.

Facilitating discussion of these films demands tremendous preparation and pedagogical design on the part of my students as social justice educators. Neither film assumes a dominant standpoint of speaking *about* the Other (Ellsworth, 1997); rather, both address audiences from within communities marginalized by the forms of discrimination under examination. That is, the films are engaged in a postcolonial, feminist, or queer "writing back" (Ashcroft, Griffiths, & Tiffin, 2002) to the dominant gaze. Their address, or perspective, thus disrupts the normalization of the dominant unmarked subject of Orientalism/Islamophobia and homophobia/heteronormativity. The films challenge audiences to examine the ways these discourses structure their own framing of the "problem" and positioning in relation to this uneven playing field of debate. Facilitating a dialogue on these films thus demands a critical reflexivity in relation to defining the very terms of discussion. That is, students need to analyze the mechanisms of Othering through which binary dichotomies of social difference (be it Western/Muslim or straight/queer) are naturalized and the dominant gaze normalized. This involves inventorying their own partial, located, and interested framing of the issue, in order to design discussion questions that interrogate rather than presume a normative, dominant subject position and standpoint.

Excerpts from the Classroom: Democratic Dialogue through Difference

The terms of the class discussion of the two documentaries were structured by the discursive contexts of their production and our viewing. Students' prior understandings and concerns vis-à-vis Kawaja's film were framed by a global context of the "War on Terror" with its resurgent Orientalist and Islamophobic discourses that construct Muslim women as a homogenized object of vilification, pity, and romanticization (Kahf, 2000). Within this context, historically salient tropes of gendered victimization coalesce around the veil's charged image: "Islam was innately and immutably oppressive to women [and] the veil and segregation epitomized that oppression" (Leila Ahmed in Kahf, 2000, p. 150). Within French republican traditions of *laïcité* and citizenship as well as retrenched gendered Orientalism, the *hijab* has been racialized as a sign of virulent patriarchy, female victimization/submission, and premodern irrational zeal (Thomas, 2006). Popular discourses in Quebec also reflect the polarized debates, both locally and in France, concerning schools' responses to veiling. Particularly salient in the provincial context was the reproduction of White Anglophone and Francophone collective identities (or a sense of "Us-ness" from Bhabha, cited in Todd, 1999) as the Francophone media framed the issue as one of secularism while the Anglophone media defined it within liberal discourses of individual rights and choice (Todd, 1999).

Within the dominant Anglophone culture of this university, the reframing of Muslim Canadian women and girls' practices of *hijab* within liberal discourses of individual rights and freedoms can be understood, in part, as reflective—and productive—of students' dominant ethnolinguistic identities. It is not surprising, then, that questions written by groups in both sessions should frame the small-group discussions within these discourses:

Were you surprised to hear Arab feminists say the veil is their choice? Why? (section A)[7]

"Do you think Muslim women who move to the West should be allowed to wear the *hijab*? Who has the right to decide?" (section A)

What seems to be at stake in these discussion questions, for example, is the status of veiling, defined either as a right protected by the *Canadian Charter of Rights and Freedoms* or as a foreign cultural practice ("Muslim women who move to the West" are presumably not authentically Canadian), which marks Canadians who veil as racial Others to the neutral, rational citizen subject who is qualified to adjudicate the rights of others. It is this very normalization of Judeo-Christian dominant authority that one group problematizes as they ask:

"Does your construction of your racial, sexual, social economic, language, religious, or ethnic identity include the clothing your wear?" Whose costumes are "ethnic"? (section B)

In their individual reflections, two students from this group reflected on the challenges they observed facilitating discussion from a social justice perspective that resists the cultural authority and presumed neutrality of Judeo-Christian dominant standpoints within liberal egalitarianism:

> Our groups also spent a long time discussing how we would teach students about inequity in society ... We came to believe that there is no easy solution to speaking with, for, or about the other [sic]. A teacher will always have to be conscious of the position of authority from which he/she is speaking and the effects this will have on students [sic] learning (Marilyn, section B).

Marilyn identifies as a White, middle-class Anglophone. She excels academically and took a leadership role in her group. In her reflection, she explicitly recognizes teaching authority as a relation of power and worries about the reciprocal construction of student identities within this relation. In her reference to Linda Alcoff's 1995 article, covered in the course, she grapples with the challenge of pursuing democratic processes of deliberation and debate when these are always already structured in relations of unequal speaking authority.

In another section (C), it was Aisha,[8] a trilingual, Muslim, Algerian Quebecker, who problematized the liberal discourses underpinning her group's discussion and interrogated the notion of individual rights as transparent, universal, and culture-neutral:

> Girls [in our group] would argue that everyone has the right to have his [sic] own belief and religion and we don't have the right to take that away from them. But then, whose right? Or better than that, according to whose standards is this right being measured? Is what I believe to be my right the same that you believe to be my right? This is a critical question that we couldn't really get the answer to.

In her use of the first person singular in her reflection, Aisha explicitly frames the debate from her embodied speaking position as a racialized subject; as both an immigrant from the global South and a Muslim woman who does not veil, she cannot assume the unmarked normative speaking position presumed within the liberal rights arguments articulated by her fellow group members. While it is not clear from her reflection if she is quoting or reproducing her group's use of "we" and "them" (the latter clearly referring to Muslim Canadians), her use of "I" puts into question the inequitable terms of voice and debate within her group's experiment in democratic dialogue.

Class discussions of the film *It's elementary* grappled with a range of public discourses circulating in the wake of Canada's legalization of gay marriage and the current Conservative government's reopening of this debate in 2006. Also influential was the Canadian Supreme Court's decision in defense of the inclusion of gay-positive children's literature in elementary schools against the objections of faith-based parents and community (see *Globe and Mail*, 2003, included in course readings).

The heteronormative terms of this debate were problematized by discussion questions designed by all three groups, as is illustrated in this example:

- Is it dangerous to teach homosexuality at a young age because of its connection with sexuality?

- or is it something you can separate?

- What about teaching heterosexuality? (section A)

As the members of this group ask their fellow students to examine the heteronormativity of elementary school curriculum (i.e., the normalization of heterosexuality as neutral, asexual, and moral), their questions demand a recognition of the ways this space of public deliberation is structured in homophobic silencing. Anne's individual postdiscussion reflection disrupts and destabilizes the ways her group's postscreening discussion was itself structured by powerful public discourses of heteronormativity:

When can we start teaching about sexual diversity in the classroom? ... One person responded that elementary school was too young, then paused and said, "Well maybe in middle school but not much younger than that ... Heteronormativity is something that is taught to us right from kindergarten in every teachable subject. I think many people began to question their own responses to this question and began to ask, if teaching heterosexuality was possible at an early age then so is homosexuality (Anne, section B).

Anne, an Anglophone student involved in global education who identifies as straight, examines the struggles of her group members to negotiate competing discourses of the role of education from a social justice perspective that recognizes collective sexual identities as integral and not exceptional to the terms of discussion. She goes on to explore the challenges in the small-group discussion of making knowledge claims from speaking positions already structured by heteronormative power relations in society.

A really interesting comment by one group member who suddenly seemed fairly flustered really struck me; she confidently spoke about how gay bashing was something of yesterday and that nowadays people... had come to "accept" them and that people were more modern now. I think that this is a common misconception amongst many people who are not exposed to the realities of being gay, lesbian, or transsexual in today's society. They might not realize the harsh conditions that a gay or lesbian student, for example, experiences everyday in high school.

The normalization of heterosexual identities as individual, "open," and unbiased by sexually based group membership is also problematized by another group's discussion questions:

- Do you believe that society has become more accepting of sexual diversity?

- Have you witnessed homophobia?

- Which do you think is worse, homophobia or heteronormativity?(section C)

Jean, a Francophone student who also identifies as straight, examines different group members' responses to the crisis in speaking authority triggered by a social justice perspective:

It was challenging facilitating discussion because everyone took a lot of time to show how they were all really open-minded and nice with homosexual *[sic]*. Some insisted on explaining their accepting attitude even when there wasn't a question about that ... I found everyone was protecting themselves *[sic]* and it was challenging for people to see how our inaction to inequalities and privileges actually reinforces discrimination and the inequalities for marginalized groups (Jean, section C).

Within liberal discourses, objectivity and authority are guaranteed through the presumption of the individual, normative subject's civility and rationality (Goldberg, 2005), uncompromised by collective group membership. Jean's fellow students exemplify these discourses when their group membership in collective relations of power is made visible, and also when a social justice perspective highlighted the ways their apparently neutral speaking positions were structured within the collective investments and power/knowledge relations of heteronormativity. In emphasizing the inequitable effects of "inaction," Jean insists on pulling the rug of neutrality and liberal openness out from under speaking positions "structured in dominance" (Hall, 1980). Like Marilyn, Jean's reflection attends to the ways speech, and other forms of participation in democratic deliberation, not only reflects but also constructs inequitable identity relations of power, authority, audibility, and silence.

This critical reflexivity led one student to remark upon the dynamic ways normativity works to continuously position marginalized sexual identities as exceptional and external to the public sphere of debate:

I also found it interesting to hear people start their sentence with "I'm not homophobic at all, I totally accept *them* and think what *they* are doing is okay but ..." It's as if we (the norm) were kind enough to tolerate "*their lifestyle*" and not seem discriminatory toward "*them*." I wanted to ask the question "what exactly are '*they*' doing?" And "what do you mean by accepting '*them*'"? What do you feel you need to "accept" exactly? The use of "*them*" as the other and "*us*" as the norm was something that was repetitive throughout the discussion. In fact, to my own embarrassment I even caught myself using these words at one point during the discussion. (Sharon, section A, emphasis in the original)

As she examines the construction of an "Us" (discussants, educators in general) and "Them," Sharon, an Anglophone Latina-Canadian student who identifies as straight, highlights the ways she and her group members continuously assert a space of heteronormativity through the normalization of a rational, unmarked, and tolerant position of authority and institutional responsibility.

Figure 1 – The Social Construction of White/Native Racialized Identity Dichotomy

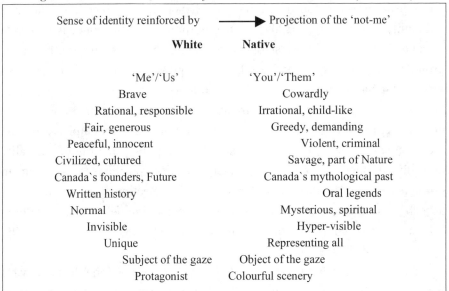

Sense of identity reinforced by	⟶ Projection of the 'not-me'
White	**Native**
'Me'/'Us'	'You'/'Them'
Brave	Cowardly
Rational, responsible	Irrational, child-like
Fair, generous	Greedy, demanding
Peaceful, innocent	Violent, criminal
Civilized, cultured	Savage, part of Nature
Canada's founders, Future	Canada's mythological past
Written history	Oral legends
Normal	Mysterious, spiritual
Invisible	Hyper-visible
Unique	Representing all
Subject of the gaze	Object of the gaze
Protagonist	Colourful scenery

Conclusion

The analysis presented in this chapter reminds us that "open-mindedness," when conceived within racially structured discourses of liberal civility and rationality, is not so much a fail-safe solution as it is a reflection of the deeper problem (Goldberg, 1993, 2002). Indeed, practices and claims of rationality, objectivity, and civility have been identified as a key strategy in securing White entitlement (Schick, 2002) and silencing any deliberation of systemic inequity and collective forms of identity and difference. This is not to argue against their inclusion in democratic education, but rather, to highlight their effects on the audibility of differently positioned subjects.

This chapter argues that civic education may well, as some authors have suggested (Galston, 2004; Hess, 2004; Oulton, Day, Dillon, & Grace, 2004), be invigorated by the discussion of "controversial issues," but that such debates will best serve our goals as educators when they are approached as spaces that do not presume rigor through the evacuation of difference, but build it through reflexively and critically situated counterhegemonic dialogue. Classroom discussion can enrich democratic education as an experiential model of collective learning, community building, and political engagement (Parker, 2006), cultivating in students the habits of democracy, not as power-blind rhetoric, but a critically reflexive, embodied counterhegemonic practice that never forgets nor accepts the playing field's tilt.

Questions for Reflection

1. Democratic dialogue generally presumes a process in which all voices have access to speaking and being heard. What assumptions does the author identify as problematic in this definition?

2. What other assumptions does the author identify in liberalism?

3. Refer to the Self/Other model (Figure 1). In relation to a particular debate concerning group rights that you have studied, use the model to identify more and less powerful collective identities. Drawing examples from mass or popular representations of this debate, identify which collective identity-based perspectives are normalized and which are presented as biased, exceptional, or irrational.

4. The author argues: "Each time I articulate experiential knowledge, I speak as a particular identity constituted within particular narratives and taxonomies of identities." Is it possible to engage in democratic dialogue when taking a purely individual or unbiased position? What dangers does the author argue arise when this is presumed?

5. Compare the author's model of critically reflexive democratic dialogue and those of other authors you have read. For example, Paulo Freire (1970) argued that education must be dialogic: "dialogue cannot occur... between those who deny other men [sic] the right to speak their word and those whose right to speak has been denied to them. Those who have been denied their primordial right to speak their word must first reclaim and prevent the continuation of this dehumanizing aggression" (p. 76).

Notes

1. Boler (2004, p. 3).

2. Following many Whiteness scholars, I use the term White to reference not an absolute identity, but as a contextually specific *practice*, a contradictory discursive form of consciousness/ignorance, a form of property, and a position of power and status vis-à-vis racialized groups constructed through modernist discourses of racial purity, moral

authority, and legal entitlement to naturalize white ethnicity as an authoritative and neutral, *unmarked* norm (Ellsworth, 1997; Levine-Rasky, 2002).

3. Citations from class discussions are drawn from field notes.

4. I follow Boler's (2004) call for a "historicized ethics" in democratic dialogue.

5. Of the students in the B.Ed. program 11.7 percent are Francophone, less than 3 percent are Allophone (their first language being neither French nor English), 35.6 percent are from outside Quebec, and <10 percent are visible minority.

6. Parker (2005, pp. 12–14) distinguishes between discussion as "seminar" and "deliberation" in democratic education. See the conclusion section.

7. This chapter cites the work of groups and individual students from three course sections (identified as section A, B, or C). All names are pseudonyms.

8. All names are pseudonyms. Aisha's country of birth has been changed to protect her anonymity. Aisha's spoken and written languages include Arabic, French, and English.

References

Alcoff, L. (1995). The problem of speaking for others. In J. Roof & R. Wiegman (Eds.), *Who can speak? Authority and critical identity* (pp. 97–119). Urbana: University of Illinois Press.

Ali, T. (2003). *The clash of fundamentalisms: Crusades, jihads and modernity*. London: Verso.

Ashcroft, B., Griffiths, G., & Tiffin, H. (2002/1989). *The empire writes back: Theory and practice in post-colonial literatures*. New York: Routledge.

Banks, J. (2004). *Diversity and citizenship education: Global perspectives*. San Francisco: Jossey-Bass.

Bhabha, H. K. (1994). *The location of culture*. New York: Routledge.

Boler, M. (Ed.). (2004). *Democratic dialogue in education: Troubling speech, disturbing silence*. New York: Peter Lang.

Burbules, N. (2004). Introduction. In M. Boler (Ed.), *Democratic dialogue in education: Troubling speech, disturbing silence* (pp. i-xxxii). New York: Peter Lang.

Chasnoff, D., & Cohen, H. (1996). *It's elementary: Talking about gay issues in school*. San Francisco: Women's Educational Media.

Chow, R. (1994). Where have all the natives gone? In A. Bammer (Ed.), *Displacements: Cultural identities in question* (pp. 125-151). Bloomington, IN: Indiana University Press.

Crosby, M. (1991). Construction of the imaginary Indian. In S. Douglas (Ed.), *Vancouver anthology: The institutional politics of art* (pp. 267–294). Vancouver: Talon Books.

Ellsworth, E. (1997). Representation, self-representation, and the meanings of difference. In R. Martusewicz & W. Reynolds (Eds.), *Inside/out: Contemporary critical perspectives in education* (pp. 100–108). New York: St. Martin's.

Foucault, M. (1980). *Power/knowledge: Selected interviews and other writings 1972–1977*. (C. Gordon, ed.). Brighton: Harvester.

Francis, D. (1992). *The imaginary Indian: The image of the Indian in Canadian culture*. Vancouver: Arsenal Pulp.

Freire, P. (1970). *Pedagogy of the oppressed* (M. Bergman, Trans.). New York: Seabury Press.

Galston, W. A. (2004). Civic education and political participation. *Political Science and Politics, 37*(2), 263–266.

Goldberg, D. (1993). *Racist culture: Philosophy and the politics of meaning.* Oxford: Blackwell.

Goldberg, D. (2002). *The racial state.* Oxford: Blackwell.

Goldberg, D. (2005). "Killing me softly": Civility/race/violence. *Review of Education, Pedagogy, and Cultural Studies, 27*(4), 337–366.

Hall, S. (1980). Race, articulation and societies structured in dominance. In UNESCO (Ed.), *Sociological theories: Race and colonialism* (pp. 305–345). Paris: UNESCO.

Hall, S. (Ed.) (1997). *Representation: Cultural representations and signifying practices.* Thousand Oaks, CA: Sage & The Open University.

Hess, D. E. (2004). Controversies about controversial issues in democratic education. *Political Science and Politics, 37*(2), 257–261.

Junn, J. (2004). Diversity, immigration and the politics of civic education. *Political Science, 37*(2), 253–256.

Kahf, M. (2000). Packaging "Huda": Sha'rawi's memoirs in the United States reception environment. In A. Amireh & L. S. Majaj (Eds.), *Going global: The transnational reception of Third World women writers* (pp. 148–172). New York: Garland.

Kawaja, J. (1999). *Under one sky ... Arab women in North America talk about the hijab.* Montreal: National Film Board of Canada.

Levine-Rasky, C. (1998). Teacher education and the negotiation of social difference. *British Journal of Sociology of Education, 19*(1), 89–112.

Levine-Rasky, C. (2002). *Working through whiteness.* New York: State University of New York Press.

Mayo, C. (2004). The tolerance that dare not speak its name. In M. Boler (Ed.), *Democratic dialogue in education: Troubling speech, disturbing silence* (pp. 33-47*)*. New York: Peter Lang.

McCarthy, C., & Crichlow, W. (Eds.) (1993). *Race, identity and representation in education* [Introduction]. New York: Routledge.

Morrison, T. (1992). *Playing in the dark: Whiteness and the literary imagination.* Cambridge, MA: Harvard University Press.

Oulton, C., Day, V., Dillon, J., & Grace, M. (2004). Controversial issues: Teachers' attitudes and practices in the context of citizenship education. *Oxford Review of Education, 30*(4), 489–507.

Parker, W. (2006). Public discourses in schools: Purposes, problems, possibilities. *Educational Researcher, 35*(8), 11–19.

Patrick, J. J. (2006). Content and process in education for democracy. *International Journal of Social Education, 20*(2), 1–12.

Razack, S. (1998). *Looking white people in the eye: Gender, race, and culture in courtrooms and classrooms.* Toronto: University of Toronto Press.

Said, E. W. (1978). *Orientalism.* New York: Vintage.

Schick, C. (2002). Keeping the ivory tower white: Discourses of racial domination. In S. Razack (Ed.), *Race, space and the law: Unmapping white settler society* (pp. 99–120). Toronto: Between the Lines.

Schick, C., & St. Denis, V. (2005). Critical autobiography in integrative anti-racist pedagogy. In L. Biggs & P. Downe (Eds.), *Gendered intersections: An introduction to women's and gender studies* (pp. 387–392). Halifax, Nova Scotia: Fernwood.

Sleeter, C. (2001). Preparing teachers for culturally diverse schools research and the overwhelming presence of whiteness. *Journal of Teacher Education, 52*(2), 94–106.

Spivak, G. C. (1988). Can the subaltern speak? In C. Nelson & L. Grossberg (Eds.), *Marxism and the interpretation of culture* (pp. 271–313). Chicago: University of Chicago Press.

Thomas, E. R. (2006). Keeping identity at a distance: Explaining France's new legal restrictions on the Islamic headscarf. *Ethnic and Racial Studies, 29*(2), 237–259.

Todd, S. (1999). Veiling the "other," unveiling our "selves": Reading media images of the hijab psychoanalytically to move beyond tolerance. *Canadian Journal of Education, 23*(4), 438–451.

C H A P T E R
9

SECULAR HUMANISM AND EDUCATION: REIMAGINING DEMOCRATIC POSSIBILITIES IN A MIDDLE EASTERN CONTEXT

Alireza Asgharzadeh

Introduction

In our rapidly globalizing world, the clash of undemocratic forces such as imperialism and fundamentalism has left a toxic trail of death and destruction in places like Iraq, Afghanistan, Lebanon, and elsewhere. While much of the Middle East is hemorrhaging from its lethal political and social wounds, it is left up to progressives and secular humanists to pick up the pieces, and reimagine a Middle East where respect for difference and diversity can become a reality. The subaltern voices in the Middle East have long been shouting that between the imperialism of major powers and the fundamentalism of the likes of Osama bin Laden, Molla Omar ,and Iran's Ayatollahs, there is, and there ought to be, a humane alternative. This alternative is, and of necessity needs to be, secular, humanist, and democratic.

In a world where Osama bin Laden identifies the Shi'a Muslims as "the most evil creatures under the heavens," or Abu Musab al-Zarqawi, the late commander of al-Qaeda in Iraq, calls them "the lurking snake, the spying enemy and the penetrating venom" who are "worse than the Jews" (Sayyed, 2005), only a secular humanism can promise a decent social order where the Jew, Christian, Shi'a, Sunni, Kurd, and Turkmen are able to live side by side as equal human beings, with equal rights and freedoms. This form of democratic and humane living condition, however, needs to be learned and internalized through sophisticated processes of socialization that public education makes possible. The arguments of this chapter are, therefore, premised on the following two main observations.

First, secular humanism is a most effective alternative for the malaise of imperialism and fundamentalism in the Middle East. The experiences of the two fundamentalist regimes of Ayatollahs in Iran and the Taliban in Afghanistan show that the idea of mixing religion with state apparatuses is a most dangerous and debilitating notion with far-reaching exclusionary and dehumanizing consequences, not only for education and schooling but also more importantly for entire communities and populations. These experiences have shown that having a religious government does not necessarily translate into having religious freedom in society, a notion that often escapes the attention of those calling for more religion in our schools and universities. The Islamic regime of Taliban, for instance, had entirely banned the education of half of the Afghan population, namely, the female gender. Similarly, under the Shi'a Islamic regime in Iran, members of the Baha'i faith are openly persecuted, a Sunni Muslim cannot become a president, and secularism is seen as a sign of disease and decadence. How can we expect such a regime to tolerate religious diversity in its schools and universities? Is there a possibility that such a regime would respect the students with secular beliefs, the nonbelievers, and the believers in other religions? What would be the experience of gay, lesbian, and transgendered students in such an environment?

Second, if implemented through a fair and inclusive education system, secular humanism can provide a democratic space where difference and diversity are acknowledged as basic features of contemporary societies. It is only in a secular space that students of different religious backgrounds and spiritual persuasions can be provided a safe environment where they can feel comfortable about their religious identity and their spirituality. Understood this way, secularism cannot be interpreted as antireligious or atheist. Rather, it is a praxis that does not favor any particular religious belief over another. According to this perspective, not only should all religious communities enjoy equal access to resources, but non-believers and also those believing in different forms of spirituality should be provided equal opportunity as well. This is a slightly different approach to secularism that, in order to distinguish it from notions such as "desecularization," "resecularization," and "postsecularism" (Berger, 1999; Ratzinger & Habermas, 2007), I propose to call "new secularism."

The development of the mind is amongst the chief tasks of education (Dewey, 1933), and fundamentalist thinking flourishes when and where education fails to uphold this major task. A respect for critical thinking and a critical engagement with difference can be implemented through democratic processes of socialization in schools and universities. The role of education is, thus, central to such engagement. In the early twentieth century Durkheim defined education as "a methodical socialization of the young generation" (1911, p. 51). As major socializing agents, schools can facilitate for young people the general process of acquiring political culture and becoming responsible global citizens. They can also positively help students to learn about the processes of democratic identity formation, peaceful coexistence, and respect for human rights, diversity, and difference.

Education and Democracy in the Middle East

The transformation of modern sociopolitical and educational systems in the Middle East can be roughly divided into three interrelated periods: World War I and the dissolution of the Ottoman Empire; the Arab-Israeli war of 1967; and the Iranian Revolution of 1978 along with the subsequent rise in Islamic Fundamentalism. Until the early nineteenth century, almost all of the Middle East and North Africa was a part of the then Ottoman Empire. As a result of World War I (1914–1918) the Ottoman Empire disintegrated into a number of dependent and semi-independent polities primarily under British and French tutelage, with Britain controlling territories like Iraq, Palestine, and Transjordan, and France taking over Syria and Lebanon. In addition, Italy maintained a colonial presence in Libya, with Spain in Morocco, and the Turkish Republic emerged as an independent entity. Of all the Arab Middle East, only Najd and Hijaz maintained a somewhat independent status, being renamed as Saudi Arabia in 1932 (see Cleveland, 2000). All the while, the conflict between the Jews and Arabs in Palestine continued to grow and gain momentum. With the rise of Nazism and fascism in Europe, the region witnessed an exodus of European Jews who were escaping Hitler's atrocities.

Being denied entry to North America and other parts of the world, the majority of them migrated to Palestine. This new development further inflamed the already existing tensions between the Arabs and Jews in the region, and eventually culminated in the United Nation's resolution on the partition of Palestine into Arab and Jewish areas on November 29, 1947 (see also Cleveland, 2000; Said, 1992).

In the periods immediately before, during, and after World War II, decolonization movements gained new momentum among various Arab communities and culminated eventually into the creation of contemporary modern Arab nations throughout the Middle East: Iraq in 1932, Egypt in 1936, and Syria and Lebanon in 1946. Meanwhile, the Arab-Israeli conflict continued to valorize sociopolitical developments in the region. These developments not only included the educational settings but, in effect, also redirected school policies and educational priorities. For much of this period, the role of education for the Arab Middle East was defined in terms of the following: an eradication of all vestiges of colonialism; the assertion of socioeconomic and political independence of the newly formed nation-states; the search for Arab unity; the promotion of a common Arab homeland and Arabic identity through language, religion, and nationality; as well as the industrialization, and the construction of strong security forces (see also Massialas & Jarrar, 1991).

Out of the ruins of the Ottoman Empire the current Turkish republic emerged as an independent entity in 1923. Mustafa Kemal Atatürk (1881–1938) laid the foundation of this new nation-state on secular republicanism, with an overt emphasis on Turkish nationalism—distancing the country, thus, from the Pan-Islamism of the Ottomans. The then-adopted Turkish Constitution of 1924, despite several amendments and ratifications thus far, still forcefully asserts that "Turkey is a secular and democratic republic," and that its founding principles of "laïcité, social equality, equality before law, the Republican form of government, the indivisibility of the Republic and of the Turkish Nation" can in no way be subject to change and modification (Constitution of the Republic of Turkey, Articles 1 and 4). Atatürk's secularism was forcefully implemented in all schools and universities throughout the Turkish republic. Amongst chief features of this particular secularism were an absolute separation of religion from the public sphere (e.g., the state apparatuses, the education system, etc.) on the one hand, and a zealous promotion of nationalism and "Turkism," on the other. Both of these notions are increasingly being challenged these days, as Turkey moves to modify its rigid interpretation of nationalism and secularism.

The Arab-Israeli war of 1967 served as another major turning point in the evolution of politics and education in the Middle East. Through this war, Israel decisively asserted its existence as a modern nation-state. Up until then, it had been a common stance of Arab states that "there was no such thing" as Israel. After its crucial victory in 1967, Israel decisively declared its existence not only to its neighbors, but also to the entire international community (Segev, 2007). As Massialas and Jarrar (1991) point out, "the 1967 defeat of the Arab regimes by Israel was a major crisis that affected the Arab intellect and identity" (p. 4). This defeat, among other things, changed the direction of the Palestinian struggle from one of reliance on Arab regimes to one of reliance on their own agency and struggle as a people.

A survey on the living conditions of the Palestinian society under Israeli occupation in Gaza, West Bank, and Arab Jerusalem indicated that 20 percent of the male population and 30 percent of the female population in these areas were secular, a figure that was higher than that of "Islamist activists" amongst the same population (Heiberg & Ovensen, 1993). The largely impartial and simply "observant Muslims" constituted the numerical majority. The study defined "secular" as a person whose life was not dictated by religion (Heiberg & Ovensen, 1993; see also Lybarger, 2007).

The 1978–1979 Islamic Revolution in Iran provided an opportunity to put into practice, for the first time, the ideology of Islamic fundamentalism, in general, and Shi'ism, in particular. Through this practice, a fundamentalist interpretation of Shi'ism became the official state doctrine in Iran. Women, racial/religious minorities, and seculars were among the first to be denied equal access to educational, economic, and sociopolitical resources. Without a doubt, this was a major phenomenon that helped shape the emergence of fundamentalist ideologies throughout the Middle East and beyond. Not surprisingly, these ideologies came to find their reflection in education systems (Massialas & Jarrar, 1991).

Fundamentalist movements have often accused current educational systems in the Middle East of corrupting the youth by infiltrating such "un-Islamic" values as feminism, democracy, and secularism. In an effort to thwart fundamentalist charges of secularization and corruption, the current Middle Eastern governments have tried to incorporate Islamic and religious studies into the curriculum. In most cases, the role of education has been redefined to promote a strong sense of devotion to Islam and religious fundamentalism. While Shi'ism and Khomeinism (Abrahamian, 1993) are the dominant fundamentalist ideology promoted through Iranian education system (and by extension amongst the Shi'a populations of Lebanon and Iraq), particular aspects of Sunnism and Wahhabism are promoted in other parts of the Middle East. Throughout the Muslim Middle East, Turkey is the only country that has maintained a fiercely secular state and education system. As Bernard Lewis (1999) has astutely observed:

> Kemal Atatürk established a secular democracy in place of the sultan; the Ayatollah Khomeini founded an Islamic theocracy in place of the shah. Their teachings and programs, Kemalism and Khomeinism, are seen by many as the two main alternative futures for the region. (pp. 133–134)

Naturally, these two contradictory political systems find their mirror images in schools and universities. Ever since the establishment of clerical rule, Iranian schools have taken up the task of promoting the values of religion, namely Shi'a Islam and increasingly what has come to be known as Khomeinism. In addition to a promotion of an Iranian version of Shi'ism, Khomeinism also promotes Persian nationalism, a nationalism based on the culture, identity, and, particularly, language of the Persian ethnic group in Iran. Conversely, the Turkish state has been trying to maintain its secular identity particularly in a region engulfed by religion and the rise of Islamic fundamentalism. In the meantime, it has been pressured by both internal struggles and external influences to modify its extreme forms of secularism and rigid notion of nationalism based on "Turkism"—a process that is increasingly identified as "post-Kemalism" (Kieser, 2006; Ozyurek, 2006).

In a Middle Eastern context, the need for the emergence of a progressive democracy has never been more pressing than now. A progressive understanding of democracy entails a way of running the affairs of one's community/society that is based on principles of human rights, equal access to resources, respect for difference, respect for freedom of expression, and, more importantly, respect for the right to self-determination of individuals, communities, and societies. This right to self-determination includes political, economic, cultural, and collective rights and freedoms at both individual and communal levels. This kind of democracy cannot be imposed either from above or outside. It has to be developed and implemented in accordance with the requirements of the local conditions, needs, and demands of every community.

Islamic fundamentalism, which has been functioning as a grand narrative of solidarity since the late 1970s, is increasingly becoming inadequate in providing a basis for social solidarity and peaceful coexistence (Asgharzadeh, 2007). Other forms of "undemocratic" expressions of identity based on nationalism, ethnicity, and nation-state-ism have produced genocidal results, not only in the Middle East, but throughout the world. In such an environment, promotion of a secular humanism through schools and universities seems to be an important democratic alternative for a variety of pernicious conditions resulting from fundamentalism, colonialism, imperialism, nationalism, and so forth. Obviously, such promotion should not entail a romanticized approach to secularism, as secularism, in and of itself, cannot be equated with democracy and progressivism. Iran under the Pahlavis, Iraq under Saddam, Egypt under Nasser, and Indonesia under Suharto, to name but a few, were clearly secular, but neither democratic nor progressive.

Fundamentalist Thinking

Fundamentalism, whether in the area of religion, nationalism, secularism, and even science, is first and foremost a product of a closed mind, a mind that resists opening up to different ideas, new possibilities and challenging viewpoints. Fundamentalists can never be critical thinkers because critical thinking requires the questioning of fixed notions of ideology, identity, and established values. The ability to doubt, to question, and to be skeptical constitutes the cornerstone of critical, independent thinking. For a fundamentalist, the absolute "sacred ideology" stands beyond criticism, questioning, and even interpretations.

Elsewhere, I have highlighted four general tendencies that fundamentalist groups, in general, and the Islamic fundamentalists, in particular, share in common (Asgharzadeh, 2004). The first of these is "absolutism," the belief in a predetermined destiny by which the purpose of life on earth is defined in the context of upholding the rule and law of God on earth. These rules and laws are written down in holy texts. They are unchangeable, unalterable through time and space, and no ordinary person can interpret them. Everything has been determined by the holy texts, and any action, deed, or thought contrary to the teachings of the sacred books is sacrilegious.

The second is "antisecularism," where secularism is seen as an attempt to challenge the absolute authority of the divine order. From a fundamentalist perspective, secularism is fostered through modernity, which is the enemy of a pure, traditional, and religious way of life. Secularism promotes corruption, heresy, and sacrilegious behavior. It gives rise to such ungodly notions as gender-equality, feminism, communism, coeducation, freedom of thought, free expression, individual rights, democratic reforms, freedom of religion, religious pluralism, and freedom from religion. As such, it should be regarded as a dangerous adversary by all "true believers."

A third feature of fundamentalist thinking is a firm belief in patriarchy. A system of religious patriarchy assigns proper places to both men and women in society. Within such a system, each gender has certain rights, duties, and a social status that are divinely sanctified. Not surprisingly, any deviation from this divine order becomes ungodly, and is oppositional to the Holy Scripture. A firm patriarchal system maintains the religious order of society, the normal hierarchy, and curtails such deviant behaviors as homosexuality and sexual expressions of any kind. Accordingly, it should be resisted by all means necessary (Asgharzadeh, 2004, 2007). Finally, a combination of all these fundamentalist visions finds its highest expression in the creation of "God's kingdom" on earth. This kingdom is a society run by God's devotees and "true representatives." For Islamic fundamentalists, this sacred society comes into being when "the true Islam" rules all aspects of life from the social to economic, scientific, spiritual, and religious realms. Under the rule of "the true Islam," God's laws are applied by the clergy and true believers. It is at this stage that ultimate salvation, perfect equality, and heavenly justice embrace the Islamic society.

Does a high degree of religiosity always lead to fundamentalism? Not necessarily. The United States, for example, is one of the most religious countries in the world, so much so that the British theologian G. K. Chesterton refers to it as the "country with the soul of a church." It is the observation of this rich religiosity that led Chesterton in the early 1900s to conclude that

> So far as [the American] democracy remains Catholic and Christian, that democracy will remain democratic. In so far as it does not, it will become wildly and wickedly undemocratic. (Chesterton, 1968, p. 307)

The majority of Americans have very religious views about topics such as abortion, same-sex marriage, and evolution. President George W. Bush, for instance, invokes religious symbols and meanings at every occasion he gets, adorning his speeches with notions such as "God Bless America," "God will watch over America," and so forth. In his speech to the United Nations on November 10, 2001, he could not help but employ the language of the Holy Scripture:

> We're confident, too, that history has an author who fills time and eternity with his purpose. We know that evil is real, but good will prevail against it. This is the teaching of many faiths, and in that assurance we gain strength for a long journey. (Bush, 2001, p. 1)

Irrespective of its strong sense of religiosity, the Religious Right in America has not been able to entirely bring down the wall that separates public and private spheres. This inability alone shows that in this era of globalization, religious-based domination of schools and universities are not easily achievable. Many American citizens continue to call for schooling that emphasizes the importance of secularism, peace, diversity, human rights, and multicultural education (Apple, 2001; Apple & Buras, 2006).

Another important area of consideration is the topic of spirituality and its relationship with religion. Despite some tendencies to limit spirituality to religion, the two are not the same. While there is a strong element of spirituality at the core of all religious beliefs, spirituality is not limited to religion and goes far beyond established religious ideas. Spirituality is an integral, inseparable part of being human, sustained through a complex web of relationships, connections, and interdependencies necessary for a fulfilling and enriching life. Spirituality is normally defined in terms of love, care, altruism, compassion, selflessness, service to others, an orientation to justice, beauty, equality, and self-sacrifice. While religiosity also entails these qualities, there are many individuals who possess these qualities but who do not necessarily consider themselves religious. In some Indigenous and Shamanist teachings certain animals such as horses and wolves are considered to be spiritual. This is to say that spirituality is not something unique to human beings, let alone to any particular faith. As human beings, we are all spiritual beings, regardless of whether we believe in a god or not.

Rethinking Secular Humanism

Literature on secularism and particularly secular humanism is considerable and growing (Asad, 2003; Lybarger, 2007; Taylor, 2007). This phenomenon owes its significance to the increasing rise in religious-based extremism, violence, and fundamentalism, on the one hand, and new transnational developments such as globalization, modernization, and diversification, on the other. In particular, the ongoing wars and religiously motivated conflicts in Iraq, Afghanistan, Lebanon, Northern Ireland, and elsewhere have drawn the attention of not only students and scholars, but also the general public, to the phenomenon of religious fundamentalism. In effect, these disastrous conflicts have attracted the interest of people from all walks of life to the nature, usefulness, and relevance of religion itself in our rapidly changing world.

Secular humanism is a most effective alternative to be used in societies plagued by religious sectarianism. It is a view that sees humanism as an alternative to religious belief. Different individuals and groups will define secular humanism somewhat differently. While some seek to define it in sharp contrast to religion and any kind of belief in god, gods, or any form of supernatural power, there are those who define it not so much in opposition to religion but alongside religion (e.g., Norman, 2004). The first group takes secular humanism to be a total rejection of belief in a god and any kind of divinity (e.g., Dawkins, 2006). To this group belongs a long line of philosophers, scholars, scientists, and thinkers such as Bertrand Russell, Jean-Paul Sartre, Karl Marx, and others. The second group considers secular humanism to be a different view of the world where human beings can live together without having any need for religion. However, at the same time, they can live with religion as well, insofar as religion does not deny them the right to live independently of religious faith. This group views secular humanism as an alternative to religion and religious belief. Instead of addressing the question of "how can we get rid of religion?" they address the question of "how can we live our lives without religion's interferences?" (see also Berger, 1999; Bruce, 2002; Ratzinger & Habermas, 2007).

This kind of humanism takes as its starting point an understanding of humans as agents of their own destiny. Thus, secularism need not mean hostility to religion in all its manifestations. Crimes and atrocities of unimaginable proportion have been committed historically in the name of both religion and secularism. While religion has caused much suffering through such infamous disasters as the Inquisition, the Crusades, and various religiously motivated sectarianisms, conflicts, and fundamentalism, secularism is also associated with such experiences as Nazism and Stalinism, for example. As such, care must be taken so that secularism is not romanticized as an ideal that always stands for democracy, human rights, peace, and progressivism. An underlying perspective behind secularism is the belief that it is, indeed, possible to live a good life without religion. To this end, the role of education is, and should be, central—an education through which the students' character, values, and self-perceptions are formed by rational discourses, critical thinking, and democratic processes of socialization.

The movement known as secular humanism has flourished in different societies in recent years. While there are somewhat different articulations of this movement in places like England, Germany, France, and North America, they all share similar attributes in their emphasis on reason, ethics, justice, and a dismissal of the supernatural. The Society of Ontario Free Thinkers (2007), for instance, summarizes the core principles of humanism as:

- That we can live full, meaningful lives, without religious doctrines, by relying on rationality, honesty, cooperation, fairness, and respect for each other;

- That we use democratic principles, logic, and scientific inquiry to find realistic solutions to problems;

- That we foster good ethics, virtues, and critical thinking in our children to help them grow to be decent, responsible, and active members of society;

- That we protect and improve the Earth for future generations by supporting scientific breakthroughs in medicine and technology and by not inflicting needless suffering on other species; and

- That total separation of religion and state is upheld in all levels of government to ensure equality and fairness for all. (p. 1)

Notwithstanding that certain religious groups may try to underestimate or undermine the sphere and scope of secularism and secular thinking in various societies, secular individuals constitute a sizeable portion of members of all communities. Secularism, in its humanist form, is defined in the context of believing in a separation between core religious beliefs and civil institutions of society, such as the government, and the education system. Obviously, this does not entail an antireligious stance; it can be viewed as an acknowledgment of difference of all sorts and kinds in society (i.e., religious, cultural, ethnic, racial, sexual, and linguistic). As such, the challenge for us becomes how to deal with diversity and how to interpret difference so that traditional forms of exclusion and marginalization are avoided. To this end, we need educational policies and practices that are geared toward universal values of human rights and peaceful coexistence.

Implications for Education

In this chapter I use a definition of secular humanism that speaks positively to issues of difference and diversity in multicultural, multiethnic, multilingual, and multireligious environments. I come from the subject position that in today's globalizing environments, religiously determined public schools are not, and cannot be, compatible with the challenge of extremely diverse student populations. If any particular religion determines or influences in any way the oversight of schools, those students and administrative personnel belonging to the dominant religion will always be placed in a position of advantage vis-à-vis those who do not share the dominant faith. This obviously goes against the principles of inclusivity and multicultural education and creates an education that does not differentiate between and among students coming from different religious, cultural, ethnic, racial, gendered, classed, and sexual backgrounds. Thus, my argument here is not to promote a sense of rejection of religion in its entirety; rather, it has to do with religion's incompatibility with, and inability to uphold, the principles of equity and equality in contemporary schools and universities.

In order to be equitable and inclusive, education should be conducted in secular spaces where students of different religious persuasions are accorded equal recognition and equal opportunity to freely develop their intellects and to grow as independent persons. Religion in this context is explored more as a marker of identity than as a belief system. More concretely, the kinds of questions to be addressed are: How can we create an education system where adherents to different religious beliefs and forms of spirituality can have equal chances with one another as well as with the nonbelievers? How can we design the education system in such a way that members of the dominant faith are not accorded more rights and privileges than other groups? What kind of education can best promote independent thinking, critical dialogue, and reflection?

This view foregrounds the possibility of shared human values and understanding as a basis for a universalistic perception of human community where crude forms of relativism and subjectivism are rejected, and the importance of shared secular moral values are emphasized: care, respect, diversity, human rights, peace, and freedom of expression. I proceed with the premise that education is not, cannot, and has never been a neutral, apolitical, and value-free enterprise. Since this has been the case, then it should promote values that enhance the local and universal human well-being, the achievement of human happiness, and the prevention or elimination of human pain and suffering.

In a democratic learning environment, fundamentalist assumptions are challenged from a variety of important epistemological, discursive, and sociocultural fronts. In a democratic society, schools are, and should be, open to all, regardless of their religious belief. While all students have the right to believe, they also have a duty to be open to various belief systems. This is why it is necessary for a democratic education system to provide a basis for respect, for the appreciation of human rights, peace, diversity, and pluralism. Schools should also provide for the equality of treatment, freedom of expression, and intercultural communication. A publicly funded school should be the place where people from different backgrounds, cultures, and religions, learn to live together, to respect diversity, and to develop through it. This function of schooling is quite consistent with the primary task of education as articulated in the context of "the development of the mind" (Dewey, 1933). It is through the ability to think independently that students will avoid falling victim to indoctrination and unhealthy fundamentalist ideologies. Schools, therefore, should promote a sense of autonomous personhood in all students. An autonomous person can be free from the mental constraints, so that he or she can think for himself or herself, and can make up his or her own mind, as opposed to having their mind made up for them. When the school denies the opportunity to learn about other traditions, it diminishes the autonomy of the learner. At the same time, the education system should try and address structural barriers to inclusion and equal treatment. A mere acknowledgment of diversity does not help to remove formidable barriers based on race, class, gender, language, citizenship, and so on.

Conclusion

Much like the rest of the world, modern education systems in the Middle East follow three general goals: development of human resources; development of national economy; development and promotion of "national" culture. The development of human resources includes such areas as the production of skilled labor, the armed forces, and human capital in general. Similarly, the development of the "national economy" emphasizes the utilization of national resources, finance, wealth, technological resources, competitiveness in global markets, and the overall economic well-being of both the country and the citizenry. Like elsewhere in the world, it is the development of what is termed "the national culture" that usually becomes problematic. This vague category includes all sorts of political, religious, linguistic, and nationalistic socialization that takes place in schools. A monolithic presentation of culture or religion becomes problematic particularly in multicultural environments characterized by difference and diversity. In general, what is normally meant by national culture, national language, and/or national/official religion are the culture, language, and religion of the dominant group in every society, masquerading as national, official, and universal. Since contemporary societies are composed of diverse ethnic, cultural, linguistic, and religious communities, it becomes a real challenge for education systems in the Middle East (and other places) to be faithful to principles of inclusivity and equity, at the same time promoting "the national/official culture." When certain religions and languages are identified as "official," other religions and languages are automatically rendered "unofficial," and hence of lesser importance.

Thus, while the emphasis on the development of human resources, national economy, and national culture may be a useful one, it does not seem to yield the desired results in the absence of promoting such essential aspects of education as intercultural communication, critical thinking, global citizenship, respect for diversity, difference, multiculturalism, and so forth. The idea of an inclusive education cannot materialize where schools tend to cater to the state's "official religion" policy. It is only in a secular space that students of different religious backgrounds can be treated as equal partners in their educational struggles. In addition to promoting issues of inclusivity and equal access within their immediate environment, schools can also help to promote the values of secularism and democracy in the wider society by utilizing their role as major socializing agents.

The sheer ferocity and magnitude of religiously motivated violence that has been unleashed in recent years in the Middle East and elsewhere make it quite possible, even attractive perhaps, for the first time, to vigorously explore the possibilities of secular humanism to be promoted in Middle Eastern schools and learning centers. To this end, it is important to interrogate issues emerging from diversity, dialogue, freedom of expression, and their centrality in challenging fundamentalist ideologies. Simultaneously, it is necessary to examine certain limitations blocking the path of independent thinking because of the current marketization of education and the politics of a corporate-based globalization. This chapter maintains that independent thinking is an antidote to fundamentalist thinking. Hence, it should be the role of education systems to promote critical reflection and independent thinking, developments that can be achieved through schools' role as major socializing agents in all societies, including the Middle Eastern ones.

Questions for Reflection

1. How can we create an education system where adherents of different religious beliefs and forms of spirituality can have equal opportunities with one another as well as with the nonbelievers?

2. How can we design the education system in such a way that members of the dominant faith are not accorded more rights and privileges than other groups?

3. What kind of education can best promote independent thinking, critical dialogue, and reflection?

4. Can the religiously centered public schools be compatible with the challenge of extremely diverse student populations, particularly in today's globalizing, multicultural environments?

5. Can fundamentalism coexist within the same learning center with such progressive sites and fields of inquiry as feminism, antisexist discourse, gay, lesbian, and transgendered studies, critical pedagogy, and postmodern educational methods?

References

Abrahamian, E. (1993). *Khomeinism: Essays on the Islamic republic.* Berkeley: University of California.
Apple, M. W. (2001). *Educating the "right" way: Markets, standards, God, and inequality.* New York: RoutledgeFalmer.

Apple, M. W., & Buras, K. L. (Eds.). (2006). *The subaltern speak: Curriculum, power, and educational struggles.* New York: Routledge.

Asad, T. (2003). *Formations of the secular: Christianity, Islam, modernity.* Stanford, CA: Stanford University Press.

Asgharzadeh, A. (2004). Islamic fundamentalism, globalization, and migration: New challenges for Canada. In Rose Folson (Ed.), *Calculated kindness: Immigration and settlement policies in Canada* (pp. 130–151). Halifax, NS: Fernwood.

Asgharzadeh, A. (2007). *Iran and the challenge of diversity: Aryanist racism, Islamic fundamentalism, and democratic struggles.* New York: Palgrave Macmillan.

Berger, P. L. (1999). *The desecularization of the world: Resurgent religion and world politics.* Grand Rapids, MI: William B. Eerdmans.

Bruce, S. (2002). *God is dead: Secularization in the West.* Oxford: Blackwell.

Bush, G. W. (2001, November 10). *President Bush speaks to United Nations: Remarks by the president to United Nations General Assembly* [Press release]. Washington, DC: The White House, Office of the Press Secretary.

Chesterton, G. K. (1968). *What I saw in America.* New York: Da Capo Press.

Cleveland, W. L. (2000). *A history of the modern Middle East* (2nd ed.). Boulder, CO: Westview.

Constitution of the Republic of Turkey. (2007). [Online document]. Retrieved May 28, 2007, from http://www.hri.org/docs/turkey

Dawkins, R. (2006). *The God delusion.* New York: Houghton Mifflin.

Dewey, J. (1933). How we think: A restatement of the relation of reflective thinking to the educative process. Boston: D. C. Heath.

Durkheim, E. (1992/1911). *Education et sociologie.* Paris: Presses Universitaires de France.

Heiberg, M., & Ovensen, G. (Eds.). (1993). Palestinian society in Gaza, West Bank and Arab Jerusalem: A survey of living conditions. Oslo: FAFO-Report 151. http://64.233.167.104/search?q=cache:ouDFAWABWcJ:www.paktoday.com/civilwar.htm+the+most+evil+creatures+under+the+heavens&hl=en&ct=clnk&cd=1

Kieser, H. L. (2006). *Turkey beyond nationalism: Towards post-nationalist identities.* London: I. B. Tauris.

Lewis, B. (1999). *The multiple identities of the Middle East.* New York: Schocken Books.

Lybarger, L. D. (2007). *Identity and religion in Palestine: The struggle between Islamism and secularism in the occupied territories—Princeton studies in Muslim politics.* Princeton, NJ: Princeton University Press.

Massialas, B. G., & Jarrar, S. A. (1991). *Arab education in transition: A source book.* New York: Garland.

Norman, R. (2004). *On humanism: Thinking in action.* London: Routledge.

Ozyurek, E. (2006). *Nostalgia for the modern: State secularism and everyday politics in Turkey.* London: Duke University Press.

Ratzinger, J., & Habermas, J. (2007). *The dialectic of secularism: On reason and religion.* (B. McNeil, trans.). San Francisco: Ignatius.

Said, E. W. (1992). *The question of Palestine.* New York: Vintage Books.

Sayyed, T. (2005, January 7). It is a civil war. *Pakistan Today*, p. 1. Retrieved May 25, 2007, from http://www.paktoday.com/civilwar.htm

Segev, T. (2007). *1967: Israel, the war and the year that transformed the Middle East.* London: Metropolitan Books.

Society of Ontario Free Thinkers. (2007). *Core principles of humanism.* Retrieved May 25, 2007, from http://kwcg.humanists.net/CMS/index.php?option=content&task=view &id=26&Itemid=55

Taylor, C. (2007). *A secular age.* Cambridge, MA: Harvard University Press.

10

Doing Democracy and Feminism in the Classroom: Challenging Hegemonic Practices

Glenda T. Bonifacio

Introduction

Feminism is intrinsically connected to democracy in education. By feminism, or more appropriately *feminisms*, I refer to the corpus of knowledge relative to different groups of women and their experiences encompassing the "multiple meanings and realities of contemporary feminism" (Coffey & Delamont, 2000, p. 5). As there are many ways to define feminism, I use its generic base to underscore the sociopolitical movement against sexism and other oppressive systems of domination, as well as the pedagogy of gender equality for social justice.

Looking back in the history of the women's movement, education serves as the key element in the struggle for gender equality. The clamor for full educational rights with men, for example, has inspired feminist activism on all fronts since the Enlightenment. Feminism, like other democratic movements, has been inspired, directly or indirectly, by education. In examining the various phases of these movements in different historical contexts, education provides the space for learning and action from which political momentum is sustained. Today, a number of structural impediments in education affecting women have been removed in many liberal-democratic countries around the world, and most universities offer Women's Studies or Gender Studies.

However, gender inequality, mediated by race and other social identifiers, largely remains in society, at different levels of education, and across disciplines (Harvey, 2003). Women in developing countries lag behind in education, and this gender gap consequently impacts their access to paid employment and political participation (Kabeer, 2003). Still, the masculinist orientation of the academy and its hegemonic learning practices reproduce gender biases that contribute to the ways in which democracy is valued and practiced between women and men (Arnot & Dillabough, 2000).

In this chapter, I present the relational praxis and pedagogy of feminism and democracy in education, and argue that teaching feminism in the classroom is inherently "doing democracy." Teaching feminism or integrating feminist discourses constructively builds on citizenship practice and grounds democratic values and processes in education. Based on my professional and personal experience of learning and teaching in three countries—Philippines, Australia, and Canada—I explore feminist teaching strategies indicative of "doing democracy" in the classroom beyond its conventional meaning of formal political participation (e.g., voting, running for office). These strategies are applicable in any classroom although the vantage point of my discussion is directed toward university classrooms pursuing Women's Studies or related disciplines.

Feminism and Democracy in Education

Education is considered a "necessity of life" (Dewey, 1916, p. 1). From it emanates the base of knowledge and action for human existence. Teaching and learning are imperative to fostering the continuity of social life. Reciprocal logic maintains that, in a democratic society, all children ought to learn about citizenship and, through education, we ensure that the next generation share our democratic tradition and create a far more inclusive society.

In view of the vital role of education in the creation and transmission of knowledge, teachers constantly engage with the content and delivery of course materials each time a new school year opens. Notwithstanding the fact that in the elementary and high school curricula the content of each subject is quite set by regulatory entities, teachers are not mere robots who simply rattle off what is prescribed. We raise questions such as: On what do we focus in this course? How are we going to deliver the content of this course? There are certainly other areas of concern in updating subject teaching areas but none require more intensive intellectual activity than content and delivery. In particular, to integrate or include controversial themes like feminism into the curriculum is, to many nonfeminists, a complex struggle between long-held beliefs about gender and academic openness, and frankly, the same dilemma faced by those teaching from an antiracist perspective.

Since education foregrounds societal values, issues, and interests, of which democracy is paramount in many regards, the gender question is crucial. It is only relatively recently in the memory of modern Western history, however, that women have been granted equal access to education as a product of "feminizing democracy" (Holton, 1986, p. 9). Despite significant educational reforms, studies reveal that the major stream of disciplines such as History, Psychology, Literature, Fine Arts, and Political Science are essentially, in the words of Martin (1998), "biased according to sex" and "fall short of the ideal epistemological equality, that is equality of representation and treatment of women in academic knowledge itself" (p. 59).

As a result of this tradition of exclusion, albeit with progress along the way, gender stereotypes persist and women's roles are mainly relegated as secondary to men in the private and public spheres (Gumport, 2002; McLeod & Allard, 2007). This social enigma of female subordination flourishes even under ultramodern democratic systems that are still patriarchal. The gender issue in policy and practice incites continued activism in many parts of the world and challenges the ways we "do" education.

Two years ago, a female student in the introductory course in Women's Studies at the University of Lethbridge raised an insightful comment about the role of education in perpetuating embedded inequalities. She commented, "we should have been taught about gender even in the elementary school so that we do not have to deconstruct ourselves today as adults." This student frames gender as a socially constructed knowledge about femininity and masculinity and the power dynamics of its construction, and whose central thesis is made famous by de Beauvoir's (1952) dictum that, "one is not born, but rather becomes a woman" (p. 267). That, essentially, the ways in which socialization is pursued in the classroom significantly shapes the gender role divide in society and women's subject position as the "other" to men.

The move toward mainstreaming gender into the school curriculum is generally directed to, and applied in, higher education. I remember signing a consent form in Australia for my daughter in the grade level to be taught "sex education," notably about anatomy and reproduction. This was not the case in Catholic Philippines. In education, relationships reflect "gender enculturation" that is, for Overall (1998), those that are "founded upon unconfirmed beliefs in the inherent sexual differences" (p. 63) between women and men. Generally speaking, primary education today has not succeeded in moving beyond a school curriculum reflective of the history of women within dominant power structures without a few exemplars in selected eras of national history. The continued reproduction of gendered knowledge in education mirrors the societal positioning of women from which feminism originates.

The past hundred years have witnessed the development of a progressive educational theory premised on the idea that for education to respond to the public interest within a democratic system "schools and classrooms must embody democratic values and processes" (Kreisberg, 1993, pp. 232–233). In reality, the educational systems in the United States and Canada, and other nations as well, fair poorly in teaching democracy and citizenship (Hennessy, 2006). Education generally maintains its focus on attaining straight mastery of the subject content disconnected from the parameters of citizenship practice. This seems to be different if we teach about feminism or if we incorporate feminism in our syllabus.

Feminism vanguards democratic values of equality, participation, rights, freedom, and liberation, among others, but its challenges to existing systems of power and domination have not been widely recognized as "public interest." Haraway (1989) posits that the theoretical and practical vision of feminism is "to explain and change historical systems of sexual difference, whereby 'men' and 'women' are socially constituted and positioned in relations of hierarchy and antagonism" (p. 290). With oppositional goals, the notion of public interest remains highly contested in the face of a popular media backlash against feminism and the rise of conservative politics after 9/11. These realities demonstrate, however, the continued relevance and challenge of teaching feminism.

Understanding the bases of power and control, and how this differentially impacts on the lives of women and men involves critical thinking, which is necessary for democracy. To be able to participate actively in human affairs, this intellectual disposition is imperative. By teaching feminism in the classroom could universalist male-oriented values of domination be negotiated in the classroom? The multifaceted aspect of feminisms and the challenge of differential politics between White, mainstream feminists and non-White feminists, for example, demonstrate the dynamics of feminist discourse. I surmise that regardless of the cleavages among feminist scholars, teaching feminism is a way of "doing democracy" that aims to empower students amidst an extant hegemonic paradigm in the academe to become active citizens in their own right.

Feminism as Democratic Pedagogy

Broadly, feminism is at the core of a democratic social revolution by altering gender relations with rights and freedom for every human being, by shaping the face of inclusive citizenship, and, by challenging normativity and fundamental traditions exploitative of the femalekind. This social revolution is unfinished. It moves, sometimes slowly like a wave, but constantly pushed to a momentum depending on the currents of the time. From the sweeping tide of the civil rights agenda, feminism has spread its base to include education. Since the 1960s, feminism has been institutionalized as "academic feminism" invariably operating in universities under different program titles (Rosser, 2000). The significance of gender as a major variable of analysis is also, to some extent, "mainstreamed" in other disciplines. In the area of development studies, Sawer (2003) contends that women are the "important index within democracy assessment" (p. 361) recognized by the United Nations and other international organizations. Their participation in public life and paid work indicate democratic advancement in nation-states.

Feminism is not only a democratic movement for social change but also a critical pedagogy; Ng (1995) uses the term "critical teaching" to refer to discourses that "challenge existing knowledge base and power relations" (p. 130) to include feminist pedagogy and antiracist education. Feminism, according to Eisenstein (1994), "unsettles traditional political theory" (p.

200) and brings forth different epistemologies. As pedagogy, feminism diverges from conventional teaching frameworks because it offers an "explicitly political stand" (Osborne, 1991, p. 80). It adopts a vision of society where gender justice reigns. Consistent with its social function, education becomes the instrument to forge a feminist vision of equality in a democracy.

Feminist pedagogy is a relatively new wave of thinking. Although defining this term is difficult in the light of the many methods applied by Women's Studies and feminist scholars, it is safe to say that feminist pedagogy fuses theory and practice, and embraces a commitment to action starting at the personal level. Teaching feminism in the classroom potentially directs this change. A feminist pedagogy motivates the translocation of idea into personal political practice through a critical consciousness or what Freire (1972) calls "conscientization."

Consciousness-raising is the "foundation for feminist pedagogy" (Enns & Forrest, 2005, p. 9), and citizenship is embodied by raising the social impact of teaching and learning about feminism. Through feminist teaching, students are made aware of the pervasive practices of sexism, racism, ageism, and other dominantly instituted practices in society by an interconnected patriarchal system. Challenging the normative assumptions in their lives with feminist discourses may result in some form of personal change, either reflective or actual. Any action of citizenship, therefore, comes from the personal sphere and its relation to the public domain. Fisher, in her book *No Angel in the Classroom* (2001), affirms the "relations between the self and the world" (p. 34) made possible by feminist ways of knowing, such as "sharing experiences, feelings, and ideas about the needs for and possibilities of liberating actions" (Fisher, 2001, p. 34).

Feminist pedagogy and democratic practice seem parallel, if not consistent, with each other. These two befit connectivity in values and goals. Democratic teaching practice is characterized by shared trust and mutual respect (Osborne, 1991). It values equal opportunity, student welfare, cooperation, and merit. Democratic teaching aims, significantly, to achieve empowerment of students, and the same could be said of feminist teaching.

Feminist pedagogy requires egalitarian ways of learning to promote inclusivity of marginalized groups, such as women and other minorities. As is the case with democratic teaching, feminist teaching adopts equality, mutual respect, community, or cooperation in the classroom. Schniedewind (1987) typifies feminist teaching values as shared leadership through participatory decision making, cooperative structures of learning and evaluation, integration of cognitive and affective learning and action. Participatory decision-making challenges hierarchical norms and places the teacher and student in a position of mutuality. The student is an autonomous and active agent in the learning process with input into a flexible, nonprescriptive curriculum as opposed to rigid top-down communication. A cooperative structure implies a holistic unit where students and teachers are involved in setting goals. One of the distinct ways of feminist teaching is the sensitivity to emotions and their impact on intellectual growth. The most vital aspect of feminist pedagogy is, however, action made possible through democratic pedagogy. Schniedewind (1987) boldly claims that "as long as we live in a sexist society, feminism inevitably implies taking action to transform institutions and values" (p. 178).

It is well documented that feminist pedagogy possesses a "transformative potential" (Coffey & Delamont, 2000, p. 39) in changing dominant ways of thinking and knowing in the classroom or, according to Sinacore and Boatwright (2005), those "experiences that do not reproduce the status quo" (p. 109). Following the Freirean approach of liberatory learning, feminist pedagogy envisions social transformation and the demise of oppressive structures and practices. With this in mind, education is best served if the teaching of feminism and its pedagogy are integrated in the learning process, using creative ways relevant to each discipline and level of education. Feminism is consistent with democratic practice, and it requires an understanding of each in a way that recognizes that we share the same aspirations in society.

Doing Democracy in a Feminist Classroom

As education is vital in a democracy, it underlies a social agenda for acceptance and continuity of democratic values and processes. In the words of Bleedorn (2005), "schools and society together are designed to continue to create our democracy" (p. 116). Consequently tied to this societal function is the training for citizenship and of learning the ways and behavior of a citizen. Grambs and Carr (1979) point out that "citizenship in a democracy demands practical, longstanding training in how to function in such a system" (p. 73). Doing democracy in the classroom behooves practicing citizenship.

Is feminism "doing democracy"? The movement for equality with men, for example, responds to the democratic value of participation; this is an established democratic virtue and vision. It makes no sense that a democratic society could keep half of its population disenfranchised, unpaid, or underpaid. Women, through the ages, like men, find it more sensible to make each member of society full participants in the affairs and benefits of the state. If feminism is a democratic exercise of inclusion and of changing power systems based on social justice, then teaching feminism is its arm in the classroom.

How, then, do we do democracy in a feminist classroom? Answering this question appears easier if we define what makes a feminist classroom. The classroom does not only cover the physical space where teachers and students meet but it is also the convergence of a feminist pedagogy and transmission of feminist values. In particular, a class, according to Crane (1995), is "a course embodied" with a "temporal, locational, dynamic, and personalized makeup" (p. xiii). A feminist classroom is continually created and engaged in an atmosphere of mutual respect, cooperation, and collaboration. Fluidity, interaction, and dialogue characterize the feminist classroom (Williams & McKenna, 2002). Although hierarchies remain because of the ascribed status of the teacher, the feminist classroom adheres to democratic processes within this structure such as having an open dialogue, employing equal opportunities for participation, and a mutually acceptable merit system by students and teachers.

In terms of space, the teacher can (re)arrange the location of learning discourse to create an ambiance of what I call "feminist spatiality." This sounds tedious because fixed structures emphasize the hierarchical position of the teacher with a front and center podium. Instructors are in some ways conscious of the impact of the physical arrangement to student-teacher exchange. I find the physical space intimidating or constraining in teaching a class of 50 students in a large or small room. Participation of students seems limited when instructors are magnetized in one location. Mobility of instructors away from the lectern or behind the desk observably stimulates students' participation as they become aware of their importance as subject-knowers.

Students form the constituency of the feminist classroom. In acknowledging mutual respect and equality, students are recognized as individuals and active contributors to the learning process. Utmost effort in calling their first names should be exercised, albeit a near impossibility with hundreds of students per semester in the university. First-name calling is a desirable practice and have long been used in the elementary and secondary schools and, apparently, dissipates in the university. The use of surnames and titles like "Mr." or "Miss" create formality and rigidity where the smooth communicative process is inhibited, reinforcing the hegemonic authority of the teacher. In contrast, a feminist classroom invites openness between students and teachers.

An essential aspect of feminist teaching is the curriculum. What do we teach? Or, "what is worth knowing?" (Gaskell, McLaren, & Novogrodsky, 1989, p. 33). A curriculum is the blueprint of a specific course and guides both the instructor and the student in classroom interaction. A feminist curriculum is holistic in scope and blends an agenda for a "transformative learning" (O'Sullivan, Morrell, & O'Connor, 2002). Although the debates on the politics of gendered curriculum remain, formulating a feminist curriculum or integrating feminism is contentious. Is feminism relevant in all subject areas? The basic idea lies in the equal epistemological treatment for sources of knowledge for women and men. In Women's Studies curricula, the different voices of women long silenced by academic traditions are emphasized, with an examination of multiple subjectivities from the perspective of women. Disciplines outside of Women's Studies or Gender Studies can formulate a feminist curriculum by promoting equal representation of women and men in texts and in examples, thereby stimulating feminist thinking.

At the elementary and secondary education the integration of feminism or, at the very least, gender-fair content is probable within approved curricular themes. I take one example in Canada using the new 2007–2008 *Curriculum Handbook for Parents* for Senior High School (10–12) in the Province of Alberta, where my daughter attends school. The Social Studies curriculum is aimed at "active and responsible citizenship" (Alberta Education, 2007, p. 32). Reading through the program guide of core courses, I surmise that feminism could very well be part of each of the subject areas. Depending on how each of these subjects is formulated and delivered, feminism can be emphasized or deemphasized. For example, Social Studies 20 (The Growth of the Global Perspective) could very well include not only the economic factors of global interdependence but also take into consideration the impact of industrialization in women's lives. Likewise, in Social Studies 30 (The Contemporary World), a gendered perspective on the roles of individuals and different groups of people could be part of the discussion on the political and economic systems since World War I.

Noddings (2001), in her work *Social Studies and Feminism*, suggests that valuing women in the Social Studies curriculum means to start with a perspective linking the dominant separation of public and private spheres. She notes that "if we had started with private life, the school curriculum would be different from the one actually developed" (p. 167). One way to be inclusive and embracing of women's knowledge within the Social Studies curriculum is to "expand the notion of citizenship" (Noddings, 2001, p. 168), encompassing the personal and the public lives of women and men. However, attempts at coming up with a feminist curriculum remain fractious and fragile. Crocco (2004) refers to this dilemma as the "long rise and rapid fall of feminist activity in social studies" (p. 153). In conservative Alberta and elsewhere, the question is whether feminism is a matter of "public interest" that would make its teaching compelling in its "contested classroom[s]" (Harrison & Kachur, 1999) and bring about transformative knowledge and values for a gender-sensitive society.

Feminist Teaching Strategies

Feminist teaching strategies indicative of "doing democracy" are different from the standard lecture format used by many professors and teachers. The following strategies are based on my experience in university instruction in the field of Social Sciences, particularly History, Political Science, and Women's Studies. I do not pretend to claim that these strategies are exhaustive and exclusive because many nonfeminist colleagues have utilized them in other disciplines. In fact, many of these strategies are common in elementary and secondary classrooms. Although common practice amongst teachers, I discuss the ways in which these strategies are used for feminist teaching. I find them stimulating in the contemporary discursive analysis of feminism as I see younger students each year responding to new challenges of the times.

Group Activities

Education portrays the values of the democratic institution it inscribes. The classroom becomes the microscopic unit for practicing values and processes in a democracy, mainly participation. One way of doing democracy in the classroom is through collaborative activities. Variants of group-based exercises are group discussion, group dynamics, and group projects.

Group discussion is effective in encouraging maximum participation of students, desirably getting all voices heard in smaller units. Consistent with democratic practice, learning is an opportunity equally shared by each student. Similarly, each member of the class is recognized as vital to the whole group. Becoming a part of the whole essentially defines democratic practice. Many students have expressed satisfaction in contributing to the discussion or providing solutions to feminist issues in manageable groups. Employing group dynamics also substitutes hierarchy with a "cooperative structure" (Schniedewind, 1987, p. 174). The completion of a group project symbolizes understanding of a common goal. Each member of the group recognizes the contribution of others toward this goal. This classroom exercise denotes that, like any other democratic process, the constituent members define the future of the group. Without a shared commitment to the common goal, the activity fails.

Participation as Attendance

To be seen and heard is vital to any participatory activity. I devise a mechanism of "participation as attendance" to encourage students to become involved regularly throughout the course. This means that a student is not considered to have attended the class without becoming a part of it. The essence of coming to class is not only "being" but "doing." The rationale behind this is that students are responsible learning agents contributing to the delivery of the course. Coming prepared to class and ready to engage with other students subsumes the potential of transformative learning.

The mechanism of "participation as attendance" correlates with most of the processes in a democratic society. For example, casting a ballot requires direct presence in the polling station or involvement in community activities. This strategy instills the value of responsibility and reciprocity, and of doing something to gain merit. In a democratic society, citizens reap the rewards of good or bad leadership by the extent of their participation in the electoral process. Experience tells us, however, that the present crop of leadership produced by a nonfeminist education has perpetuated systems of dominance that consequently marginalize women and other groups. Instilling the value of democratic participation as practiced continually in classrooms orients women's equal voice in the polity and their contribution to political life. When students recognize their role and the value of participation in systems of representation, a new generation of progressive leadership is plausible.

Experiential Learning

A useful teaching strategy to connect with and find social relevance is experiential learning. Albeit criticized by Michelson (1996) for its idealist assumptions of human nature, I find merit in Kolb's (1984) definition of experiential learning as a "holistic integrative perspective on learning that combines experience, perception, cognition, and behavior" (p. 21). Of the teaching strategies, only feminist pedagogy emphasizes women's personal experiences as a valid source of knowledge (Macdonald, 2002). Women have particular ways of knowing that define knowledge itself and challenge dominant paradigms of male thinking. Through experiencing the political in the personal, women give academic discourse a different voice.

In a feminist classroom, there are other ways to undertake experiential learning such as attending a parliamentary session, casting a vote in student elections, or doing placement at the women's shelter. Connecting with the processes and procedures affecting gender relations allows students to make their own judgments and action. Rosenthal (2002) concludes in her study on experiential learning that "when [the] classroom helps students make those connections, the learning is rich and rewarding" (p. 36).

Community Outreach

Gilbert and Taylor (1991) contend that "social reality is ideological" (p. 135). Our societies are enmeshed with a set of ideas prescribing social interactions and behavior, each holding a particular world view shaped by history, religion, and others. A feminist classroom engages with the social environment as its epistemic base. Feminism shows the many aspects of social life where gender, intersecting with race, class, ethnicity, and other markers of identity impact students' understanding of their lives and others in their own communities.

While we have a fixed classroom for our regular lectures and discussion, learning does not only come about within its four walls. The sense of connection with the outside world becomes more meaningful if we include, even once, the community as a source of learning. A community outreach activity is an interactive process wherein students directly undertake what Orr (2002) calls "challenging the academic/real world divide" (p. 36). I call this community-classroom connection as the "open class" model. There are many ways of opening up our classroom to others who might be interested to participate in certain topics. At the university level, I usually hold one session at the public library to discuss a particular topic and invite the "interested public" to share their views with the students. Or, as part of a group project, students invite other students and faculty to the classroom to provide what I call "other informed voices" in the discussion.

Other examples of community-linked activities include students' presentation to the community, student-public dialogue like an open forum or a roundtable discussion. The "open class" concept allows students to experience the feminist duo of "theory and praxis." Elementary and secondary schools have traditionally had their own ways of involving the community. Most schools use sports activities and other fun ways to learn, but seem to be lacking in gradually introducing a systematic approach to incorporate gender and its related issues appropriate to the students' level of understanding.

Extending the classroom to the community is one way of practicing citizenship or doing democracy. Students, with their own particular social locations, are able to ground the abstract knowledge with reality and make the learning experience worthwhile. Feminism is discursively engaged simultaneously in the classroom and the community providing the nexus for a feminist "transformational politics" (hooks, 1989, p. 19) and change.

Conclusion

Democracy is an ideal for society, one that is in constant transformation and subscribes to recognized values, processes, and participation of different groups of people. Feminism underscores a democratic practice of inclusion for women and offers an alternative social order based on gender equality and social justice. The forging of this vision has expanded to the academy. Education, ideally, fosters the transmission of democratic values, and the teaching of feminism and its pedagogical practice is a challenge to hegemonic teaching practices.

Teaching feminism in the classroom is good pedagogy and can be considered doing democracy. With an inclusive epistemology valuing women's knowledge and experiences, feminism connects with democracy in education through a vision of equality and shared practices of respect, mutuality, cooperation, and collaboration. Its holistic curriculum and feminist strategies of participation allow students to connect theoretical discourse with practical experiences and chart the journey toward transformation and action. Feminism encourages simultaneous learning of the interconnectivity between the personal and the public through different ways of participatory learning such as experiential learning and community outreach activities.

The challenge of feminism is a challenge to everyone living in a democratic society. Those of us with the opportunity to advance feminism in the academy are cognizant of the many ways in which the teaching of feminism is essentially doing democracy in the classroom. In this way, the function of education to train its citizens—especially women—for active participation in society is achievable. A democratic education does not only imply the process employed for teacher-student interaction but also openness, if not willingness, to teach feminism.

Questions for Reflection

1. What would the social impact be if feminist classrooms become the norm in education?

2. What are the boundaries in practicing or doing democracy in the classroom?

3. Should educators become feminists to be democratic in teaching?

4. What are the institutional challenges of a feminist classroom?

5. How can we evaluate and recognize feminist classrooms in the performance of democracy in education?

References

Alberta Education. (2007). *2007–2008 Curriculum handbook for parents*. Retrieved October 15, 2007, from http://www.education.gov.ab.ca/parents/handbooks/srpub.pdf

Arnot, M., & Dillabough, J. (2000). *Challenging democracy: International perspectives on gender, education and citizenship*. London: RoutledgeFalmer.

Bleedorn, B. (2005). *Education is everybody's business*. Lanham: Rowman & Littlefield.

Coffey, A., & Delamont, S. (2000). *Feminism and the classroom teacher: Research, praxis, pedagogy*. New York: RoutledgeFalmer.

Crane, D. (1995). A personal postscript. In J. Gallop (Ed.), *Pedagogy: The question of impersonation* (pp. ix–xiv). Bloomington, IN: Indiana University Press.

Crocco, M. S. (2004). Women and the social studies: The long rise and rapid fall of feminist activity in the National Council for the Social Studies. In C. Woyshner, J. Watras, & M. S. Crocco (Eds.), *Social education in the twentieth century: Curriculum and context for citizenship* (pp. 142–159). New York: Peter Lang.

de Beauvoir, S. (1952). *The second sex*. New York: Bantam.

Dewey, J. (1916). *Democracy and education: An introduction to the philosophy of education*. New York: Macmillan.

Eisenstein, Z. R. (1994). *The color of gender*. Berkeley, CA: University of California Press.

Enns, C. Z., & Forrest, L. M. (2005). Toward defining and integrating multicultural and feminist pedagogies. In C. Z. Enns & A. L. Sinacore (Eds.), *Teaching social justice* (pp. 3–23). Washington, DC: American Psychological Association.

Fisher, B. (2001). *No angel in the classroom*. Lanham, MD: Rowman & Littlefield.

Freire, P. (1972). *Pedagogy of the oppressed*. Ringwood, Australia: Penguin.

Gaskell, J., McLaren, A., & Novogrodsky, M. (1989). *Claiming an education*. Toronto: Our Schools/Our Selves Education Foundation.

Gilbert, P., & Taylor, S. (1991). *Fashioning the feminine.* Sydney: Allen & Unwin.

Grambs, G., & Carr, L. (1979). *Modern methods in secondary education.* New York: Holt.

Gumport, P. J. (2002). *Academic pathfinders: Knowledge creation and feminist scholarship.* London: Greenwood.

Haraway, D. (1989). *Primate visions: Gender, race and nature in the world of modern science.* London: Routledge.

Harrison, T. W., & Kachur, J. L. (Eds.) (1999). *Contested classroom: Education, globalization, and democracy in Alberta.* Edmonton, AB: University of Alberta Press.

Harvey, W. (2003). *Twentieth annual status report on minorities in higher education, 2002–2003.* Washington, DC: American Council on Education.

Hennessy, P. H. (2006). *From student to citizen.* Toronto: White Knight Books.

Holton, S. S. (1986). *Feminism and democracy.* Cambridge, UK: Cambridge University Press.

hooks, b. (1989). *Talking back.* Boston: South End Press.

Kabeer, N. (2003). Gender mainstreaming in poverty eradication and the millennium development goals. London: Commonwealth Secretariat/IDRC/CIDA.

Kolb, D. A. (1984). *Experiential learning: Experience as the source of learning and development.* Englewood Cliffs, NJ: Prentice Hall.

Kreisberg, S. (1993). Educating for democracy and community: Toward the transformation of power in our schools. In S. Berman & P. LaFarge (Eds.), *Promising practices in teaching social responsibility* (pp. 218–235). Albany, NY: State University of New York Press.

Macdonald, A. A. (2002). Feminist pedagogy and the appeal to epistemic privilege. In A. A. Macdonald & S. Sanchez-Casal (Eds.), *Twenty-first century feminist classrooms* (pp. 111–133). New York: Palgrave Macmillan.

Martin, J. R. (1998). Excluding women from the educational realm. In C. A. Woyshner & H. S. Gelfond (Eds.), *Minding women: Reshaping the educational realm* (pp. 59–76). Cambridge, MA: Harvard Educational Review.

McLeod, J., & Allard, A. (Eds.) (2007). Learning from the margins: Young women, social exclusion, and education. New York: Routledge.

Michelson, E. (1996). "Auctorite" and "experience": Feminist epistemology and the assessment of experiential learning. *Feminist Studies, 22*(3), 627–656.

Ng, R. (1995). Teaching against the grain. In R. Ng, P. Stanton, & J. Scane (Eds.), *Anti-racism, feminism, and critical approaches to education* (pp. 129–152). Westport, CT: Bergin & Garvey.

Noddings, N. (2001). Social studies and feminism. In E. W. Ross (Ed.), *The social studies curriculum* (rev. ed., pp. 163–175). Albany, NY: State University of New York.

O'Sullivan, E., Morrell, A., & O'Connor, M. A. (Eds.) (2002). *Expanding the boundaries of transformative learning.* New York: Palgrave.

Orr, C. (2002). Challenging the "academic/real world" divide. In N. Naples & K. Bojar (Eds.), *Teaching feminist activism* (pp. 36–53). New York: Routledge.

Osborne, K. (1991). *Teaching for democratic citizenship.* Toronto: Our Schools/Our Selves Education Foundation.

Overall, C. (1998). *A feminist I.* Toronto: Broadview.

Rosenthal, C. S. (2002). Teaching about gender through experience: A pedagogy of engagement. In J. DiGeorgio-Lutz (Ed.), *Women in higher education* (pp. 21–36). London: Praeger.

Rosser, S. (2000). *Women, science and society.* New York: Teachers College Press.

Sawer, M. (2003). Constructing democracy. *International Feminist Journal of Politics, 5*(3), 361–365.

Schniedewind, N. (1987). Feminist values: Guidelines for teaching methodology in women's studies. In I. Shor (Ed.), *Freire for the classroom* (pp. 170–179). Portsmouth, NH: Boynton/Look.

Sinacore, A. L., & Boatwright, K. J. (2005). The feminist classroom: Feminist strategies and student responses. In C. Z. Enns & A. L. Sinacore (Eds.), *Teaching and social justice* (pp. 109–124). Washington, DC: American Psychological Association.

Williams, T., & McKenna, E. (2002). Negotiating subject positions in a service-learning context. In. A. A. Macdonald & S. Sanchez-Casal (Eds.), *Twenty-first century feminist classrooms* (pp. 135–154). New York: Palgrave Macmillan.

SECTION III

CASE STUDIES FOR UNDERSTANDING DEMOCRACY IN EDUCATION

11

PRIMARY EDUCATION FOR GIRLS: MIS/INTERPRETATION OF EDUCATION FOR ALL OF KENYA

Njoki Nathani Wane

Introduction

Kenya attained its political independence from Britain in 1963. The country inherited a colonial education system based on segregation and exclusion in terms of race, culture, class, and gender. Forty-four years later, there is a very significant gender differentiation in access to education. Every successive government has education reforms emphasizing issues of social justice and equitable redistribution of Kenyan educational resources. Experience, however, shows that if reforms are implemented without explicit identification of girls as targets, gender disparities will most likely not be reduced, and may even widen. Attempts to improve the status of girls and women call for changing deeply ingrained genderized attitudes and practices. It also requires serious efforts and initiatives to develop enabling environments where girls and other disadvantaged groups can participate.

The 1990 Education for All (EFA) Conference in Jomtien, Thailand, drew the world's attention to gender discrimination and the gross inequities between girls' and boys' education throughout the developing world. At the primary level, far more girls than boys were out of school (Wane & Gathenya, 2004). Kofi Annan, the UN secretary general at the time, stated that one of the ways to reduce poverty was to educate girls (as cited in Wane & Gathenya, 2004). This was echoed by Lawrence Summers, former World Bank chief economist and U.S. Treasury secretary, who stated that educating girls would strengthen the economy of a country. What are the barriers of implementing equitable educational policies that dwell on democratic rights of the people? What does it actually mean in relation to our African culture, philosophy, and indigenous education? Why have democratic educational policies failed to bring gender equity that was intended?

Drawing from the shifting socioeconomic and political scenario in Kenya, this chapter examines some of the democratic policy reforms of education, as well as their impact or lack of impact for girls. I discuss primary education and examine the gender enrolment rates at primary level since independence. I also provide a brief background on indigenous African education before colonization, an education that I believe was democratically conceptualized and implemented. It was an indigenous education where all the members of society had a role to play in ensuring there was equitable distribution of knowledge in relation to roles, gender equity, and age. I conclude with a discussion that tries to make sense of why girls' education has been compromised despite democratic policies that have been introduced since attainment of political independence in 1963. In particular, I scrutinize the exclusion of girls from the lower socioeconomic groups, showing how these measures have, in essence, replaced the racial segregation of the colonial system with the cultural and class-based inequities of postcolonial society. Using an anticolonial discursive framework, I analyze multiple equity issues arising from cultural and class dynamics and their implications for access to education for girls.

Democracy as it is conceptualized within the Western paradigm is very different from the way democracy is conceptualized among many Kenyans, and especially those from marginalized communities. However, democracy in its meaningful sense, if I can use that word, ought to include in its narrow definition accountability, political institutions that reflect societal values as established and changed through formal and legislative mechanisms, and freedom to associate and organize politically (Sifuna, 2000, p. 215). The practice of democracy, according to Sifuna, "belongs to ... the cultural patrimony of the people; where culture means what a person learns from, and in relation to his/her material and social environment" (p. 216). Democracy cannot be a top-down directive, with captions that one can do whatever one likes, regardless of the consequences of their actions to others (Kaunda & Kendall, 2002). According to Kaunda's and Kendall's study in Malawi, this type of democracy has destroyed the cultural values, and the groups that become victims of it are the young generation. According to their study, the participants felt there has to be a correct definition of democracy, not the one that is aligned with Western notions of citizen rights. As one participant said, "democracy is a foreign thing to Malawi. It was brought here by foreigners … even those at the top… curse each other in Parliament … we see it even in our children (p. 39).

Although this was made in reference to Malawi, it is very applicable to Kenyan situation. This is clearly articulated by Dr. Sifuna, a professor from one of the universities in Kenya, who feels that "the organizational mode of current formal education systems in Africa, is basically Western and trapped in its colonial historic origins in particular, have been lacking in promoting tolerance and democratic values … the authoritarian school structures have encouraging unquestioning acquiescence of authority" (2000, p. 214). Sifuna goes on to explain that this undemocratic governance is felt not only within the education system, but by citizenry. This is articulated by the following quotation from a woman elder in a rural village: "When will this independence pass away so that we can enjoy the peace and the life we loved so much when we were young? We used to grind our corn when and in a manner we wanted. We could make our own soap and salt" (Hagan, as cited in Sifuna, 2000, p. 215). According to Sifuna, many rural people in Kenya feel that they have retrogressed since independence when democracy was made the rule of the land and when no changes were made in the colonial educational structures. This is because colonial education, as Sifuna (quoting Mamdani) writes,

> was not education, but training; not liberation, but enslavement. Its purpose was not to educate a person to understand the objective limits to the advancement of individual and collective welfare, but to train a person to accept even administer the limits in an "efficient, reliable and honest way." (p. 221)

This doctrinaire attitude has not left our school system; hence, it is the reason I situate my argument in anticolonial theoretical framework.

Anticolonial Theoretical Framework

In confronting the concepts and conditions of colonial and neocolonial education in Africa, it is important to move beyond the internal conflicts or decaying social structures and examine the psychological impact of colonialism. Colonialism has left numerous psychological traces in colonized subjects. The essence of anticolonial thought is to challenge ideas or ideologies that are presented in unworkable abstracts, or in idealistic forms, which are more damaging to the psyche than the visible legacy of the original colonial rule.

It is, therefore, crucial that I employ a holistic approach when interrogating colonial and neocolonial education. In the field of postcolonial thought, Frantz Fanon (1967), Edward Said (2003), Linda Smith (1999), and Ngugi Wa Thiongo (1982), just to name a few, are vigorous narrators of the colonized subject. However, I argue that the narratives of colonial knowledge and colonial powers simply cannot be assembled within postcolonial thought because histories of economic exploitation, political coercion or military conquest play a far more constitutional part in anticolonial educational thought.

The agency of anticolonial thought is to search for ways of dismantling colonialism and neocolonialism, both visible and invisible. It is necessary for us to go back to the source and ask ourselves: How has colonialism as a theory, a project, praxis, and discourse, managed to produce and reproduce itself, politically, socially, culturally, materially, and ideologically? I think, as a starting point, we need to take stock of the traces of colonialism in ourselves. To start with, in the field of education, we should note that the cultural apparatus, that is, the language of instruction and the method of delivery are overwhelmingly European.

In order to rupture this doctrinaire attitude, some educators have suggested setting up school councils where students will be introduced to participation in the governance of schools. This way, students, as part of the stakeholders, will be involved in democratic decision making in an education that impacts their lives.

Kenya at Independence

In 1963, Kenya inherited a colonial education that was described as a caste system with rigid boundaries, providing separate and unequal schools for Europeans, Asians, and Africans. Ninety-nine percent of the colonial education budget was spent on European and Asian schools, and just one percent on African schools. The colonial system posed many problems and challenges in terms of quantity, quality, equity, relevance, and utility in the educational structure and philosophy. The colonial system encouraged families to send only boys to schools. What most families resulted in doing was to send only one male child, and especially a child who was not deemed to be lazy when it came to working on the land. Today, majority of families in Kenya send all their children to school regardless of gender. Currently, there is a strong belief that it is essential for girls to attain an education because, as the saying in my Kiembu language states, *Wathomithia muiretu, ni wathomitha mbururi,* which translates to "when you educate a girl, you educate a whole nation."

In 1965, the Kenyan government made a commitment that education would be accessible to all Kenyans without regard to religion, ethnic background, gender, geographical location, race, or class. As I have stated elsewhere (Wane & Opini, 2006), however, in the last two decades the living conditions of the vast majority of Kenyans have stagnated or even worsened. This stagnation is reflected in outcomes in the education system. Many school leavers are unemployed, are dissatisfied with educational services, and those who drop out find themselves on the streets of the major cities (Sifuna, 2000; Wane & Gathenya, 2004; World Bank, 2000). In particular, the number of girls on the street is on the rise. What went wrong? In order for us to understand how education is intertwined with the social, economic, and political structure of the Kenyan state, I provide an overview of precolonial, colonial, and postcolonial educational systems since Kenya attained its political independence in 1963.

African Indigenous Education

To introduce a discussion on democratic indigenous education system in Africa and in particular Kenya may be seen as romanticizing the past, a past that is not quarantined in time and space. Therefore, when I discuss the notion of democratic education among African indigenous people, it must be made clear that this is in relation to what many African scholars such as Cheikh Anta Diop (1996), Aime Cesaire, (1996), Jomo Kenyatta (1965), Asante Molefi (2007), Ifi Amadiume (1987), and George Dei (2000), just to name a few, are reconstructing and arguing for its centrality in African ways of educating their young. There may be similarities and differences; however, there are certain elements that may be applicable to most African societies. Africa is a vast country; however, there are relevant African systems of education and systems of governance, as has been shown by the writings of the above scholars.

Every society, whatever its level of development, has some form of purposeful education. As defined in its broadest sense, education encompasses a conscious attempt to help people live in their society and participate fully and effectively in its organization in order to ensure a continued existence (Wane, 2002). Within most Kenyan communities the purpose of indigenous education was to train youth for the responsibilities of adulthood within that society. The methods of instruction included oral narratives, myths, fables, legends, riddles, and proverbs, as well as observation and participation (Kenyatta, 1965). Both the specific and the broad aims of indigenous education were closely tied to the sociocultural and physical environment of the learner; "it was effective, utilitarian, and relevant to everyday life" (Otiende et al., 2001, p. 9). Indigenous education has been categorized as involving the nonformal, formal, and informal (Bogonko, 1992). Nonformal education involved explicit planning and was implemented through apprenticeship.

There were definite venues, durations, and instructors to carry out indigenous formal education where the participants were provided with knowledge of curative plants (e.g., for headaches, stomachaches, and malaria), as well as plants from which poison could be extracted for killing animals (Otiende et al., 1992, p. 12). Both boys and girls were trained to observe norms and duties that ensured consensus and social stability among the members of society (Kenyatta, 1965; Otiende et al., 1992).

The rites of passage were the final "institutions" of learning. The piercing of the ears for both boys and girls marked the passage from childhood to girl/boyhood. Before this ritual, both boys and girls were under the mother's care. After the piercing of the ears, the boys were placed under the guidance of their fathers, who taught them how to prepare digging sticks, the names of various plants, roots, and their uses especially those that were used as antidotes for insect or snake bites, while the girls were left behind to learn, through role playing, imitation, and observation, their future roles as wives and mothers (Kenyatta, 1965; Sifuna, 1990; Wane, 2005).

As I have mentioned elsewhere (Wane, 2002), these institutions are no longer in place. Between 1993 and 1995, while in Embu interviewing women for my doctoral work, most of the above rites were no longer practiced, either because the practices had been made illegal, the economic hardship could not permit the lavish ceremonial celebrations, or, quite simply, the rite had lost its significance. The loss of traditional practices and the resulting breakdown of the social structures they transmitted and sustained manifest itself in many fissures. The older women complained that the younger generation had lost respect for their elders, and that it was obvious that more boys were given European education than the girls.

For a very long time, Africa has been portrayed in the media, in textbooks, in our schools, and even in informal conversations as a "dark continent." The question that begs to be answered as I listen to these conversations, or watch media representations of the negative aspects of Africa, is: What is the agenda? Why should a continent from which we all originated be condemned overwhelmingly by the majority of peoples in the world? Is it ignorance, or is it done on purpose?

I do not have space in this chapter to articulate Africa's contributions to world civilization, and in particular in the area of education. However, Molefi Kete Asante's (2000, 2007) work provides engaging information about the philosophical thought of ancient Africa, as well as the history of Africa. Unfortunately, such books will not find themselves in our school system. Cheikh Anta Diop (1986) is another scholar who has provided detailed structures of what Africa was, how it was destroyed, and how much it has contributed to what we have around the world today. However, again, none of these contributions is acknowledged in our education system. Is it any wonder, then, that in people's imagination of Africa, all that they can see is backwardness and primitivity? Many scholars of African ancestry have stressed various aspects of indigenous education and how it can be incorporated in today's education system.

Democracy is not genetic, and according to Harber and Serf (2006), it is learned behavior. However, unless our education system has a clear idea of what sort of democratic person it hopes to cultivate, in relation to their culture and background, the outcome will be a citizenry that is very undemocratic in its governance as well as in ways of thinking. According to Harber and Serf (2006),

> a democratic person should celebrate social and political diversity, work for and practice mutual respect between individuals and groups, regard all people as having equal social and political rights as human being, respect evidence in forming their own opinions and respect the opinion of others based on evidence. (p. 987)

As mentioned above, this is not what we are witnessing today in Africa. There is a rupture between the traditional and modern social structure. The older women resent the fact that they have no say in shaping the lives of the future generation. They can feel the resistance when they try to talk to them and offer advice. In most instances, they are ignored and regarded as ignorant and backward because they were not schooled in the European modes of education (Wane, 2003). What this means is that all decisions about education are not conceptualized democratically. If education has to promote a democratic way of thinking, there needs to be input not only from the students, but also from the elders in the villages who have never been to anybody's school. Maruatona (2006) indicates that democracy can be achieved in Africa as a whole despite its diversity and difference. Maruatona makes the argument that "it is possible to organize effective educational programs that engage African communities in deliberative democracy for social transformation" (p.11), and that this type of democracy involves "the interaction of all voices within a community in the making and executing collective decisions" (p. 11).

Colonial Education

It is important to highlight that any discussion on colonial education has raised many questions in relation to whether it benefited the indigenous people—in this particular case, African—or if it robbed them of their very existence (Wane, 2006a, 2006b). Different studies have indicated that colonial education improved the lives of African women. However, Chege and Sifuna (2006) state that, "while the existence of a dominant patriarchal arrangement was true for many traditional African communities, the claim that the underlying ideology translated exclusively into the exploitation of women is inaccurate" (p. 19). They suggest that such claims are conspicuously silent on matriarchal societies in Africa where gender relations comprised a type of balance of a power between female and male. In addition, most studies do not address the ways in which colonial administrations used models of Western education to propagate female inferiority, exploitation, and oppression (Chege, 2001).

The encounter between the colonizer and colonized resulted in an education that completely ignored the customary and cultural relevance of traditional African education. The presence of gendered communities provided the missionaries, as well as colonial administration, with easy spaces in which indoctrination could take place. It was in these spaces that missionaries deconstructed African masculinities and femininities and reconstructed them as polar opposites (Chege & Sifuna, 2006). The men were offered a type of education that prepared them to be vocational and blue-collar workers, while the women were introduced to domestic "science" designed to cater to low intellectual ability, with the aim of gradually transmitting values of humility and low ambition (Assie-Lumumba, 1994, p. 27). This education entailed learning to be a good wife, bake cakes, clean and look after the children. It did not take into consideration that women had to take care of the family plot, since the formal indoctrination for men took them away from family settings into cities or settler farms. The outcome was a

> complex scenario in which traditional gender relations were transformed in a manner
> that has been difficult to undo, even several decades after the attainment of political
> independence. The effects of colonial and missionary gendering processes that were

ingrained in, and perpetuated through, Western education have continued to plague
the Kenyan education system into the 21st Century. (Chege & Sifuna, 2006, p. 19)

The gender discrimination in education in the pre-independence period
shows that the colonial, capitalist economy was designed around racial and
gender ideologies of oppression and exploitation. The African woman, more
than the man, was systematically and deliberately discriminated against
(Chege & Sifuna, 2006). The colonial administration deemed the domestic
work performed by females did not need formal education to do it. Chege
and Sifuna also noted that the colonial administration was quick to blame
traditional cultural norms for the low participation of females in formal
education. It is important to note that the colonial administration did not act
alone in enforcing education policy that discriminated against girls. The
traditional leaders, who were benefiting from colonial administration, wholly
supported the systemic marginalization of girls. The new system favored
men, and, as a result, many parents did not send their daughters to school,
preferring to educate their boys.

Education since 1963

Since independence in 1963, the Kenyan government has expressed its desire,
in various policy documents, to provide education to all citizens. Soon after
independence, it responded to the problem of human resource development
with a major expansion in both primary and secondary education. The 1964
Ominde Report (Sifuna, 2000) was the first of such initiatives, providing a
framework for a unified education system in independent Kenya. There have
been subsequent education commissions, such as the Gachathi Report (1976),
the Mackay Report (1981), the Kamunge Report (1988), and the Kenya
Country Report (1999), along with others, all of which emphasized the
educational goals laid down in the 1964 report: foster national unity; promote
social justice and social obligations and responsibilities; foster positive
attitudes and consciousness toward other nations; and provide and equip the
youth with knowledge, skills, and expertise to enable them to play an
effective role in the life of the nation.

The 8–4–4 System of Education Curriculum

The current 8–4–4 system of education consists of 8 years of primary, 4 years of secondary, and 4 years of a basic bachelor's degree. The overall responsibility of managing education in the country rests with the Ministry of Education. With the 8–4–4 system, standard eight school-leavers have opportunities for further technical training, which would enable them to attain higher technical skills or be self-employed. Government policy for financing education is shaped around the principles of cost sharing where parents, the communities, NGOs, religious organizations, donors, and the government all provide resources. However, even though there is this kind of partnership, currently the heaviest responsibility lies with parents, religious organizations, and community efforts (Chege & Sifuna, 2006).

Assessment of Primary Education

Primary education in Kenya is supposed to be universal and free but is not compulsory. Attaining Universal Primary Education (UPE) by 2005 was a national goal in Kenya. Prior to 2003, primary education was a mirage for most Kenyan children, many of whom could not afford registration fees, books, and charges for the maintenance of facilities. The basic goals of primary education are to impart literacy and numeracy, develop an understanding of economic production factors and their relationship with social context and the natural environment, promote social equity, including females, in disadvantaged communities, and lay a firm foundation for lifelong learning.

The purpose of these goals is to have a citizenry that is schooled with democratic values. Notwithstanding the fact that education does not always produce the citizenry we want, properly planned education experiences are prerequisites for involvement of all members of the community in the political process. I believe that it is the responsibility of all educators to facilitate an education that empowers people through their democratic participation at all levels of governance. As Maruatona (2006), arguing for adult education, states, "educators need to engage the citizenry in process of deliberative democracy by working with them to extend the 'public spaces' in their countries" (p. 20).

In 2003 when the government introduced Free Primary Education (FPE), enrolment in primary education increased by 17.9 percent, from 6.131 million in 2002 to 7.2003 million in 2003. The primary completion rate for 2000/01–2002/03 was 56 percent (Chege & Sifuna, 2006; Sifuna, 2000). In spite of the rising number of pupils enrolled in primary schools, the gross enrolment rate (GER) has declined from 48.7 percent in 1990 to 48.5 percent in 2003. The percentage of girls' enrolment also increased to 48.5 percent, implying that gender parity in enrolment in primary schools at the national level has nearly been achieved. The completion rate is also one of the measures of retention in school. In Kenya, completion rates reached the 50 percent mark in 2001, meaning that, out of the children who enroll in the first year, over 47.4 percent do not complete the primary school cycle. Significantly, the completion rate has risen from 43.2 percent in 1990 to 52.6 percent in 2001, representing a 9 percent increase. The gender imbalances have been minimal, in favor of boys for most years except for 1998, 2000, and 2001, where the girls' enrolment rate was higher.

Transition from primary to secondary school has never gone beyond 40 percent since 1990. In addition, the rate for girls has always been lower than that of boys. This implies that girls are dropping out of the education system before reaching secondary level of education more often than boys.

Discussion

Women have been denied equal access to education with men since colonial times. The colonial administration wanted to ensure that women participated in mostly reproductive services at the family level and also as providers of cheap casual labor. The relative enrolment rates for girls in both primary and secondary schools have, however, improved over the four decades. It is interesting to note that it costs more to educate a girl than a boy because of the so-called opportunity cost. In most communities children participate in farming, selling produce in the market, and domestic chores. Although all children are expected to participate in family labor, when it comes to childcare, girls are more likely to be involved than boys. Therefore, when girls are sent to school, it costs the family twice as much, since they lose her labor as well as having to pay fees. In addition, poor rural families send their daughters to cities to work as domestic help in exchange for regular cash income. In most cases, this income is used to educate the boys. It is important to note that when money is scarce, parents prefer to invest in their sons' education to higher levels because of the anticipated economic returns. Most families elect to have boys sent for further studies because of patrilineal inheritance systems. Parents are committed to the continuation of their family names and they are aware that the education given to the girls is lost to the family once they get married and take up the husband's family name (Odaga & Heneveld, 1995).

In some cases, families are forced to choose as to who should be sent to school due to scarcity of resources and they usually decide to send the best-performing children. Often girls do not do well because of the many responsibilities imposed on them. In most cases girls face inequities in the classroom; as well, teachers use them to assist with cooking and cleaning the teacher's house. Girls often have higher dropout rates than boys because of household responsibilities, child labor, higher opportunity cost to the family, long distances to schools from girls' homes, early marriage and/or pregnancy, the threat of sexual harassment and violence in school and en route to school (see Wane & Opini, 2006), lack of girl-friendly facilities, gender discriminatory teaching and learning methods, and parents and communities who are convinced of the value of education for girls. Poverty is clearly interrelated with child labor; one of the most common reasons for children, especially girls, not to attend school is that their families need them to work.

While walking long distances, often through remote fields and forests away from the main thoroughfares, girls are more susceptible to sexual harassment and other forms of violence than boys, making parents cautious. In many cases, it is often deemed appropriate for girls to be accompanied by a parent or relative if the school is far from the village. In provinces in the arid and semi-arid regions, enrolment is low. The people who live in these regions are pastoralists, and during the colonial period they had very little contact with colonial economy or missionaries. Their way of life was least affected by the capitalist economy and, as a result, they remained insulated from some of the more direct impacts of colonialism (Nathani, 1996).

To achieve educational goals, the government of Kenya needs to rekindle the spirit of *Harambee*, self-reliance, in an environment of improved professional work ethics and commitment to providing basic services both for individual and public good. The African philosophy of mutual respect, responsibility, and accountability means the government can count on its peoples' support and vice versa, only if both parties are ready to keep their side of the bargain. Only then can the government hope to deliver the promise made at the attainment of independence in 1963 to ensure equitable distribution of resources including equal access to education regardless of class, race, creed, ethnicity, and geographical location.

There is a powerful correlation between low enrolment, poor retention, and unsatisfactory learning outcomes and this requires nothing less than the integration of gender, class, regional, and other equality concerns into the design and implementation of relevant intersector policies and strategies. The importance of gathering and carefully analyzing reliable desegregated data at local, national, and international levels is evident. Flexible instruments for such data collection and analysis mean better representation of peripherized groups. According to Wamahiu (1997), a multiplicity of interrelated factors contributes to the underparticipation (nonenrollment, lower persistence, and poorer performance) of girls in formal and nonformal education programs in Kenya. A complex interplay of macro-level policy and micro-level practices, beliefs, and attitudes determine whether households and communities feel it profitable to educate their daughters. A pervasive patriarchal ideology influences policy and practice at the national, community, and school level, marginalizing Kenyan girls in education. This situation is a major contributor to Kenya's current social problems and its exponential effects are steadily eroding the country's ability to develop, grow, and become self-sustaining.

Questions for Reflection:

1. What are the barriers to implementing equitable educational policies that dwell on democratic rights of the people?

2. What do equitable democratic policies mean in relation to African culture, philosophy and indigenous education?

3. Why have democratic educational policies failed to bring about gender equity in Kenya?

4.   Discuss the relative power of teachers, students, administrators, school boards and communities to make decisions with regard to the implementation of democratic policies in education. Who does and does not have power?

5.   Discuss the complexities of negotiating the boundaries between indigenous forms of education and contemporary, Western forms of education.

References

Asante, M. K. (2000). *The Egyptian philosophers: Ancient African voices from Imhotep to Akhenaten*. Chicago: African Images.

————. (2007). *Cheikh Anta Diop: An intellectual portrait*. Los Angeles: University of Sankore Press.

Assie-Lumumba, N. T. (1994). Demand, access, and equity issues in Africa higher education: Past policies, current practices, and readiness for the 21st century. Paper prepared for Donors to African Education Working Group on Higher Education, New York, and Cornell University.

Bogonko, S. N. (1992). *Reflections on education in East Africa*. Nairobi, Kenya: Oxford University Press.

Chege, F. (2001). Gender *values, schooling and transition to adulthood: A study of female and male pupils from two urban primary schools in Kenya*. Unpublished doctoral dissertation, University of Cambridge, UK.

Chege, F., & Sifuna, D. (2006). *Girls' and women's education in Kenya: Gender perspectives and trends*. Nairobi, Kenya: UNESCO.

Harber, C., & Serf, J. (2006). Teacher education for a democratic society in England and South Africa. *Teaching and Teacher Education, 22*, 986–997.

Kaunda, Z., & Kendall, N. (2002). Prospects of educating for democracy in struggling third wave regimes: The case of Malawi. *Current Issues in Comparative Education, 4*(2), 36–51.

Kenyatta, J. (1965). *Facing Mount Kenya*. New York: Vintage.

Maruatona, T. (2006). Adult education, deliberative democracy and social re-engagement in Africa. *Journal of Developing Societies, 22*(11), 11–19.

Nathani, N. (1996). *Sustainable development: Indigenous forms of food processing technologies: A Kenyan case study*. Unpublished doctoral dissertation, University of Toronto.

Odaga, A., & Heneveld, W. (1995). *Girls and schools in sub-Saharan Africa: From analysis to action* [Technical Paper No. 298]. Washington, DC: World Bank.

Otiende, J., Okello, G., & Bennaars, G. (2001). *Peak revision KCSE social education and ethics*. Nairobi: East African Educational.

Republic of Kenya. (1964/1965). *Kenya education commission report, Part I & II* [aka Ominde Report]. Nairobi, Kenya: Government Printer.

————. (1965). African socialism and its applications to planning in Kenya. Nairobi, Kenya: Government Printer.

————. (1988). Report of the presidential working party on education and manpower training for the next decade and beyond [aka Kamunge Report]. Nairobi, Kenya: Government Printer.

————. (1999). *Report of the presidential commission on the review of the education* [aka Koech Report]. Nairobi, Kenya: Government Printer.

Sifuna, D. N. (1990). Development of education in Africa: The Kenyan experience. Nairobi, Kenya: Initiatives.

Sifuna, D. N. (2000). Education for democracy and human rights in African schools: The Kenyan experience. *African Development, 25*(1/2), 213–239.

Wamahiu, S. P. (1997). *The empowerment of girls and women through education: The Kenya situation.* Background paper prepared for the Forum for African Women Educationalists, International Women's Day, Nairobi, Kenya.

Wane, N. N. (2002, March). *The quest for education in postcolonial Kenya: Sharing educational experiences.* Paper presented at the 46th annual meeting of the Comparative and International Education Society, Orlando, FL

————. (2005). Claiming, writing, storing, sharing African indigenous knowledge. *Journal of Thought, 40*(2), 27–46.

————. (2006a). Inclusive education and anti-racist classroom practice in a teacher education program. In G. S. Dei and M. Lordan, (Eds.), *Poetics of anti-racist education* (pp.130–148). Halifax, Nova Scotia: Fernwood.

————. (2006b). Social organization and primary and secondary teacher education in Africa. In A. A. Abdi & A. Cleghorn (Eds.), *Sociology of education: African perspectives* (pp. 275–296). New York. Palgrave MacMillan.

Wane, N. N., & Gathenya, W. (2004). The yokes of gender and class: The policy reforms and implications for equitable access to education in Kenya. *Managing Global Transitions, 1*(2), 169–194.

Wane, N. N., & Opini, B. (2006). An exploration of gendered violence in Kenyan schools. *Eastern African Journal of Humanities and Sciences, 6*(2), 44–66.

World Bank. (2000). Ecuador gender review: Issues and recommendations. Washington DC: World Bank.

12

THE ROLE OF SCIENCE EDUCATION IN FOSTERING DEMOCRACY: PERSPECTIVES OF FUTURE TEACHERS

Sarah Elizabeth Barrett and Martina Nieswandt

Introduction

An important aspect of fostering democracy through education is teaching for social justice; translating into an education in civic ethics with the responsibility to promote both economic justice and the equitable distribution of political power within society. Such an education seeks to develop in students (1) a sense of ethical responsibility to fellow citizens; (2) empowerment to act; and (3) knowledge to act wisely. It follows that teaching *science* for social justice involves the consideration of, and developing courses of, action to address the following issues:

> (a) the environmental ramifications of science and technology, (b) the uneven distribution of the benefits of science and technology to those who are less economically powerful, (c) the under-representation of women and minorities in science and technology fields and science curricula and for those contemplating a career in science, (d) becoming scientists who consider the ramifications of their experimental and theoretical work and take some responsibility for the applications of their research. (Barrett, 2007, p. 1)

This emphasis on the interactions between science and society and the social aspects of science practice can be seen as a science education that attempts to help students "read the world" (Freire, 2000b). By portraying science as practice, subject to the same ethical considerations as any other human endeavor rather than treating science as a canon of knowledge extracted from nature, teachers can help students make connections between their science study and issues related to science (socioscientific issues) in their lives.

A case in point is climate change and the interactions between individual citizens, the media, the scientific community, privately funded think-tanks, industry, the United Nations, and individual governments tackling the problem. The fundamental background knowledge with respect to climate change is chemistry. However, now that the science behind the problem has essentially been settled (Intergovernmental Panel on Climate Change, Working Group 1, 2007), controversy remains over what should be done.[1] Citizens will be making important decisions on these issues in the near future and science education should support their participation in the debate.

To engage students in critical discussions about socioscientific issues requires science teachers who are transformative intellectuals (Giroux, 1988), who encourage students to be critical of the assumptions underlying everything they learn in school. To navigate the inevitable resistance of students and the system to such fundamental critique requires a great deal of skill and support (hooks, 1994).

Advanced studies in the physical sciences are a problematic place from which to learn those skills. Socioscientific issues are rarely discussed in senior physical science courses in high schools (Cross & Price, 1996), possibly because science teachers assume that students will take what they learn in science, and apply it to the content of social studies courses, where controversial issues are expected to be discussed. Unfortunately, we suspect that it is rare that science-related issues are raised in social studies classes. Also, the form of science education, especially in the senior grades, does not support these discussions. Science courses are traditionally taught using a transmission model of instruction where students are encouraged to be passive recipients of prepackaged knowledge as opposed to engaged creators and interrogators of knowledge. This "banking method" (Freire, 2000a) of teaching can act as a barrier to fostering agency in students. With very little recognition of ethical issues involving interactions between the overlapping groups of scientists, governments, citizens, and industry (Cross & Price, 1996) and little acknowledgment of vested interests, winners and losers, or societal consequences (Bencze, 2001), an intellectual disconnect is created between science content and societal issues, which can seriously undermine students' ability to connect the skills and knowledge gained through social studies courses with what is learned in science courses (Somerville, 2006).

Therefore, science teacher candidates arrive at teacher education programs with little experience tackling socioscientific issues in science classrooms and varying degrees of understanding of what teaching science for social justice would entail. This chapter analyzes the efforts of three teacher candidates to reconcile their understandings of teaching science for social justice with the demands of the existing school context.

Methodology

After obtaining the necessary consents, we interviewed 12 teacher candidates enrolled in physics and chemistry curriculum method courses in a 9-month teacher education program at a large university in Southern Ontario. The interviews occurred three times throughout the 9-month program: in September, October, and March. The first interview focused on their academic background, the second on their experiences both at the faculty of education and during their practice teaching, and the third focused on reflection about their experiences (Seidman, 1991). In every interview, the participants were asked to clarify their answers from the previous interview, express their beliefs about the place of ethics in science education. Triangulation was achieved through this prolonged engagement and working with 12 teacher candidates with respect to the same concept (Lincoln & Guba, 1985). All interviews were audiotaped and fully transcribed.

We used a constant comparative method of analysis (Strauss & Corbin, 1990) to discern themes from the transcripts. These were collapsed into larger themes. One of the major themes was teaching for social justice, on which we focus in the following results.

Findings and Analysis

Through analysis of the interview data, we discerned three different approaches taken by teacher candidates attempting to teach science for social justice. In the following, we concentrate on the interview data of 3 out of the

12 participants, chosen because they provided vivid representations of these three approaches.

• *Nadeem's Cognitive Approach*

Nadeem[3] is a South Asian man in his early 40s. A certified engineer, he was deeply concerned about social and economic oppression and environmental degradation. He attributed this awareness to his having grown up in a developing country—a place where people are relatively poor and relatively expensive energy tends to be conserved—and immigrated to Canada—a place where people are relatively wealthy and relatively cheap energy tends to be wasted (Monbiot & Prescott, 2006).

Nadeem had earned a Master's degree in electrical engineering, specializing in telecommunications. As in all contemporary engineering programs, discussions about social responsibility and ethics were a mandatory part of his studies. Upon reflection, he interpreted this aspect of his studies in the following way, as pertaining to

> how you would use your skills for the betterment of the society and the nation and humanity in general … and not to use this knowledge or apply it to things that are detrimental to the society or the country.

Thus, Nadeem's conception of an engineer involved having a professional responsibility, not only to avoid harm, but also to improve society. It was not difficult for him to take the next mental step and assume that this was the role of scientists as well. He was a great admirer of scientists and philosophers, such as Galileo, Socrates, and Einstein. In his view, they had changed the course of history by remaining faithful to the social, spiritual, and political implications of their research rather than giving in to those in power who felt threatened by those implications or chose to ignore them. He attributed their conviction to clear thinking saying:

> Science can never be stifled. Science is a product of human curiosity. By passing a dictum or making a law today or rule today, nothing can ever be stopped. That experiment has been tried and failed…. Such things always fail.

Thus, Nadeem seemed to believe that science education could support democracy by teaching students to think clearly and honestly about issues:

> Understanding science helps you to think logically. This skill you can apply to other issues in life.... And I believe that when you have clarity of thought, it carries on. It is not just restricted to that particular academic course. You apply those skills to other facets of your life.

Though perhaps naïve about clarity of thought automatically translating into ethical action (Martin, 1994), he was obviously aware of the ways science practice could be politically manipulated or its discoveries misrepresented for the sake of money or power. Here, he discusses the automobile:

> This has caused so many problems. It degrades our environment. It is ruining our atmosphere ... yet the Orthodox Fossil Fuel Lobby still latches onto it.... Alternate methods are not encouraged because their economy would be cut.... Students at the high school level or even earlier at the middle school level should be made aware of all these issues.

To this end, Nadeem's planned strategy was to bring issues into his teaching to make students aware of them and to provide time for discussion. However, once Nadeem began practice teaching, he seemed to be pressured to cover the traditional content in the curriculum—theories, equations, and facts. With regard to senior physics courses, he noted:

> I initiated the dialogue on nuclear power. How whether it is okay.... I wanted to even discuss the nuclear waste disposal. But then I didn't have time. I was there only for a month and I did not want to digress very much from the topic because, actually, it was not my class.

One can see here that he either viewed the nuclear waste disposal question as a diversion from the prescribed curriculum or assumed his associate teacher would see it as so. Yet, within the Ontario curriculum, the learning expectation pertaining to nuclear power is described in the following way:

Analyze, using their own or given criteria, the *economic, social, and environmental impact* of various energy sources … and energy-transformation technologies (e.g., hydroelectric power plants and energy transformations produced by other renewable sources, fossil fuel, and *nuclear power plants*) used around the world [emphasis added]. (Ontario Ministry of Education and Training, 2000, p. 94)

Like many science teachers (Hughes, 2000), Nadeem ignored the official curriculum even though it supported his professed agenda. Instead, he enacted the traditional conception of science education, where facts and theories are the priority and applications and context are extras (Carlone, 2004). Clearly, the pressure to prioritize abstract over context did not come solely from the official curriculum. Nadeem recognized one other source but it is worth quoting him at length to show how he interpreted it:

The heat was always left on [in the portable] even when there was no class....but then when I did bring it up in the classroom, many students said, "Who cares whether I switch it off or not? I don't care." Which I thought needed more debating, but then there was no time for it because … actually the curriculum load is so much that there is less time for anything other than what is in the curriculum. And as a teacher, you are always racing against time to reach the curriculum expectations. So very little time is left for any other kind of a debate.

Here, faced with student apathy, Nadeem again invokes the problem of a loaded curriculum and time constraints, and this time he was teaching mathematics during his practice teaching. He does not consider the ways that schooling itself encourages students' apathy (Freire, 2000a). Nor does he question the legitimacy of the traditional prioritizing of abstract theories and facts over the socioscientific issues of energy conservation that he has already shown he understands to be urgent. He also appears to assume that a debate, a weighing of different viewpoints, was all that was necessary to address the students' attitudes. Nadeem said that, once he had his own class, it would be sufficient to introduce the topic and give students some time to talk about it with each other. Given his conception of scientists as active citizens and science as unstoppable in its quest for knowledge, Nadeem appeared to believe two things: (1) science, when done properly, is clear, unprejudiced thought, and (2) if you train the mind, appropriate actions will follow. Yet we know that science, because it is done by people, can never be completely unprejudiced (Bell & Lederman, 2003). Also, science students do not tend to connect their science knowledge to thinking about socioscientific issues without explicit instruction (Sadler, 2004). Nadeem's cognitive approach that aims only to provide students with skills to think and facts to inform that thinking leaves much to be desired.

Maura's Activist Approach

Maura is a White woman in her late 20s. She majored in physics in university, and worked in engineering for a while before leaving to teach English as a Second Language (ESL) abroad and locally. She then entered the Bachelor of Education program. She did not recall ever talking about ethical issues in science courses. Instead, she developed a sense of activism from her friends in high school and university. She described one incident in her late adolescence that has shaped her view of citizenship. She related the incident in the following way:

> [My friend, Carol] ... tried to get everyone to stop drinking Pepsi[4] in high school.... It became maybe the first stand that I took on something.... Pepsi actually left Burma.... [Carol] really fought really hard and actually made a difference. And to think that I had participated in that, in some way, was definitely very moving.

Maura went on to describe other incidents in the university where she and her friends had been activists on one issue or another. Throughout her life, Maura's parents also encouraged her to participate in causes that were important to her, whether they were protecting the rainforest in British Columbia from destruction, Amnesty International, or product boycotts. However, she complained that the high school should have been more involved in helping her to be an active citizen, and she wanted to correct this through her own teaching. She declared:

> Teachers should be responsible for helping students become good citizens and socially responsible and it would be careless and irresponsible not to consider ethical issues related to science and technology.

Maura's strong words indicate dissatisfaction with her own experiences as a student. Her political activities had been completely separate and in spite of her studies in physics. Her first recognition of this gap occurred one summer, when she worked at a nuclear power plant as a researcher and teacher.

> When I would be using the resources at [the Nuclear Power Plant] to plan my lessons or my research, [I was] looking at it and thinking, "How much of this is propaganda and how much of this is science?" That was kind of shocking for me, thinking that way. I had been so used to—just coming out of university—not thinking about that, about my resources, whether they're biased or not.

This was perhaps the first time that Maura had considered the ways in which politics and/or vested interests are involved in the reporting of scientific data. She had never before considered that the origin of scientific statements might be relevant. Yet she still did not focus on the politics of science. She stated that the most important thing for her to encourage her students to do was to act. She said:

> The only way for people to get involved in making decisions or instigating change in the world is through action. I think a lot of people aren't active because [issues] can be intimidating or it can be difficult to figure out where to put that action in order to get change. It's not easy to give students hope that their action can be successful in instigating change, that their voice does matter.

Maura, then, seemed to believe that recognizing issues was not enough. She needed to help her students to feel empowered to act. With encouragement and guidance from significant adults, such as their teachers, students might be able to handle the difficulties that were sure to arise. This aspect of her role as a teacher was essentially extracurricular. That is, disconnected from the science that she would be teaching:

> It's just so hard to get through everything that you need to get through to meet the curriculum expectations from the Ministry and to get all your topics and to make them fun but to realize you have to move on to the next unit and then you only have a certain amount of time.... But I still think these things are obviously important. I'm just realizing that they definitely get shoved to the back when you're a new teacher.

Maura has failed to acknowledge that socioscientific issues are already a part of the "curriculum expectations from the Ministry." Also, we would argue that Maura had trouble imagining what fostering democracy through science teaching would look like because she had always separated her science studies from her political activities. Consequently, she did not teach her students to make connections between science concepts/topics and social justice issues, as defined in this chapter's introduction. Instead, she emphasized skills her students would need to be effective activists in society.

It is unclear whether Maura was aware of the resistance she might encounter if she attempted to do this in a school. Activist teachers are often marginalized within their schools and are prone to burn-out (hooks, 1994). Their emphasis on the school community and broader social issues is seen as undermining their ability to teach what is valued by the system (Sernak, 2006). Yet, Maura's focus seemed to be on issues safely removed from her own life and work; therefore, we suspect that the school system would regard her efforts as benign. Maura's activist approach to teaching for social justice, then, was to emphasize action without making explicit connections to school curriculum or even, necessarily, to students' personal lives.

Richard's Critical Approach

Richard is a White man in his late 20s. He grew up near a First Nations reserve, an experience that he claimed sharpened his awareness of economic inequities. After completing a master's degree in chemistry, Richard taught English overseas before returning to Canada to attend the Faculty of Education. Richard viewed civic ethics in terms of power relations related to socioeconomic status. To him, science was suspect because of its privileged status, and needed to be overhauled. Therefore, Richard wished to change science by teaching his students to critique what he called a *culture of privilege*:

> One of the big problems with the society we have is that science has become like the new religion. It's not questioned enough. The answers are given and also considered to be as good as gospel. And I think that we need to start teaching students that it's not always the right answer that's given to you so you need to ask more questions.

Thus, Richard viewed science as inherently political. He was keenly aware of the ways that his being White, male, heterosexual, and middle class made it easier for him to become a part of that culture. He said that he wanted to help his students to understand and recognize their privilege, as well:

> Saying, by example, that I'm a privileged White male … I will use that language often in a class just to get them to understand that I really do see myself as someone who has had that extra privilege and with that privilege I have a responsibility. So, when I carry myself in that way, a lot of students end up nodding their heads and they start to talk to me about the sorts of things that I'm passionate about and they start to get the feeling that maybe these things are important to think about.

Of all of the participants, Richard was most successful at bringing societal issues into his science teaching. In his first practicum, he began each class with what he called "Taste of Reality." This activity involved introducing stories that had appeared in the news and initiating discussions with students. For a special program designed for at-risk students[5] in which he taught, he also designed a Web quest for students to calculate their ecological footprints and begin to determine ways to reduce them. With his senior chemistry class, he initiated discussions about the ways scientists needed to take responsibility for their research. He said his "at-risk" students seemed to respond enthusiastically to his approach while the senior academic students gave him the answers they thought he wanted without seeming to understand. He explained this in the following way:

> It's pretty easy to get students that don't have privilege to recognize that they don't have privilege. It's very difficult to get students who have privilege to recognize that they have privilege.

Langhout, Rosselli, and Feinstein's (2007) research on perceptions of classism found that, while those of lower social classes were definitely more aware of classism than the middle-class students, upper-class students were also aware of classism which suggested to the researchers that what is considered normal (i.e., middle class) is invisible to students. There are similar findings with respect to race and gender (see O'Brien, Kopala, & Martinez-Pons, 1999). What all of this indicates is that Richard's interpretation of his students' reactions to his approach may have been oversimplified.

What was problematic about Richard's approach was his denial of his own power over the students because of his authority as a teacher. He stated that, due to time constraints, he did not make a point of presenting a balanced view about the issues discussed in class. That is, his lessons were designed to give a specific political message with respect to the consequences of privilege and the problematic nature of current science practice. In the face of this obvious bias, his senior students may have sought to avoid conflict in order to protect their marks.

At the end of his first practice teaching experience, he seemed quite confident in his approach to teaching for social justice. During his second practicum, however, Richard was removed from the school after only one day. The principal and his associate teacher did not appreciate the way he taught so as to challenge "the hierarchy between student and teacher," as he described it. This experience made him a little more cautious:

> It's going to be a juggling act. You have to have balance in there. So, before I thought, "Oh, [ethics] needs to be in every lesson. It needs to be there. It has to be in there. Brainwash these students...." I'm beginning to realize that there has to be a mix in there.... You have to have that kind of mix of social justice, global education and then you also have to worry about them being able to be successful in university. So, I guess I'm learning more about the combination of everything and how it's got to work.

The interesting aspect of this quote is that Richard seemed to conclude that teaching science for social justice was at odds with preparing students to be successful in university. Richard's approach lacked a recognition that even the school system in which he would eventually be teaching was deeply invested in the culture of privilege that he wished to challenge. Indeed, Barton and Yang (2000) described the culture of science education as a *culture of power* designed to teach students to fit into a predetermined hierarchy. Further, in his enthusiasm to get on with his project to encourage the students to restructure an unjust society, Richard may have undermined his students' ability to think about issues he introduced by not presenting different perspectives (Fine, 1993). He essentially attempted to encourage critique with knowledge designed to produce foregone conclusions, and his own actions were ineffective because he lacked political savvy.

Conclusions: Three Aspects of Teaching for Social Justice

At the beginning of this chapter, we described teaching for social justice as seeking to develop in students: a sense of ethical responsibility to fellow citizens; empowerment to act; and knowledge to act wisely. When the three approaches of the teacher candidates are placed together, as they are in Table 1, one can see how each approach has one of the aspects of teaching for social justice as its defining goal.

Table 1 - Three approaches to teaching science for social justice

Approach	Emphasis for student learning	Goals for student outcomes
Cognitive	Developing clear thought and analyzing information	Knowledge to act wisely
Activist	Learning to enact their political agendas in their lives and communities	Empowerment to act
Critical	Questioning the power relations inherent in science practice and society	Sense of responsibility for fellow citizens

Each of the teacher candidates' approaches to teaching science to foster democracy was somewhat ineffective because it neglected one or more aspects of teaching for social justice. Nadeem's focus on knowledge left the problematic social structures—from which science is not immune—intact without helping students to channel what they had learned into action. Maura's approach focused on action but made no connection to science knowledge and involved very little critique. Richard's approach downplayed information that did not support his agenda, leaving his students unprepared to respond to societal resistance and translate their critique into action. Richard, himself, was a case in point due to his own underestimation of the effects of hegemony within the school system. In short, neither cognitive, activist, nor critical approaches are effective on their own. We hesitate to view cognitive, activist, and critical approaches in some sort of developmental hierarchy, however. Each approach is an important aspect of teaching for social justice—knowledge, action, and critique. If one is deemphasized, the entire effort suffers (Bogdan, 1994; Delpit, 1988; Hodson, 1999).

Implications

As teacher educators, the purpose of this analysis is to help determine what each teacher candidate needs to teach science successfully for social justice. Teacher candidates espousing a cognitive approach, as most teachers do (Hodson, 2003), need to be made aware of the ways that the structure of science education and schooling itself renders the possibility of students acting on their knowledge unlikely without more support and guidance. Activist teachers, while politically savvy about how to get things done, need help recognizing science's implications in social justice issues. All teacher candidates need help recognizing and working around the hegemony within the school system.

Strategies that can be used in teacher education programs include examining case studies, reading and discussing books like this one, and/or pairing teacher candidates in their practice teaching to provide support and ongoing debriefing of their experiences in small group settings (see Solomon & Levine-Rasky, 2003, for an example of such a strategy). To be successful at teaching for social justice, teacher candidates need help implementing all three aspects—knowledge, action, and critique. The key is for teacher educators to recognize that their students arrive with limited experience viewing science education in this way. Supports need to be provided throughout the first few years of teaching whenever possible and becoming a transformative intellectual (Giroux, 1988) needs to be viewed as a work in progress.

Questions for Reflection

1.   Describe the pros and cons of the three different approaches to teaching for social justice.

2. Why does the way science is taught affect the way science issues are considered by society?

3. Given the seriousness of science-related issues, such as climate change, should science teachers be forced to bring these topics into their teaching? To what extent should social justice issues related to this or any topic be mandated within the science curriculum?

4. Teachers encouraging their students to be politically active is controversial. Yet, some argue that the school is the perfect place for young people to practice activism in a safe environment. In what ways could teaching activism foster or undermine democracy?

5. Discuss ideas about how to integrate teaching for social justice into teacher education and professional development programs.

Notes

1. See Monbiot and Prescott's (2006) book, *Heat*, for a description of how the oil industry and its representatives successfully lobbied the governments of industrialized countries not to do anything about climate change.

2. Many authors have already done so. See, for example, Barrett and Pedretti (2006), Bencze (2001), Carter (2005), and Pedretti and Hodson (1995).

3. All names are pseudonyms.

4. Burma's politics at the time allowed workers to be employed at wages that were considered to be unacceptable by the international community. Pepsi was a company that had factories in Burma at the time.

5. Richard was unclear about the criteria used to identify these students as "at risk" and did not seem to question it. He said that according to his associate teacher, all of the students had a high risk of dropping out of school. Based on student comments about their personal lives, Richard stated that this was because of their low socioeconomic status and living in neighborhoods with a high concentration of public housing and high level of crime.

References

Barrett, S. E. (2007). *Teacher candidates' beliefs about including socioscientific issues in physics and chemistry*. Unpublished doctoral dissertation, University of Toronto, Toronto.

Barrett, S. E., & Pedretti, E. (2006). Contrasting orientations: STSE for social reconstruction or social reproduction? *School Science and Mathematics, 106*(5), 21–31.

Barton, A. C., & Yang, K. (2000). The culture of power and science education: Learning from Miguel. *Journal of Research in Science Teaching, 37*(8), 871–889.

Bell, R. L., & Lederman, N. G. (2003). Understandings of the nature of science and decision making on science and technology based issues. *Science Education, 83*, 352–377.

Bencze, L. (2001). "Technoscience" education: Empowering citizens against the tyranny of school science. *International Journal of Technology and Design Education, 11*, 273–298.

Bogdan, D. (1994). When is a singing school (not) a chorus? The emancipatory agenda in feminist pedagogy and literature education. In L. Stone (Ed.), *The education feminism reader* (pp. 349–358). New York: Routledge.

Carlone, H. B. (2004). The cultural production of science in reform-based physics: Girls' access, participation and resistance. *Journal of Research in Science Teaching, 41*(4), 392–414.

Carter, L. (2005). Globalisation and science education: Rethinking science education reform. *Journal of Research in Science Teaching, 42*(5), 561–580.

Cross, R. T., & Price, R. F. (1996). Science teachers' social conscience and the role of controversial issues in the teaching of science. *Journal of Research in Science Teaching, 33*(3), 319–333.

Delpit, L. D. (1988). The silenced dialogue: Power and pedagogy in educating other people's children. *Harvard Educational Review, 58*(3), 280–298.

Fine, M. (1993). "You can't just say that the only ones who can speak are those who agree with your position": Political discourse in the classroom. *Harvard Educational Review, 63*, 412–433.

Freire, P. (2000a). *Pedagogy of the oppressed* (M. B. Ramos, trans., new rev. 20th anniversary ed.). New York: Continuum.

———. (2000b). Reading the world and reading the word: An interview with Paulo Freire. In W. Hare & J. P. Portelli (Eds.), *Philosophy of education: Introductory readings* (pp. 145–152). Calgary: Detselig.

Giroux, H. A. (1988). *Teachers as intellectuals: Toward a critical pedagogy of learning*. Granby, MA: Bergin & Garvey.

Hodson, D. (1999). Going beyond cultural pluralism: Science education for sociopolitical action. *Science Education, 83*, 775–796.

———. (2003). Time for action: Science education for an alternative future. *International Journal of Science Education, 25*(6), 645–670.

hooks, b. (1994). *Teaching to transgress: Education as the practice of freedom*. New York: Routledge.

Hughes, G. (2000). Marginalization of socioscientific material in science-technology-society science curricula: Some implications for gender inclusivity and curriculum reform. *Journal of Research in Science Teaching, 37*(5), 426–440.

Intergovernmental Panel on Climate Change, Working Group 1. (2007, April 30). The physical basis of climate change. Retrieved May 11, 2007, from http://www.ipcc.ch

Langhout, R. D., Rosselli, F., & Feinstein, J. (2007). Assessing classism in academic settings. *The Review of Higher Education, 30*(2), 145–184.

Lincoln, Y. S., & Guba, E. G. (1985). *Naturalistic inquiry*. Beverly Hills, CA: Sage.

Martin, J. R. (1994). *Changing the educational landscape: Philosophy, women and curriculum*. New York: Routledge.

Monbiot, G., & Prescott, M. (2006). *Heat: How to stop the planet from burning*. London: Penguin.

O'Brien, V., Kopala, M., & Martinez-Pons, M. (1999). Mathematics self-efficacy, ethnic identity, gender, and career interests related to mathematics and science. *Journal of Educational Research, 92*(4), 231–235.

Ontario Ministry of Education and Training. (2000). *The Ontario curriculum—Grades 11 and 12: Science*. Toronto: Queen's Printer for Ontario.

Pedretti, E., & Hodson, D. (1995). From rhetoric to action: Implementing STS education through action research. *Journal of Research in Science Teaching, 32*(5), 463–485.

Sadler, T. D. (2004). Informal reasoning regarding socioscientific issues: A critical review of research. *Journal of Research in Science Teaching, 41*(5), 513–536.

Seidman, I. (1991). *Interviewing as qualitative research: A guide for researchers in education and the social sciences.* New York: Teachers College Press.

Sernak, K. (2006). School reform and Freire's methodology of conscientization. *International Electronic Journal for Leadership in Learning, 10*(25). Retrieved September 2, 2007, from http://www.ucalgary.ca/~iejll/volume10/socjusted.htm

Solomon, R. P., & Levine-Rasky, C. (2003). *Teaching for equity and diversity: Research to practice.* Toronto: Canadian Scholars' Press.

Somerville, M. A. (2006). *The ethical imagination: Journeys of the human spirit.* Toronto: House of Anansi Press.

Strauss, A., & Corbin, J. (1990). *Basics of qualitative research.* Newbury Park, CA: Sage.

CHAPTER
13

TOWARD A CRITICAL ECONOMIC LITERACY:
PREPARING K-12 LEARNERS TO BE
ECONOMICALLY LITERATE ADULTS

Mary Frances Agnello and Thomas A. Lucey

Introduction

An important factor in economics education has been *No Child Left Behind*
(NCLB) accountability-driven policies that take time away from the social
studies (McGuire, 2007; Siskin, 2003). However, we cannot underestimate
teacher candidates' lack of preparedness to teach issues and problems in
economic relations. Depicting the dearth of coverage of economic class in
both public school textbooks and university teacher preparation texts, we
consider several factors that affect economic education and that have
significant implications for democracy.

After reporting on the state of economics education in the United States,
we utilize Banks' (2000) five dimensions of multicultural education to
critically structure several of the National Council on Economic Education's
economic education standards. We present ways to move students
progressively from knowledge to application, then to empowerment to act on
economic information through a transformative pedagogy (Banks, 2000;
Freire, 1970).

Economic Contexts

Kennickell's (2006) study of the changes in the distribution of wealth
emphasizes the United States' various economic demographics, revealing a
highly inequitable and stratified population. Economic and, therefore,
political inequality is manifest at several levels, exemplified by holdings of
Black or Hispanic families, which are substantially below the corresponding

distributions for all families (p. 34). Females still earn only 70 cents to the dollar that males earn doing comparable work (Dey & Hill, 2007). According to the U.S. Department of Labor, Bureau of Labor Statistics (2005), employees of "Nursing and Residential Care Facilities" earn approximately two-thirds of employees of "Offices of Physicians." A recent report discloses that CEOs from more than three-fourths of the Fortune 500 corporations averaged earnings of nearly $11 million (Institute for Policy Studies, 2007), "over 364 times the pay of the average American worker" (p. 5). Gross disparities between the rich and poor in the United States have widened, and continue to do so. The top 10 percent of families received more combined income than the bottom 90 percent in a year (Council on International and Public Affairs, 2007).

The Problematic of Dealing with These Issues in School

The capacity for schools to deal with these gross inequities depends on three forces: (1) teacher knowledge about these inequalities, (2) teacher willingness to teach with these issues, and (3) a democratic curriculum transformation focused on social justice.

Teacher willingness to teach about inequality requires the ability to see the societal macrocosm and juxtapose economic and political practices to the classroom conditions where educators and students find themselves. Many teachers who lack critical literacy skills adhere to American myths of equality, unable to see the political and social system problematic (Agnello, 2001, 2006b; Kincheloe, Slattery, & Steinberg, 2000). Others experience challenges acknowledging or articulating criticisms of the political economy (Agnello, 2001; Lucey & Laney, 2007).

Educational policy dictates a hierarchy of accountability mandates that increase teachers' employment obligations (Valli & Buese, 2007), to quantify their teaching and control curriculum and instruction. High stakes testing emphasis prompts undue pressures upon educators and administrators to show acceptable performance. These conditions lead to cheating and other unethical practices, as well as distracting learning from content of untested subjects (Nichols & Berliner, 2007). Moral economics and the necessary values for developing such a perspective would fall into the deemphasized content areas of social studies (Pedulla et al., 2003). Pockets of resistance to scientific formal practices that have driven the curriculum that tests "expert" knowledge (Kincheloe & Steinberg, 1993) exist, but truly democratic teaching rarely occurs without teacher acumen to address testing preparation, along with an informed economic and social studies curriculum.

Ultimately, however, teachers cannot act unless they possess the knowledge and skills to initiate such processes. Lucey and Hill-Clarke (in press) argue that the teacher education community has a moral obligation to empower teachers to discuss moral and social justice issues in their classrooms and to recommend activities to prompt candidates' conversations about these issues. Lucey (2008) reports that after experiencing an activity designed to enable creative expression about the relationships of economics to societal perspectives, preservice teachers were mostly neutral in their agreement with items concerning specific topics concerning economic statements related to social justice (e.g., regulation of credit card companies and permanence of economic structures). In a follow-up study, Lucey and Laney (2007) find that preservice elementary school teachers' agreement with these economic items related to social justice was influenced by respondents' economic status and developmental settings (suburban versus nonsuburban—including urban and rural). There was more disagreement with items among those from higher economic contexts and suburban settings than with those from lower economic contexts and nonsuburban settings. If teacher educators have a moral responsibility to empower teacher discussion of moral and social justice issues, then the associated processes need to address the patterns of knowledge that candidates bring to their preparations.

A curriculum concerned with economic justice should incorporate related environmental contexts and, accordingly, enable students' appropriate responses. Price and Valli (2005) illustrate how teaching for change represents a subjective predisposition that preservice teachers must interpret within the contexts of their own background understandings and abilities. McDonald (2005) describes the problems with preparation, and training focused on conceptual content, rather than promoting candidates' experiential awareness of such issues. Bridging the theoretical and practical social justice gap necessitates preparations that provide authentic material for exploration, facilitate safe conversations about these topics, enable community examination of their applications, and engender individual reflection about personal connections for practice.

Challenging the gross inequalities and disparities in economics requires critical literacy (Agnello, 2001). Such literacy juxtaposes that which would seemingly be fair, good, and just with a reading of "real" social conditions, and facilitates an articulation of the contradictions between the real and the ideal. Oakes and Lipton (2007) point out that the concept of "real" has many meanings. Thus, educators need a balance of instructional strategies. Gay (2000) writes that "communication is a dynamic, interactive, irreversible, and invariably contextual ... It is a continuous ever-changing activity ... governed by the rules of the social and physical contexts in which it occurs" (p. 79). Developing citizens who critically interpret traditional economic philosophy require an openness to such pedagogies that invite such patterns of thought.

A critical Freirean literacy differs greatly from a procedural literacy that teachers promote through their scripted lessons, bubble practice tests, and commercialized curricula. Extensive ties among education lobbyists, textbook publishers, state textbook adopters, and producers of packaged reading software assure a tightly controlled literacy that is sold to schools chosen to be Reading First fund grantees under the *NCLB* through a competitive grant funding process (Agnello, 2006a, in press).

The combination of weak teacher transformative literacy knowledge or critical awareness about social discrepancies, bureaucratic procedure, and a tightly controlled curriculum agenda makes classroom discussion about the moral issues of a democratic economy seem remote. Educators tend to hedge questions about power and economic relations and use language that avoids the social class problem. They discuss inequality, poverty, wealth, regressive taxation, and resource distribution without connecting exercise of power to allocation of goods and services.

Furthermore, teachers possess a highly sensitive individual and collective righteous thermostat when discussing economics and morality. Teacher education processes may reinforce this problem. Lucey and Maxwell (2005) reported some successes in lowering teacher candidates' resistance to discussion about financial inequalities. Nevertheless, the connections between economics and morality are not readily apparent within economic education, although Siegler and Thompson (1998) reveal that students begin to develop abilities to see the inequality or immorality of certain economic or social issues as early as fourth grade. Nonetheless, it appears that teachers lack the willingness or ability to discuss the value distinctions that children realize.

Policy Initiatives

Some activity and economic policy initiatives in the United States are insubstantial when compared to those in many developed countries, and related programs do little to engender substantial economic betterment. The following overview of legislative efforts describes these challenges.

No Child Left Behind. Subpart 13 of the *No Child Left Behind* legislation (*Excellence in Economic Education*) "promote[d] economic and financial literacy among students in kindergarten through grade 12," and provided funding for education efforts (U.S. Department of Education, 2001). While this legislation affirmed the federal government's acknowledgment of ineffective financial learning in schools, it did not provide curricular direction, but only funded unspecified curricular exploration.

According to the National Council on Economic Education's *Survey of the States* (2007b), educational standards of all states require economics. A total of 41 adhere to these standards, up from 34 in 2004 and 28 in 1998. Yet only 17 states require students take an Economics course for graduation, and only 22 states administer testing of student knowledge in economics. Personal finance is now included in the educational standards of 40 states, with 28 requiring the standards' implementation, and only 7 requiring the class for graduation.

Texas Education Code. The Texas Legislature required the Texas Education Agency to provide each member of the legislature with a report on the implementation and effectiveness of the personal financial literacy pilot project 41 by January 1, 2007 (Texas Education Agency, 2006). The

Financial literacy pilot program aimed to "establish and implement a financial literacy pilot program to provide students in participating school districts with the knowledge and skills necessary as self-supporting adults to make critical decision relating to personal finance matters" (Texas Education Agency, 2006). The bill contained the following 10 goals:

1. avoiding and eliminating credit card debt,

2. understanding rights and responsibilities of renting or buying a house,

3. managing money to make the transition from renting a home to home ownership,

4. starting a small business,

5. being a prudent investor in the stock market and using other investment options,

6. beginning a savings program,

7. bankruptcy,

8. the types of bank accounts available to consumers and the benefits of maintaining a bank account,

9. balancing a check book, and

10. types of loans available to consumers and becoming a low-risk borrower.

In the fall of 2006, about 500 Texas secondary students took this course but data are not yet available to determine its effectiveness (Texas Education Agency, 2006). While this program involves financial management and practice, none of the goals facilitates student awareness of social or human values.

Rhetoric versus (immoral) reality. Local, state, national, and international policies and practices seem to defy a communitarian approach to people providing needed goods and services in an equitably accessible fashion. Just as social class should be taught in social studies (Loewen, 1995), so should world history address the displacement of people throughout the world and enable students to examine globalizing economic policies (O'Sullivan, 1999) and their relationship to class structures. Economic abuses occurred early in the formation of North American political economy and continue to the present. For example, the taking of indigenous peoples' land, the unjust gentrification of property values to unaffordable levels, the tolerance of cost controls by special interests in the field of medicine, and the petroleum industry's corruption of U.S. foreign policy inform us that the abominable exercise of social and economic power represents an immoral continuance that educators should discuss.

In a text-dependent traditionally instructed classroom, the silence of social studies texts about economic class issues perpetuates the ignorance that develops through specialized and corporate-driven educational, social, and economical policies. Loewen's (1995) analysis of social studies texts finds nominal or no discussion about class. Our review of nearly 20 social studies and social studies methods texts (See Tables 1–3) resulted in similar findings.

Table 1 depicts findings of our review of social (economic) class coverage in textbooks commonly used for teaching social studies. While only 5 of the 14 (35.71 percent) texts addressed socioeconomic class, none discussed this issue within a modern U.S. context. In a sense, history texts portray class structures as social challenges of the past, ignoring their contemporary American presence.

Table 2 depicts findings that most of the social studies methods texts do not cover social class. Martorella, Beal, and Bolick (2005) discuss social concerns and moral stage theory (e.g., Kohlberg); however, they do not discuss social class. Maxim (2006) discusses social class, but limits the content to the comparative severity of this discriminatory basis, and a discussion of achievement and tracking issues. Parker (2005) addresses social class within the discussion of diversity and sociology issues, and provides examples of how teachers can intervene in conversations that demean rural or working-class students. Social studies texts that support teacher preparation often soften the topic by discussing systems and interrelationship (e.g., Diaz, Massialas, & Xanthopoulous, 1999); an exception to this is O'Sullivan (1999).

As depicted in Table 3, no texts delved into social class. We believe that two reasons for this situation exist. First, such coverage would inform developing citizenry of social reasons for economic disparities that they experience or observe. Rather than presenting such situations as societal problems, students learn that these situations result from individuals. Individuals "earn" their societal places, rather than occupy contexts reinforced through patterns of social law. Because the *No Child Left Behind* legislation deemphasizes social studies in elementary schools, math and literacy curricula condition children to think linearly. Children learn social studies concepts through role models defined by prescriptive literature, rather than active discovery. This narrow pedagogy challenges children's abilities and willingness to realize, acknowledge, and challenge the classicism that society practices.

This textbook dependent setting in which many teachers find themselves prepares neither pre- nor in-service teachers to discuss social class and related moral issues with their public school students. Universities tend to relegate social class to courses in foundations, multicultural education, diversity, and perhaps some sociology and history or special topics courses. Teacher preparation programs treat classicism and morality as normal topics when teachers' everyday classroom management processes directly affect societal attitudes toward future citizenry. Such processes leave teachers susceptible to simplistic interpretations of how society works (e.g., Ruby Payne, 1995, and her highly commercialized reinforcement of economic class stereotypes).

Table 1—Secondary American and World History/Civilizations Textbooks

Textbook Title	Author	Publisher	# of pages	Index Mention of Social Class
The American Nation in the Modern Era	Lankiewicz and Miller (Eds.)	Bedford St. Martin's	Workers 8 Labor 6	None
Modern American History: Pathways to the Present	Cayton, Perry, Reed and Winkler	Prentice Hall	None	None
The Americans: Reconstruction to the 21st Century	Danzer, Alva, Krieger, Wilson, and Woloch	McDougall Littell	None	None
America Past and Present	Divine, Breen, Fredrickson, and Williams	Longman	None	None
World History: Connections to Today	Ellis and Esler	Prentice Hall	None	None
The Earth and its People: A Global History	Bulliet, Crossley, Headrick, Hirsch, Johnson, and Northrup	Houghton-Mifflin	None	None
World History	Upshaw, Terry, Holoka, Goff, and Cassar	Wadsworth Thompson	Industrial Revolution 2	None

Traditions & Encounters: A Global Perspective on the Past	Bentley, and Ziegler	McGraw Hill	40 pages in ancient and other civilizations; 1 for socialism and labor under industrialization; 2 under labor refer to trade unions, work, working class	Yes
Western Civilization	Thompson and Spielvogel	Wadsworth Thompson	28 references in various civilizations, not US; industrialization 8 pages; workers and working class (39 references)	Yes
World Civilizations: The Global Experience	Stearns, Adas, Schwartz, and Gilbert	Longman	social class in various civilizations including Latin America, not US (36 references)	Yes
World Geography: Building a Global Perspective	Baerwald and Fraser	Prentice Hall	None	None

Table 2 - Middle and elementary school Social Studies methods textbooks

Title	Author(s)	Publisher	Coverage	Index Mention of Social Class
Teaching Social Studies for Middle and Secondary Schools	Martorella, Beal, & Bolick	Pearson Merrill Prentice Hall	None	None
Children and Their World, Strategies for Teaching Social Studies	Welton	Houghton Mifflin	None	None
Social Studies for the Elementary and Middle Grades: A Constructivist Approach	Sunal & Haas	Pearson Merrill Prentice Hall	None	None
Dynamic Social Studies for Constructivist Classrooms: Inspiring Tomorrow's Social Scientists	Maxim	Pearson Merrill Prentice Hall	3 pages	Yes
Powerful Social Studies for Elementary Students	Brophy and Alleman	Thomson and Wadsworth	None	None
Social Studies in Elementary Education	Parker	Pearson Merrill Prentice Hall	10 pages	Yes

Table 3 - U.S. Economics Textbooks

Title	Author	Publisher	Coverage	Index
Economics: Principles and Policy	Baumol & Blinder	Harcourt College Publishers	None	None
Economics Principles and Practice	Clayton	Glencoe McGraw Hill	None	None
Introduction to Economics	Lieberman & Hall	South-Western College Publishing	None	None
Economics Principles, Problems, & Policies	McConnell & Brue	McGraw-Hill	None	None
Economics Today and Tomorrow	Miller	Glencoe-McGraw-Hill	None	None
Economics	Pennington	Holt, Rhinehart, & Winston	None	None

Instruction. Forming a public (Parker, 1991, 2006) is a requisite of social studies education to sustain a democratic system. In this system, classrooms should employ regular dialogues, interfacing, and voting at all grade levels in order to develop an active and participatory citizenry. The Center for Research on Education, Diversity, and Excellence (http://www.crede.org) promotes five standards for effective pedagogy: teachers and students working together; developing language and literacy skills across all curricula; connecting lessons to students' lives; engaging students with challenging lessons; and emphasizing dialogue over lectures. Implementing such instructional tenets in teacher preparations and K-12 settings offers potential benefits for classroom discussions of economics and morality. Such innovation would differ from present practices whereby policy makers and authorities, including teachers, shape democracy to preserve hierarchical power structures, rather than engender full democratic participation.

Moral Framework for Economic Education

In Table 4, we present a critical and democratic framework for teaching four of the National Council on Economic Education standards (2007a) by framing them within Banks' five dimensions of multicultural education (2000). The concepts developed here include Standard 10 (Role of Economic Institutions), Standard 12 (Interest Rates), Standard 13 (Role of Resources in Determining Income), and Standard 15 (Growth). We chose these standards for this model for teaching economics democratically to illustrate a method of encouraging students' movement beyond the typical low-wage earner perspectives of looking at financial institutions, labor markets, stock returns, or salary increases. Students at the bottom rungs of the social economic ladder may not have had home experiences with economic institutions, such as nonprofits, labor unions, and corporations as legal systems. Standard 12 inspires thought and discussion about interest rates and their roles in the personal, local, and larger home buying and selling market. Students consider resources discussed in Standard 13 in a larger framework that determines their future and potential earnings as more than what the political economy deems their value is individually. Students can begin to ponder economic equity as inspired by the concepts outlined in Standard 15. They may not have considered that health, nutrition, and savings can all be interrelated in the care of individuals, families, and communities—small and large.

These standards encourage students' visualization of these concepts as avenues for their financial economic advancement; however, they do not engender their comprehension of these topics as vehicles for economic repression. Because prices tend to increase, the real value of money decreases. For example, $20 will purchase more CDs today than they would next year. Economic curricula justify interest, dividends, and growth as compensation for the use of money over time. Prudent use of (financial) resources enables one to control the terms of the money that he or she lets others use. If one earns and saves enough money, he or she controls the amount of interest income and interest expense he or she gains or loses.

Using Banks' (2000) five dimensions of multicultural education as a guide, we provide some suggestions for study within these economic standards. The problem with traditional treatment of economic concepts is that inequity is assumed to be normal and acceptable. For example, substantial interest income benefits the affluent, while substantial interest expense challenges many. Similarly, economic curricula inform students how to succeed at the game of financial oppression, but they do not educate the students about their humanitarian responsibilities in this process. The media saturate the lower and middle class psyche with the conviction that personal luxury (e.g., cell phones, cosmetics, and attire) is necessary. It portrays credit as cool, easy, and controlling, while 7,000 CEOs and powerful people, most of whom are from the top 20 percent of the socioeconomic economic ladder, control most of the power and economic influence in this country (Dye, 1966; Tozer, Violas, & Senese, 2002).

Transforming the Economics Curriculum—
Making Connections to Social Justice

The activities and recursive learning generated through engagement with this framework can promote more social justice awareness and action. Doing action research following a "Look, Think, and Act" model (Stringer, 2004) can empower students to examine their contextualized settings, make sense of their cultural and economic involvement, and then act to transform the present circumstances into future possibilities. In the thinking stage, they consider alternative realities, conditions, institutions, and policies that would correct the immoral, misdirected, and undemocratic economic policies that people and nations face. In order to design alternative systems, students should engage in short- and long-term planning, taking into considerations the moral implications for utopian versus individual and group economic acts while analyzing the political foundation of economic power.

Table 4 - Banks' dimensions of multicultural education and four NCEE standards

	Standard 10 (Role of economic institutions)	Standard 12 (Interest rates)	Standard 13 (Roles of resources in determining income)	Standard 15 (Growth)
Content integration	Examine financial reports of international banking institutions. Analyze the debtor countries and their major exports	Using maps explore the patterns of inflation, produce, and poverty in different countries	Examine what a proper price would be for any human. Discuss why a society of one person, one vote would allow different compensation for different jobs	Discuss whose standards of living increase from factories and whose decrease. Examine how technology affects people of different socioeconomic classes
Knowledge construction	Examine both the processes for developing different kinds of economic institutions and utilizing their services. Explore whether such institutions are temporary or permanent entities	Research the characteristics of people who obtain high interest loans and those who obtain low interest loans, and their traits	Predict future earnings based on current plans for education, training, and career options. Ask parents about their childhood plans as children and their development	Explore the opportunity costs of higher taxes and more social and economic infrastructures

Equity pedagogies	Attend union rallies and other gatherings of solidarity economic empowerment groups. Discuss the applications on global and personal levels	Encourage parent participation in discussions about large credit purchases, their advantages, and disadvantages	Facilitate conversations about the ideas of the rights to work, to be respected, and to be compensated fairly	Research, debate, and synthesize ideas about the attainability of uniform growth
Empowering school/social structures	Simulate efforts for democratic school economic policy. Involve parents and other community members	Investigate patterns of school lending, borrowing, and benefiting	Encourage community participation in career day and network with university recruitment programs	Start health awareness and fitness programs that benefit teachers and students, connecting prevention to the availability of social services

Questions for Reflection

1. Is a critical economic literacy important for understanding and supporting democracy? If so or if not, why?

2. How important is it to advance from including multicultural economic topics in the curriculum to empowering students within schools?

3. Why do you think that social class might not be a major area of focus in K-12 or teacher education?

4. To what extent do you think a literacy of control precludes development of a critical economic literacy?

5. What are the similarities and differences between the moral and ethical aspects of educating about economic issues from a multicultural perspective and your

understandings? How do you feel about these similarities and differences? How do your socioeconomic backgrounds relate to your feelings?

References

Agnello, M. F. (2001). *A postmodern literacy policy analysis*. New York: Peter Lang.
———. (2006a). Rise of scientific measurement of literacy: Implications for citizenship and critical literacy development. In J. Kincheloe & R. Horn (Eds.), *Encyclopedia of educational psychology* (pp. 805–813). New York: Greenwood.
———. (2006b, April). *Economic education: A multicultural mission*. Paper presented at the annual meeting of the American Educational Research Association, San Francisco, CA.
———. (in press). Literacy for sale: War on literacy. In T. Giberson & G. Giberson (Eds.), *Knowledge economy: The commodification of knowledge and information in the academic system*. New York: Greenwood.
Banks, J. A. (2000). Multicultural education and curriculum transformation. In F. W. Parkay & G. Hass (Eds.), *Curriculum planning: A contemporary approach* (7th ed., pp. 254–263). Boston: Allyn & Bacon.
Council on International and Public Affairs. (2007). *Too much: A commentary on excess and inequality*. Retrieved on July 23, 2007, at http://www.cipa-apex.org/toomuch/index.html
Dey, J. G., & Hill, C. (2007). *Behind the pay gap*. Washington, DC: American Association of University Women Educational Foundation.
Dye, T. (1966). *Politics, economics, and the public: Policy outcomes in the American states*. Chicago: Rand McNally.
Diaz, C. F., Massialas, B. G., & Xanthopoulos, J. A. (1999). *Global perspectives for educators*. Boston: Allyn & Bacon.
Friere, P. (1970). *Pedagogy of the oppressed*. New York: Seabury.
Gay, G. (2000). *Culturally responsive teaching: Theory, research, & practice*. New York: Teachers College Press.
Institute for Policy Studies. (2007). *Executive excess 2007: The staggering cost of U.S. business leadership*. Retrieved October 22, 2007, from http://www.ips-dc.org/reports/070829-executiveexcess.pdf
Kennickell, A. B. (2006). Currents and undercurrents: Changes in the distribution of wealth, 1989–2004. Washington, DC: Federal Reserve Board.
Kincheloe, J. L., & Steinberg, S. (1993). A tentative description of post-formal thinking: The critical confrontation with cognitive theory. *Harvard Educational Review, 63*, 296–320.
Kincheloe, J. L., Slattery, P., & Steinberg, S. (2000). *Contextualizing teaching: Introduction to education and educational foundations*. New York: Addison-Wesley Longman.
Loewen, J. (1995). *Lies my teacher told me: Everything your American History textbook got wrong*. New York: Touchstone.
Lucey, T. A. (2008). Fence sitting: Preservice teachers' agreement with tenets of economic responsibilities and social justice. In C. J. Craig & L. F. Deretchin (Eds.), *Imagining a renaissance in teacher education. Teacher education yearbook XVI* (pp. 237-251). Lanham, MD: Rowman & Littlefield.

Lucey, T. A., & Hill-Clarke, K. Y. (in press). Considering teacher empowerment: Why it is moral. *Teacher Education and Practice.*

Lucey, T. A., & Laney, J. D. (2007, April). *Preservice teachers' agreement with tenets of economic and social justice: Views from two institutions.* Paper presented at the annual meeting of the American Educational Research Association, Chicago, IL.

Lucey, T. A., & Maxwell, S. A. (2005, October). *Pre-service teachers' interpretations of social justice within financial education.* Paper presented at the annual meeting of the National Council on Economic Education, San Antonio, TX.

Martorella, P. H., Beal, C., & Bolick, C. H. (2005). *Teaching social studies in middle and secondary schools* (4th ed.). New York: Prentice Hall.

Maxim, G. W. (2006). *Dynamic social studies for constructivist classrooms* (8th ed.). New York: Prentice Hall.

McDonald, M. A. (2005). The integration of social justice in teacher education: Dimensions of prospective teachers' opportunities to learn. *Journal of Teacher Education, 56*(6), 418–435.

McGuire, M. (2007). What happened to the Social Studies? The disappearing curriculum. *Phi Delta Kappan, 88*(8), 620–624.

National Council on Economic Education. (2007a). *National standards.* Retrieved on July 27, 2007, from http://www.ncee.net/ea/standards/

National Council on Economic Education. (2007b). *Survey of the states: Economic and personal finance education in our nation's schools in 2007—A report card.* Retrieved on July 27, 2007, from http://ncee.net/about/survey 2007/NCEE Survey2007.pdf

Nichols, S. L., & Berliner, D.C. (2007). *Collateral damage: How high stakes testing corrupts America's schools.* Cambridge, MA: Harvard Education Press.

O'Sullivan, E. (1999). *Transformative learning: Educational vision for the 21st century.* New York: Zed Books.

Oakes, J., & Lipton, M. (2007). *Teaching to change the world* (3rd ed.). New York: McGraw-Hill.

Parker, W. C. (1991). *Renewing the social studies curriculum.* Alexandria, VA: Association for Supervision and Curriculum Development.

———. (2005). *Social studies in elementary education.* New York: Pearson.

———. (2006). Public discourses in schools: Purposes, problems, and possibilities. *Educational Researcher, 35*(8), 11–18.

Payne, R. K. (1995). *A framework: Understanding working with students and adults from poverty.* Baytown, TX: RFT.

Pedulla, J. J., Abrams, L. M., Madaus, G., Russell, M. K., Ramos, A., & Miao, J. (2003). *Perceiving effects of state-mandated testing programs on teaching and learning: Findings from a national survey of teachers.* Chestnut Hill, MA: National Board on Educational Testing and Public Policy.

Price, J. N., & Valli, L. (2005). Preservice teachers becoming agents of change. *Journal of Teacher Education, 56*(1), 57–72.

Siegler, R. S., & Thompson, D. R. (1998). "Hey, would you like a nice cold cup of lemonade on this hot day?" Children's understanding of economic causation. *Developmental Psychology, 34*(1), 146–160.

Siskin, L. (2003). Outside the core curriculum: Accountability in tested and untested subjects. In M. Carnoy, R. Elmore, & Y. L. S. Sisskin (Eds.), *The new accountability: High schools and high-stakes testing* (pp. 87–98). New York: RoutledgeFalmer.

Stringer, E. (2004). *Action research in education.* Columbus, OH: Pearson.

Texas Education Agency. (2006). *Implementation and effectiveness of the personal financial literacy pilot program.* A report to the 80th Texas Legislature.

Tozer, S. E., Violas, P. C., & Senese, G. (2002). *School and society: Historical and contemporary perspectives on education.* New York: McGraw-Hill.

U.S. Department of Education. (2001). *Subpart 13—Excellence in economic education* (Sections 5531-5537 of the *No Child Left Behind Act*). Retrieved July 31, 2002, from http://www.ed.gov/print/policy/elsec/leg/esea02/pg78.html

U.S. Department of Labor, Bureau of Labor Statistics. (2005). *Career guide to industries: Health Care.* Retrieved October 10, 2007, from http://www.bls.gov/oco/cg/cgs 035.htm

Valli, L., & Buese, D. (2007). The changing roles of teachers in an era of high-stakes accountability. *American Educational Research Journal, 44*(3), 519–558.

CHAPTER

14

DEMOCRACY OR DIGITAL DIVIDE?: THE PEDAGOGICAL PARADOXES OF ONLINE ACTIVISM

Karim A. Remtulla

Introduction

A rift between people and formal politics flourishes under a climate of cynicism, suspicion, and apathy (Amutabi et al., 1997; Bennett, 2004; Dahlgren, 2004). Yet people must have a voice in the societies they live. They also deserve to learn how to overcome the social inequities that exclude, marginalize, and prevent them from democratic participation,[1] whether these inequities are based on age, gender, race, income, education, occupation, language, sexual orientation, religious beliefs, or some other reason. Spurred on by this "democratic deficit" (Gaventa, 2006), social activists (Holst, 2007), regardless of their particular cause for social justice, strive to empower people to recognize these social inequities and also struggle with the disenfranchised to overcome their exclusion and marginalization through increased civic engagement (Adler & Goggin, 2005), be it in the forms of education, action, or resistance (Folely, 2004; Holst, 2007; Norris, 2002; Schugurensky, 2005).

Recognizing a crisis of democracy in the formal systems of political engagement, Dahlgren (2004) points to civil society (Habermas, 1989, 1996; Salter, 2003). In civil society, the potentials for increased civic engagement with the assistance of the Internet and other information and communication technologies (also known as "ICTs")[2] seem to provide strong hope for social activists and their aspirations for social justice brought about by greater democratic participation: "the new ICTs are playing a much more significant role in the extra-parliamentarian context … enabling forms of participation that would not have been possible without them" (Dahlgren, 2004, p. xiii).

This chapter explores the dynamics of augmenting civic engagement with online activism[3] for a future that is increasingly digitally mediated. Yet this amalgamation of the Internet with civic engagement is not altogether benign. Some of the pitfalls of the Internet as a contested space are also elaborated. Against a backdrop of the neo-liberal, capitalist, and hegemonic forces currently vying for control over the Internet, the digital divide—and this notion is more fully developed later in the chapter—persists for those who are already silenced, voiceless, and overlooked, due to social inequities despite the optimistic claims to the contrary about the Internet and its potential for enhancing democratic participation (Norris, 2001). Online activism can be said to contribute to *both* democratic participation and the democratic deficit when considering democracy *and* the digital divide in an increasingly digitally mediated future. Ultimately, this duality presents critical, pedagogical challenges for teaching online activism as a means of civic engagement in civil society. Nevertheless, Mojab (2000) posits that "the question is not rejecting civil society as a site of struggle. It is rather a recognition of the web of conflicts that constitute this space, both real and virtual" (p. 117).

Civil Society, Civic Engagement, and the Internet

With assistance of the Internet and other ICTs, social activists are expanding their channels of civic engagement in civil society in order to enhance democratic participation for social justice. Whether as localized social action and resistance, in partnership with institutions of higher education, through community-centred development programs, or under the auspices of global, transnational, non-governmental organizations, those individuals and organizations involved in civic engagement for social justice are increasingly using the Internet as a means to bring about greater democratic participation (McCaughey & Ayers, 2003; Trigona, 2007; van de Donk, Loader, Nixon, & Rucht, 2004).

Can online activism contribute to a more inclusive, participatory, and democratic society that is socially just and politically engaged? Burgeoning coalitions of activists, citizens, social movements, select governments, and private enterprises that aim to address environmental devastation and the global ecological crisis serve as powerful exemplars of (a) the coming together of civic engagement, civil society, and the Internet; and, (b) how people around the world may be brought together in the public sphere (Habermas, 1989, 1996) in a massive demonstration of global solidarity (van de Donk et al., 2004).

There are three general categories of online activism (Rosenkrands, 2004; Van Aelst & Walgrave, 2004; Vegh, 2003). The first type of online activism, "awareness/advocacy" (Vegh, 2003), views the Internet and other ICTs as a channel of access to independent and alternative media groups for information that tends to be ignored or often suppressed by mainstream media. The Independent Media Center (www.indymedia.org) (hereafter Indymedia) is a well-known, alternative news media. On their "Frequently Asked Questions" web page, in response to the question, "Of what are you 'independent'?" they reply:

> No corporation owns Indymedia, no government manages the organization, no single donor finances the project. Indymedia is not the mouthpiece of any political party or organization. People involved with Indymedia have a wide variety of political and personal viewpoints. Anyone may participate in Indymedia organizing and anyone may post to the Indymedia newswires. (Indymedia's Frequently Asked Questions (FAQ), n.d., Of what are you "independent"? section, para. 1)

As a second form of online activism, "community-oriented sites" (Rosenkrands, 2004), seek to build relationships and share dialogue. Grupo Alavio and their web site, Ágora TV (www.agoratv.org) make a good case in point. For Grupo Alavio, "the basis for the project is to adapt internet technology and put it to use for the benefit of the community" (Trigona, 2007, Alternative Agenda: A Working Class Point of View section, para. 2). Digital video productions from all over Latin America dealing with labour conflicts, social movements, indigenous struggles, and experimental video art populate this site. In short, "the objective of Ágora TV is for the audience to appropriate the media and use it as a tool for social change" (Trigona, 2007, Alternative Agenda: A Working Class Point of View section, para. 1). This serves as a distinctive example of the convergence of various digital technologies to strengthen community and voice.

The third variety of online activism, "action groups" (Van Aelst & Walgrave, 2004), try to raise public support in favour of specific social causes. In this respect, for online activism to contribute to civil society, there must be some translation from online to the real world (Dahlgren, 2004). The global justice movement, also known as the anti-globalization movement, which brings together a number of issues including human rights, poverty, equality, access, and the environment, is constantly forging temporary alliances enhanced through the use of the Internet. The protests against the World Trade Organization in Seattle in December 1999, and more recently, against the World Bank and International Monetary Fund, serve as fitting illustrations of how the Internet facilitates partnerships and rapid mobilization over geo-spatially dispersed areas (Dahlgren, 2004; van de Donk et al., 2004).

As shown by these examples of online activism, the Internet facilitates for social activists the establishment of, or at least the potential to establish, collaboration as well as raising public awareness, building popular consciousness, communication, and coordination of action and the sharing of knowledge.

Neo-liberalism, Capital, Hegemony, and the Internet

The Internet is a highly disputed terrain, and its presumed benefits for social justice and democratic participation are far from settled. The significance of the Internet, as the space for online activism, cannot be side-stepped in this discussion for it shapes how online activism is conceived, perceived, and, ultimately, carried out. Normative/dominant perspectives praise the Internet as contributing towards the development of civil society and beneficial for civic engagement and democratic participation. Yet, to accept the Internet as neutral space for civic engagement and a transparent context for online activism may be tantamount to silencing and marginalizing the very voices, communities, and social causes that have come together in civil society in the first place. The Internet is equally susceptible to neo-liberal ideology and to manipulation by the forces of capital and hegemony. Critical/subaltern points of view on the Internet decry the potential hazards of such manipulation for social justice and democratic participation.

The Internet, together with transnational, social movement, and networked activists all exist within an environment of globalization and cultural control by giant media corporations known as "dominant media" (King, 2003; Mojab, 2000; Steven, 2004). "Cultural control" alludes to the term "hegemony" (Gramsci, 1971) which is the cultural situation where the power of the elite and dominant in a society is maintained through the privileging of certain beliefs, values, and practices to the exclusion of others, and, restricting the way new ideas are either accepted or excluded based on their alignment with the dominant. Therefore, online activism must also be historicized and placed into such a context to truly get at its meanings and implications for civic engagement and democratic participation

If the World Wide Web and other online spaces do aspire to establish a public sphere (Habermas, 1989, 1996), it is a public sphere progressively delimited by the blatant conflation of commercial and state powers under the doctrine of neo-liberalism (Bousquet & Wills, 2003). Dahlberg (2005) puts forward the argument that "the Internet's potential for extending strong democratic culture through critical communication is being undermined by a corporate colonization of cyberspace" (p. 160). Steven (2004) asserts that "the dominant media have the power to set political agendas and shape the cultural landscape" (p. 37), further documenting that "most empirical studies reveal a significant overlap of media owners and managers with the political elite" (p. 53). Such a colonizing trend jeopardizes the expansion of democratic culture on the Internet and in society overall, privileging certain consumer content and market practices while concurrently marginalizing many voices and critical forms of participation. Amutabi et al. (1997) emphasize that "the distinction between civil society and economy is becoming more blurred" (p. 5). Under these conditions, one of the many fears of social movements, activists, and civil society is the ability of the dominant to "co-opt" and appropriate social causes to reinforce and maintain the power of capital and hegemony by manipulating the message of social justice and democratic participation into their opposites. All this only exacerbates the "democratic deficit" discussed earlier.

The normative/dominant discourses of the Internet also portray the Internet as an open space that allows social movements and activists to network across borders freely and unencumbered. When looked at more critically, one central question becomes apparent: Are all online spaces, and are the communities that form online in those spaces equally open and accessible to everyone? If online activism is vulnerable to the machinations of neo-liberalism, capital, and hegemony, what does this imply for the openness and inclusiveness of online activism as a means to enhance social justice and democratic participation?

Nakamura (2000) analyses the ways in which telecommunications companies portray racial and ethnic differences through their advertising of digital services including the Internet and other ICTs. As Nakamura (2000) states, ironically, "the ad gestures towards a democracy founded upon disembodiment and uncontaminated by physical difference.... Diversity is ... what the product will eradicate" (p. 16). Instead of promoting democratic participation to eradicate racial conflict, this ad co-opts the social cause of racism and appropriates the use of Internet and other ICTs to justify the erasing of *race* as a worthy social cause that is equivalent to eradicating racial conflict. This serves as a primary example of the manipulation of social causes for corporate profits.

McPherson (2000) presents a cultural anthropological analysis of neo-Confederate web sites and their common yearning for a renewed independence and identity of "the South." From McPherson's (2000) point of view, although neo-Confederate web sites commonly eschew racism, their efforts only succeed in re-entrenching a celebration of White patriarchy perpetrated by a subtler form of racism. The "overt racism" of the past, which openly portrayed "White" supremacy over "coloured" people is now replaced by the covert racism of the present, which suppresses all discussion of race and difference behind the rhetoric of equality and civil rights. This serves as an apt example of the manipulation of the social cause of racism to reinforce racist views in favour of a dominant, White hegemony.

Access to the Internet and other ICTs is also not readily available in the Caribbean, Latin America, Asia, and Africa, as it might be in North America and Europe (Dahlberg, 2005; Lindsay & Poindexter, 2003; Mojab, 2000;

Wright, 2004). As such, the online activism originating from the Northwestern hemisphere may not reach the very populations they may be trying to represent. These online activism are also primarily in English and indicative of the White male gaze, thus marginalizing non-English speaking activists, and, potentially gender-biasing and possibly misinterpreting events that take place in other cultures (McPherson, 2000; Radcliffe, Laurie, & Andolina, 2004; Wright, 2004).

Furthermore, a problem comes to light when trying to determine which causes deserve attention and who makes such a determination (Wright, 2004, p. 86). Those with fewer resources may be silenced and excluded online from participating in the resolution of the very social problems that most affect them. At the same time, the more dominant voices of the North and the West bring with them perceptions and conceptions of democratic participation that may not be focused on the needs of those who continue to remain "unheard." Mojab (2000) roundly disputes the notion that "the current communications revolution has changed the balance of forces in favour of civil society" (p. 106).

Combining Nakamura's (2000) observations around the erasing of race in cyberspace, and McPherson's (2000) focus on the transition from *overt* racism in American culture to *covert* racism in cyberculture, and Niell's take on the role of power, reveals a very specific pedagogy of citizenship education (Schugurensky, 2005). Online, the very idea of "difference" is *preemptively* subverted by the forces of neo-liberalism, capital, and hegemony, thereby diminishing the reality that disparity (e.g., poverty, homelessness, and illiteracy) precludes all citizens from exercising their rights in an even and just way. The integrity of notions like "citizenship" and "global citizen," which bring diverse peoples together, without calling for the *disappearance* of their differences, now becomes distorted in cyberspace through a neo-liberal, ideological lens:

> The possibility of a new cosmopolitanism constituting all the necessary requirements for a global citizen who speaks multiple languages, inhabits multiple cultures, wears whatever skin colour or body part desired, elaborates a language of romantic union with technology or nature, and moves easily between identification with movie stars, action heroes, and other ethnicities or races … and above all, consuming subject is offered as the model of future cyber-citizenship. (Gonzalez, 2000, p. 48)

More so, it is now vital to determine whether cyberspace serves as a catalyst for the spread of democracy around the globe. On the other hand, the virtual may implode civil society, perpetuate an ersatz online activism leading to an artificial change, and in so doing, continue to exacerbate democratic deficits (Gaventa, 2006). There remain fundamental questions as to whether the potential of cyberspace for forming communities online will actually result in more civil and social cohesion in society. Hill and Hughes (1998) add that "true, the Internet does carry with it the potential to create a global community that can influence politics.... But it also carries just as large a potential to tribalize the world" (p. 14).

Pedagogical Paradoxes for Democracy in Education

Teaching online activism as civic engagement is both appropriate and essential for any discussion on democratic participation given a future that is increasingly digitally mediated. However, this raises a philosophical question when considering the ontology of the learner and their *situatedness* in a *digitized* world.

Dewey's (1897) doctrine on "education being a social process" (ARTICLE II—What the school is section, para. 1) deems that learning must contribute to the good of the community of which the learner is a part. Dewey's (1897) insistence that education is learning by "doing" places great emphasis on "experience" as pedagogy (Dewey, 1897; Fenwick, 2001). Dewey (1897) proclaims: "I believe that all education proceeds by the participation of the individual in the social consciousness of the race" (ARTICLE I—What education is section, para. 1).

Dewey's thinking serves as a widely accepted explanation and justification for *doing* democracy in education. If democracy, education, and action are all inter-connected as Dewey (1897) upholds, then does online activism fit? In a world that is increasingly digitally mediated, does democracy in education, based on action and "doing," fit? When contemplating democracy in education, if democracy is learned by "doing" good for society, then what (type of) democracy is the learner "experiencing" by "doing" online activism?

The ontological dictates the pedagogical. Yet, in a future that is increasingly digitally mediated, how do educators conceive of "the learner" as they decide on pedagogical practices to teach about online activism? Therein rest two pedagogical paradoxes that online activism poses for democracy in education: (a) Is the learner a "consumer" as the neo-liberal, capitalist, and hegemonic forces encourage, or, is the learner an "agent" capable of making social justice happen from increased democratic participation in civil society; and, (b) is the learner seen as "virtual" or "corporeal"?

For the first paradox, what is really at issue is the relationship between online activism and the "digital divide":

> The digital divide is understood as a multidimensional phenomenon encompassing three distinct aspects. The *global divide* refers to the divergence of Internet access between industrialized and developing societies. The *social divide* concerns the gap between information rich and poor in each nation. And finally within the online community, the *democratic divide* signifies the difference between those who do, and do not, use the panoply of digital resources to engage, mobilize, and participate in public life. (Norris, 2001, p. 4)

Given that online activism takes place as a result of the Internet and other ICTs, any and all online activism trigger the digital divide at one level or another. Even though social justice advocacy may be a central motivation behind online activism, there remains a sizeable chasm between online activism as a means for civic engagement and democratic participation, and online activism as a force that drives social change.

Through the power of capital and hegemony exerted over the Internet and bound together by neo-liberal ideology, social justice is represented as a consumer good that may be bought, sold, traded, and discarded at a whim, for those who can afford to and have the means to do so. Through co-optation, appropriation, and manipulation of online spaces, the forces of capital and hegemony, through the lens of neo-liberalism, portray social justice online as something that does not (need to) matter online or in reality—as a "non-issue." The outcome of online activism that champion social justice are now at risk of becoming politically and ethically contradictory to and undermining of their own original intentions.

This "consumer–agent" paradox captures the defining characteristic of the relationship between online activism and the digital divide. The very same social inequities such as income and education, which contribute to the digital divide, also make online activism possible (Norris, 2001; van Dijk, 2005). The implications of this paradox for *doing* democracy in education portray social justice as a consumable good and the learner as "consumer." "Democracy" now becomes a metaphor for "a marketplace," and "democratic participation," a metaphor for "consumption." Interestingly, even the term "democratic *deficit*" harkens this paradox.

A second pedagogical paradox occurs in the "juxtaposition" of the notions of "online" with "activism." The conjoining of these two terms is almost an oxymoron. The *isolated and solitary keystroke* of the "online" somehow *nullifies* the ideas of *movement, aggregation,* and *embodiment* as signified by "activism." In the "online," glimpses of people crouched in front of keyboards come into view, *transfixed* by their computer screens, interacting with numerous *disembodied* others through their mutual manipulation and negotiation of secret codes and programming languages known only to them (Balsamo, 1996).

The pedagogical implications for this "virtual–corporeal" paradox for *doing* democracy in education are manifested in whether or not civic engagement and democratic participation from online activism have affected the social causes that demand society's attention? McCaughey and Ayers (2003) surmise that

> the Internet allows us to interact with others without our voices, faces, and bodies. In the absence of meat bodies ... the traversing of spatial and temporal boundaries raises questions about what presence, essence, or soul we think we are on the Net ... where is the body on which that traditional activism has relied? Indeed, a substantial component of political activism has always been the activist's willingness to put her body on the line. Can you really put your body on the line online? If not, how do social-change efforts online actually work? (p. 5)

Is the "virtual" sufficient to convey the complexity of "corporeal" social justice issues such as women's rights, poverty, and AIDS, or, is what is conveyed a perversion of the virtual that has fallen prey to neo-liberalism, capital, and hegemony; an opiate and distraction meant to tantalize the masses from society's very real and mounting challenges? Mojab (2000) cautions that, "recognizing the contradictions and limitations of the real and virtual spaces of civil society enhances our ability to create alternative forms of knowledge" (p. 106).

Conclusions

The Internet and other ICTs, and their increased influence on society, are no longer in dispute. What are the implications of this influence? The relationship between democratic participation and online activism becomes paradoxical when the forces of neo-liberalism, capital, and hegemony, and the power they exert over the Internet and cyberspace, are factored in. The objective of this chapter is not to resolve the "virtual–corporeal" or the "consumer–agent" paradoxes, but to raise them and present them in a critical manner. A pivotal enquiry now transpires for future research and contemplation: How does social change happen, and what does that process look like when the virtual (online) and the real (activism) come together in civil society to enhance democratic participation? For educators, academics, social activists, and concerned citizens, the understanding of online activism and the digital divide, and how their interaction may be pedagogically understood for the sustaining of civic engagement and democratic participation in an increasingly digitally mediated future, is paramount to answering this question of the salience of a digitally divided world.

Questions for Reflection

1. What is the conceptual relationship between online activism and democratic participation?

2. Visit the following social activist web sites: Greenpeace (www.greenpeace.org); Amnesty International (www.amnesty.org); CorpWatch (www.corpwatch.org); TakingITGlobal (www.takingitglobal.org); (RED) (www.joinred.com); and Make Poverty History (www.makepovertyhistory.org). What category of online activism are they? Explain.

3. Do you agree with the following statement: "Even though social justice advocacy may be a central motivation behind online activism, there remains a sizeable chasm between online activism as a means for civic engagement and democratic participation, and online activism as a force for social change"? Why or why not?

4. Is it necessary to resolve the pedagogical paradoxes in order for online activism to be

effective for civic engagement and democratic participation? Why or why not?

5. How may social change happen, and what might that process look like when the virtual (online) and the real (activism) come together in civil society for civic engagement and democratic participation in a future that will be increasingly digitally mediated?

Notes

1. This chapter defines "democratic participation" as "responding to the democratic deficit (Gaventa, 2006) through greater civic engagement (Adler & Goggin, 2005)."

2. This chapter takes Hill and Hughes' (1998) definition for the Internet as "a series of widely dispersed and linked computer networks" (p. 18), which also closely resembles Salter's (2003) view of the Internet as "network of computer networks" (p. 118). The term "Internet," more commonly referred to as "the World Wide Web" or "the net," is also used interchangeably with ICTs—an umbrella term that includes the Internet but also computers, mobile phones, and other micro-chip–based digital devices that integrate and link via the World Wide Web (Internet, ICTs, and World Wide Web are used interchangeably in this chapter) (van de Donk et al., 2004).

3. "Online activism" is a contested and varicoloured notion (McCaughey & Ayers, 2003; Vegh, 2003). For the purposes of this chapter, online activism is taken to mean "civic engagement (Adler & Goggin, 2005) done with the assistance of the Internet and other information and communication technologies as an intentional means of political action."

References

Adler, R. P., & Goggin, J. (2005). What do we mean by "civic engagement"? *Journal of Transformative Education, 3*(3), 236–253.

Amutabi, M., Jackson, K., Korsgaard, O., Murphy, P., Quiroz Martin, T., & Walters, S. (1997). Introduction. In S. Walters (Ed.), *Globalization, adult education and training: Impacts and issues* (pp. 1–12). London: Zed Books.

Balsamo, A. (1996). The virtual body in cyberspace. In D. Bell & B. M. Kennedy (Eds.), *The cyberculture reader* (pp. 489–503). New York: Routledge.

Bennett, W. L. (2004). Communicating global activism: Strengths and vulnerabilities of networked politics. In W. van de Donk, B. D. Loader, P. G. Nixon, & D. Rucht (Eds.), *Cyberprotest: New media, citizens and social movements* (pp. 123–146). New York: Routledge.

Bousquet, M., & Wills, K. (Eds.). (2003). *The politics of information: The electronic mediation of social change*. Stanford, CA: Alt-X.

Dahlberg, L. (2005). The corporate colonization of online attention and the marginalization of critical communication? *Journal of Communication Inquiry, 29*(2), 160–180.

Dahlgren, P. (2004). Foreword. In W. van de Donk, B. D. Loader, P. G. Nixon, & D. Rucht (Eds.), *Cyberprotest: New media, citizens and social movements* (pp. xi–xvi). New York: Routledge.

Dewey, J. (1897). My pedagogic creed [electronic version]. *The School Journal, 54*(3), 77–80. Retrieved May 17, 2007, from http://www.infed.org/archives/e-texts/e-dew-pc.htm

Fenwick, T. (2001). *Experiential learning: A theoretical critique explored through five perspectives (Information series no. 385)*. Retrieved March 4, 2006, from http://www.eric.ed.gov/ERICDocs/data/ericdocs2/content_storage_01/0000000b/80/26/30/a1.pdf

Folely, G. (Ed.). (2004). *Dimensions of adult learning: Adult education and training in a global era*. Berkshire, UK: Open University Press.

Gaventa, J. (2006). *Triumph, deficit or contestation? Deepening the "deepening democracy" debate (Working paper 264)*. Retrieved November 7, 2006, from http://www.ntd.co.uk/idsbookshop/details.asp?id=944

Gonzalez, J. (2000). The appended subject: Race and identity as digital assemblage. In B. E. Kolko, L. Nakamura, & G. Rodman (Eds.), *Race in cyberspace* (pp. 27–50). New York: Routledge.

Gramsci, A. (1971). *Selections from the prison notebooks*. New York: International.

Habermas, J. (1989). *The structural transformation of the public sphere* (T. Burger, trans.). Cambridge, MA: MIT Press.

Habermas, J. (1996). *Between facts and norms: Contributions to a discourse theory of law and democracy* (W. Rehg, trans.). Cambridge, MA: MIT Press.

Hill, K. A., & Hughes, J. E. (1998). *Cyberpolitics: Citizen activism in the age of the internet*. New York: Rowman & Littlefield.

Holst, J. D. (2007). The politics and economics of globalization and social change in radical adult education: A critical review of recent literature [electronic version]. *Journal for Critical Education Policy Studies, 5*. Retrieved May 15, 2007, from http://www.jceps.com/?pageID=article&articleID=91

Indymedia's Frequently Asked Questions (FAQ) (n.d.). *Welcome to the Indymedia Documentation Project*. Retrieved May 5, 2007, from http://docs.indymedia.org/view/Global/FrequentlyAskedQuestionEn

King, K. (2003). Women in the web. In M. Bousquet & K. Willis (Eds.), *The politics of information: The electronic mediation of social change* (pp. 303–313). Stanford, CA: Alt-X.

Lindsay, B., & Poindexter, M. T. (2003). The Internet: Creating equity through continuous education or perpetuating a digital divide? *Comparative Education Review, 47*(1), 112–122.

McCaughey, M., & Ayers, M. D. (Eds.) (2003). *Cyberactivism: Online activism in theory and politics*. New York: Routledge.

McPherson, T. (2000). I'll take my stand in Dixie-net: White guys, the south, and cyberspace. In B. E. Kolko, L. Nakamura, & G. Rodman (Eds.), *Race in cyberspace* (pp. 117–132). New York: Routledge.

Mojab, S. (2000). The feminist project in cyberspace and civil society. *Convergence (Toronto, ON), 33*(1–2), 106–119.

Nakamura, L. (2000). "Where do you want to go today?" Cybernetic tourism, the internet, and transnationality. In B. E. Kolko, L. Nakamura, & G. Rodman (Eds.), *Race in cyberspace* (pp. 15–26). New York: Routledge.

Norris, P. (2001). *Digital divide: Civic engagement, information poverty, and the internet worldwide*. New York: Cambridge University Press.

———. (2002). New social movements, protest politics, and the Internet. In P. Norris (Ed.), *Democratic phoenix: Reinventing political activism* (pp. 188–214). Cambridge, UK: Cambridge University Press.

Radcliffe, S. A., Laurie, N., & Andolina, R. (2004, Winter). The transnationalization of gender and re-imagining Andean indigenous development. *Signs: Journal of Women in*

Culture and Society, 29(2, Development Cultures: New Environments, New Realities, New Strategies), 387–416.

Rosenkrands, J. (2004). Politicizing *homo* economicus: Analysis of anti-corporate websites. In W. van de Donk, B. D. Loader, P. G. Nixon, & D. Rucht (Eds.), *Cyberprotest: New media, citizens and social movements* (pp. 57–76). New York: Routledge.

Salter, L. (2003). Democracy, new social movements, and the internet: A Habermasian analysis. In M. McCaughey & M. Ayers (Eds.), *Cyberactivism: Online activism in theory and politics* (pp. 117–144). New York: Routledge.

Schugurensky, D. (2005). *Citizenship and citizenship education: Canada in an international context.* Retrieved November 1, 2006, from http://fcis.oise.utoronto.ca/~daniel_schugurensky/courses/4.citizenship&citized.doc

Steven, P. (2004). *The no-nonsense guide to global media.* Toronto, ON: New Internationalist.

Trigona, M. (2007). *Community television in Argentina: Ágora TV, a window for liberation.* Retrieved May 6, 2007, from http://www.zmag.org/content/showarticle.cfm?SectionID=42&ItemID=12741

Van Aelst, P., & Walgrave, S. (2004). New media, new movements? The role of the internet in shaping the "anti-globalization" movement. In W. van de Donk, B. D. Loader, P. G. Nixon, & D. Rucht (Eds.), *Cyberprotest: New media, citizens and social movements* (pp. 97–122). New York: Routledge.

van de Donk, W., Loader, B. D., Nixon, P. G., & Rucht, D. (Eds.). (2004). *Cyberprotest: New media, citizens and social movements.* New York: Routledge.

van Dijk, J. A. G. M. (2005). *The deepening divide: Inequality in the information society.* London: Sage.

Vegh, S. (2003). Classifying forms of online activism: The case of cyberprotests against the World Bank. In M. McCaughey & M. Ayers (Eds.), *Cyberactivism: Online activism in theory and politics* (pp. 71–96). New York: Routledge.

Wright, S. (2004). Informing, communicating and ICTs in contemporary anti-capitalist movements. In W. van de Donk, B. D. Loader, P. G. Nixon, & D. Rucht (Eds.), *Cyberprotest: New media, citizens and social movements* (pp. 77–93). New York: Routledge.

SECTION IV

TEACHING ABOUT AND FOR DEMOCRACY

CHAPTER
15

TEACHING AND LEARNING DEMOCRACY IN EDUCATION: INTERWEAVING DEMOCRATIC CITIZENSHIP INTO/THROUGH THE CURRICULUM

Suzanne Vincent and Jacques Désautels

Introduction

The School[1] undoubtedly has a vital contribution to make to developing democratic practices among young people, and to providing them with an education in *"le vivre-ensemble"*—an active principle of community participation and belonging.[2] Further, citizenship education, also commonly referred to as "civic education," represents a unique avenue for translating this objective into reality. As a rule, citizenship education is thought of in connection with specific types or areas of knowledge or with the contents contained in the formal curriculum, but it is also apparent in the overall culture of the School, especially concerning the organizational set-up and practices of diverse educators and administrators. Similarly, the question remains as to how best to approach or assess the thrust of today's citizenship education? How, for example, do the many individual issues surrounding this form of education meet up with the infinite demands to recast the social contract underpinning modern democratic societies? What frameworks and practices are currently being mobilized by the contemporary School to meet the objectives of citizenship education? Given the pivotal role of knowledge and power in contemporary society, what curricular approach should be given priority by the School? More specifically, how should this relationship to knowledge frame educational practices so as to enable students to more fully grasp and gauge the sensitive issues accompanying the explosion of new socio-technical developments?

This chapter attempts to address such questions in four distinct sections. The first section describes a number of dysfunctions of democracy and also documents efforts to promote a renewed form of citizenship based on participation and deliberation. The second section outlines the particular contribution that the School may make in educating tomorrow's citizenry, focusing particularly on several dynamic, school-based initiatives adopted with the objective of furthering the socialization of an increasingly diverse populace. Adopting a critical perspective, the third section analyses and then links with the socio-epistemological frameworks built into school curricula, especially in relation to the type of relationship to knowledge promoted in the School. The fourth section discusses the deconstruction of the hierarchy of school subject-disciplines against the backdrop of a broader programme aimed at revitalizing education for democracy.

Concerning the Need to Re-configure the Foundation of Democratic Societies

Western models of democracy have, on the basis of such principles as the rule of law, the formal recognition of human rights and freedoms, and the separation of various powers, made it possible to manage the body politic and society as a whole with a certain degree of harmony. However, these democracies are by no means uniform, nor can they be considered as having been entirely perfected or, indeed, as being representative of the only viable route to full-fledged democratic governance. Furthermore, much criticism can be levelled at the political authorities who are ostensibly charged with the stewardship of our democracies and their underlying ideals. Ultimately, the political process is at risk of being judged powerless to transform society (Innerarity, 2002), or incapable of assuring for citizens the basic conditions of the "good life,"[3] to borrow from Honneth (2000).

The governance of societies has, in addition, become more complex as the result of global changes—the most prominent of which is globalization itself—that have re-configured the economic, social, and cultural landscape everywhere, and that have also de-structured/re-structured political life in the process (Held & McGrew, 2000). Together, these phenomena have modified the dynamics driving the relationships between governments, as well as those occurring between the state and the institutions of civil society. They have also produced major repercussions on individuals' views, attitudes, and lifestyles, as well as on social relationships. Actions and behaviours, relating to individuals' social identity and feelings of belonging, their willingness to co-operate and interest in taking an active part in the life of the community around them, have all been re-configured—as have their bonds and ties to various institutions (i.e., the government, schools, public services, etc.). Social relationships have, moreover, been instrumentalized along consumerist lines, thus placing many people in conflict with their civic duties.

It is important to view these structural changes against the backdrop of a social climate that is becoming increasingly brittle in response to the looming dangers of the environment, mushrooming healthcare requirements, widening socio-economic gaps, spiralling violence in the Middle East and elsewhere, and the spread of terrorism, to name but a few examples. Governments no longer appear to be capable of actively or proactively managing society's development, or even of ensuring the welfare of their populations (Dubet, 2000). This partially accounts for not only the erosion in the confidence of citizens in their elected representatives and public administration, but also their growing disinterest in public affairs. In their defence, it must be said that many individuals, when confronted with a market economy that operates according to impersonal rules over which they have no control, are no longer able to fathom the resulting social context; thus, they become unable to see any point to their engaging with it. Instead, they may well prefer to withdraw into the autonomous self, or take refuge in the comforts the domestic sphere, in keeping with specific attitudes and conceptualizations mediating the emergence of today's post-national society (Vibert, 2002). All such trends point in the direction of a certain dilapidation of the historical legacy of democracy (Barber, 1984), which explains why some observers believe that the time has come to engage in efforts to place social practices on new foundations with a view to re-configuring the political community (Michaud, 2006).

However, while a concern for re-humanizing the bonds of society provides ample grounds for re-thinking the architecture of democracy, to borrow from Reynolds (2002), it is vital to account for two pre-conditions of a primarily political nature: first, the requirement for greater transparency on the part of governments, and, second, the political will to establish greater balance among the inputs accorded consideration when arbitrating society-wide choices, particularly in relation to techno-scientific developments. At stake is nothing less than a redefinition of the role of citizens in political life, which must proceed hand-in-hand with a reinterpretation of the social contract on which our divided societies are founded. Efforts to give shape to this "new citizenship," which some have characterized as being participative or deliberative in nature, must necessarily evolve in full respect of traditional rights and freedoms. To this end, deliberation must be organized for the purpose of facilitating debate over socially sensitive issues, including such forms as popular symposia, citizens' advisory committees, public hearings agencies, focus groups, and referenda (Rowe & Frewer, 2000). At the risk of stating the obvious, all such objectives bring into question, de facto, the role of the School in relation to the political socialization of young people.

Democratic Citizenship as an Educational Agenda for the School

Through its mission of contributing to the socialization of the citizens of tomorrow, the School plays a vital role in the development of democracy. Nonetheless, as has been shown by research in the sociology of education, the School can also be viewed as constituting a microcosm that is riven with the same issues that frame and indeed drive the development of democracy in the society around it (Forquin, 2000). It is also important to point out that the work enacted in the School prefigures the symbolic power exerted in society at large; moreover, the School manages to exert this influence effects through both the basic learnings that it provides to students and the legal authority that it exercises over a diverse enrolment (Mabilon-Bonfils & Saadoun, 2001). Therefore, the School's work of "providing an education" can be considered to be a socio-political project or agenda in that it evinces the intentions underlying not only a given society's preferred model of development, but also the type of citizen that this same society aspires to produce. Now, such intentions are of particular interest to the purposes of our present analysis—and about which further space will be dedicated below—

for they are articulated or "given voice" in the curriculum, particularly in the form of the type of knowledge being promoted. They are also expressed through a relationship to knowledge, as revealed by an entire range of systems, organizations, and educational practices that structure educational action.

The Many, Weighty Social Needs Requiring Educational Action

The expectations or indeed the ambitions that surround the School in our time have been affected by such troubling issues as an upsurge in classroom violence, inappropriate aggressiveness, and early school leaving, especially among boys (Berthelot, 1994; Duru-Bellat, 2000). Considering how the School refracts the social tensions and injustices that originate outside its walls (and that nevertheless resound within them), a range of actors from within and outside the educational community have begun, increasingly, to voice their concerns and to devise and debate new courses of action. In particular, many educators have come forward to decry what they diagnose as the inadequate socialization of young people—the result, among other things, of society's "mushy" values (Grand-Maison, 1999), families' weak supervisory capacities, and the mediocre, media-touted role models beloved of youth. Likewise, they challenge the present-day emphasis on rights at the expense of responsibilities, young people's occasional difficulty tolerating differences (e.g., religious, ethnic, etc.), and their lax commitment to schooling proper. At the same time, these observers and critics have linked their concerns to the potential impact on students of society's encouragement of "care-less" attitudes, individualism, and behaviours that instil or entrench competitiveness, consumption, and exclusion—ills that are all the more worrisome in view of the School's traditional specific expectations respecting personal effort and application, co-operative attitudes, and respect for people and things. Thus, when envisioning any future role for the School in re-casting social bonds and revitalizing democracy, it is clear that the battle will first have to be joined on the School's home turf, so to speak.

In that connection, it is worth noting that many countries have demonstrated their determination to strengthen the School's educational work in respect of the social education provided to young people.[4] Accordingly, and within the framework of the neo-liberal educational reforms introduced on the eve of the twenty-first century, the perspective referred to as the "new citizenship" in policy directives of various international and national organizations has emerged as the pole of reference concerning citizenship education (e.g., Conseil supérieur de l'éducation du Québec, 1998; Council of Europe, 1997). Policy statements and reports emphasize the importance of education in positioning democracy: democratic values (namely, instruction in rights and responsibilities, familiarization with the deliberative process, and the development of critical judgment); developing student's sensitivity to pluralism as well as the diversity of identities; familiarizing students with civics-related knowledge and practices in various subject-areas; and affording them the opportunity to actively take part in and commit to the School's educational project.

A Plethora of Citizenship Education Initiatives

Similar directives frame the choices respecting citizenship education set out in the Quebec Ministry of Education's most recent Educational Policy Statement (Ministère de l'Éducation, 1997). In particular, teachers and school administrators are encouraged to direct their actions towards creating or implementing various organizational and teaching frameworks, and/or predispositions within the school setting with a view to shaping either learning content or teaching approaches. In several communities, these educational objectives have been integrated into the mission of local schools, in keeping with efforts to translate into practice the perspectives outlined in the *History, Geography and Citizenship Education* components of Quebec's Education Program, and which contain recommendations for developing specific competencies among students.

There are a variety of initiatives targeted at achieving a broad array of objectives, as can be seen from a review of projects inventoried by school boards or through the research on school socialization. A number of them are conducted in adherence with comprehensive social or humanitarian causes, whereas others are focused on particular aspects of the internal workings of the school, including the school's local outreach and influence. These initiatives can generally be classified according to any one of the following educational objectives:

- Developing harmonious interpersonal relationships in the school;

- Acknowledging and accepting differences in the school and in society;

- Preventing conflict and promoting non-violent, conflict-resolution practices;

- Stimulating mutual support and co-operation through classroom, cultural, or sports-related activities in the school;

- Establishing inter-school networks or connections via the web;

- Developing attitudes of openness to the world, sensitive to controversial issues;

- Learning democratic practices in the classroom and in the school; and

- Building awareness of the workings of various political institutions and bodies.

It is important to place any assessment of these projects within a context that is broader yet more limiting. While efforts to integrate the objectives of an education anchored in democratic life may well prove crucial to the success of teachers and administrators as they supervise and regulate student conduct, there can be no denying that schools are held accountable for discharging two main duties: first, they must carry out prescribed educational activities; second, they must mediate or arbitrate, on the one hand, the interpersonal relationships of students hailing from a diversity of backgrounds and, on the other hand, the hierarchical relationships occurring between adults and young people. Thus, the pedagogical and curricular options of a school, however valuable they may be for the purposes of identifying and furthering its objectives pertaining to citizenship education, provide evidence of a deeper political or ideological enterprise originating in the School's very definition. If it is allowed that the School's educational agenda may be considered to be overtly or implicitly "political" from the outset, then it is worth examining just how the programmes are designed to build socialization or provide citizenship education, or both. However laudable or necessary they may be otherwise, these programmes are likely to be buttressed by a web of representations and practices loaded with unspoken socio-epistemological assumptions.

Concerning the precise role of the School in citizenship education, there can be no escaping the question of what meaning or finality should be ascribed to this form of learning. It is generally accepted that citizenship education can be readily conceived of in terms of preparing and readying future generations of responsible citizens. Nevertheless, the question remains as to the spirit or vision that informs particular learning choices that then stimulate diverse educational actions. For example, for some schools it might be very tempting to acquiesce to the social pressure implicitly conveyed by the notion that, in order to solve the ills of society, efforts should first be dedicated to restraining social behaviours, rather to assist students in constructing their conducts. At that point, the choice may likely be to educate with a view to achieving conformity rather than personal responsibility. Some schools' efforts to socialize students for democracy may be likened to a project of subjugating minds, as opposed to liberating them. If that, indeed, is the case, these schools may well elect to invoke their authority or to cloak themselves in a rhetoric of "doing their duty" of simply passing on knowledge.

It is germane at this point to draw on the concept referred to by Vincent (1994) as the "school form" and which this author defines as both a mindset (or *Gestalt*) and a set of rules that all actors in the school setting adhere to. Moreover, as has been noted by Larochelle (2007), the school form enshrines "the implementation and maintenance of disciplinary power" tending to predominate among a range of other, actual, or potential modes of relating to oneself and to the world. As such, the school form constitutes, in our view, a first level of institutionalization of the School as both the outcome and the history specific to its development. At the same time, it offers an organizational and attitudinal framework that is reinforced and re-produced by virtue of its function of tacitly reconfirming legitimated social conducts.

At a second level of institutionalization, the school form is also moulded by the individual representations constructed and maintained by teachers and school administrators (Vincent, Lavallée, & Sounan, 2003), who translate into practice their own positions and attitudes with respect to political, social, economic, or cultural issues, as well as their own way of conceptualizing the position and role that ought normally to fall to citizens. They accomplish this work of translation and interpretation through their choices and preferences with respect to course content, class organization, and classroom interactions. It is important to note, however, that, for complex structural reasons, this "personal input" on the part of teachers is not as free-wheeling or even as conducive to challenging the school establishment as might first be thought.

More than embodying and enforcing a particular space–time configuration among a well-defined set of actors, the "school form" also tends to impose a stereotypical scenario of knowledge (i.e., knowledge construction), as well as highly specific expectations concerning students' cognitive and behavioural commitments. The cumulative result is, too often, to point the actions of educators in the direction of standardizing knowledge, to instil a consumerist conception of knowledge (i.e., respecting the ends and applications of knowledge), and to inculcate conducts of docility in response to the ambient social discourse with an emphasis on "performance." The very absence of reflexive or critical stock taking that, as a rule, characterizes the school form thus undermines the pursuit of democratic ideals as well as the development, among students, of a personal capacity to weigh evidence and make logical connections. Ultimately, the negative implications of this de facto situation are as numerous as they are varied: students may become prone to constructing relationships to knowledge—which themselves bear witness to a kind of relationship to the world and to others—that possess few emancipative qualities; they may, indeed, become marginalized subjects, ill-equipped to deal with the school culture or simply obedient citizens.

School Subject-disciplines, the Curriculum, and the Relationship to Knowledge

> Any system of education is a political way of maintaining or modifying the appropriation of discourses, along with the knowledges and powers which they carry. (Foucault, 1981/1971, p. 64)

This apparently straightforward quotation from Michel Foucault in fact compels a radical re-vision of curriculum design and implementation, urging us to view this process as being a fundamentally political one (Petrina, 2004). It carries forward the argument above in relation to the socio-epistemological underpinnings of educational directives, implying that a central component of pursuing any school's instructional agenda consists of the manifest and tacit decisions concerning what types of knowledge are deemed to possess the requisite legitimacy. Ultimately, Foucault's words argue for a different kind of educational project in which students are enabled to gain awareness of the stakes and issues surrounding the organization of school subjects, such that they may also grasp the meaning of their involvement in a process and a system framed by considerations of power.

Some recent controversies surrounding attempts at curriculum reform offer telling illustration of the scope of factors and potential impacts that can be associated with such changes in education systems. For example, in Quebec, the publication of a new secondary school history curriculum was met with a storm of protest on the part of some historians. In their view, this programme had glossed over or omitted several main episodes and features of Quebec nationalism (Laperrière, Robichaud, Southam, & Vandal, 2006). Here, the relationship between the proposed history curriculum and citizenship education is clear-cut, for the notion of nationhood presented in the classroom is likely to shape students' ways of conceiving their role as citizens. The epistemological issues arising in connection with one version of knowledge thus constitute *socio-political* issues. Further, we cannot help but point out that what holds for the history curriculum is also true for the other subject-disciplines.

An excellent illustration of the intertwining of epistemological and socio-political stakes can be found in the account by Blades (1997) of one recent attempt at reforming a secondary science curriculum. In particular, this author describes the irony-inflected reaction that greeted the Alberta Ministry of Education's announcement of a shift away from narrow discipline studies towards an STS (Science-Technology-Society) curriculum featuring an emphasis on the social relationships underlying the techno-sciences. While these jibes (e.g., "Mickey Mouse science" and *"Reader's Digest* science") provide insight into the stance of this project's opponents, they must also be considered in terms of their strategic importance in the ensuing political conflict that ended in the rejection of the proposed reform. Rightly or wrongly, opponents perceived this project as providing students with a watered-down version of the traditional content of high school science education. Such was the basis of the alliances that were subsequently struck between the Alberta Medical Association, the Alberta Teachers' Association, and the university science faculties with a view to taking the battle over the Education Ministry's reform to the political sphere. Benefiting from considerable media coverage, these groups succeeded in alarming public opinion with their claims that, if enacted, the project would cause considerable harm. This alleged damage would come not only in terms of the impoverished scientific education provided to Alberta's youth, generally, but also of an imminent shortage of adequately trained scientists and engineers. United, these groups wielded enough political clout to force the government to back-pedal on this project, which was never carried out.

There are many lessons to be learned from this incident. To begin with, where science teaching is concerned, it would appear that scientific groups adhere to a certain orthodoxy and feel themselves to be the most fully qualified to assess the quality of this education. Furthermore, politically speaking, they adroitly leverage all such powers and authority as may be invested in them. In particular, they make or shape many of the decisions concerning the admissions standards in force at university science faculties. Such clout also explains, in large part, the continued marginalization of curricula that either portray scientific knowledge as social artefacts or that propose to make room for studying the socio-ethical issues surrounding the production of this knowledge. As there is a discernable worldwide trend towards standardizing the hierarchy of disciplines in schools (De Brabander, 2000), political realities such as these thus argue for reflecting on the relationships that may be established between the preservation of subject-based orthodoxy in science teaching, the relationship to knowledge (as constructed by experts, educators, and students), and citizenship education.

To begin with, however, it is important to recall that our societies are fraught with many controversies in existing or projected socio-technical developments (e.g., xeno-transplantation, nuclear waste, etc.). Resolving such controversies or dilemmas will oblige us to devise ways and means whereby citizens may share more fully in the decision-making process. In our view, where socio-technical developments are concerned, it is simply no longer possible to conduct debates or develop policies behind closed doors, be they in high-ranking government offices or in academic isolation. Likewise, it is patently clear the extent to which the techno-sciences are intertwined with politics. By way of demonstration, one need only consider the rapid development of biotechnology knowledge and humankind's evolving capacity to intervene in the processes of human reproduction (e.g., cloning, embryo selection, freezing of egg cells, etc.), which will completely re-configure centuries-old filiation processes.

Efforts to foster active participation in the decisions concerning controversial techno-scientific developments will entail allowing the greatest possible number of citizens to acquire an emancipative relationship towards scientific knowledge, as well as towards those who possess it. Among other things, this objective requires that citizens view themselves as constituting legitimate partners in the problem-definition process itself. Efforts to achieve this objective need not detract from recognizing the robustness of the scientific knowledge at issue, or the value of experts' contributions to defining and framing a given controversy. At the same time, however, it is readily apparent that such an option can only become feasible if the social hierarchy of knowledge reflected in schools' discipline-based curricula is seriously thrown open to question.

Deconstructing the Hierarchy of School Subject-disciplines

The success of any project to deconstruct the hierarchy of subject-disciplines will depend on the extent to which the related issues become broadly shared by the populace, and can, at that point, become the subject of society-wide debates. Such a process is eminently political in nature, as was noted by Foucault, and is also prone to encounter strong resistance, attested by the above-mentioned cases. The very question of the epistemological terrain to be staked out as a legitimating force in the curriculum debate becomes key. Curriculum design could conceivably be pursued according to procedures similar to those characterizing citizens' forums held with the objective of making decisions concerning socio-technical issues. If this vision appears to be somewhat utopian, it is worth noting that an initiative of this kind, concerning science teaching in Aboriginal communities in Saskatchewan, has already been conducted and has proven to be feasible. Aikenhead (1996), for one, in collaboration with community teachers and elders, successfully constructed a series of modules that integrated endogenous knowledge, which is now a part of the local school's curriculum. At this school, moreover, the legitimacy of endogenous knowledge is acknowledged to the same extent as is "official" scientific knowledge, although care is taken to associate both types of knowledge with two different worldviews. Students are encouraged to work in two different universes, and to cross back and forth across the border separating them, without any opportunity to establish a hierarchy between the *knowledges* stemming from the two cultures of reference.

Beyond meeting the challenge of curriculum construction, teachers must also question themselves concerning the epistemological stakes surrounding the forms of knowledge brought into contact with one another, such that teachers are able, in turn, to prompt their students to do the same. This pedagogical criterion is not exactly commonplace, as school disciplines are customarily viewed as self-evident bodies of knowledge whose origin and foundations lend themselves more or less well to scrutiny. Yet a number of recent educational experiments indicate that an opening of this kind into a form of "epistemological democracy" is indeed viable.

A team of researchers recently reported on a series of experiments designed to engage students in debates about socially sensitive issues, such as the fallout of the new biotechnologies, the potential harmfulness of cell phones, stem cell research, the legalization of marijuana, and so on (Legardez & Simonneaux, 2006). It is worth noting from the outset that none of these potentially "hot topics" can be covered exclusively within the framework of any single traditional school discipline because such issues bring into play a whole array of *knowledges*, including lay knowledge, and because they presuppose receptiveness to the interdisciplinary perspective. The teachers involved in conducting these experiments drew on a range of teaching strategies, including classroom debates, role-playing exercises, laboratory experiments, conversations in the field not only with experts and specialists but also with citizens, and participation in public debates held in the community. Where students were given both sufficient leeway and appropriate support, they showed themselves capable of taking on the complex situations presented to them. On many occasions, moreover, they displayed a capacity to establish a critical stance towards experts, noting in particular how the latter's judgement was at risk of being influenced by the sensitive relationship of the dependency linking research interests to industry funding. It was also abundantly clear, however, that when the time came to identify the appropriate action to be taken whenever scientific experts expressed disagreement, students were generally inclined to reiterate the school rhetoric around science and to deploy the characteristic empiricist arguments, as may be seen from the following excerpt of a conversation between students:

> Student 19: It will take another research study.
>
> Student 20: At the same place, at the very same place. Both groups of scientists will have to do their work at the same place. At that point, they have no choice but to come up with the same things. (Bader, 2001, pp. 120–121)

One of the lessons to be had from these experiments is the need to tackle epistemological questions directly with students if the objective remains to allow them to develop the conceptual tools needed to interrogate the hierarchy of school disciplines. Is it, in fact, realistic to engage such efforts with primary and secondary students? Wouldn't these young people be prone to embracing a simplistic form of scepticism and to espousing the view that "In the end, it's all relative"? In view of the experiments conducted with the objective of providing secondary students with an introduction into the "game" and issues of epistemological reflexivity, there are grounds for thinking that young people are well equipped to grapple with such questions. One particularly persuasive illustration of this capacity is cited by Désautels and Roth (1999). Indeed, we are forced to admit that some students are far from naïve—on the contrary, some are quite savvy—in how they go about interpreting discourses with respect to school knowledge and, with this, the limitations imposed by the "school form," as is suggested in the following excerpt:

Student 11: You know, usually, based on the categories of what they teach us at school, you figure that there can't be two different versions of one and the same reality. (Bader, 2001, p. 184)

When invited to tackle socially sensitive questions or to wrestle with the ins and outs of the production of scholarly knowledge, students can manage quite well to establish a certain distance towards the hierarchy of school disciplines. They show no signs of being de-stabilized at the realization that what counts as knowledge is relative to the socio-historical conditions of production underpinning this knowledge. Nor, for that matter, do they appear to adopt a position of nihilistic relativism towards knowledge. The above-mentioned studies show that while it is possible to achieve critical distance taking among students, success will very much depend on the skill with which teachers take up the challenge of this kind of education, which admittedly breaks with time-tested classroom approaches and socially approved techniques.

Conclusion

Today's societies are ripe with numerous conflicts and disturbances that have caused social bonds to grow brittle, thus jeopardizing efforts to make good on the ideal or objective of democracy. Against this backdrop, the School, in its capacity as an institution of socialization, carries out a variety of initiatives and projects designed to provide youth with an education in *"le vivre-ensemble."* The School will prove to be incapable of developing citizenship skills among young people if it continues to disregard the question of how to engage them in activities of critical deliberation whereby they are empowered to challenge prevailing ideas. Following from this premise, the School must seek to create those conditions for which students are able to question the hierarchy of school disciplines and, also, to gain some awareness and insight into how this hierarchy tends to reflect the arbitrary division of power in society. Indeed, if the School does not see to this responsibility, who will?

Questions for Reflection

1. In their dual capacity of citizens and social actors, teachers and school administrators are compelled to take part in the construction of a society that is open, pluralistic, just, and

democratic. What perspective frames their appropriation of the abundance of sensitive issues or controversies with which our societies are currently grappling and that often pose a thorny challenge to the democratic ideal?

2. How may educators reconcile their dual role as guide/director to students, and also be a source of support to students throughout the process of the social construction of identity?

3. By what means, and under what conditions, could the School become a genuine place of critical expression, debate, and position taking, all the while remaining mindful of its mandate and the numerous constraints surrounding its work?

4. What sort of curriculum design would prove conducive to stimulating reflection among students and teachers concerning the relationship to knowledge in our societies?

5. What directions and procedures ought to be accorded priority in pre-service teaching programmes with a view to integrating a concern for citizenship education, regardless of the track or specialization embarked upon? What place should the study of epistemology and the sociology of knowledge occupy in these programmes?

Notes

The authors wish to thank our translator Donald Kellough for his contributions to both the form and content of this chapter.

1. "School" (with a capital "s") is understood in this chapter to refer not only to the institution from a sociological perspective but also, from a narrative perspective, as constituting an actor in a web of discourse pertaining to knowledge, power, and, of course, education.

2. In a sense, "*le vivre-ensemble*" recalls the notions underlying the now seemingly antiquated English term of "commonweal"—namely, the active sharing in the life of one's community and the envisioning of oneself as a member of the body politic.

3. The original term, in German, is *Sittlichkeit*, which is also translated as "(right) ethical life."

4. Interestingly enough, the notion that citizenship education has the potential to influence renewal of the social dynamic is one of the driving assumptions of these educators' efforts to date in an attempt to underscore the relationship between education for socialization and citizenship education.

References

Aikenhead, G. S. (1996). Science education: Border crossing into the subculture of science. *Studies in Science Education, 27*, 1–52.

Bader, B. (2001). *Étude de conversations estudiantines autour d'une controverse entre scientifiques sur la question du réchauffement climatique.* Unpublished doctoral dissertation, Université Laval, Québec, QC.

Barber, B. R. (1984). *Strong democracy: Participatory politics for a new age.* Berkeley: University of California Press.

Berthelot, J. (1994). *Une école de son temps: un horizon démocratique pour l'école et le collège.* Québec, QC: Centrale de l'enseignement du Québec.

Blades, D. W. (1997). *Procedures of power and curriculum change: Foucault and the quest for possibilities in science education.* New York: Peter Lang.

Conseil supérieur de l'éducation. (1998). *Éduquer à la citoyenneté: Rapport annuel sur l'état et les besoins de l'éducation 1997–98.* Sainte-Foy, QC: Le Conseil.

Council of Europe. (1997). *Project: Education for democratic citizenship: Seminar on basic concepts and core competences.* Strasbourg, France: Council for Cultural Cooperation.

De Brabander, C. J. (2000). Knowledge definition, subject, and educational track level: Perceptions of secondary school teachers. *American Educational Research Journal, 37*(4), 1027–1058.

Désautels, J., & Roth, W.-M. (1999). Demystifying epistemological practice. *Cybernetics and Human Knowing, 6*(1), 33–45.

Dubet, F. (2000). *Les inégalités multipliées.* Paris: L'Aube.

Duru-Bellat, M. (2000) Les inégalités face à l'école en Europe, L'éclairage des comparaisons internationales. In A. Van Zanten (Ed.), *L'école, l'état des savoirs* (pp. 322–330). Paris: La Découverte.

Forquin, J. C. (2000). *Sociologie de l'éducation: Nouvelles approches, nouveaux objets.* Paris: Institut national de la recherche pédagogique.

Foucault, M. (1981/1971). *L'ordre du discours.* Paris: Gallimard. [English translation: "The Order of Discourse" in R. Young (Ed.), *Untying the text: A poststructuralist reader* (I. McLeod, trans.) (pp. 48–78). Boston: Routledge & Kegan Paul.]

Grand-Maison, J. (1999). *Quand le jugement fout le camp: Essai sur la déculturation.* Saint-Laurent, QC: Fides.

Held, D., & McGrew, A. G. (Eds.). (2000). *The global transformations reader: An introduction to the globalization debate.* Oxford, UK: Blackwell.

Honneth, A. (2000). *The struggle for recognition: The moral grammar of social conflicts.* Cambridge, UK: Polity Press.

Innerarity, D. (2002). *La démocratie sans l'état: Essai sur le gouvernement des sociétés complexes.* Paris: Climats.

Laperrière, G., Robichaud, L., Southam, P., & Vandal, G. (2006, August 25). Nouvelle mouture du programme d'histoire au secondaire–Du programme à l'enseignement. *Le Devoir* (Montreal), p. A-9.

Larochelle, M. (2007). Disciplinary power and the school form. *Cultural Studies of Science Education, 2*(4), 711–720.

Legardez, A., & Simonneaux, L. (Eds.). (2006). *L'école à l'épreuve de l'actualité: Enseigner des questions vives.* Paris: ESF.

Mabilon-Bonfils, B., & Saadoun, L. (2001). *Sociologie politique de l'école.* Paris: Presses universitaires de France.

Michaud, Y. (2006). *Précis de recomposition politique: Des incivismes à la française et de quelques manières d'y remédier.* Paris: Flammarion.

Ministère de l'Éducation. (1997). *L'école, tout un programme: Énoncé de politique éducative.* Québec, QC: Government of Quebec.

Petrina, S. (2004). The politics of curriculum and instructional design/theory/form: Critical problems, projects, units and modules. *Interchange, 35*(1), 81–126.

Reynolds A. (2002). *The architecture of democracy: Constitutional design, conflict management, and democracy.* New York: Oxford University Press.

Rowe, G., & Frewer, L. J. (2000). Public participation methods: A framework for evaluation. *Science, Technology, and Human Values, 25*(1), 3–29.

Vibert, S. (2002). La démocratie dans un espace «postnational»? Holisme, individualisme et modernité politique. *Anthropologie et Sociétés, 26*(1), 177–194.

Vincent, G. (1994). *L'éducation prisonnière de la forme scolaire? Scolarisation et socialisation dans les sociétés industrielles.* Lyon, France: Presses universitaires de Lyon.

Vincent, S., Lavallée, M., & Sounan, C. (2003). Approche de la représentation sociale de la citoyenneté et de l'éducation à la citoyenneté chez de futurs enseignants du secondaire au Québec. In M. Lavallée, S. Vincent, C. Ouellet, & C. Garnier (Eds.), *Les représentations sociales. Constructions nouvelles* (pp. 373–391). Montreal, PQ: Université du Québec à Montréal. Retrieved August 23, 2007, from http://www.unites.uqam.ca/geirso/frameset/publications.html

16

TOMORROW'S TEACHERS:
THE CHALLENGES OF DEMOCRATIC
ENGAGEMENT

Beverly-Jean Daniel and R. Patrick Solomon

Introduction

Tomorrow's teachers are ideally located, either to reproduce the social order and its inherent inequities or engage in critical democratic schooling that will transform Canadian society. Education policies and practices in Western societies appear to be counterproductive to the preparation for democratic schooling. Current teacher preparation is characterized by the standardization of teacher-education curriculum; the marginalization of divergent knowledge forms; teacher testing for proof of competency to teach; and teacher induction and the transmission of dominant values, traditions, and perspectives. Giroux and McLaren (1986) characterize these practices as "entirely removed from a vision of a set of practices dedicated to the fostering of critical democracy and social justice" (p. 227).

In this chapter we explore preservice teachers'[1] understandings of democratic engagement in their multiple sites of preparation: the university classroom, field-based practicum classrooms, and the extended school-community practicum. We identify the challenges they encounter in moving from theorized versions of critical democracy to actualized practices in the schools and communities where they develop their craft. The overwhelming premise of this chapter is that if preservice teachers are not provided the opportunities to engage democratically in the process of learning to teach, it is unlikely that they will teach for democracy and social justice when they assume full responsibility teaching in their classrooms. This ominous projection has tremendous implications for teacher educators and institutions that participate in the preparation of the next generation of teachers.

Theorizing Teacher Preparation for Democratic Schooling

Contemporary and twentieth-century scholars, such as John Dewey, Paulo Freire, Henri Giroux, Stuart Hall, Ben Levin, and bell hooks among others, have provided a range of ideas on the topic of democracy and education. Arising from these visions of democracy, Portelli and Solomon (2001) have distilled the common elements to be "critical thinking, dialogue and discussion, tolerance, free and reasoned choices, and public participation ... a conception of democracy which is associated with equity, community, creativity and taking difference seriously" (p. 17). In this chapter we draw from those foundational ideas and believe that teachers play a central role in enacting democracy in classrooms and in society at large. Teacher education is perceived by critical scholars as central to the development and maintenance of a democratic society. Hartnett and Carr (1995) argue:

> Society is dependent upon the quality of their [teachers'] judgments, values, knowledge and sensitivities in particular in social contexts to negotiate acceptable solutions to issues of authority in education; to sustain the development of democratic values in the wider society.... They are a critical pivot between the state, parental power, institutional power and the development of democratic values and attitudes in each new generation. (p. 43)

But according to the critics of teacher education, Hartnett and Carr's idealized notion of democratic teacher education is far from being actualized (Darling-Hammond, 1998; Giroux & McLaren, 1986; Menter, 1989). Giroux and McLaren (1986) contend that traditional teacher education is weak in fostering critical democracy and does not lead to the transformation of schools and society. Instead, it tends to reproduce societal norms, values, and ways of operating; it plays the role of service institutions preparing students to fit into, rather than transform, hierarchical, corporate-driven structures. Giroux and McLaren urge teacher educators to "adopt a more critical role of challenging the social order so as to develop and advocate its democratic imperatives" (p. 224).

The field-based component of teacher preparation is particularly sensitive to antidemocratic practices. Critics argue that the social and political contexts of school-based practice tend to restrict candidates' engagement in reflective, critical, and enquiring practice. Established school culture and its intertwined power relations tend to tether pre-service teachers to the bottom of the school hierarchy and impede the practice of democracy (Grant & Zozakiewicz, 1995; Menter, 1989; Solomon, 2000). This is particularly troubling since Su's (1992) research on sources of influence in preservice teacher socialization highlights that student teaching and cooperating (mentor) teachers are the most important sources of such influence, while the course curriculum at the university is less influential.

Zeichner (1991) states that "we cannot build tomorrow's schools in today's unequal society" (p. 374). We concur and add that we cannot democratize schools without democratically engaged teachers. In the sections that follow we provide a brief overview of a teacher preparation initiative that integrates the principle of democracy in its theoretical framework, and document the challenges, tensions, and contradictions preservice teachers experience as they move from idealized to actualized democratic education.

Teacher Preparation Setting

Preservice teachers in this 1-year post-baccalaureate B.Ed. program reflect the diversity in the larger urban population from which they are drawn. Most are Canadian born, and some are immigrants who were schooled in their country of origin before migrating to Canada. This initiative moves beyond traditional teacher preparation and integrates into its philosophy and practices an inclusive curriculum and pedagogy; opportunities for professional development across "social difference", and an engagement with community, thereby building university-school-community partnerships as a "community of learners." The field-based practicum constitutes over 60 percent of the teacher preparation time, positing it to have a major impact on candidates' induction into the profession; candidates are involved in varying ways with the entire school community, including parents and community organizations. In addition, each candidate is assigned to a mentor-teacher whose role, among other duties, is to provide ongoing modeling of effective teaching and to assist candidates to integrate theory and practice.

The democratic education initiative infuses issues of equity, diversity, and social justice into the curriculum content; theories of education (social, cultural, philosophical, and historical); and field-based practicum courses. Some of the key questions for educators that are explored include What is democratic education? What is social justice? What is citizenship education? What is critical pedagogy? (Hare & Portelli, 2005). Here, candidates are provided a theoretical grounding in issues that are central to democratic schooling. More importantly, the challenges of moving from theory to practice in schools and communities are made evident.

Preparing tomorrow's teachers for democratic schooling is central to the initiative from which the data for this study are drawn. Responses of 15 teacher-education candidates who had graduated from the teacher-education program the previous year and who responded to an online questionnaire were analyzed. The participant sample was quite diverse and included participants who included were of African, South Asian, and Eastern European ancestry. The participants were asked to discuss their understanding of democracy as a philosophical approach to education; the way in which issues of social justice inform their thinking about democratic education; to identify the ways in which democratic education was evidenced in their practicum, university classroom, and community placements; and the obstacles to enacting democratic education. The specific responses from the teacher-candidates are included in block quotes in the text.

Findings and Discussion: Conceptualizing Democracy

Based on the responses from the teacher-candidates, democratic education has to be discussed using two frames that are both complementary and, at times, contradictory. The construct of democratic education emerged along two fronts, theorized and actualized. Theorized democracy was based on TCs' conceptualization of democratic education informed by course reading materials (e.g., Friere, 1993; Glass, 2005; Hare & Portelli, 2005). The following quotes were provided by the TCs:

Democracy in its philosophical approach to education is rooted ... within the framework of equity, social justice and diversity. This ideology ... can only be practiced within a setting where democratic approaches are made at every level. (Linda, White female).

Democracy ... implies that all participants in the education system can have a say in the way that education is delivered. (Tamara, Black female)

Actualized democracy was perceived more as the practice of democracy in given contexts. To this end, TCs cited their own willingness to have parental involvement in the schooling process as well as openness to having students involved in determining the educational trajectory within the context of their classroom.

Giving students, their families and their communities opportunities to become invested in the school through recognition of the contributions and cultural and social practices and background showed me a... understanding of what it means to practice democracy in education. (Nancy, White female)

These ideas reflect Hartnett and Carr's (1995) idea that teachers' judgments, beliefs, and critical understanding of social institutions significantly inform their ability to engage in democratic educational practices.

TCs theoretical understandings also became an essential reference point for their critique of actualized democracy. They critiqued the gap between the theory and the practice of democracy and challenged the possibility of truly democratic engagement. Further, TCs believed that the theory of democracy in effect served to obfuscate the true nature of everyday schooling practices. Some participants were convinced that the actualized version of democracy was devoid of the theorized notion of democracy. One student explicitly stated that "the term 'democracy' is sometimes used as a smoke screen to pacify the under privileged" (Sharon, Black Female).

The participants believed in the possibility of democratic engagement within education. However, people's unwillingness to push the boundaries of traditional schooling, fear of reprisals, and the level of power and control that gatekeepers in school possessed, limited their options for true democratic engagement. The results of this research reflect the willingness on the part of the teacher-candidates to adopt more socially just practices in the development of their craft; however, the traditional structure, development, and delivery of the teacher-education program can actually limit their ability to engage in transformative practices (Giroux & McLaren, 1986).

There were concrete examples of actualized democratic engagement that participants provided, which served to bridge the theory/practice divide. For example, one TC discussed her observations regarding the practice of democracy by the host teacher in her interactions with students in the classroom and stated: "At my practicum school I had a marvelous experience with my second mentor teacher and will incorporate a number of things I learnt from her in my own class" (Sharon, Black female). She also spoke of the way in which the mentor-teacher invited the informed participation of students:

> Students in my practicum school and classrooms were treated with respect.… A high level of academic achievement and character education of the students was held in high esteem. For example, teachers spoke to students, as they wanted to be spoken to…" (Karen, White female)

The ability of the mentor-teachers to model positive teacher-student interaction provided the TCs with experiences that strengthened their ability to move democratic education from theory to practice. This observation highlights the importance of experiential learning, the need to have effective and engaged mentor teachers who move beyond simply naming expected practices such as diversity, inclusion, and democracy and enacting these practices in the context of everyday schooling, to validate authentic engagement. The data from this study replicates Su's (1992) research, which underscores the importance of the role of mentor teachers.

The teacher-candidates in this study conceptualized democratic education as consisting of the following terms: collaboration, inclusion, facilitating the inclusion of multiple voices in a manner that is safe and requires the involvement of all educational stakeholders. Additionally, democratic education involves the development of responsible citizens (Glass, 2005), who are informed, analytical, and keenly aware of the power they have to change the events in their lives and society in general. Another key idea that framed the candidates' conceptions of democratic education is ensuring that each party has a safe space to voice their concerns and question existing social situations and contexts. "Doing democracy," therefore, requires an engagement with and practice of democracy.

These conceptualizations of democratic education are central, and candidates' theoretical notions of democratic education provide them with an effective lens for critiquing educational practices within varied contexts, including their teacher-education program, their practicum school, and community placements. el-Ojeili and Hayden (2006), in their discussion of critical theories, the school of thought within which democratic education is located, indicate that

> Uncritical approaches to theory regard social reality as a pure "fact," an objective given that can be apprehended in a neutral or value-free sense, critical theory considers the social order and our knowledge of it as being historically constituted and contingently situated. This has two implications: first, our understanding of the social and political world cannot be disconnected from the historically contextualized beliefs and assumptions that inform our interpretations of that reality; and, second, our interpretations and theories do not simply describe reality but also shape and produce it. (el-Ojeili & Hayden, 2006, p. 11)

The teacher-candidates' conceptions of democratic education also provide an effective foundation for providing them with the tools that are necessary to enact democratic practices in their future classrooms (Portelli & Solomon, 2001). el-Ojeili and Hayden (2006) further indicate that "theory is not a neutral instrument for passively disclosing reality, but a lens through which agents actively analyze their world and propose alternative ways to shape and reshape it" (p. 11).

Another aspect of the participants' conceptualizations of democratic education is that it enables them to engage in a critical examination and interrogation of the observed practices and interactions (Glass, 2005) that were evidenced in the multiple sites of the teacher-education program. They develop the ability to observe and critique existing social relations of schooling; to identify the aspects of in-service teachers' practices and the overall culture of the schools that promote and limit the application of democratically enhanced educational practices; and to see the challenges that will impact their efficacy at incorporating democratic education into their teaching repertoire (Daniel, 2003). This experience effectively encapsulates peer learning practices (Eisen, 2001; Valentino, 1998), given that teacher-candidates are learning from their peers, their mentor-teachers, other teachers, and school administrators and members of community organizations who engage with democratic as well as undemocratic practices (Eisen, 2001; Su, 1992). Additionally, candidates' site-based experiences expose them to the daily manifestations and resistances to democratic education.

The teacher-candidates are uniquely positioned to engage theory and practice of democratic education and enact them in a way that can serve to improve the lives of their students (Harnett & Carr, 1995; Zeichner, 1991). Further, these experiences can serve to sharpen their critique of existing social relations of schooling and map out possible strategies that then can be employed to circumvent the obstacles they will face in their future classrooms.

Teacher Preparation Sites of Engagement

The teacher-candidates are provided with three primary sites of learning and engagement during the tenure of their teacher-education program: the university classroom, placements in local community organizations, and the practicum school. The university classroom provides opportunities for theoretical learning; the community involvement provides candidates opportunities to learn in, from, and about communities from which students come; and, finally, the practicum school where they are under the tutelage of a mentor-teacher and can learn the art and practice of pedagogy. In effect, the teacher-candidates are provided with opportunities to learn about and witness the multiple aspects of democratic education thereby providing a trifecta effect.

The University Classroom

When discussing the interactions of their peers in the university classroom, the participants were critical of the ways in which their peers mouthed the trope of democratic education, primarily in an attempt to buttress their grading. However, the ideas that were articulated in the presence of the instructors or those that were included in written assignments belied the truth of their interactions and statements in the smaller groups. One student stated, "You felt from the outset that 'it was a competition' in order to outdo the next person. People were not always willing to share and the minority groups were made to feel very uncomfortable at times by [dominant group] colleagues."[2]

Statements and reflections such as these belie the fallacy of assuming that the ability to engage with a particular discourse of social justice equates a belief in or a willingness to engage in and enact socially just practices. The teacher-candidates indicated that their peers engaged in practices that are undemocratic and engaged in marginalizing practices in the program that included silencing voices of immigrant students, as well as dissenting voices. The trope of democracy was used as a smoke-screen essentially to fulfill course requirements, as the following quotes reveal:

> Democracy existed as much as the "natives" pretended for course directors to see it, mostly for grades sake. (Karen, White female)

> In the university classroom this year, I saw many incidents where democratic education ironically (considering the material that we studied) was under great strain. Often during group work, dominant personalities would control the direction of a presentation while at the same time some individuals would not shoulder their responsibilities. I also found, during the classroom discussions, that many of the students felt intimidated to speak their mind on a variety of controversial issues raised during the year. I can think of a few different classes where dissenting opinions were often met with such shock by classmates, guest speakers and even instructors. As a result of this kind of uproar, many students produced views on paper which reflected the course instructor's views rather than their own. (John, White male)

The above quotes highlight the need to provide the TCs with multiple opportunities for self-analysis and for teacher-educators to address the trope of democratic engagement versus an ideological and applied commitment.

The Practicum School

Similarly, participants observed undemocratic behaviors in their practicum settings. They spoke of the marginalizing practices of the members of the school community, which served to remind them of their outsider and subordinate status (Grant & Zozakiewicz, 1995) and underscored their unwillingness to challenge the culture of the organization. The following quote was provided by a teacher-candidate as an example of marginalizing, undemocratic teacher-student interaction:

> I could just have assumed that the Black students just "stuck with their own kind" and they "just hate people who are not like them ..." I noticed that the teachers, mostly White, tended to lecture and discipline the Black male students in the class the most. After a while, I could see how any student would lose their self-esteem after countless lectures by teachers and trips to the office. (Brandon, White male)

The teacher-candidates also spoke of the comments that were openly stated in the staff lunchrooms regarding their assessments of some of the students in their classrooms: "Some White teachers actually feared these groups (Black males) of students to the point of avoidance, even to the point of occasionally portraying these students as gangs in staff room discussions" (Brandon, White male). This fear of Black males by White teachers is well documented in the research literature (Noguera, 2003; Sewell, 1997; Solomon & Palmer, 2006). This has led to differential and undemocratic treatment of Black youth under such initiatives as the Safe Schools—often labeled "zero tolerance"—policies in Ontario and other jurisdictions.

The instances of undemocratic practices were also evidenced in the hierarchical structure of the relationship between the in-service and preservice teachers, which limited preservice teachers' ability to practice democratic education. One teacher complained:

> My group members opined that it was really hard to teach democratically using a prescribed curriculum that is totally undemocratic. Moreover, schools have a fixed hierarchical structure, which does not allow staff and students to have democratic opportunities while making inside and outside decisions. (Shanti, South Asian female)

Oftentimes in my practicum school certain teachers were treated in a more respectful manner than some other teachers because of seniority. The whole notion of seniority … continues the perpetual cycle of undemocratic education. (Ranjin, South Asian male)

The practicum site behaviors TCs perceived as undemocratic may be summarized as the hierarchical school culture and the structure of relationships between in-service and preservice teachers (Menter, 1989); the implementation of standardized curriculum with little regard for locally generated curriculum and pedagogy (culturally relevant pedagogy); and the differential treatment of students, based on markers of social difference such as race. Further, these factors limit the possibility of developing democratic teachers when they are honing their craft in undemocratic classrooms.

Community Involvement

The structure of organizations, as earlier indicated, is often hierarchically constituted (Grant & Zozakiewicz, 1995; Menter, 1989; Solomon, 2000) and is organic. That is, movement and change are often built in to return the environment to a form of stasis to ensure that the organization continues to function in a manner that is self-perpetuating. Many organizations fall into a structural-functionalist model, which proscribes the given roles and relations that govern the overall functioning of the organization. People who are regarded as being foreign to the existing model of organizational culture are expected to conform to the behaviors of the existing system, and primarily become assimilated.

Teacher-candidates who are grounded in the philosophy and practice of democratic education are likely to be opposed to the culture of such organizations. They may be deemed a threat and, as such, the organic nature of the environment reformulates itself to circumvent or at least neutralize the perceived threat: "People might see you as a trouble-maker trying to stir things up" (Sharon, Black female). Therefore, the interaction with teacher-candidates may be informed by organizational norms that limit their ability to effectively engage in democratic practices in their community engagement.

Community organizations may replicate the hierarchical structure of the school (Hartnett & Carr, 1995) and, in much the same way that those who are considered to be members of the organization are regarded as having an insider perspective and by default a more informed perspective, their input may be valued over that of the teacher- candidates. The construction of the teacher-candidate as neophytes serves to stultify their experience and limit the potential impact that they may have in their community work. According to a teacher-candidate:

> At times I feel communities are more open to new people coming in if they are not seen as a threat, unlike in schools where you are seen as the new kid on the block who is trying to show off. You are made to feel like "what is it that you are going to show me that I haven't already seen before?" even before you try anything. (Sharon, Black female)

Neophytes are learning first hand about the potential obstacles to the practice of democratic education. This allows them to develop a set of strategies for circumventing the culture of resistance that is often evidenced. If the candidates are prepared to critically evaluate their experiences in these placements (Giroux & McLaren, 1986), and develop the skills of effective response, rather than a focus on the barriers to their engagement and promotion of socially just practices, they can enter their teaching careers with a more informed and realistic understanding of the ways in which they can enact democratic education.

Within the context of the teacher-education course that is explicitly grounded in democratic education principles and practices, candidates are encouraged to become advocates and to be politically involved. This form of political involvement is marked as a central aspect of critical theory that, according to el-Ojeili and Hayden (2006), is "especially concerned with addressing the forms of systemic exclusion associated with the social, economic and political status quo, insofar as the established system often replicates entrenched power relations which have detrimental effects on systematically excluded groups." As a part of their teacher-education program candidates are obliged to collaborate with organizations in the development of services and supports that meet the needs of the students and their parents. However, when their democratic approaches contradict the "systems approach" to intervention, tensions develop between candidates and the members of the community organizations.

Challenging systemic inequities while reifying the norms of a particular system are incongruent and, therefore, can complicate the practice of democracy in the field, again underscoring the divide between theorized and actualized democracy. What we do learn from these contestations is the importance of recognizing that there are no pure systems, and that, in order for any system to be enacted, one remains in a constant state of challenge, negotiation, and change. The idea that one can simply move into a system that is organic, and enact unidirectional change with limited resistance, is at best a fallacy. Another candidate stated that:

> It is not easy to implement change, and ... true democracy fosters change, allowing people to exchange their views which stomps out old routinized ways. With the exchange of diverse ideas, education for democracy and social change can come into play. (Shauna, White female)

The implication for teacher-educators here is that cross-institutional negotiation and conflict management skills are essential to bringing about democratic change in organizations.

Voice and Safety

The teacher-candidates underscored the importance of voice and safety across their learning sites in teacher preparation:

> I believe that democratic education is where all individuals are participating and given the right and freedom to speak his/her mind. Furthermore, educators must also create an environment where it is safe to embrace different viewpoints and discuss them without prosecution..." (Ranjin, South Asian male)

Another indicated:

> Democracy implies that power is held by the people of a particular group. Each individual has a voice ... that his or her voice can have an impact on the conditions within the group. (Tamara, Black female)

The participants affirmed their belief in the importance of ensuring that all members of the school and wider community be assured the space to voice concerns and engage in informed critiques of the existing systems in the society. The right to have a voice should also be accompanied by a sense of safety, thereby ensuring that there were no penalties for voicing one's concerns. Yet another teacher-candidate stated that democratic practices involve "Freedom to express oneself in a safe environment without our feeling foolish, wrong or having to follow or agree with what is being talked about. Feeling safe in disagreeing because you will not feel ridiculed" (Sharon, Black female).

Feminist authors believe that voice and speech are central aspects of resistance for oppressed groups (Anzaldua, 1990; hooks, 1990), as such there are multiple attempts of those who hold power in society to silence those voices. According to hooks (1990), when she has chosen to speak through her writings, she "had expected a climate of critical dialogue ... not a critical avalanche that had the power in its intensity to crush spirit, to push one into silence" (p. 339). She goes on to say:

> Moving from silence into speech is for the oppressed, the colonized, the exploited, and those who stand and struggle side by side, a gesture of defiance that heals, that makes new life, and new growth possible. It is that act of speech, of "talking back" that is no mere gesture of empty words, that is the expression of moving from object to subject, that is the liberated voice. (p. 340)

Voice then, which is equated with speech, becomes an important and central aspect of challenging hegemonic discourses of schooling and schooling practice. Therefore, given the oppressive nature of schooling, there are varying attempts to silence the voice. The participants spoke not only of the silencing of the students, but also of the ways in which they as teacher-candidates are also silenced by the gatekeepers through varying technologies of marginalization, such as limiting their input in the classrooms, or in the development and delivery of the curriculum. One TC posits:

> I think the greatest obstacles I faced and will still face relate to administrative bottle-neck and resistance to new ideas by colleagues and (possibly) parents of my students. As a teacher candidate I had a number of ideas that I wanted to make use of around the school but couldn't because I faced opposition from the administration and I even witnessed the same thing sometimes being done to regular staff. It is hard to come up with new and innovative ideas when the atmosphere is not conducive or people are not open to trying new things!" (Sharon, Black female)

Voice is an important aspect of democratic citizenship. If we fail to give people a voice, we are literally dumbing down the citizenry (Lather, 1990) and scaring them into nonparticipation through various strategies of fear. Another TC reflects:

> For the last 15 years here I was doing everything in my power to help raise the awareness around democracy and democratic education. I have not done too much, mostly because of lack of co-operation and fear of stating a simple democratic opinion that could cost you with isolation from the rest of the community, school, etc. By being silent you actually help discrimination to continue, most people live their "little" lives scared of losing their jobs, positions, benefits…" (Karen, White female)

Learning to think critically emerges through an engagement with dialogue. Put another way, the failure to facilitate dialogue becomes a form of silencing and contributes to the failure to develop analytical critical thinking skills. However, "the more that citizens participate in the wide range of activities that form a just community, the more these conflicts find voice and possible resolutions within democratic institutions" (Glass, 2005, p. 86). By supporting an engagement with democracy, tomorrow's teachers can play a central role in that process, and "facilitate the formation of … citizens who intentionally embody their power to make history and culture in the quest for a just pluralistic democracy" (Glass, 2005, p. 86).

Implications for Schooling

This research underscores several implications for preparing teachers for democratic schooling. The study highlights the primacy of a theory-practice alignment for true educational democracy to be realized. The connection between theorized and actualized democracy should be evidenced within and across all sites of teacher preparation, including the university classroom, the practicum school, and community placements. It is important, therefore, that teacher educators develop a more engaged and comprehensive process of ensuring that the philosophical positioning that is grounded in teacher-education is articulated to all stakeholders in the schooling process.

With that said, however, the exposure to undemocratic practices in the three learning sites became opportunities for the development of learning strategies to overcome resistance and to identify effective strategies for enact-

ing democracy in their future classrooms. Because of their grounding in the
theory of democracy, the candidates in this study were effectively prepared to
address the inconsistencies and contradictions of democratic schooling.
However, we cannot assume that all candidates will be able to effectively
navigate this morass without adequate preparation. In addition, there were
indications that some of the candidates learned the language of democracy
and social justice but superficially applied it in an attempt to "pass" as democratic teachers. Unfortunately it can be difficult to separate the true
practitioners from the ones who are focused on self-maintenance; however,
teacher-educators have to be aware of these discrepancies.

Tomorrow's teachers have to learn to navigate the politics inherent in
these multiple sites of political democratic engagement and recognize that
enacting democracy requires constant negotiations. Destabilizing the existing
power relations and hierarchical structures that exist at the sites of engagement is an ongoing process that involves multiple challenges and resistances.
Developing the skills to work around such obstacles is an integral aspect of
learning. There are multiple tensions that emerge when change is afoot and
the sites of privilege are deemed to be shifting. The primary point is that
teachers of tomorrow have to be involved in the negotiation of democracy.

Questions for Reflection

1. The hierarchical culture of schools makes it challenging for new teachers to effect democ-
    ratic change. Explore "points of entry" to start the process of democratization.

2. To move from theorized to actualized democracy teachers must be "critical pivots be-
    tween the state, parental power and institutional power." What competencies must they
    develop to engage with these power groups?

3. How may teachers develop democratic relationships across the institutional borders of
    school and community so that these sites provide mutual benefits in the schooling proc-
    ess?

4. Taking "social difference" seriously is a hallmark of critical democracy. How do we ex-
    pose those who masquerade as democratic practitioners and engage them in the true
    practice of democracy?

5. The challenges of engagement often force new teachers to delay democratic classroom
    practices. What are some of the dangers of "putting democracy on ice?"

Notes

1. In preservice teacher-education programs. The labels "tomorrow's teachers," "preservice teachers," and "teacher-candidates" (TCs) are used interchangeably throughout this chapter.

2. Although a specific program objective was to foster interdependent and collaborative learning, TCs who were socialized in a competitive, capitalist culture found it problematic to disengage from competitive behaviors. By the same token, TCs (usually immigrants) from "collectivist" cultures felt discomfort in engaging competitively. See Hofstede (1986) for his work on cultural differences in teaching and learning.

References

Anzaldua, G. (1990). How to tame a wild tongue. In R. Ferguson, M. Gever, T. T. Minh-ha, & C. West (Eds.), *Out there: Marginalization and contemporary cultures* (pp. 203–212). Cambridge, MA: MIT Press.

Daniel, B. M. (2003). *Cohort group membership and individual agency in teacher education: Implication for addressing issues of race, gender and class.* Unpublished doctoral dissertation, University of Toronto, Toronto.

Darling-Hammond, L. (1998). Education for democracy. In W. C. Mayers & J. Miller (Eds.), *A light in dark times: Maxine Green and the unfinished conversation* (pp. 78–91). New York: Teachers College Press.

Eisen, M.-J. (2001). Peer-based learning: A new-old alternative to professional development. *Adult Learning, 12*(1), 9–10.

el-Ojeili, C., & Hayden, P. (2006). *Critical theories of globalization.* New York: Palgrave Macmillan.

Freire, P. (1993). *Pedagogy of the oppressed* (rev. 20th anniversary ed.). New York: Continuum.

Giroux, H., & McLaren, P. (1986). Teacher education and the politics of engagement: The case for democratic schooling. *Harvard Educational Review, 56*(3), 213–238.

Glass, R. D. (2005). What is democratic education? In W. Hare & J. P. Portelli (Eds.), *Key questions for educators.* Halifax, Nova Scotia: Edphil Books.

Grant, C. A., & Zozakiewicz, C. A. (1995). Student teachers, cooperating teachers and supervisors: Interrupting the multicultural silences of student teaching. In J. M. Markin & C. E. Sleeter (Eds.), *Developing multicultural teacher education curricula* (pp. 259–278). Albany, NY: State University of New York Press.

Hartnett, A., & Carr, W. (1995). Education, teacher development and the struggle for democracy. In J. Smyth (Ed.), *Critical discourses on teacher development* (pp. 39-53). Toronto, ON: OISE Press.

Hare, W., & Portelli, J. P. (Eds.). (2005). *Key questions for educators.* Halifax, Nova Scotia: Edphil Books.

Hofstede, G. (1986). Cultural differences in teaching and learning. *International Journal of Intercultural Relations, 10*(3), 301–320.

Hooks, B. (1990). Talking back. In R. Ferguson, M. Gever, T. T. Minh-ha, & C. West (Eds.), *Out there: Marginalization and contemporary cultures* (pp. 337–340). Cambridge, MA: MIT Press.

Lather, P. (1990, April). *Staying dumb? Student resistance to liberatory curriculum.* Paper presented at the American Educational Research Association, Boston, MA.

Menter, I. (1989). Teaching practice stasis: Racism, sexism and school experience in initial teacher education. *British Journal of Sociology of Education, 10*(4), 459–473.

Noguera, P. (2003) The trouble with Black boys: The role and influence of environmental and cultural factors on the academic performance of African American males. *Urban Education, 38*(4), 431–459.

Portelli, J., & Solomon, R. P. (2001). *The erosion of democracy in education: From critique to possibilities.* Calgary, AB: Detselig.

Sewell, T. (1997, March). *Teacher attitude: Who is afraid of the big, Black boy?* Paper presented at the Annual Meeting of the American Educational Research Association, Chicago, IL.

Solomon, R. P. (2000). Exploring cross-race dyad partnerships in learning to teach. *Teachers College Record* (special issue on Multicultural Education), *102*(6), 953–979.

Solomon, R. P., & Palmer, H. (2006). Black boys through the school–prison pipeline: When "racial profiling" and "zero tolerance" collide. In D. Armstrong & B. McMahon (Eds.), *Inclusion in urban educational environments: Addressing issues of diversity, equity and social justice* (pp. 191–212). Greenwich, CT: Information Age.

Su, J. Z. (1992). Sources of influence in pre-service teacher socialization. *Journal of Education for Teaching, 18*(3), 239–258.

Valentino, L. R. (1998). *Teacher study groups: A case of teacher groups and their influence on teachers' attitudes towards student achievement and social justice issues.* Unpublished doctoral dissertation, University of California, Los Angeles, CA.

Zeichner, K. M. (1991). Contradictions and tensions in the professionalization of teaching and democratization of schools. *Teachers College Record, 92*(3), 363–379.

17

TEACHING STUDENTS TO SPEAK UP
AND LISTEN TO OTHERS: FOSTERING
MORAL-DEMOCRATIC COMPETENCIES

Georg Lind

Introduction

Every journey, even the longest, starts with a first step. Every democracy, even the most advanced one, begins with speaking up about things that really matter for and to us as well as listening to those who may disagree. The very essence of democracy relies on resolving our conflicts through discussions based on shared moral principles such as justice and mutual respect, rather than by using brute force. All institutions in a democracy, ideally, operate on the same premise, focusing on mediating conflicts in a peaceful way, namely by speaking up and listening to others, and coming to an agreement that is fair and respects the worth of each individual regardless of wealth and social power. This is, as the philosopher Immanuel Kant (1785) stated, the highest "standard" of democratic life: Act as if the principle on which your action is based were to become by your will a universal law of nature, and treat humans in every case an end, never as a means only. An updated and communicative extension of this democratic standard has been presented by philosophers like Jürgen Habermas (1990), who states that a "moral" solution to a conflict excludes any use of power or violence, and must rest only on reason and dialogue.

Most, or possibly all, people value the high moral ideal of democracy. The authors of the American *Declaration of Independence* "hold these Truths to be self-evident, that all Men are created equal, that they are endowed by their Creator with certain unalienable Rights, that among these are Life, Liberty, and the Pursuit of Happiness." As many surveys show, the democratic *ideal* is not confined to North America or Europe but can be found around the globe, regardless of cultural and religious background. The agreement on these ideals is documented in many international declarations—for example, the *UN Convention on the Rights of the Child*—and most national constitutions refer to unalienable democratic ideals as the ultimate standard for policy making, law enforcement, and education.

Yet, daily media reports about violent conflicts, corruption, and other criminal offenses highlight that people are still far from being able to live in harmony with their democratic ideals. In fact, more often than we like, we do not live up to these ideals. All too often, people resort to power, violence, or wars to resolve differences of opinion, or constrain debate in order to avoid a conflict rather than coping with it.

In this chapter I argue that, in order to narrow this gap between the moral ideal of democracy on the one side, and everyday life on the other, we need to cultivate democratic competencies through education. Ultimately, it does not suffice to only teach about democratic ideals and institutions, but we also need to foster democratic competencies in everyday life. This raises two important questions: First, how can we find out about these competencies and perhaps measure them? Second, can we educate about them and, if so, how can we do this?

The Meaning and Measurement of Democratic Competencies

Without doubt, democratic ideals, values, and beliefs are essential for developing and maintaining a democratic society. If people would not value the ideals of democracies higher than other forms of government, and if they would not believe that this is the best form of government, it certainly would not prevail. The World Values Surveys indicate that most people all over the world aspire to hold democratic values. For example, citizens of Islamic countries do not differ with regard to their democratic ideals from citizens from the United States or from other Western countries (Inglehard & Norris, 2003). Importantly, it should be clear that democracy would not prevail if these ideals remain simply ideals and, moreover, if citizens are unable to apply these ideals to everyday decision making.

In a democracy, the rule of powerful people, such as a king/queen (as in a monarchy), a dictator (as in a tyranny), or a group of wealthy people (as in an oligarchy), has been replaced by the rule of moral principles (e.g., justice, mutual respect, and liberty) on which there is general agreement. Therefore, in a democratic society citizens cannot solve conflicts by simply appealing to some authority, but they must be engaged in a democratic, nonviolent discourse on the basis of these shared principles; "the problem lies in the appeal to any authority whose conclusions are impervious, in principle as well as practice, to the standards of logical consistency or to reliable methods of inquiry that themselves should be mutually acceptable" (Gutmann & Thompson, 1997, p. 56). The most basic democratic competence, then, is to engage in a rational, moral discourse with other people, especially with opponents.

The psychologist and educator Lawrence Kohlberg (1964) has identified an essential part of this paradigm as *moral judgment competence*, and defined it as "the capacity to make decisions and judgments which are moral (i.e., based on internal principles) and to act in accordance with such judgments" (p. 425). Habermas (1990), one of the most eminent philosophers of our time, extends Kohlberg's definition through his *theory of communicative ethics*. Yet, he extends the concept in an important way by stating that a true democratic discourse must be free of violence and the use of force or social power, and be restricted only by universal ethical principles. "Moral reason," Habermas asserts, "implies the deletion of those power relationships which are included invisibly in communications and which prevent conscious conflict resolution and consensual conflict solutions through intra-psychic as well as through personal barriers of communication" (Habermas, 1976, p. 34; translated from German by the author). This means that a democratic citizen should be able (a) to use and accept arguments as a means of conflict solution; (b) to use commonly accepted moral orientations or principles to evaluate arguments; and (c) to do this even when challenged or confronted by opponents or those who are in disagreement.

True Democratic Competencies Are Rooted in Our Tacit Knowledge

Democratic competencies, like other competencies, are not limited to, and are not identical to, conscious knowledge, that is, the knowledge about which we can discuss. On the contrary, to be effective, democratic competencies must be rooted in an unconscious cognitive structure. On the one hand, we may believe that we are more democratically competent than we really are. We *believe* that we are engaged in our own views and interests, and that we do listen to others but may, in fact, keep quiet when we should speak up and turn our back on people who do not share our point of view. On the other hand, we often "know" more than we believe. For example, we "know" whom to trust as a politician and whom not. But if we should explain why we should not trust a certain politician, we may have no meaningful explanation.

In science, these distinctions are very important. The philosopher Ryle (1949) highlighted the difference between "knowing that" and "knowing how." The philosopher Polanyi (1966) called the latter *tacit knowledge* in contrast to *overt* knowledge (see also Gigerenzer, 2006). In psychology, tacit knowledge is referred to as *cognitive structure*. Piaget (1976) stated that, "cognitive structures are not the conscious content of thinking, but impose one form of thinking rather than another…. The subject is only conscious of their results…. He has no access to the internal mechanisms that direct his thinking" (p. 64).

Competencies and Ideals Are Distinct but Inseparable Aspects of Democratic Behavior

We believe that democratic behavior is not only determined by (tacit) democratic competencies (or cognitions), but also by (tacit) democratic ideals and emotions (or affects). We call this the Dual Aspect Theory (Lind, 2000, 2002). For a long time we used to view them as separate *entities* or *components* of human functioning, which can be located in different areas of the brain, and which could be assessed only through different assessment instruments. In their influential taxonomies of educational objectives, Bloom and his associates (Bloom, Engelhart, Hill, Furst, & Krathwohl, 1956; Krathwohl, Bloom, & Masia, 1964) saw democratic and moral objectives as clearly separate from the cognitive domain, and published them under the title "affective objectives" in a separate volume. This separation of "affective" democratic behavior from the "cognitive" domain seems to explain why researchers have developed hundreds of democratic attitude and value scales but rarely established a democratic competency test.

Today, we are more aware of this separation of affect and cognition as two *separate* domains and, also, how separating the components of behavior is erroneous. Ultimately, all human behavior have an affective as well as a cognitive side. Piaget (1981) noted: "It is impossible to find behavior arising from affectivity alone without any cognitive elements. It is equally impossible to find behavior composed only of cognitive elements.... Although cognitive and affective factors are indissociable in an individual's behavior, they appear to be different in nature" (p. 2). This "distinct but inseparable aspects model" is confirmed by modern neurobiological research (Damasio, 1994).

Like cognition, affect and emotion do not need to be conscious. Often, we find some politicians very pleasant without being able to say for sure why. Sometimes, we think we "know why" only to realize later that we have erred. Piaget (1976) speaks of this as "affective unconsciousness."

These two distinctions lead to a fourfold conceptual model of democratic behavior that is depicted in Figure 1. While most of the literature in this area focus on the upper part of the model, namely on conscious reports of participants about their moral values and overt behavior, we know little about the lower part, namely on the assessment and education of *tacit* or *procedural* democratic knowledge, which is the knowledge on which we mostly rely in everyday life.

People's declarative democratic attitudes and beliefs hardly let us predict behavior. People are poor judges of their own emotions and competencies, and we often have reasons to hide them if we are aware of them. We must remember that people can pretend almost anything and also falsify attitude and belief scales in any desired direction. In contrast, people's competencies are a much better base for predicting their behavior. They are a good predictor of nonviolent conflict resolution, resistance against immoral authority, and helping behavior (Candee & Kohlberg, 1987) as well as abstinence from drug consumption (Lenz, 2006).

Measuring Moral Judgment Competence: The Moral Judgment Test (MJT)

The MJT has been developed to simultaneously measure moral *orientations* and *competencies*. The standard version of the MJT contains two short stories (the "workers' dilemma" and the "doctor's dilemma") in which someone is confronted with a moral dilemma. The participant is to judge whether the protagonist's decision was right or wrong. By doing so, he or she reveals a commitment to certain opinions about the issues at stake. Then the participant is confronted with six arguments *in favor* of the decision and six arguments *against* it. All arguments have been carefully selected or drafted to represent each of the six moral orientations that Kohlberg (1984)[2] identified. All of this constitutes a moral task for people, for which we can distinguish three different levels of difficulty.

Figure 1 - Dual aspect model of democratic behavior (Aspects of behaviour[1])

	Affective aspects	*Cognitive aspects*
Overt knowledge (knowing that, declarative knowledge)	Expression of democratic Values	Expression of democratic beliefs and "knowing that"
Tacit knowledge (knowing how, procedural knowledge)	Manifestations of democratic Affects	Manifestations of democratic competencies

The lowest level of difficulty of the MJT is to go beyond mere opinions and to deal with arguments. Some may be surprised by the number of people for whom this is very challenging. The second level of difficulty for the participant then is to recognize that the arguments differ with regard to their moral quality. People with low moral judgment competence accept all supporting arguments without qualification. The development of their judgment competence becomes visible only when they start to accept some supporting arguments less, or even reject them, because they represent an inadequate moral orientation or principle. For example, someone may argue that the doctor in one of the dilemmas should not do mercy killing because he may get into trouble. Although this is a supporting argument, from a moral point of view, this is not an adequate or compelling argument against mercy killing because it does not refer in any way to the value of life or to the suffering of the person who asks for it.

The third and highest difficulty level for the participants is to make a differentiated judgment about the arguments that *oppose* his or her opinion on the dilemma. Most people are unable to cope with this task. They find it extremely difficult even to listen to an opponent, and nearly impossibly to weigh on an opponent's arguments. Such a task causes *cognitive dissonance* (Festinger, 1957) and cognitive imbalance or *disequilibrium* (Piaget, 1976). From the research by Keasey (1974), we know that most people tend to assimilate arguments to their own opinion on a particular issue, and also judge all arguments on the basis of agreement or disagreement with their opinion. Situated at low levels of democratic competence, people here hold opinions on political and moral issues so strong that their moral ideals and principles have no bearing on their behavior. Their opinions seem so deeply anchored in their emotions, and reinforced by their social environment (and the mass media to which they expose themselves), that their own moral orientations are suppressed. Only when higher-order cognitive processes—like deliberation and discourse—have developed, they will be able to judge and behave according to their own moral and democratic principles.

If a participant cannot discern the moral quality of the arguments, because he or she is preoccupied with defending his or her opinion against an opponent, he or she gets zero C-points ("C" stands for competence). A C score of zero is reflected in the pattern of judgments of the fictitious "Person A" on the left side of Figure 2. A participant who rejects supporting arguments that are inadequate, and accepts counterarguments because of their high moral adequacy (like Person B in Figure 2), will get the highest score of 100 C-points.

Figure 2: The response patterns of two participants with different Competence-scores

Person: Opinion:	Person A "The decision was right"		Person B "The decision was right"	
Arguments on	**Contra**	**Pro**	**Contra**	**Pro**
Stage 1	✗ -3 -2 -1 0 +1 +2 +3 +4	-4 -3 -2 -1 0 +1 +2 +✗ +4	✗ -3 -2 -1 0 +1 +2 +3 +4	✗ -3 -2 -1 0 +1 +2 +3 +4
Stage 2	✗ -3 -2 -1 0 +1 +2 +3 +4	-4 -3 -2 -1 0 +1 +2 +✗ +4	-4 ✗ -2 -1 0 +1 +2 +3 +4	✗ -3 -2 -1 0 +1 +2 +3 +4
Stage 3	✗ -3 -2 -1 0 +1 +2 +3 +4	-4 -3 -2 -1 0 +1 +2 +3 ✗	✗ -3 -2 -1 0 +1 +2 +3 +4	-4 -✗ -2 -1 0 +1 +2 +3 +4
Stage 4	✗ -3 -2 -1 0 +1 +2 +3 +4	-4 -3 -2 -1 0 +1 +2 +3 ✗	-4 -3 -✗ -1 0 +1 +2 +3 +4	-4 -3 -2 ✗ 0 +1 +2 +3 +4
Stage 5	✗ -3 -2 -1 0 +1 +2 +3 +4	-4 -3 -2 -1 0 +1 +2 +3 ✗	-4 -3 -2 -1 ✗ +1 +2 +3 +4	-4 -3 -2 -1 0 ✗ +2 +3 +4
Stage 6	✗ -3 -2 -1 0 +1 +2 +3 +4	-4 -3 -2 -1 0 +1 +2 +3 ✗	-4 -3 -2 -1 0 +1 ✗ +3 +4	-4 -3 -2 -1 0 +1 +2 +3 +✗

C-score: 0.4
Low judgment competence

C-score: 92.2
High judgment competence

The methodological rationale of the MJT is outlined in greater detail elsewhere (Lind, in press).[3] In many respects, the MJT contrasts sharply with traditional psychometric instruments. With the MJT, the unit of study is the *individual person* and not the responses of a *sample* of people. The main index, the C score, is based on an analysis of the total response pattern, and not on atomized answers that are stripped from their meaning. Finally, the MJT allows us to measure both aspects of democratic behavior—competence and orientation—simultaneously. The MJT, therefore, provides several measures for cognitive and affective aspects of moral judgment behavior, for which the most central is the "C score" (Lind, in press). The C score reflects the degree to which the participant rates the 24 arguments of the MJT with regard to their moral quality rather than in relation to their opinion, agreement, or other aspects of the situation-like dilemma context.[4] The C score ranges from zero, meaning that the participant is not able to attend to the moral quality of the arguments, to one hundred, inferring that he or she has rated the arguments exclusively by their moral quality.

The Konstanz Method of Dilemma Discussion: The Need for Democratic Education

The task of living and working together in an ever more complex and changing world with people from different cultural and religious backgrounds is a huge challenge, especially for future generations. Today children are born into a world of unprecedented diversity and moral challenges. They are faced with problems that the older generation had not even known to exist when they were young. Each child will have to figure out his or her own way to cope with diversity and pluralism. In order to acquire the basic competencies for this challenge, society needs to provide students with a "favorable learning environment" (Schillinger, 2006) throughout their development—in kindergarten, elementary and secondary school, college, and beyond. Some children are blessed with favorable genes and parents, yet in a democracy, *all* people need to cooperate and live together peacefully and, therefore, *all* need to acquire basic democratic competencies. This is why we cannot do without democratic education at schools.

Educators (and the public) hold various beliefs about the nature of democratic personality, resulting in different views on the role of schools. Some believe that moral-democratic competencies are inborn and the only thing school can do is to select the students accordingly. This theory lays the groundwork for highly selective school systems as well as much of our testing policies. Some educators believe that moral and democratic competencies are not totally fixed at birth but unfold as the child gets older in an invariant sequence. School, they believe, does little to intervene in relation to the students' development. In contrast, behaviorists believe that children are born as "blank slates" and need to be molded through rewards and punishment to become the kind of citizen that a particular society values. The school's task, then, is to "socialize" the child by using social pressure or force.

According to my reading of the research literature, neither theory is adequate. Moral and democratic competencies are not inborn, nor are they instilled in children through social force. The existing evidence, rather, suggests that (a) deep in their hearts, most, if not all, people believe in the moral ideal of democracy and want to live by it; (b) they often face a formidable task when time constraints, social forces, or other issues impact with their ideal; and (c) they are more likely to cope with these tasks if they had learned to solve conflicts through free deliberation and discourse with opponents. This, in sum, is our "education theory" of moral and democratic development (Lind, 1987, 2002, 2003, 2005). This theory implies that it is not merely the amount of education, but its quality that fosters moral democratic competencies. Education must provide opportunities for responsibility taking and guided reflection in order to be effective (Sprinthall, Reiman, & Thies-Sprinthall, 1993). In a longitudinal study Lind (2002) found that the absence of such opportunities in the learning environment of university students leads to a decrease of students' moral judgment competence (see also Schillinger, 2006). The importance of good education for the development of democratic competence had already been shown by Torney et al. (1975) in their 10-country study: "Morally knowledgeable, less authoritarian and more interested students came from schools where they were encouraged to have free discussion and to express their opinion in class" (p. 18).

Schools Do Not Always Do the Right Thing

In spite of the general desire for deliberative democracy and the need for the respective competencies, we see little of this in our classrooms. Teaching in most schools is confined to the conveying of declarative textbook knowledge. It seems that many teachers and educational policy makers have not understood the dimension and the urgency of the task. Often teachers who praise the value of democratic government, at the same time, behave autocratically in their classroom. Of the many standards meant for guiding civic education, only a few, if any, refer to basic democratic competencies. Among the hundreds of policy *standards for civics teaching*, collected across the United States,[5] the vast majority, namely 426 out of 427, pertain to *declarative* knowledge about democratic institutions, and only one addresses the acquisition of procedural democratic knowledge. None of the standards listed in the *Compendium K-12 Standards* (Kendall & Marzano, 2004) mentions competencies such as speaking up and listening to others in a democratic discussion.

A few standards do, however, come close. One standard requires that the child "understands and applies the basic principles of presenting an argument." Yet, this standard is not meant as a democratic virtue but only as an instrument for "me" winning the "others." Students should "understand that people are more likely to believe a person's ideas if that person can give good reasons for them" and that, therefore, they should "back up their ideas with good reasons." It does not seem to be important whether the arguments given are true and sincere. Democratic competencies are also more than just the ability to use "conflict-resolution techniques" or display "effective interpersonal communication skills." These skills and techniques can be helpful but without interpersonal agreement on common ethical grounds and without emphatic understanding of each other, no genuine cooperation is possible. This is not a unique problem to the U.S. educational system alone.

Therefore, we should not be surprised that people often do better in speaking about freedom and democracy than living by these ideals. Keasey (1974) highlighted that most adolescents find it difficult to listen to, and appreciate, counterarguments. Lind (2002) also found that most people are so preoccupied with defending their opinions against others that they cannot appreciate the quality of their arguments. We sometimes even encounter individuals who cannot even differentiate between an "argument" and the opinion for which it is given: "Why do you ask us again to say what we think about this issue?" It is not inconceivable to predict that such individuals will have difficulty achieving an agreement on a controversial issue by nonviolent ethical discourse. It seems more likely that they might either use brute force to make their opinion dominate over all others or give up their opinion if their opponent is seen as more powerful. In fact, *low* judgment competency correlates strongly with blind submission to authority, as seen in the Milgram experiments (Kohlberg, 1984) and with an inclination for violence (Lind, 1998).

If we are concerned only with backing up our ideas with "convincing reasons," and with conflict-resolution techniques, we are "rationalizing" but are not, necessarily, rational. Rationalizing means that we use arguments, and the moral principles to which they appeal, just to back up our intuitive opinions, and that we will change our reasons rather than our opinion if they do not agree. In contrast, being rational means that we examine our opinions and action-choices on the basis of our shared moral principles, and adapt our opinion to our principles rather than the other way round. Rational also means that we listen to the arguments of opponents (or even enemies), and judge their arguments according to their moral quality, rather than only to their opinion-agreement.

It seems that the importance of schooling for the maintenance and development of a democratic society is best understood at times of threat, controversy, and social disaster. Confronted with the task of building up a nation after the War of Independence, Jefferson, one of the first U.S. presidents, clearly noted the importance of schooling for democracy: "I know no safe depository of the ultimate powers of the society, but the people themselves and if we think them not enlightened enough to exercise their control with a wholesome discretion, the remedy is not to take it from them, but to inform their discretion by education" (as cited in Boyer, 1990, p. 5).

A New, Effective Method of Democratic Education

Dilemma discussions have shown to be one of the most effective ways to stimulate democratic competencies. If they are well designed, they provide what Schillinger (2006) calls a "favorable learning environment." There are many methods using the dilemma-discussion format. Yet, not all are equally effective. Over the years, we have developed a particularly effective method, one that we now call the *Konstanz Method of Dilemma Discussion* (KMDD; Lind, 2003, 2005). It grew out of the method first suggested by Blatt and Kohlberg (1975), which showed to be more effective than previous methods (Higgins, 1980; Lockwood, 1978). In a meta-analysis of 141 intervention studies, for which sufficient information was given, Lind (2002) found a remarkable average effect size ($r = 0.40$). No negative effects were found, and the effects were sustained over a longer period of time.

However, the Blatt-Kohlberg method also had its drawbacks (e.g., Berowitz, 1981; Lind, 2002). One critical aspect concerns the so-called plus-one convention, which demands that the teacher confront his or her students with arguments exactly one "stage" above the reasoning level in order to stimulate upward development. Not only could this requirement encounter difficulty in being fulfilled but the plus-one convention also seemed to rely too much on the authority and prescription of the teacher. This convention and the presentation of several dilemmas within 45 min leave too little room for autonomous learning.

Therefore, we introduced several changes. Among other things, we gave up the plus-one convention in favor of counterarguments, which were shown to be very effective for stimulating cognitive growth (Piaget, 1929). In order to allow for more child-centered teaching, we also reduced the number of dilemmas to one, and increased the minimum session time to 90 min. While experimenting with these changes, three basic principles of democratic learning turned out to be essential.

First, there is the *constructivist principle of learning*. A good dilemma discussion works like a vaccination. By confronting the organism with a semi-real virus it develops all the capacities to cope later with a real virus. Similarly, by confronting the learner with a semi-real "educative" moral dilemma, he or she is stimulated to develop many of the abilities needed when being confronted with a similar dilemma in real life later. The educative dilemmas we use are especially designed for stimulating learning.[6] Yet we should keep in mind that dilemmas are cognitive construction and each learner defines them in a different way depending on his or her level of cognitive-moral competence (Lind, 2006). This makes communication often very difficult, if not impossible. Therefore, becoming aware of, and coping with, these differences in meaning construction have become major objectives of the KMDD.

Second, there is the *principle of maintaining an optimal level of arousal through alternating phases of support and challenge*. Through challenges, students get emotionally aroused. They are eager to solve problems or to ease bad feelings. Yet, challenges must never last for too long, or get too strong, because too much arousal (like anxiety) prevents learning. Before this happens, the teacher switches from the phase of challenge to a phase of support, in which the participants are reassured, and their emotions then can calm down to allow intellectual activities and reflection to recuperate.

Third, the *principle of mutual respect and free moral discourse in the classroom* is fundamental. Above all, this principle requires the teacher to see him or herself as a facilitator, not as a master of students' learning. With regard to the moral and democratic learning, it is especially important that teachers do not use their authority to impose their aims, and their pace of learning, upon students. Teachers must provide their students with opportunities for a free discourse (Habermas, 1990) by respecting each learner equally, regardless of his or her power and status.

Based on these three principles of democratic and moral learning, the KMDD has become a highly effective method. In a carefully designed, randomized intervention experiment with Thai college students, Lerkiatbundit, Utaipan, Laohawiriyanon, and Teo (2006) found high and sustainable effects of the KMDD on moral judgment competence. The experimental group gained 12 C score points on the MJT, and this gain could still be observed 6 months after the end of the intervention. The high average gain is remarkable as the MJT showed a high stability in a separate "reliability" study ($r = 0.90$) (Lerkiatbundit et al., 2006), and the C score remained almost unchanged in the control group. Other studies found similar gains. For comparison, the gains with the Blatt Kohlberg method were, on average, about six percentage points per year (Lind, 2002). The effect sizes of both intervention methods compare favorably to average effect sizes of "effective" psychological, educational, and medical treatments (Lipsey & Wilson, 1993).

Conclusion

"Deliberative democracy," concludes Gutmann (1999), "underscores the importance of publicly supported education that develops the capacity to deliberate among all children as future free and equal citizens" (p. xii). Speaking up and listening to others can, indeed, be taught. However, this "teaching" must be different from traditional instruction and classroom management. To be effective, democracy education must be democratic itself (Dewey, 1966). Teaching must not only attend to the curriculum but it must also respect the learner and adapt to his or her special needs.

Questions for Reflection

1. What kind of knowledge is underrepresented in our schools' curriculum and standards?

2. Why is there often a gap between people's high democratic ideals and their behavior?

3. How can children be supported to speak up in school in relation to democracy?

4. What makes it so difficult for many teachers to be an effective democratic educator?

5. How can democratic competencies be measured?

Notes

1. To be consistent with our own model of human behavior, we speak here of inseparable (yet distinguishable) aspects or properties of behavior rather than of components. See the first section of this paper for a theoretical explication of the aspect model.

2. Kohlberg reduced his six-stage model at one point but returned to it later (Kohlberg, 1984).

3. The MJT is available in 30 languages (http://democracy-education.net). It can be ordered from the author for research and program evaluation. The prospective user of the MJT should have a background in moral and democratic psychology.

4. As Kohlberg (1984) notes, "in studying moral behavior we are concerned with studying action in which the subject gives up something or takes risks where not doing so would appear to be to his or her immediate advantage.... Thus, it is the overcoming of these situational pressures on either a verbal or a physical level that constitutes the test of moral behavior" (p. 522).

5. Source: http://www.mcrel.com (October 12, 2004).

6. Educative moral dilemmas for various teaching objectives can be found in Lind (2003); see also http://www.uni-konstanz.de/ag-moral/home-e.htm. KMDD instructors are taught how to develop educative moral dilemmas for particular educational objectives as part of their training.

References

Berkowitz, M. W. (1981, March). A critical appraisal of the "plus-one" convention in moral education. *Phi Delta Kappan*, 488–489.

Blatt, M., & Kohlberg, L. (1975). The effect of classroom moral discussion upon children's level of moral judgment. *Journal of Moral Education, 4*, 129–161.

Bloom, B. S., Engelhart, M. D., Hill, W. H., Furst, E. J., & Krathwohl, D. (1956). *Taxonomy of educational objectives. Handbook I: Cognitive domain*. New York: David McKay.

Boyer, E. L. (1990). Civic education for responsible citizens. *Educational Leadership, 48*, 4–7.

Candee, D., & Kohlberg, L. (1987). Moral judgment and moral action: A reanalysis of Haan, Smith, and Block's Free Speech Movement data. *Journal of Personality and Social Psychology, 52*(3), 554–564.

Damasio, A. (1994). *Descartes' error: Emotion, reason and the human brain*. New York: G. P. Putnam's Sons.

Dewey, J. (1966). *Democracy and education. An introduction to the philosophy of education*. New York: The Free Press.

Festinger, L. (1957). *A theory of cognitive dissonance*. New York: Harper & Row.

Gigerenzer, G. (2006). *Gut feelings: The intelligence of the unconscious*. New York: Viking.

Gutmann, A. (1999). *Democratic education*. Princeton, NJ: Princeton University Press.

Gutmann, A., & Thompson, D. (1997). *Democracy and disagreement*. Cambridge, MA: Harvard University Press.

Habermas, J. (1976). Was heißt Universalpragmatik? In K.-O. Apel (Ed.), *Sprachpragmatik und Philsophie* (pp. 174–272). Frankfurt, Germany: Suhrkamp.

Habermas, J. (1990). *Moral consciousness and communicative action*. Cambridge, MA: MIT Press.

Higgins, A. (1980). Research and measurement issues in moral education interventions. In R. Mosher, (Ed.), *Moral education: A first generation of research and development* (pp. 92–107). New York: Praeger.

Inglehard, R., & Norris, P. (2003, March/April). The true clash of civilizations. *Foreign Policy, 67*–74.

Kant, I. (1975). *Grundlegung zur Metaphysik der Sitten* (Principles of the metaphysics of ethics). Werkausgabe Bd. VII (Weischedel). Frankfurt. Germany: Suhrkamp. (translation from the Microsoft® Encarta: "Immanuel Kant")

Keasey, C. B. (1974). The influence of opinion-agreement and qualitative supportive reasoning in the evaluation of moral judgments. *Journal of Personality and Social Psychology, 30*, 477–482.

Kendall, J. S., & Marzano, R. J. (2004). *Content knowledge: A compendium of standards and benchmarks for K-12 education*. Aurora, CO: Mid-continent Research for Education and Learning. Retrieved June 30, 2007, from http://www.mcrel.org/standards-benchmarks

Kohlberg, L. (1964). Development of moral character and moral ideology. In M. L. Hoffman & L. W. Hoffman (Eds.), *Review of child development research* (vol. 1, pp. 381–431). New York: Russell Sage Foundation.

———. (1984). The meaning and measurement of moral development. In L. Kohlberg (Ed.), *The psychology of moral development. Essays on moral development* (vol. 2, pp. 395–425). San Francisco: Harper & Row.

Krathwohl, D. R., Bloom, B. S., & Masia, B. B. (1964). *Taxonomy of educational objectives. Handbook II: Affective domain*. New York: David McKay.

Lenz, B. (2006). *Moral judgment competence as a determinant of drug consumption of youth*. Unpublished Master's Thesis, Department of Psychology, University of Konstanz, Germany.

Lerkiatbundit, S., Utaipan, P., Laohawiriyanon, C., & Teo, A. (2006). Randomized controlled study of the impact of the Konstanz method of dilemma discussion on moral judgement. *Journal of Allied Health, 35*(2), 101–108.

Lind, G. (1987). Moral competence and education in democratic society. In G. Zecha & P. Weingartner (Eds.), *Conscience: An interdisciplinary approach* (pp. 91–122). Dordrecht, Germany: Reidel.

———. (1998). Gewalt und Krieg als niedrigste Stufe der Konfliktbewältigung [Violence and war as the lowest stage of conflict resolution]. In W. Kempf & I. Schmidt-Regener (Eds.), *Krieg. Nationalismus, Rassismus und die Medien* (pp. 273–282). Münster, Germany: LIT-Verlag.

———. (2000). The importance of role-taking opportunities for self-sustaining moral development. *Journal of Research in Education, 10*(1), 9–15.

———. (2002). *Ist Moral lehrbar? Ergebnisse der modernen moralpsychologischen Forschung* [Can morality be taught? Research findings from modern moral psychology] (2nd ed.). Berlin: Logos-Verlag.

———. (2003). *Moral ist lehrbar. Handbuch zur Theorie und Praxis moralischer und demokratischer Bildung* [Morality can be taught. Handbook on theory and practice of moral and democratic education]. (English ed. forthcoming). München, Germany: Oldenbourg.

————. (2005). Moral dilemma discussion revisited: The Konstanz method. *European Journal of Psychology*. Retrieved June 30, 2007, from http://www.ejop.org

————. (2006). Das Dilemma liegt im Auge des Betrachters. Zur Behandlung bio-ethischer Fragen im Biologie-Unterricht mit der Konstanzer Methode der Dilemmadiskussion. *Praxis der Naturwissenschaften. Biologie in der Schule, Januar*, 1/55, S. 10–16.

————. (in press). The meaning and measurement of moral judgment competence revisited: A dual-aspect model. In D. Fasko & W. Willis (Eds.), *Contemporary philosophical and psychological perspectives on moral development and education* (pp. 185–220). Cresskill, NJ: Hampton.

Lipsey, M. W., & Wilson, D. B. (1993). The efficacy of psychological, educational and behavioral treatment: Confirmation from meta-analysis. *American Psychologist, 48*, 1181–1209.

Lockwood, A. L. (1978). The effects of value clarification and moral development curricula on school-age subjects: A critical review of recent research. *Review of Educational Research, 48*, 325–364.

Piaget, J. (1929). *The child's conception of the world*. London: Routledge & Kegan Paul.

————. (1965). *The moral judgment of the child*. New York: The Free Press.

————. (1976). The affective unconscious and the cognitive unconscious. In B. Inhelder & H. H. Chipman (Eds.), *Piaget and his school* (pp. 63–71). New York: Springer.

————. (1981). *Intelligence and affectivity: Their relation during child development*. Palo Alto, CA: Annual Reviews. (Originally published 1954.)

Piaget, J., & Inhelder, B. (1969). *The psychology of the child*. New York: Basic Books.

Polanyi, M. (1966). *The tacit dimension*. New York: Doubleday.

Ryle, G. (1949). *Concept of mind*. Chicago: University of Chicago Press.

Schillinger, M. (2006). *Learning environments and moral development: How university education fosters moral judgment competence in Brazil and two German-speaking countries*. Aachen, Germany: Shaker-Verlag.

Sprinthall, N. A., Reiman, A. J., & Thies-Sprinthall, L. (1993). Role-taking and reflection: Promoting the conceptual and moral development of teachers. *Learning and Individual Differences, 5*(4), 283–299.

Torney, J. V., Oppenheim, A. N., & Farnen, R. F. (1975). *Civic education in ten countries: An empirical study*. New York: Wiley.

CHAPTER

18

DON'T TEACH ME WHAT I DON'T KNOW: FOSTERING DEMOCRATIC LITERACY

Heidi Huse

In true democracy every man and woman is taught to think for himself or herself.
—Mohandas K. Gandhi

Regardless of what society we are in, in what world we find ourselves, it is impermissible to train engineers or stonemasons, physicians or ... machinists, educators ... farmers or philosophers ... without an understanding of our own selves as historical, political, social, and cultural beings—without a comprehension of how society works.
—Paulo Freire

Introduction

As a first-year university composition professor, I believe that effective writing necessarily requires extensive awareness, along with the critical thinking also essential to the well-being of a democratic society. However, I have noticed a significant lack of awareness about, if not disinterest in, national and global concerns on the part of many students. What these students do not realize is that their disengagement with thoughtful investigation can seriously undermine a democratic society's well-being and progress. Elizabeth Beaumont (2007), writing for the *Carnegie Foundation for the Advancement of Teaching*, implies a direct correlation between education and quality of citizen civic action:

> Rather than focusing narrowly on whether young adults vote at lower or equally low rates as the rest of Americans, we need to also be concerned with the quality of participation. Being concerned with the quality of participation means working to increase relevant political knowledge, skills, and motivations that can support engaged and effective citizenship. (paras. 4–5)

A report by CIRCLE (Center for Information and Research on Civic Learning and Engagement, 2006) also confirms that poor civic knowledge translates to lower voter registration and turn out, and lower community involvement. The report further notes that lack of awareness of current events from available news media likewise results in lower rates of civic action of any kind (pp. 24–26). So what can educators do to reconnect students to rigorous learning and a commitment to actively engage in democratic civic action?

In this chapter, I discuss the seeming epidemic of indifference many of today's students present toward attaining an education that goes beyond the minimum necessary for a lucrative career. Along with the experiences of other educators, I place my own experiences with student apathy into a historical context of American democratic progress. I then discuss how educators might reinspire students to transformative knowledge as well as to participation in democratic life.

What We Don't Want to Know Can Hurt Us

In preparing for a literacy conference panel on the relationship between depth of knowledge and effective academic writing, in 2006, I distributed to all my classes a first-day writing "ice-breaker." I gave students a list of around 40 random historical and current leaders, dates, and events, including:

Apartheid	Kim Jong-il
Jim Crow	Mahmoud Ahmadinejad
Darfur	John Glover Roberts
Hiroshima & Nagasaki	Dust Bowl
December 7, 1941	FEMA
Trail of Tears	Abu Ghraib
Roe v. Wade	Sandra Day O'Connor
Manifest Destiny	Lorraine Motel

I asked students to select 10 items from the list and write 2–4 sentences identifying and briefly explaining each selection. Three classes were first-year writing courses consisting of traditional, nontraditional, underprepared, and international students. My fourth class was an upper-division writing course that included education majors from various disciplines, some of whom were in their final semester of coursework before moving on to their student teaching and into their own classrooms as teachers. Less than half of the students could respond to even 10 items at all; of those who tried to take on the task as assigned, most responded to their chosen 10 items incorrectly, despite the fact that I had asked for only superficial responses.

In recent years I have also begun to regularly surprise students with a "news quiz," in which they must identify a news story they have heard about in the previous week and respond to it in a 5-min writing exercise—again, they are not being asked to offer in-depth knowledge, just some awareness. When they are unable to identify even one news event, their justifications mirror those given by the students embarrassed by their inability to respond to my 2006 list: "I don't own a TV," "I don't have time for the news," "I don't have a computer at home," "we don't subscribe to any newspapers," and so on.

On the other hand, when I remind them that they may not write about sports scores or the latest celebrity gossip, there are groans around the classroom—that information many could have readily provided. So it appears that what many students are aware of is selective. Why are so many students so uninformed and seemingly uninterested in national or global concerns? Have "we" educated interest in the world around them right out of them somehow? Will they become more engaged and aware as they mature, presumably as we did when we graduated and entered adulthood? And if so, will they be engaged and aware enough to vote knowledgably? To become future national and world leaders? To participate actively as informed citizens in the democratic process—attending school board and town meetings, writing letters to their elected officials, engaging in sociopolitical activism, or perhaps even starting their own charitable or advocacy organizations—and to teach their children to do the same?

Surfing the channels one afternoon, I happened upon *Tucker*, a cable news talk show. The guest host that day referred to a recent poll regarding Saddam Hussein's role in the 9/11 attacks. The host reported that 6 years after the event, 41 percent of Americans polled still believe Saddam Hussein planned the attack and that the terrorists involved came from Iraq—despite the plethora of information published refuting any Iraqi role. Expressing his dismay that such gross misinformation was still so prevalent in a supposedly literate society, he asked his guest panelists: "Isn't there a threat to a democracy when you have an electorate ... that misinformed?!" In the case of cable news talk shows such as *Tucker*, the often aggressive banter likely alienates many viewers, preventing their access to the kernels of accurate information provided by the politically oppositional "talking heads," but the host's question is nevertheless relevant. What is the problem? Do Americans simply not learn about national or global history and current events? Or despite the abundance of information available at their fingertips through multiple communications technologies, do Americans just not care? Such questions cannot be answered in simple "yes" or "no" terms.

The Problem in a Larger Context

Today's increasing lack of sociopolitical awareness and resistance to in-depth learning would likely rattle the United States' founders. In one online report, the National Endowment for the Humanities (2002) chair, Bruce Cole, notes that for James Madison "the diffusion of knowledge is the only true guardian of liberty" (para. 12). But Cole (National Endowment for the Humanities, 2002) laments that "studies have shown that Americans of all ages have a dangerously poor understanding of American history and culture," and he warned that "when a nation fails to know why it exists and what it stands for, it cannot be expected to long endure" (para. 2).

In the anthology *Making Good Citizens: Education and Civil Society*, Diana Ravitch (2001) offers a historical overview of the value placed on education for America's democratic evolution from the start. For example, she notes that early in America's development, Daniel Webster saw in public education the means of fostering "a strong sense of national identity" (p. 16), while Thomas Jefferson, like Madison, believed education was a means of protecting the nation against tyranny by those in power. Later, as Ravitch continues, Horace Mann "argued that popular education was integrally connected to freedom and democratic government" (p. 17), then John Dewey brought the notion into the twentieth century, believing that students could study virtually any subject, "in ways that made it valuable, especially if students understood its social significance" (p. 23). Finally, Ravitch herself brings the relationship between education and democracy into the twenty-first century, arguing that those who value education for propagating democratic ideals "must attend to the strengthening of civil society, humane culture, and our democratic institutions" (p. 27). She fears that current generations have already begun to take their democratic freedoms for granted, if not devaluing them altogether. Ravitch advocates curricular breadth:

> The schools must teach youngsters about our history, our civic institutions, and our Constitution ... they must give students the intellectual tools to comprehend science, mathematics, language, the arts, literature, and history ... Democratic habits and values must be taught and communicated through the daily life of our society.... The best protection for a democratic society is well-educated citizens. (p. 28)

Damon (2001) shares Ravitch's concerns. He argues that "it is on the inauspicious front of young people's minds and morals that the battle for democracy will be won or lost" (p. 123) and, like Ravitch, he has observed that this battle front seems to be losing ground. According to Damon, "young people ... have been disengaging from civic and political activities to a degree unimaginable a mere generation ago.... Today there are no leaders, no causes, no legacy ... or accomplishments that inspire much more than apathy or cynicism from the young" (p. 123). He offers as one example voting statistics for 18-year-olds from the 1972 presidential election, the first election in which 18-year-olds could vote in the United States. He contrasts the 47 percent 18-year-old voter turnout then with the 27 percent 18-year-old voter turnout in the 1996 presidential election, and he adds that for later elections the trend appears to continue downward. Damon (2001) further notes that until recently, "there has never been a time in American history when so small a proportion of young people ... have sought or accepted leadership roles in local civic organizations," and he finally laments that the "lack of interest" of today's youth "is reflected in the sorry state of their knowledge (p. 123).

To discover reasons for youth disinterest and lack of knowledge, Damon (2001) explains that his Center on Adolescence at Stanford interviewed several teenagers, 14–18 years old, from "heartland American communities," in addition to reading essays from "hundreds of other students ... written about the laws and purpose of life in today's world" (p. 124). What Damon and his staff discovered is what I have found to be true of many of the college students in my classes: "They showed little interest in people outside their immediate circle of friends and relatives (other than fictional media characters and entertainment or sports figures); little awareness of current events; and virtually no expressions of social concern, political opinion, civic duty, patriotic emotion, or sense of citizenship in any form" (p. 124).[1]

Damon (2001) argues that students' "civil disaffection" may arise from yet another problem, a lack of genuine appreciation for one's own society or country, which he defines as "patriotism." Unfortunately, patriotism of late has developed a negative connotation, according to Damon, becoming strongly aligned with "chauvinistic and super-militaristic passions"; as a result, love of country is not stressed in educational curricula. In fact, he explains, "when patriotism does come up in education, the goal is usually to find ways to guard against its dangers" (p. 133).[2] Damon agrees that the ability to knowledgeably critique flaws in one's own country for the sake of its future health is crucial; however, he also argues that patriotism as love of community and country is equally essential, and that fostering healthy "patriotism" can be an important function of education (p. 133):

> A positive emotional attachment to a particular community is a necessary condition for sustained civic engagement…. For full participatory citizenship in a democratic society, a student needs to develop a love for the particular society, including its historical legacy and cultural traditions. The capacity for constructive criticism is … essential … for civic engagement … but … this capacity must build upon a prior sympathetic understanding of that which is being criticized. (p. 135)

Many educators would likely take no issue with Damon's argument, but on the basis of their classroom experiences, they might point out that establishing that foundational "sympathetic understanding" in the classroom may prove challenging.

As 15-year veteran anthropology professor, Rebekah Nathan[3] (2005) learned first hand that, by the time many young people reach college, especially their upper division classes, they are not necessarily pursuing the material in enough depth to truly understand it, let alone cherish it. Instead, they are developing expertise in academic performance, learning only what they need to successfully complete their coursework and enter the professional world. In her book *My Freshman Year*, Nathan (2005) recounts her experiences as a second-time first-year college student, undertaken during a faculty sabbatical. She decided that by becoming a student herself, she might find some answers for her own frustrations with students' seeming disengagement with the coursework, with their unwillingness to participate in class discussion, and with their sporadic attendance and poor preparation. Nathan immersed herself in the first-year experience (ostensibly as a nontraditional student due to her age), from registration and orientation to dorm life and coursework. As a student, she spoke with first-year to graduating students about their priorities, their academic choices, and actions (class attendance and preparation, study prioritization, engagement in class discussions and activities, etc.), their extracurricular obligations relative to their coursework, and their ultimate goals for their education.

Nathan (2005) also gained new perspectives on American students and their lack of awareness from conversations with international students from an array of nations. She notes that "the single biggest complaint international students lodged about U.S. students was, to put it bluntly, our ignorance … the misinformation and lack of information that Americans have both about other countries and about themselves" (p. 84). Nathan explains that the international students with whom she spoke generally had positive academic experiences in the United States. Nevertheless, they found the American students' lack of knowledge and their apparent lack of concern about their own ignorance noteworthy.

Some also expressed discomfort with the American students' blind arrogance about their country. Nathan (2005) cites, for example, one German student's observation that "Americans seem to think they have the perfect place to live, the best country, the best city … I used to think you just got that from politicians, but now I see it's from regular people too. The patriotism thing here really bothers me" (p. 87). It might seem that the patriotism Damon calls for—positive regard for one's homeland—is alive and well, but the problem for this student was that such patriotism is based too heavily in ignorance, of both the American students' homeland and the world around them.

Nathan (2005) leaves educators with questions that reflect Freire's focus on education for liberation and transformation: "Will the liminal life of college culture allow students to arrive at inspired new ideas for society and transformative visions of our world? Or will it simply train young people to become adults who take their place in line in the workforce of the existing society?" She points out that just as society shapes the university, the students passing through our universities, educated and aware—or not—will shape our democratic societies one way or another (p. 148).

So What Do We Do?

How do we create and implement effective means of engaging students in self-motivated knowledge making and, in the "practice of true democracy" as Gandhi (1946) put it—or in Freire's (1994a) words, in "becoming beings of insertion in the world and not of pure adaptation to the world" (p. 91). How do we as educators move students to "cherish the material" enough to "invest attention" and "pursue it on their own" (Damon, 2001, p. 137) as engaged participants in the democratic process, and further, as engaged future parents, civic leaders, and educators modeling civic involvement to future generations?

First, as educators we must infect students with enthusiasm for knowledge and civic responsibility, which calls upon us to become more inspired ourselves, particularly on the occasions when we wish to turn students' attention to areas in our democracy's evolution where critical evaluation and change is necessary. Damon (2001) adds that placing our criticisms within a larger and more positive context may encourage students' appreciation for their homeland and their desire to act in its continued transformation and productive growth. He offers an example:

> A landmark civil rights demonstration can be presented either as an indicator of our society's racism or as a sign that there have been people in our society who have been determined—and permitted by our democratic system of governance—to correct that racism. Which orientation is more likely to encourage students themselves to get involved in constructive civil action? Which is more likely to instill civic affiliation rather than cynicism and apathy?..... A society's successes and failures can always be presented in a context of appreciation for the society's highest ideals. (p. 139)

On the one hand, perhaps Damon's approach can move students to rise above what seems, in our age, to be a pervasive cynicism. During election years, I regularly ask students whether they plan to vote and if they are even yet registered to vote. Too many of them offer responses bespeaking individual powerlessness; they believe that their voices and votes have no currency in a nation and world overrun by powerful corporate entities. "Why bother?" they ask, an attitude they also express toward liberal education and sociopolitical knowledge: "What's the point? The news is always bad, and there's nothing we can do about it anyway." The difficulty here might be that they will no longer believe in those higher, democratic ideals.

On the other hand, in addition to drowning in deep cynicism, in America we currently seem to be living in a sharply divided, contentious atmosphere of blind devotion to specific political affiliations and perspectives. In the aftermath of 9/11, patriotism has become synonymous with flag-waving revelry in *only* that which is glorious about America. American citizens, much like the rest of the world, are presented with two possible identities: either we are "for us," meaning we endorse, without question, virtually everything our leaders say or our nation does; or, if we offer any degree of critique, we are labeled as traitors, members of an anti-American "axis of evil."

In such a strident, narrowly constructed environment, creating a curriculum in which students willingly move from engagement with the glories of their homeland, to a scholarly and honest examination of its more unpleasant realities is difficult. Many students already appreciate, far too uncritically, America's better qualities, believing that America's democratic ideals are universal realities. With the time constraints imposed on educators by the clock and academic calendar, democracy educators may need all their time to help students confront the less attractive matters of national and global significance, in order to promote positive social change. The authors of *Educating Citizens* (Colby, Ehrlich, Beaumont, & Stephens, 2003) maintain that our best chance for ensuring that students will take the educational ball we hand them and productively run with it lies in our being "self-conscious and intentional" about what we offer to them (p. 5). Our goals must include providing students with a heartfelt affiliation with greater society, which will lead them to see that society's problems are their own and then to take responsibility for finding solutions; an ability to intelligently and productively "make and justify civil and moral judgments; and a willingness to act when necessary" (p. 17). Further, they argue that

> there are some values that ... colleges and universities ought to promote and support if they are committed to graduating engaged and responsible citizens. These values include respect and tolerance for others ... respect for civil liberties ... an interest in politics and in contributing to positive social change, however that is defined. (p. 113)

Hopefully, effective institutional and curricular goals will enhance student motivation to learn and to actively participate in civic activities and society.

It's Not All Bad News

Peter Levine (2005) offers cause for hope, particularly for college educators, challenging Damon's rather depressing statistics about youth voter turnout. In his online article, "Youth voting in 2004: The myths and the facts," he rejects lamentations about poor youth voter turnout in the 2004 elections. According to Levine (2005), while turnout for 18–24-year-olds in the 2000 election was only around 36 percent, turnout for this age group increased significantly in the 2004 election, to 47 percent, almost half of the registered voters for that demographic (Was Voter Turnout Flat? section, para. 1). Moreover, Levine adds that those young people in college or who have attended college show greater tendency to vote than those who have not attended college. Levine (2005) might also offer an additional explanation for youth cynicism and lack of involvement in civic matters. He puts it in simple terms: youth don't care and don't act because they are not asked to, and he resists such deliberate oversight.

Field experiments by Yale professors Donald Green and Alan Gerber, and their students, found that young people are more likely to vote when they are asked to. In an era of targeted campaigning, however, under-25s are not asked. After elections, legislators emphasize issues of interest to older voters. Young people feel left out of the national debate and rarely experience any sense of political influence. Meanwhile, reporters ignore young people as active participants in formal politics (Left out of the Debate section, para. 1).

Further, educator skepticism about youth interest in sociopolitical issues may not be entirely warranted either. Levine (2005) points to a 2004 election poll, by MTV and CIRCLE, which shows that "81 percent of young registered voters closely followed the campaign in September 2004, the highest level at a comparable point in the election cycle since 1992" (Mobilizing Young Voters section, para. 3). In another survey during the same election, Levine (2005) notes that 62 percent of the respondents not only voted themselves, but "encouraged or helped someone else to vote" (Mobilizing Young Voters section, para. 3). So according to Levine, we can take heart. While he agrees that, up until 2000, there was cause for alarm about youth civic engagement, such concern is currently not the case. However, he also offers the warning that if our society, political leaders, and news media continue to complain about youth apathy and ignore the voices, votes, and concerns of younger citizens, we might just lose their growing interest in national civic affairs. We must encourage their awareness, interest, and active participation, and then acknowledge and respect their efforts when they follow through.

My own frustrations with student disinterest in in-depth, self-motivated learning and civic involvement are also not without occasional silver linings. For example, I center one of my first-year writing courses around the theme of animal rights and human morality. An "animal rights" theme is somewhat risky at my university, which is located in a rural, agricultural, conservative setting where hunting is a virtually sacred family tradition, cattle and hog farms—and slaughterhouses—abound, and rodeo is a highly successful collegiate sport. So I was surprised when one particular collaborative group of students focused their research project on factory farming and assembly-line slaughter, and decided to engage in "primary research" by visiting a local hog slaughterhouse. The experience was, needless to say, shocking and transformative for them, confirming with their own eyes what they had encountered in the assigned course reading. They became aware of the world immediately around them and in which they had grown up in new and profound ways because they chose to take on a deeper investigation.

Similarly, I recently showed the film *Iron Jawed Angels* (Von Garnier, 2004), a fictional representation of Alice Paul's activism for women's suffrage, which portrayed Paul's unconstitutional arrest, imprisonment, and brutal mistreatment while in jail. Hollywood special effects did not disappoint during the prison scenes, prompting one student, who shared little in common with a feminist standpoint, to investigate Alice Paul online for herself between the end of the movie and our next class. During class discussion, she admitted assuming the women's abuses in prison were Hollywood fiction, to enhance the drama, so she was stunned to learn that the scenes were based in reality. She reported that her research challenged her assumptions about feminism and the history of the women's movement, as well as about the actions our democratically elected leaders in government might be willing to take under duress.

In both cases, students engaged thoughtfully with the course material in ways that were meaningful for them, and I want to believe that as a result they became both better learners and more aware as voting-age citizens. Yet, have these students retained these educational moments in their lives? Have they transferred their self-motivated learning in these specific instances to more direct democracy education and civic action? I don't know. Rebekah Nathan's first-hand research of today's college students implies that many do not take what they respond to in the classroom beyond the classroom door. Additionally, isolated anecdotes about individual self-motivated learning do not translate into an educated citizenry. What occurred for these few individuals obviously needs to occur with greater regularity for all students. But the chances of deeper, more widespread learning are higher if we provide such opportunities for self-motivated education.

Ultimately, our educational goal needs to be to get students excited about being productive participants in the democratic process: registering to vote, researching candidates and legislative propositions, and showing up at the polls on election day; serving on juries; attending community civic meetings; running for local political offices; joining and actively supporting sociopolitical organizations, even while they are still in school, and not just during senior year because such membership "looks good" on a job resume; and so on. Hopefully, they will then become committed to being knowledgeable citizens. Hopefully, they will become eager to learn and willing to question, to engage in productive research, to keep abreast of current events, to express their views and engage in debate that will ultimately offer them additional knowledge from multiple perspectives. Hopefully, their educators will likewise demonstrate their own well-informed, active participation in civic life. After all, we are as responsible for the well-being and progress of democracy as we expect our students to be.

Questions for Reflection

1. How might fostering "patriotic" commitment to one's community and country, as Damon calls for, engage students in productive interaction with historical and current sociopolitical issues?

2. What might you identify as contributing factors for the 20 percent drop in 18-year-old voter turnout between 1972 and 1996? How might we ensure that the increasing numbers of youth voters, that Levine reports of the 2004 election, be well informed as well as multiplied?

3. How would you answer the questions posed early in the chapter regarding student disinterest in national and global matters as well as the reasons for student disengagement?

4. Many colleges and universities offer institutional mission statements that indicate a desire to foster student "critical thinking," to instill a sense of civic responsibility, and to prepare students for their roles as informed citizens. Since concerned educators are often limited in what they might accomplish by bureaucratic constraints, how might democracy education be more actively promoted at the institutional level?

5. How might students' attraction to entertainment or sports events or celebrities be harnessed to foster greater sociopolitical awareness?

Notes

1. Since the book was published in 2001, the interviews were likely conducted and the students' essays written before 9/11 (and before the Iraq/Afghanistan military conflicts). Many of these "heartland" students now know someone directly impacted by the "War on Terrorism" militarily, or some have perhaps enlisted for military service themselves. Certainly, 9/11 and the Middle East conflict have affected what the students know and care about, though the results from my Fall 2006 exploration of what students know about history and current events, including 9/11 and U.S. involvement in Afghanistan and Iraq, were disappointing. Nevertheless, it is important to point out that the world has changed since Damon conducted his research with students.

2. Again, in a post–9/11 environment, patriotism as love of country has rebounded. However, it rings of the superior and "super-militaristic" sensibility Damon notes, an

"us" or "them" mentality fostered by strong, aggressive speeches by national leaders. The flag waving arising in the United States following 9/11 might demonstrate renewed patriotic fervor, though not necessarily patriotism based in knowledge of historical or current events or in critical thinking.

3. *My Freshman Year* was published under the pseudonym Rebekah Nathan. However, in the paperback edition of her book, Nathan reveals her identity as Cathy Small, a faculty member at Northern Arizona University in Flagstaff, where she undertook her study.

References

Beaumont, E. (2007). *Engaging students politically goes beyond the voting booth.* Retrieved October 10, 2007, from http://www.carnegiefoundation.org/perspectives/sub.asp?key=245&subkey=573

Center for Information and Research on Civic Learning and Engagement. (2006). *The 2006 civic and political health of the nation: A detailed look at how youth participate in politics and communities.* Retrieved October 10, 2007, from http://www.civicyouth.org/Popups/2006_CPHS_Report_update.pdf

Colby, A., Ehrlich, T., Beaumont, E., & Stephens, J. (2003). *Educating citizens: Preparing America's undergraduates for lives of moral and civic responsibility.* San Francisco: Jossey-Bass.

Damon, W. (2001). Restoring civil identity among the young. In D. Ravitch & J. P. Viteritti (Eds.), *Education and civil society* (pp. 122–141). New Haven: Yale University Press.

Freire, P. (1994a). *Pedagogy of hope: Reliving pedagogy of the oppressed* (R. Barr, trans.). New York: Continuum.

———. (1994b). *Pedagogy of the oppressed* (20th anniversary ed.) (M. B. Ramos, trans.). New York: Continuum.

Gandhi, M. (1946). "Essence of democracy." *Harijan, 14*(7), 220. Retrieved June 30, 2007, from http://www.mkgandhi.org/momgandhi/chap72.htm

Levine, P. (2005). Youth voting in 2004: The myths and the facts. *Wingspread Journal.* Retrieved October 10, 2007, from http://www.johnsonfnd.org/Publications/WSJournals/2005/WSJournalDemocracy05.pdf

Nathan, R. (2005). *My freshman year: What a professor learned by becoming a student.* New York: Penguin.

National Endowment for the Humanities. (2002). *President Bush announces NEH American History Initiative.* Retrieved July 21, 2007, from http://www.neh.gov/news/archive/20020917.html

Ravitch, D. (2001). Education and democracy. In D. Ravitch & J. P. Viretti (Eds.), *Making good citizens: Education and civil society* (pp. 15–29). New Haven: Yale University Press.

Von Garnier, K. (2004). *Iron jawed angels* [Compact Disc]. New York: HBO Films.

19

A PEDAGOGY FOR SOCIAL JUSTICE:
CRITICAL TEACHING THAT GOES
AGAINST THE GRAIN

Shazia Shujah

Introduction: Why Social Justice Education?

Paulo Freire (1985) perceptively notes the nature of education as a discourse of power when he states that "education is a political act" (p. 188). The process of education exists within a societal context, with a particular bias, purpose, and outcome. Knowing that school culture is merely a microcosm, and mirror, of the larger culture, we understand that social categories, such as race, class, gender, and culture, influence the schooling that students receive. In this sense, "knowledge is socially constructed, culturally mediated, and historically situated" (McLaren, 1998, p. 185). Highlighting the relationship between schooling and inequality, Apple (1990), Giroux (1997), and McLaren (1999) have all argued that schools are sites that reproduce social inequality. This chapter, first, establishes why social justice education is necessary in the Canadian landscape. Second, it explores what *doing* democracy looks like from a critical perspective in Ontario's elementary schools. Finally, I note the challenges of engaging in social justice pedagogy, one that seeks a democratic classroom.

History of Colonization

Canada has a known history of colonization and exclusion (Alladin, 1996). From the outset of public education in the nineteenth century, streaming for the benefit of the White middle class has occurred (Gidney, 1999). To prevent class mobility, the poorest students were excluded altogether or received a differentiated education geared toward preparing them to be obedient factory workers (Curtis, Livingstone, & Smaller, 1992). Likewise, today's gender gap can be traced to the fact that women were initially excluded, later segregated until 1917, and then shunned from particular fields (Gaskell, McLaren, & Novogrodsky, 1989). Likewise, when minoritized bodies were permitted to attend public school, they were separate and unequal (Winks, 1971). A poignant example of indoctrination is the federally run Indian Residential schools that were blatantly intended to assimilate First Nations people into Anglo culture, religion, and language (Frideres, 1987).

In fact, we know that cultural imposition and imperialism continue today in complex and subtle ways. School curriculum continues to reinforce a hegemonic perspective, one that privileges a White, Western identity (Dei, 2000; Giroux, 1997). First published by the Conservative government (1997, 1998) and partially updated by the Liberals (2004, 2005, 2006), the current Ontario school curriculum is exclusive in its format and content.

The Ontario curriculum's formulaic language, generic format, and standardized testing are disadvantageous to anybody whose experiences and knowledge do not fit into its fixed model (Wein & Dudley-Marling, 1998). Likewise, its content can be considered Eurocentric. In this sense, racialized bodies are marginalized and disadvantaged from the outset (Shujah, 2005): "What 'standard' curriculum, report cards, and testing have been consistent in doing is to continue to breed inequality in education" (Shujah, 2005, p. 1). The fact that Ontario's students are diverse learners from diverse backgrounds raises the challenge and need to provide an educational process that is inclusive.

Unequal Outcomes

Emphasizing the need for a more democratic approach to education is the fact that unequal access continues to result in unequal outcomes. Alladin (1996) notes that while education in Canada is assumingly undiscriminatory—it is free and compulsory to all—factors such as race, class, and gender continue to affect student achievement (p. 14). Statistics highlight the discrepancies between rich and poor neighborhoods. In the GTA, the lowest income neighborhoods (essentially high immigrant) have 39% of students at risk of underachievement compared to only 11% in

GTA's highest income area (Duffy, 2004, p. A11). Poor and minority students continue to be informally segregated through curriculum, special education, ability grouping, and formal tracking. Furthermore, the "hidden curriculum" of school environment and teacher interaction all contribute to a cycle of disadvantage in urban areas (Anyon, 1983). Marginalized, these bodies are more likely to tune out and drop out (Dei, Mazzuca, McIsaac, & Zine, 1997). Knowing that particular bodies continue to be disadvantaged in the schooling process, democratic education is even more a necessity to ensure the success of every student.

My Background

With these starting points, I come to this chapter. I am a Muslim female and visible minority. I have 18 years experience working with the Toronto District School Board, including 10 years as an educator. Working in inner-city Toronto with students, families, and communities—while maintaining my academic and theoretical grounding—has helped me to establish a deep commitment to equity and social justice pedagogy. In my teaching experience, I have watched students overcome personal adversity; I have supported families through crisis and have witnessed the effects of poverty and crime on students. Yet, I continue to be fuelled by what Freire calls a "pedagogy of hope" (1994). This hope is fundamental for all critical educators.

Critical Framework

The framework used in this chapter for examining power, difference, and schooling is rooted in Foucault (1980, 1984) and Freire (1970). To deconstruct power, I specifically use a critical antiracism perspective. Critical theory derives from Foucault's (1980) examination of the relationship between knowledge and power. He notes how individuals are produced through social practices and language, which shapes perception and reality (Foucault, 1984, p. 205). Specifically examining education, Freire (1970) outlines the duality of the schooling process: education has both oppressive and transformative potential.

Naming the social categories that influence power, critical antiracism theory unmaps how power operates, and how we can work within and beyond the boundaries of school culture as change agents. Dei (1996) argues that while "a multifaceted analysis [of race, class, gender, sexuality, etc.] is useful in capturing the nuances and complexities of social experience," the primacy of race must be placed in the foreground (p. 20). Using critical race theory, this chapter commences with the understanding that education is influenced by the primacy of race and its intersections with gender, class, ability, and other social markers. The remainder of this chapter examines what democratic education looks like in everyday practice, specifically in Ontario's urban areas, as well as the challenges of teaching outside the established curriculum limits.

Toward Social Justice Education

To begin to explore what democratic pedagogy and teaching looks like we need to re-address fundamental questions: What do we teach? How do we teach? For me, doing democracy is a critical pedagogy that is inclusive of multiple perspectives and content. It respects diversity and is empowering to the bodies in the classroom and beyond. For me, democratic education is synonymous with social justice pedagogy and these terms are interchanged in this chapter.

In seeking to empower students, Mohanty's (1990) definition of resistance is significant here: "Resistance lies in a self-conscious engagement with dominant, normative discourses and representations and in the active creation of oppositional analytic and cultural spaces" (p. 185). If we are to seek democratic schooling first, we should "engage" in, rather than disregard, the current curriculum. Second, although we should teach dominant discourses, we need to do so in a meaningful manner. Third, a "self-conscious" engagement with curriculum means that students need to develop critical skills to understand various "texts" including television, and the Internet. Simultaneously, we must "actively" continue to broaden the curriculum, what Mohanty (1990) describes as "uncovering and reclaiming subjugated knowledges" (p. 185). Curriculum must be inclusive: it must incorporate learners' histories and experiences. Finally, to truly do democracy students need to become active citizens in a democratic society beyond the classroom (Freire, 1985); students need to feel like positive change agents in their communities. Each of these key aspects of critical pedagogy is detailed below.

The Culture of Power

While the Ontario school curriculum is arguably biased in its content (Shujah, 2005), it does contain the cultural knowledge and language skills that students need to be academically successful in this society, what Delpit (1995) labels "the culture of power" (p. 25). The culture of power is advantageous to those who have it. In fact, it can be argued that resistance entails mastering the language of the dominant, and then using it critically for political change. As Freire (1987) explains, "because of the political problem of power, you need to learn how to command the dominant language, in order for you to survive in the struggle to transform society" (p. 73). Students need to acquire the language of power, and then use the power of language for critical thought and action.

Knowing that students from nondominant backgrounds come to school with codes other than (*not* inferior to) those which form the culture of power, we must explicitly teach these codes. After all, we know that students will ultimately find themselves held accountable for them (Delpit, 1995). By helping my students acquire the skills and knowledge by which they will be measured and judged academically and socially, I am ensuring their success. For example, knowing how to write a formal essay like this requires a certain knowledge of language and grammar. If I ensure that my students acquire the tools and rules of standard English, then I have helped them to empower themselves. As Corson (2001) notes, the culture of power is a "commodity ... for social selection" (p. 23). To benefit all learners we must teach and maintain high expectations for all of our students. While we do arguably have different degrees of access to the language of power (through social markers such as class), Freire (1985) lucidly notes that literacy is a key to empowerment.

Lived Identities

With fixed outcomes for a generic student, the Ontario school curriculum fails to account for the multiplicity of students' backgrounds, experiences, and varied learning styles (Shujah, 2005). However, a democratic curriculum must be fluid enough to validate all learners. Students need to be able to make the crucial link between school knowledge and their own histories, experiences, and perspectives. For example, for Valentine's Day, students not only learn the traditional story of St. Valentine, but they are also introduced to another love story, that of the Taj Mahal; Shah Jahan built this wonder of the world as a token to his wife Mumtaz. Inspired, students are asked to research love stories from their cultures and family histories. Here, students' home cultures are regarded as "cultural enrichment" not "cultural baggage" (Dei, 1996, p. 84). With such an approach, neither the curriculum plan nor teacher is deemed the expert. Rather, a reciprocal relationship between teacher and student ensues (Freire, 1985). Through multiple content, teaching methods, and assessment, a democratic classroom is established, one that is relevant and reflective of our multicultural society.

Striving toward inclusive teaching and learning, Haymes (1995) notes that we cannot separate learners from the neighborhood in which the school is entrenched. Likewise, antiracist spatial theory emphasizes the link between identities, dominance, and the physical spaces that we occupy (Razack, 2002). Educators need to be cognizant of what messages their physical classroom and their teaching practices portray about its students. As educators are faced with teaching a plethora of curriculum expectations under a tight time line, textbooks and photocopied materials can seem appealing. On the other hand, linking lessons directly to the students in the classroom may require more thought, creativity, and effort. For example, as a culminating task for a grade three "Urban and rural studies" unit, students created a City Mural on our classroom wall. The mural reflected and validated these students' understanding of urban space; alongside structures such as the CN Tower and the Rogers Centre were neighborhood sites such as a Portuguese churrascaria restaurant, a Dufferin Mall, and a High Park.

Finally, part of ensuring that learning is linked to students' lives, students need to see themselves reflected in positive role models. Events such as a

Career Fair using community members as guests is one way to inspire students in an authentic manner.

Critical Learners

Beyond meaningful learning, students need to develop critical language in order to critique school knowledge and the world around them. As Darder (1991) notes, students should be introduced to the "language of theory" that represents a critical language of social analysis. Students should be able to recognize bias, stereotypes, and victimization (Darder, 1991, p. 104). Part of teaching students to become critical thinkers is to help them develop awareness that knowledge is not neutral, that "all knowledge reflects the power and social relations within society" (Banks, 1993, p. 9). This critical examination of power relations is absent in school curriculum.

Contextualizing curriculum within past and present power relations ensures that students gain a more representative perspective. Thus, knowing that knowledge of Impressionist art is a part of the culture of power, I do teach it. However, I do so in a critical manner whereby students are aware that this knowledge is specific to class, place, time, gender, race, and more. Simultaneously, students learn about various types of art and artists such as Islamic geometric art, Ancient Egyptian art, and current female North American artists.

To develop a deeper understanding of how power operates, I engage my students in a 4-week program called WHORM, World History of Racism in Minutes (McCaskell, 1986). Through language and the integrated arts, students learn how power relations between civilizations have shifted through time. Using Drama and oral language, students learn that the world's first university was in Africa, that India was once a powerful and independent empire, and that China built the spectacular Great Wall. Thus, while mandated Social Studies topics, such as "Early civilizations," "Early settlements in Upper Canada," and "Medieval times" (Ontario, 2004, p. 20), are covered, we go beyond a superficial historical analysis of artifacts to understand how European "exploration" and conquest resulted in a profound shift of power and wealth. From here, media studies are used to develop awareness of current human rights issues, such as negative stereotypes against Muslims.

Challenging the Media

Beyond exploring systematic inequality throughout history, students need to develop critical language and skills to analyze the media. However, the Ontario government only added "Media literacy" to the curriculum in 2006. Understanding, reflecting on, and creating various media forms is a direct part of current mandates (2006, pp. 13–14). However, a critical examination of bias and stereotypes in the media such as gender role stereotypes should be at the fore.

Analyzing and critiquing media texts—such as the Internet, newspapers, and television—for bias is necessary for social justice teaching. To develop critical awareness I have had students analyze their favorite storybook illustrations for gendered, racial, and classist stereotypes. Beyond this, we analyze TV shows, newspapers, magazines, and advertisements with a broader discussion of not only gender and race, but issues of ableism, body size, and ageism. Students explore questions such as: Who is represented? Who is missing? What messages are conveyed about certain people? Through personal logs and diaries, students quickly discover that White males are more represented as are blond haired and blue-eyed individuals. They are more likely to be the heroes or the "beautiful" ones. Nevertheless, as with any discussion, critical educators need to be careful to not isolate such students in the classroom; we need to acknowledge that all features are beautiful and valid.

Finally, just as students learn about selling techniques and audience in advertisements, they also need to develop awareness of stereotypes and power. Thus, I have had students create their own, more inclusive, advertisements. These have included senior citizens, large-sized bodies, various ethnicities, as well as people in wheelchairs. The personal becomes the political (Smith, 1987) as students create images of people who are reflective of themselves and their families. Likewise, students make the shift from being passive consumers to active participants in their community and society, a key aspect of democratic education. Critical awareness provides students with a framework for analyzing power and inequality in their lives and beyond.

New Knowledges

To ensure democratic teaching and learning, we must broaden curriculum content. The Eurocentric content of the curriculum needs to be ruptured to emphasize other knowledges. We need to uncover and reclaim histories and to examine their intersections (Dei, 1996; Mohanty, 1990). In a democratic classroom, alternative and oppositional paradigms should flourish. Thus, curricular borders are extended to incorporate multiple perspectives and values.

An example of extending these boundaries is with the grade five Social Studies topic of government (Ontario, 2004). Students should learn about the Canadian Charter of Rights and Freedoms, which is part of the curriculum (Ontario, 2004, p. 44), but they should also learn about when and to whom these rights have been denied, which is not mandated. Students should be taught about Canada's mistreatment of First Nations people, slavery, Chinese immigrant workers, as well as females' political struggles. Students should learn about Aboriginal self-government, as well as other forms of world government. Using a variety of instructional methods, we can and must teach a more balanced story of Canada, one where students can weave their own stories into the larger portrait. Doing democracy requires that subjugated voices and histories be brought to the fore.

In this sense, if we are to achieve a democratic classroom, we need to move beyond mere tokenism to truly integrate, multiple perspectives and histories into the school curriculum. As Rosemary Sadlier (Equity Department, Toronto District School Board, 2005) states, shifting beyond hegemonic Eurocentric history is a crucial step for Canada as a diverse nation, "to arrive at an understanding of ourselves as Canadians in the most accurate and complete socio-historical context that we can produce" (p. 5). After all, only one voice and one perspective will be disadvantageous, disrespectful, and disempowering to the bodies who do not see themselves reflected in the stories, histories, and people around them.

Citizens for Change

Nevertheless, to truly empower students, a shift from critical knowledge to critical action for change needs to occur. While the Ontario curriculum focuses on skills and knowledge, citizenship and values are essentially nonexistent in the school curriculum. Personal skills are relegated a small space at the bottom of the provincial report card. However, as Giroux and McLaren (1986) have outlined, empowerment must move beyond a personal level for students, toward political/social awareness and action. Students should not only acquire critical knowledge to understand their immediate world, but also acquire the courage to transform it (p. 229). Especially after learning about past and current racism and discrimination, students need to feel like change is possible.

Students need to become active citizens who are part of positive change and they need to learn the skills that will enable them to take such action. For inspiration, students should first study current and past role models around the world who use peaceful change strategies. Next, students should choose a cause that they are personally interested in. As citizens in a democratic society, students should work for positive change using a peaceful strategy such as letter writing, poster campaigning, or conducting interviews.

Likewise, every classroom in every school should pick one project a year where they actively seek to improve the community; it can be as simple as planting trees, volunteering, or fundraising for a community cause. With past classes, I have helped them to organize events such as community planting, fundraising for the South Asia earthquake victims (2005), and a Sock Drive for the homeless. In this sense, the boundaries of teaching shift beyond the curriculum to a transformative level; math, language, organizational skills, cooperative skills, and citizenship become lived experiences where students contribute in a real way to positively altering our world. As a key aspect of inclusive schooling, schools become sites of social activism and community engagement (Dei, James, James-Wilson, Karumanchery, & Zine, 2000). If democracy is to flourish, then active engagement at all grade levels must be encouraged.

The Challenges of Shifting Borders

As a critical antiracist educator I acknowledge the challenges and limitations of this daily work. Inclusive education means changing staffing practices, teacher education programs, professional development funding, and learning materials, all over which I do not have control.

In the classroom, a major challenge I have faced is a lack of resources at my inner-city school. The discrepancies between rich and poor schools have been dubbed as "savage inequalities" by Kozol (1991). I have struggled for classroom "basics," such as a world maps, calculators, and textbooks. With an "equal" funding formula first established by the former Conservative government (Gidney, 1999, pp. 234–253)—the same amount of money per child, regardless of needs—the compounding needs of inner-city schools lose priority. Increasing the gap between rich and poor, private schools have increased by 40 percent (Dei, 2004, p. 188), and private fundraising by parents raises over $39 million (People for Education, 2004). The differential resources in different neighborhoods contribute to differential academic outcomes.

Second, the principal, as leader, needs to establish clear expectations around equity beyond token gestures to simply fulfill a School Improvement Plan or a School Profile. An environment that fosters inclusion needs to be established through an Equity Committee, school expectations, curriculum, and support for educators and parents. From my experience, I have had principals who were conscientious and entirely supportive of inclusive education and some who have been unsupportive and even hindering to social justice work. It is disheartening and frustrating when an administrator tunes out equity issues, especially where the bodies in our schools oblige us to keep it at the forefront.

A third challenge to critical work is dealing with the intersecting oppressions of race, culture, social class, gender, religion, and others that affect students' lives. The complex issues and cycles of poverty, discrimination, abuse, and violence can sometimes prove to be overwhelming for students and families. Due to a lack of initiatives at the school level, combined with limited Ministry and Board funding for social workers, after-school programs and parenting centers, I have found it a challenge to support parents beyond a personal level. These inner-city challenges have been noted by others (Dei et al., 2004).

Fourth, we know that to empower minority students, a strong school-community partnership is fundamental (Cummins, 1986). From my experience, parents of the dominant background are more comfortable and more likely to be members of the School Parent Council, while parents from various ethnicities face language and cultural barriers. In this sense the council is not always representative of the school demographics (Dei et al., 2000). School administrators need to strategize to involve a diversity of parents, such as by using translators. In order to promote mutual respect, a Parent/Literacy Centre should be mandatory for all schools. This should be a physical space where parents are welcome to visit and have their queries answered. I recently visited an "inner-city" school in its sixth year of receiving special ministry funding. From my observations, a key factor in its success was the ease with which parents, from a variety of ethnic and linguistic backgrounds, were integrated into school life.

Finally, even as self-reflective pedagogues, we too are fallible. We must acknowledge our own positions of privilege and our own flaws. For example, I am aware of gendered communication patterns and the fact that teachers usually spend more time interacting with boys than girls (Sadker & Sadker, 1994). However, I have caught myself doing the same at times. I have found myself paying less attention to the girls who were working quietly in class and spent more time reacting to negative behaviors of boys. Knowing that quiet and well-mannered students should not be denied teacher attention, this is one issue of which I continue to be self-conscious.

Conclusion

In summary, as educators doing democracy we are helping to shape the citizens of tomorrow. To truly teach in a democratic manner, we must acknowledge that race, class, gender, sexuality, and ability—among other social markers—are all factors that continue to influence education. To enable and enrich every student we need to establish an inclusive pedagogy and practice that validates multiple voices, values, and knowledges (Dei et al., 2000).

We can only accomplish inclusive education if students are instilled with hope, pride, and critical literacy. As Giroux (1988) states, educators "must create the conditions that give students the opportunity to become citizens who have knowledge and courage to struggle in order to make ... hope practical" (p. 128). In a democratic schooling process, all students have the right to maintain dignity in their own identities and histories.

Finally, all stakeholders in education must continue to dialogue and strategize for concrete improvements to our education system. After all, in a truly democratic society, all classes, all races, all people have a voice. Likewise this voice and agency must be a fundamental right given to all of our students.

Questions for Reflection

1. How can you justify to parents of the dominant background the need for inclusive education?

2. In what ways is a standard curriculum beneficial? Disadvantageous?

3. Describe the key aspects of social justice pedagogy as outlined in this chapter. Which element would you argue is the most important? Why?

4. Why is there a current need for critical media studies? How can educators work to counter the negative influences of the media?

5. From your perspective, what is a key area of marginalization that you see in education today? How could you work as a change agent to correct this?

References

Alladin, I. (1996). *Racism in Canadian schools.* Toronto: Harcourt Brace.

Anyon, J. (1983). Social class and the hidden curriculum of work. In H. Giroux & D. Purpel (Eds.), *The hidden curriculum and moral education: Deception or discovery?* (pp. 143–167). Berkeley, CA: McCutchen.

Apple, M. (1990). *Ideology and curriculum* (2nd ed.). New York: Routledge.

Banks, J. (1993). Approaches to multicultural curriculum reform. In J. Banks & C. M. Banks (Eds.), *Multicultural education: Issues and perspectives* (2nd ed., pp. 63–70). Boston: Allyn & Bacon.

Corson, D. (2001). *Language diversity and education.* Mahwah, NJ: Lawrence Erlbaum Associates.

Cummins, J. (1986). Empowering minority students: A framework for intervention. *Harvard Educational Review, 56*(1), 18–36.

Curtis, B., Livingstone, D. W., & Smaller, H. (1992). *Stacking the deck: The streaming of working class kids in Ontario schools.* Montreal, PQ: Our School/Our Selves Foundation.

Darder, A. (1991). *Culture and power in the classroom: A critical foundation for bicultural education.* Toronto: OISE.

Dei, G. J. S. (1996). *Anti-racism education: Theory and practice.* Halifax, Nova Scotia: Fernwood.

Dei, G. J. S. (2000). Towards an anti-racism discursive framework. In G. J. S. Dei & A. Calliste (Eds.), *Power knowledge, and anti-racism: A critical reader* (pp. 23–40). Halifax, Nova Scotia: Fernwood.

Dei, G. J. S. (2004). The challenge of promoting inclusive education in Ontario schools: What does educational research tell us? In B. Kidd & J. Phillips (Eds.), *From enforcement and prevention to civic engagement: Research on community safety* (pp. 184–200). Toronto: University of Toronto.

Dei, G. J. S., James, I. M., James-Wilson, S., Karumanchery, L. L., & Zine, J. (2000). *Removing the margins: The challenges and possibilities of inclusive schooling.* Toronto: Canadian Scholars' Press.

Dei, G. J. S., Mazzuca, J., McIsaac, J., & Zine, J. (1997). *Reconstructing "dropout": A critical ethnography of the dynamics of Black students' disengagement from school.* Toronto: University of Toronto.

Delpit, L. (1995). *Other people's children: Cultural conflict in the classroom.* New York: New Press.

Duffy, A. (2004, October 3). Black students still poorly served: Study. *Toronto Star*, pp. A1, A11.

Equity Department. (2005). *African heritage resource guide.* Toronto: Toronto District School Board.

Foucault, M. (1980). *Power/knowledge.* New York: Pantheon.

Foucault, M. (1984). The means of correct training. In P. Rabinow (Ed.), *Foucault Reader* (pp. 188–205). New York: Pantheon.

Freire, P. (1970). *Pedagogy of the oppressed.* New York: Seabury.

Freire, P. (1985). *The politics of education, culture, power, and liberation.* South Hadley, MA: Bergin & Garvey.

Freire, P. (1987). *A pedagogy for liberation: Dialogues on transforming education.* South Hadley, MA: Bergin & Garvey.

Freire, P. (1994). *Pedagogy of hope.* New York: Continuum.

Frideres, J. S. (1987). Native people and Canadian education. In T. Wotherspoon (Ed.), *The political economy of Canadian schooling* (pp. 275–290). Toronto: Methuen.

Gaskell, J., McLaren A., & Novogrodsky, M. (1989). *Claiming an education: Feminism and Canadian schools.* Toronto: Our School/Our Selves Foundation.

Gidney, R. D. (1999). *From hope to Harris: The reshaping of Ontario's schools.* Toronto: University of Toronto.

Giroux, H. (1988). *Teachers as intellectuals: Towards a pedagogy of learning.* Hadley, MA: Bergin & Garvey.

Giroux, H. (1997). Rewriting the discourse of racial identity: Towards a pedagogy and politics of Whiteness. *Harvard Educational Review, 67*(2), 285–320.

Giroux, H., & McLaren, P. (1986). Teacher education and the politics of engagement: The case for democratic schooling. *Harvard Educational Review, 56*(3), 213–238.

Haymes, S. N. (1995). *Race, culture, and the city: A pedagogy for Black urban struggle.* Albany, NY: State University of New York Press.Kozol, J. (1991). *Savage inequalities: Children in America's schools.* New York: Crown.

McCaskell, T. (1986). *World history of racism in minutes: WHORM.* Toronto: Toronto Board of Education.

McLaren, P. (1998). *Life in schools: An introduction to critical pedagogy in the foundations of education* (3rd ed.). Los Angeles: Addison-Wesley Longman.

McLaren, P. (1999). *Schooling as a ritual performance: Toward a political economy of educational symbols and gestures*. Oxford: Rowman & Littlefield.

Mohanty, C. (1990). On race and voice: Challenges for liberal education in the 90s. *Cultural Critique, 14*, 179–208.

Ontario Ministry for Education and Training. (2004). *The Ontario curriculum: Social Studies grades 1 to 6; History and geography grades 7 and 8, revised*. Toronto: Queen's Printer.

Ontario Ministry for Education and Training. (2006). *The Ontario curriculum grades 1–8: Language, revised*. Toronto: Queen's Printer.

People for Education. (June 2004). *Elementary schools tracking results*. Toronto: Author.

Razack, S. H. (2002). When place becomes race. In S. H. Razack (Ed.), *Race, space, and the law: Unmapping a White settler society* (pp. 1–20). Toronto: Between the Lines.

Sadker, M., & Sadker, D. (1994). *Failing at fairness: How America's schools cheat girls*. New York: Maxwell Macmillan International.

Shujah, S. (2005). *The Ontario school curriculum: A critical overview*. Toronto: University of Toronto.

Smith, D. (1987). *The everyday world as problematic. A feminist sociology*. Toronto: University of Toronto.

Wein, C., & Dudley-Marling, C. (1998). Limited vision: The Ontario curriculum and outcomes-based learning. *Canadian Journal of Education, 23*(4), 405–420.

Winks, R. W. (1971). *The Blacks in Canada: A history*. New Haven, CT: Yale University Press.

SECTION V

AFTERWORD

AFTERWORD

THE TWIN PROJECT OF WIDENING AND DEEPENING DEMOCRACY: IMPLICATIONS FOR EDUCATION

Daniel Schugurensky

I am very grateful to Darren Lund and Paul Carr, the editors of this book, for inviting me to write a short text on the topic of democracy, citizenship and education. In these few pages I will argue, taking a cue from the title of this book, that any educational project that strives for political literacy and social justice must be connected to a larger undertaking of societal democratization that includes two main projects. The first one, widening democracy, has to do with having a substantive democracy in which all human beings have equal opportunities to develop their full potential, and in which non-humans are also considered as subjects with rights (including animal rights and ecological justice). The second one, deepening democracy, has to do with doing democracy while cultivating effective processes of participatory democracy in a variety of communities.

The Widening Democracy Project

The publication of this book coincides with the 60th anniversary of the Universal Declaration of Human Rights, arguably one of the most important documents of the 20th century. The Declaration was produced, discussed and approved during a lucid, creative and responsible moment of humankind after the tragedy and madness of World War II. Today, in its 60th anniversary, it is pertinent to refresh our collective memory by briefly revisiting the 1948 declaration and examining where we stand in relation to it.

The Declaration is organized in a beautiful preamble and 30 articles. The articles in the first two-thirds of the declaration (1 to 21) deal with basic human, civil and political rights, from the right to life, liberty, equality, dignity and security, to the right to enter marriage with the free and full consent of the intending spouses, the right to freedom of expression and association, the right to seek, receive and impart information through any media, and the right to vote and be elected to government office. Those articles also ban slavery, servitude, torture and any form of cruel, inhuman or degrading treatment or punishment, as well as arbitrary arrest, detention or exile, and clearly state that these rights apply to all human beings, without discrimination of any kind, such as race, color, sex, language, religion, political or other opinion, national or social origin, property, birth or other status. Several of these rights can also be found in the legislation of many individual nation-states, and sometimes even in their Constitutions and Charters.

One of the most important contributions of the Declaration can be found in articles 22 to 28 because, for the first time in human history, it addressed issues of economic, social and cultural democracy, and articulated them in terms of fundamental rights for all human beings.

Article 22 states that all members of society have the right to social security and are entitled to the economic, social and cultural rights indispensable for their dignity and the free development of their personality.

Article 23 states that everyone has the right to work, to free choice of employment, to just and favorable conditions of work, to protection against unemployment, and to equal pay for equal work without any discrimination. It also states that everyone who works has the right to just and favorable remuneration ensuring an existence worthy of human dignity, and supplemented, if necessary, by other means of social protection. Moreover, this article notes that workers have the right to form and to join trade unions to protect their interests.

Article 24 states that everyone has the right to rest and leisure, including reasonable limitation of working hours and periodic holidays with pay.

Article 25 deals with the right to a standard of living adequate for individual and family health and wellbeing, including food, clothing, housing and medical care and necessary social services. It also notes the right to security in the event of unemployment, sickness, disability, widowhood, old age or other lack of livelihood in circumstances beyond our control. This article pays special attention to mothers and children, who are entitled to special care and assistance, and notes that all children, whether born in or out of wedlock, should enjoy the same social protection.

Article 26 is about education. Among other things, it clearly specifies that education is a right and should be free, at least at the elementary level, and the higher education should be equally accessible to all on the basis of merit. This article also refers to the mission of education with words that can reflect the hope of peace and tolerance after the pain of two world wars:

> Education shall be directed to the full development of the human personality and to the strengthening of respect for human rights and fundamental freedoms. It shall promote understanding, tolerance and friendship among all nations, racial or religious groups, and shall further the activities of the United Nations for the maintenance of peace.

Article 27 deals with the right to freely participate in the cultural life of the community, to enjoy the arts and to share in scientific advancement and its benefits.

Article 28 is particularly interesting because it assumes a call against colonialist and imperialist tendencies as well as a call for planetary democracy: "Everyone is entitled to a social and international order in which the rights and freedoms set forth in this Declaration can be fully realized."

The 1948 declaration put great hope in educational institutions to promote awareness about the newly proclaimed rights. From the outset, the Preamble of the Declaration asked every person and every social organization "to strive by teaching and education to promote respect for these rights and freedoms." Moreover, immediately after the approval of the Declaration in December of 1948, the General Assembly of the United Nations called upon all member countries to disseminate it widely, especially in schools and other educational institutions. I attended one elementary school and two secondary schools during the 1960s and 1970s, and I don't recall any lesson or class discussion on the Universal Declaration of Human Rights. Perhaps the main reason for this silence was that I attended those schools in Argentina during a time in which that country was often ruled by military dictatorships but I wonder what proportion of students in schools around the world had the opportunity to read, reflect on and discuss the declaration as part of the school curriculum.

The team that prepared the text of the Declaration worked under the direction of a Canadian human rights advocate named John Peters Humphrey. The Chair of the Commission was Eleanor Roosevelt, who called the Declaration the international Magna Carta of humankind. She argued that the acceptance of these rights throughout the world were a precondition for peace by creating an atmosphere in which peace could grow, and wisely noted that "the destiny of human rights is in the hands of all our citizens in all our communities."

Today, we can observe with disappointment that most of the rights proclaimed in the Universal Declaration sixty years ago are far from being a reality. First, the social rights proclaimed in the second part of the declaration have often been considered "soft law" by member states. This means that, as a non-binding agreement, the articles of the Declaration are seldom translated into enforceable legislation. Probably the most illustrative expression of this stance can be found in the famous statement made by Jeanne Kirkpatrick, U.S. Ambassador to the United Nations during the government of Ronald Reagan, who argued that certain economic and social rights cannot be considered human rights and then called the Universal Declaration "a letter to Santa Claus."

Unfortunately, it is not only the social, economic and cultural rights of the declaration that are ignored. Today, even many of the basic civil and political rights mentioned in the first 21 articles of the declaration are still being ignored everyday in many parts of the world. To begin with, the fundamental notion of the equality of all members of the human family that is explicitly stated on the first line of the text flies in the face of reality in a world characterized by obscene inequalities. A recent study coordinated by Branko Milanovic (a leading economist of the World Bank) found that global inequality between world citizens is even higher than previously thought. While article 15 asserts that everyone has a right to a nationality, presently there are more than 11 million stateless people around the world who have very limited rights.

Although slavery is explicitly prohibited in the Declaration, millions of people around the world (especially children) are confined by contemporary forms of slavery, such as forced and bonded labor, forced prostitution, child soldiers, and human trafficking. The same can be said about daily occurrences of torture, exile, and arbitrary arrest, which, in many countries, are accompanied by the suspension of *habeas corpus*, hence interrupting a democratic tradition that can be traced back to the 1215 Magna Carta. Other basic rights noted in 1948 such as the right to enter marriage with the free and full consent of the intending spouses are also violated today when women are forced to accept arranged marriages, running the risk of honor killing if they refuse.

In this context, the project of widening democracy has to start with the struggle to ensure that the minimum core of basic civil rights enshrined in the 1948 Universal Declaration of Human Rights and in most national constitutions are respected in every corner of the planet. The project must also call for a comprehensive approach to citizenship that covers not only basic civil rights, but also the political and social rights detailed in the 1948 Declaration. As T.H. Marshall argued in the seminal *Citizenship and Social Class* (1950), citizens are only full citizens when they possess these three kinds of rights. This implies a transit from soft law (a "Letter to Santa Claus" in Kirkpatrick's words) to enforceable legislation, complemented with the implementation of redistributive policies that address social inequalities. The project of widening democracy, then, is both about inclusiveness and inclusion. On the one hand, it is about an inclusive approach to human rights that encompasses civil, political and social rights (and we could add cultural rights as well). On the other hand, it is about the real inclusion of all human beings as full citizens in our societies, regardless of their class, gender, race, and other differences. Moreover, one of the pending debates of the 21st century is to determine whether alien immigrants, children, animals, and plants should also be subjects of rights, and if so, what type of rights should they have. The claim that children, animals and plants should have rights may sound strange to many ears today but we need to remember that in other periods of history it probably sounded strange to many ears to claim that slaves, women, blacks, and indigenous peoples were entitled to the same rights as anybody else. The U.N. Convention on the Rights of the Child (1989) and the Earth Charter (2000) are encouraging steps in this direction.

The Deepening Democracy Project

The deepening democracy project has to do with democracy as a way of life. As John Dewey once noted, a democracy is more than a form of government: it is primarily a mode of associated living, of conjointly communicated experience of community in the making. The deepening democracy project also has to do with political justice. As Erik Olin Wright argues in the Envisioning Real Utopias project, in a politically just society all people would have broadly equal access to the necessary political means to collectively control those decisions that affect their common fate. The notions of democracy as a way of life and political justice lead almost naturally to the principles and practices of participatory democracy. This is not a new idea. Participatory democracy was practiced in a variety of societies throughout history, from Athens 2500 years ago to indigenous communities in North America before the conquest to workers' cooperatives and municipal budgets in more recent times.

Participatory democracy is proposed as a complement of representative democracy, and not as a substitute for it. For simple reasons of scale, it would be impossible to avoid some degree of representative democracy in any process that involves thousands or millions of people. However, the limits of representative democracy in terms of transparency, accountability, accessibility and the like have generated an almost universal distrust in politicians and political institutions. In 2005, in one of the largest surveys of public opinion ever on the topic of democracy and power that included more than 50,000 people in 68 countries, Gallup International found that politicians are generally the least trusted group: globally, only 11% trust politicians – less than military, religious and business leaders. This alarmingly low confidence in representative democracy goes hand in hand with an increasing gap between ordinary citizens and elected politicians as well as the crisis in the social contract that binds them. The deepening democracy project can address this situation by opening more democratic spaces for citizen participation, by promoting more and better transmission belts between citizens and elected representatives, and by improving the quality of democratic processes. This is about the building of vibrant democracies in which citizen participation involves more than going to the ballot box every few years.

Citizen participation, however, is not just about tokenistic exercises of pseudo-consultation. Four decades ago, in her short and influential article "A ladder of citizen participation," Sherry Arnstein argued that citizen participation is citizen power, and identified eight rungs of participation that allowed her to distinguish between manipulation exercises and genuine citizen control. Participatory democracy, hence, is about genuine, respectful and inclusive processes of deliberation and decision-making that are grounded on agreed upon principles. Participatory democracy has a great potential to further democratize and deepen our thin and superficial democracies, but also has a great educational potential. This is an important consideration for all those interested in promoting education for democracy inside and outside schools.

Rousseau, one of the most perceptive observers of the pedagogical dimension of participatory democracy, contended that the regular practice of democracy at the community level nurtures a sense of both empathy and efficacy on the part of individuals who participate. Empathy emerges as a consequence of the fact that an individual must take more into consideration than simply immediate self-interest if the support of others is to be secured. Put differently, the nature of a democratic process teaches an individual to take the interests of others into account, thereby nurturing an appreciation of the linkage between public and private as well as a sense of belonging to a broader community. Efficacy, which is the confidence that people have in their possibilities to influence decisions, is promoted through democratic decision making processes because the social relations characterizing these processes (i.e. equality and consent) permit individuals to have some control over decisions that affect the quality of their lives. For Rousseau, such opportunities are a prerequisite for the attainment of freedom because the norm of intrinsic equality nestled at the core of democratic practice affirms the inalienable right of each individual to be heard. In this sense, democratic institutions breed a sense of efficacy because the simple act of empowering individuals to participate implicitly recognizes and reinforces their autonomy and equality as individuals.

Following Rousseau, Carole Pateman advanced two related propositions. The first is that the major function of participation is educative in the broad sense, including both the psychological aspect and the gaining of practice in democratic skills and procedures. The second is that democracy is self-sustaining through the educative impact of the participatory process. This means that participation develops and fosters the very qualities necessary for it, because the more individuals participate, the better able they become to do so. In this sense, a reciprocal relation exists between citizenship learning and participatory democracy. In a sort of virtuous circle, good democratic processes nurtures positive citizenship learning, and citizenship learning nurtures healthier and more effective democracies. In other words, citizenship learning is both a prerequisite and an outcome of participatory democracy. As John Dewey aptly noted, the cure for the problems of democracy is more –not less– democracy. Moreover, by developing new relations of understanding and solidarity under conditions of equality, participatory democracy can help to address one of the key challenges for the 21st century noted in the Delors Report: learning to live together.

Final remarks

In the final sentences of this piece, I would like to re-assert the direct connection of these two projects with educational endeavors. In relation to the widening democracy project, it is pertinent to remember—as the Global Campaign for Education constantly reminds us—that although education is a basic human right and a fundamental activity for promoting human dignity and freedom, for 72 million children and 774 million adults, that right is violated everyday. It is not that human societies have no resources to address these and other issues and accomplish the Education for All goals and the Millennium Development Goals. Human societies produce enough resources to feed and educate every person on this planet. Unfortunately, most of these resources are unequally concentrated (the gap between rich and poor among and within nations has increased in the last decades). Moreover, significant resources that could be used for educational and social development are channeled every year to military expenditures. The United Nations estimates that only a small fraction (about 5%) of what the world spends today on arms and other means of destruction would be enough to provide primary education, low-cost water, sanitation and public health facilities, and reproductive health, family planning and clinical services to all those in need. It is for this reason that the project of democracy cannot be isolated from peace efforts, and that citizenship education and peace education efforts should go hand in hand.

In relation to the deepening democracy project, it is pertinent to point out that schools and other educational institutions are very good places for implementing participatory democracy principles and practices. If we accept the premise that one of the best ways of learning democracy is by doing democracy, then schools should not provide a holistic citizenship education that combines informative and critical content, dialogical methods, and a democratic classroom and school environment. Moreover, educators also have a role outside of schools, supporting capacity building efforts for local democracies in neighbourhoods, public housing units, community organizations, municipal governments and the like. Good quality democratic participation does not happen spontaneously. It often requires, among other things, a good understanding of democratic principles and processes, an informed and critical understanding of the issues being considered, a capacity to listen respectfully to others, an inclination to engage responsibly in a collective process, and a good facilitation process for deliberation and decision-making activities. All these things cannot happen without high quality educational resources and committed, democratic educators.

In today's world, there is an overemphasis on the role of educational systems to produce efficient and productive workers that are competitive in the global economy. A productive labor force is indeed an important facet of any society but it should not be the end goal of society. As John Dewey pointed out, "the ultimate aim of production is not production of goods, but the production of free human beings associated with one another on terms of equality."

References

Arnstein, S. (1969). A ladder of citizen participation. *Journal of the American Institute of Planners, 35*(4), 216-24.

Chomsky, N. (2002). *Chomsky on democracy and education* (edited by Carlos Otero). New York: Routledge.

Gallup International. (2005). *Voice of the people 2005: Trends in democracy: Global summary*. Zurich, Switzerland: Gallup International.

Marshall, T. H. (1949/1992). Citizenship and social class. In T. H. Marshall & T. Bottomore (Eds.), *Citizenship and social class* (pp. 1-51). London: Pluto Press.

Milanovic, B. (2006). *Global income inequality: What it is and why it matters*. (The World Bank Policy Research Working Paper Series, Paper 3865). Washington: World Bank.

Unesco. (1997). *Learning: The treasure within* (Delors Report to UNESCO's International Commission on Education for the Twenty-first Century). Paris: Unesco.

Unesco. (2008). *Global monitoring report: Will we make it?* Paris: Unesco.

United Nations. (1948). *Universal declaration of human rights*. Paris: United States General Assembly.

Wright, E. O. (2008). *Envisioning real utopias*. Retrieved January 15, 2008, from http://www.ssc.wisc.edu/~wright/

CONTRIBUTOR BIOGRAPHIES

Mary Frances Agnello is an Assistant Professor in Secondary Education in the College of Education at Texas Tech University, USA. She received her doctoral degree from Texas A&M University in Curriculum and Instruction with a focus in language, literacy, culture, and foundations of education. Her book *A Postmodern Literacy Policy Analysis* (2001) as well as several subsequent publications address literacy policy and several discourses of literacy and literate identity development of preservice teachers. Her research in teacher education, in addition to curriculum that addresses issues of race, class, and gender, led to her interest in critical economic literacy. She has published in *The Social Studies*, *Teacher Education Quarterly*, *Journal of Thought*, and *Community Education Journal*. She has a chapter in *The Praeger Handbook of Education and Psychology*, and another one upcoming in *Knowledge Economy: The Commodification of Knowledge and Information in the Academic System*.

Alireza Asgharzadeh teaches the sociology of knowledge, the sociology of education, and comparative educational systems in the Department of Sociology at York University, Toronto, Ontario, Canada. His areas of concentration and research include social theory, sociology of education/knowledge, as well as societies and cultures of the Middle East. His latest book, *Iran and the Challenge of Diversity: Islamic Fundamentalism, Aryanist Racism, and Democratic Struggles,* was published in June 2007 by Palgrave Macmillan.

James A. Banks is the Kerry and Linda Killinger Professor of Diversity Studies and Director of the Center for Multicultural Education at the University of Washington, Seattle. His books include *Teaching Strategies for Ethnic Studies* (8th edition), *Educating Citizens in a Multicultural Society* (2nd edition), the *Handbook of Research on Multicultural Education* (2nd edition), and *Diversity and Citizenship Education: Global Perspectives*. Professor Banks is a past president of the National Council for the Social Studies (NCSS) and of the American Educational Research Association (AERA). He was a Spencer Fellow at the Center for Advanced Study in the Behavioral

Sciences at Stanford in 2005-2006 and is a member of the National Academy of Education.

Sarah Elizabeth Barrett is an Assistant Professor in the Faculty of Education at York University, Toronto, Ontario, Canada. Her research focuses on student and teacher identity with respect to science, the professional identity of teachers in general, and making teaching for social justice an integral part of teacher education and professional development. She was a secondary school teacher for 10 years.

Glenda T. Bonifacio is an Assistant Professor in Women's Studies at the University of Lethbridge, Alberta, Canada. She completed her Ph.D. in Political Science from the School of History and Politics at the University of Wollongong, Australia, in 2004. She holds a B.A. in Social Sciences and an M.A. in Asian Studies from the University of the Philippines. Her research interests focus on gender, migration, and citizenship in the lives of racialized women in Australia and Canada.

Paul R. Carr is Assistant Professor in the Beeghly College of Education at Youngstown State University in Ohio, USA. Originally from Toronto, he continues to conduct research on antiracism, equity, and policymaking in education in, and on, Canada as well as within an international context. For 17 years he was a Senior Policy Advisor in the Ontario government, primarily in the Ministry of Education, where he worked on a range of equity in education policies, programs, and initiatives. With Darren E. Lund, he recently coedited a book entitled *The Great White North? Exploring Whiteness, Privilege and Identity in Education* (Sense). He is presently involved in collaborative research on democracy in education and environmental education.

Beverly-Jean Daniel is an Assistant Professor in the Faculty of Education, York University, Ontario, Canada, where she teaches in both the graduate and undergraduate programs. Her interests in the field of education include preparing teachers for working within an urban school setting, structuring antiracist pedagogy within teacher education curriculum, and a focus on women and gender studies in education. Some of her recent publications include "Developing educational collectives and networks: Moving beyond the boundaries of 'community' in urban education" and "The discourse of denial: How white teacher candidates construct race, racism and 'white privilege.'"

Jacques Désautels is a Professor at Université Laval's Faculty of Education in Québec City, Québec, Canada. For more than 30 years, he has been concerned with the pedagogical and ideological dimensions of science teaching. He has authored or coauthored several works and articles in the field of science education written from a socioconstructivist perspective. One of his main research interests is the type of power/knowledge relationship fostered by science teaching, particularly when viewed in terms of the encompassing "scientific literacy for all," an objective that appears to have achieved consensus in the field of science education. More specifically, he is interested in understanding how science education can aid social actors to develop the intellectual instruments, potential for action, and ability to mobilize that are required to participate in the politics of the technosciences. He coedited, with Roth, *Science Education as/for Sociopolitical Action* (2002).

Alexandra Fidyk is an Assistant Professor in the Department of Educational Foundations and Inquiry at National Louis University in Chicago, USA, where she teaches graduate courses in social justice in education, interpretive/critical research, and curriculum studies. She has worked in multicultural education in Canada with the Canadian International Development Agency in Kosovo and has taught secondary Language Arts (including ESL) in international schools in Japan, Colombia, and Egypt. Her interests lie in the areas of philosophy, identity, poetics, and ethics, with particular focus on silence and love in education.

Reinaldo Matias Fleuri is a Professor at the Sciences Education Centre of Santa Catarina Federal University (UFSC). He earned a doctorate in

Education from Campinas University, SP, Brazil, and has done postdoctorate work at Universitá di Perugia, Italy, and USP, Brazil. Since 1992 he has participated in the *Grupo de Trabalho de Educação Popular* (Popular Education Work Group) of the *Associação Nacional de Pesquisa e Pós-graduação em Educação* (National Association of Research and Post-Graduation in Education). He is president of the *Association pour la Recherche Interculturelle* (ARIC); he is a collaborator researcher of *Centre de Recherche sur l'intervention éducativ—CRIE* (Canadá); coordinates the research nucleus *Mover–Educação Intercultural e Movimentos Sociais* (UFSC); and is also a CNPq researcher and consultant. Reinaldo has published over a hundred articles in several national and international periodicals and specialized journals. Among his published books are *Universidade e Educação Popular* (NUP/CED/UFSC, 2001), *Educar para quê?* (Cortez, 2001), *Educação intercultural: Mediações necessaries* (DP&A, 2003); and *Disciplina e rebeldia na escola: Olhar da complexidade* (Liberlivros, 2008).

Dave Hill is Professor of Education Policy at the University of Northampton, England. For 20 years he was a regional political and trade union leader. He recently completed an International Labour Organisation global report on the impacts of neoliberal education policy on equity, democracy, and workers' rights, and lectures worldwide on this, and on Marxism and Education, to Trade Unions and Academic and Activist conferences. He is Chief Editor of the international refereed academic journal, the *Journal for Critical Education Policy Studies* (www.jceps.com). He cofounded the Hillcole Group of Radical Left Educators in Britain and, among other books, coedited a trilogy on schooling and inequality for Cassell and Kogan Page publishers. His most recent edited book, with Peter McLaren, Glenn Rikowski, and Mike Cole, is *Marxism against Postmodernism in Educational Theory* (Lexington Books, 2002). He has a number of forthcoming books on Marxism and Education, and Globalization/Neoliberalism/Education. He has published around a hundred journal articles and book chapters. He chairs the *Marxian Analysis of Schools, Society, and Education Special Interest Group* (MASSES) of AERA and is Series Editor for *Routledge Studies in Education* *and Neoliberalism*, and also Routledge Series Editor for *Studies in Education and Marxism.*

Heidi Huse is an Assistant Professor in the Department of English at the University of Tennessee at Martin, Tennessee. She teaches in-class and online writing and rhetoric courses. Her article critiquing "virtuous violence" rhetoric was recently published in the online journal *In Factis Pax.* She also coauthored an article, published in the *Journal of Basic Writing*, detailing her involvement in the design and implementation of a first-year writing program that addresses the needs of a diverse underprepared student population including international and nontraditional students. She has been an active member of the American Democracy Project at the University of Tennessee at Martin (UTM) since its inception on campus.

Georg Lind, born in 1947, is professor of psychology at the University of Konstanz, one of the six 'universities of excellence' in Germany, where he has been conducting research and teaching in the area of moral psychology, democratic education, and educational research for over 30 years. Dr. Lind has developed the *Moral Judgment Test* (MJT), a new method of measuring moral judgment competence, which has been translated into 30 languages, and is used world-wide for research and program evaluation. He created the highly effective *Konstanz Method of Dilemma Discussion* (KMDD) for fostering basic moral and democratic competencies, which is is used and taught in many countries, from grade school to professional schools, teacher education and also in other institutions (see his website at http://democracy-education.net). Dr. Lind is married and has three children.

Thomas A. Lucey is an Assistant Professor in the Department of Curriculum and Instruction at Illinois State University. He holds an educational doctorate from the University of Memphis in Instruction and Curriculum Leadership. His research areas include teacher education, financial education, and related social justice issues. He has several works in press, including chapters in the *Handbook of Research on Instructional Systems and Technology* (coauthored by Michael M. Grant) (Idea Group), and *Imagining a Renaissance in Teacher*

Education: Teacher Education Yearbook XVI. His edited textbook (coedited by Kathleen S. Cooter), *Financial Literacy to Children and Youth*, is scheduled for release in 2008.

Darren E. Lund is an Associate Professor in the Faculty of Education at the University of Calgary, Alberta, Canada, where his research examines social justice activism in schools, communities, and teacher education programs. Darren was a high school teacher for 16 years and formed the award-winning *Students and Teachers Opposing Prejudice* (STOP) program. For his doctoral research at the University of British Columbia, Darren won the *2002 Outstanding Dissertation Award* from the *American Educational Research Association* (Curriculum Studies). He has published numerous articles and book chapters and is creator of the popular online *Diversity Toolkit* project. Darren has been recognized with a number of honors for his social justice work, including being named a *Killam Resident Fellow*, the *Exemplary Multicultural Educator of the Year*, and a *Reader's Digest National Leader in Education*. He recently coedited a book with Paul R. Carr, entitled *The Great White North? Exploring Whiteness, Privilege and Identity in Education* (Sense).

Gregory Martin is a Lecturer in the Faculty of Education at the University of Technology in Sydney, Australia. His research interests include Marxist theory, critical pedagogy, and participatory activist research. He is currently a member of Australia's National Tertiary Education Union and the Gold Coast branch of Socialist Alliance.

Martina Nieswandt is an Assistant Professor of Science Education in the Department of Curriculum, Teaching, and Learning at OISE/UT, Toronto, Canada. She received her Ph.D. from the Christian-Albrechts University of Kiel, Germany. Since her immigration to North America her research has focused on the influence of motivation, affects, and social factors on meaningful understanding of high school science. Utilizing mixed-method approaches her classroom-based research integrates teacher professional development with an emphasis on teaching science through the integration of Science-Technology-Society in student-centered, inquiry-based approaches.

Michael O'Sullivan is an Assistant Professor who teaches international and comparative education and global citizenship education at Brock University in Saint Catharines, Ontario, Canada. Over the years Michael has worked as a social activist, human rights educator, and program officer in Latin America doing international community development work in partnership with popular organizations. He has taught at the elementary, secondary, college, and university levels. His current research interests include the challenges facing educators who teach from a social justice perspective, social movements, and education and social change in Latin America.

Jason M. C. Price is an Assistant Professor at the University of Victoria and is a former K-12 teacher, school administrator, alternative school founder, and international development executive. Dr. Price is of working class Irish/Scot and Aboriginal ancestry. He has lived, taught, studied, and traveled extensively in the "Fourth World" and has studied with Indigenous Elders in Canada, Central and South America, Ethiopia, Kenya, India, and South East Asia. Dr. Price has also taught in the Aboriginal Teacher Certification Program at Nipissing University in North Bay, Ontario, Canada.

Karim A. Remtulla is a doctoral candidate in the Department of Adult Education and Counseling Psychology at the Ontario Institute for Studies in Education at the University of Toronto. He holds a Master of Business Administration (York University) and a Master of Science in Information Resources Management (Syracuse University) degree. His research interests include activism and learning; humanism and constructivism in education; and the impact of the intersection of libratory pedagogies on education and learning in civil society. He has published in the *International Journal of Baudrillard Studies* and has presented at the World Conference on Educational Multimedia, Hypermedia, and Telecommunications, as well as the International Research Foundation for Development World Forum—

Conference on Digital Divide, Global Development, and the Information Society.

Ali Sammel works at Griffith University on the Gold Coast in Australia. Ali's research and teaching focus include the teaching and learning of science with a particular interest in social, environmental justice, and political issues; community-based activism; and the impacts of White privilege in education. She explores the world through the lenses of critical pedagogy and feminist poststructuralism.

Daniel Schugurensky is the Coordinator of the Graduate Program in Adult Education and Community Development at the Ontario Institute for Studies in Education of the University of Toronto (OISE/UT), and Associate Director of the Centre for Urban and Community Studies (CUCS), University of Toronto. Born and raised in Argentina, he studied at the Universidad de Buenos Aires, the Universidad Nacional Autónoma de México, and the University of Alberta. After working as a visiting professor at the UCLA Graduate School of Education and Information Studies, he joined OISE/UT in 1998. He teaches courses in popular education, sociology of education, citizenship learning, participatory democracy, education policies and politics, community development, research methods, Latin American education, and comparative education. He has published widely on a variety of educational and social issues. Last year, he co-edited the book *Ruptures, continuities and re-learning: The political participation of Latin Americans in Canada*. He lives in Toronto with his wife Laurie and their children Alejandro and Ana. For more information, Daniel's website is: http://www.oise.utoronto.ca/research/edu20/home.html .

Shazia Shujah is a Toronto native committed to social justice as a critical pedagogue, academic, and community activist. With an M.A. in Sociology and Equity Studies in Education (OISE/UT), her thesis critiques the Ontario curriculum from an antiracism perspective. Also, as an Urban Diversity specialist, she is currently a full-time elementary school educator committed to a pedagogy of empowerment for all of her students, one where they are encouraged to become active citizens of change. While teaching for over nine years in inner city Toronto, she has organized and engaged in numerous community events to help empower students and parents. Simultaneously, she has maintained her academic involvement at OISE, and has presented at various conferences and workshops.

R. Patrick Solomon is an Associate Professor in the Faculty of Education, York University, Ontario, Canada. His professional career as an educator includes teaching in elementary and secondary schools in Jamaica and Canada, being a school administrator in special education settings in Jamaica and Canada, and teaching at the university level in Canada. His current research projects include the impact of educational reform on teacher preparation for equity and diversity work in schools and communities, and community involvement, with a service learning approach to teacher education in Jamaica. Some of his book publications include *Urban Teacher Education and Teaching*: *Innovative Practices for Diversity and Social Justice* (2007) (with D. Sekayi); *Teaching for Equity and Diversity: Research to Practice* (2003) (with C. Levine-Rasky); *The Erosion of Democracy in Education: Critique to Possibilities* (2001) (with J. Portelli).

Lisa Karen Taylor is an Associate Professor at Bishop's University in Quebec, Canada. She completed her doctoral degree at the OISE/University of Toronto. As an ESL, EFL, and social justice educator of 20 years, she conducts research in critical multicultural, multilingual and "multi-literacies" education in multilingual contexts, as well as critical race, feminist poststructuralist, and postcolonial theory in education and teacher education. She has published in special issues on Critical Race Theory and Postcolonial Theory in *TESOL Quarterly* and *International Society for Language Studies Journal*. She is currently coediting a special issue of *Intercultural Education* on feminist anticolonial pedagogies and the reception of Muslim women's literary and cultural production.

Jennifer A. Tupper is an Assistant Professor in the Faculty of Education at the University of Regina in Regina, Saskatchewan, Canada, where she teaches in the area of social studies and curriculum. She is a former high school teacher and has worked in British Columbia, Alberta, and Saskatchewan. She received her Ph.D. in 2004 from the University of Alberta, where she was a Killam scholar. Jennifer's research interests include the intersections of citizenship education, race, culture, and gender as they inform curriculum; the challenges of transformative teaching in social studies; and the possibilities of treaty education in fostering student understanding of historical and contemporary relationships between First Nations and non–First Nations people in Canada. She is currently the principal investigator of a SSHRC funded research project titled "21st Century Citizens: High School Students Understandings and Experiences of Citizenship."

Suzanne Vincent is a Professor at Université Laval's faculty of education in Québec City, Québec, Canada. Her area of expertise deals particularly with sets of issues and problems pertaining to classroom interventions, school practices and knowledge, aspects of social and school exclusion amongst students, and social representations of citizenship. Her knowledge of socioeducational perspectives bearing on various institutional cultures, and the practices and actors found within them draws not only from the various research projects she is pursuing but also from her academic background in two distinct fields, education and political science, as well as her professional experience as a coordinator and researcher with different Québec government bodies (Conseil supérieur de l'Éducation and Ministère de l'éducation), where she carried out various analysis on behalf of the Quebec Minister of Education (briefs and annual report on educational management), and as an evaluator of the organizational models of administrative units on behalf of school boards.

Njoki Nathani Wane is an Associate Professor at the University of Toronto in the Department of Sociology and Equity Studies at the Ontario Institute for Studies in Education. Her areas of specialization include, but are not limited to, African Indigenous knowledge production, Black Canadian feminist thought, antiracist education, spirituality and schooling, and cultural knowledges and representations. She has published widely in the areas of the role of women in African Indigenous knowledge production, decolonization, antiracist education, and Black Canadian feminist thought. Her recent publications include: "Is decolonization possible?" in G. J. S. Dei & A. Kempf (Eds.), *Anti-colonialism and education: The politics of resistance* (2006, Sense); and "Black Canadian feminism thought: Renewed imagined possibilities," in N. Massaquoi & N. Wane (Eds.), *Theorizing empowerment: Canadian perspectives on Black feminist thought* (2007, Inanna).

Index

ABOUT THE EDITORS

Darren E. Lund (left) is an Associate Professor in the Faculty of Education at the University of Calgary, Alberta, Canada, where his research examines social justice activism in schools, communities, and teacher education programs. Lund was a high school teacher for 16 years and formed the award-winning Students and Teachers Opposing Prejudice (STOP) program. For his doctoral research at the University of British Columbia, Lund won the 2002 Outstanding Dissertation Award from the American Educational Research Association (Curriculum Studies). He has published numerous articles and book chapters and is creator of the popular online Diversity Toolkit project. Darren has been recognized with a number of honors for his social justice work, including being named a Killam Resident Fellow, the Exemplary Multicultural Educator of the Year, and a Reader's Digest National Leader in Education. He recently co-edited a book with Paul R. Carr, entitled *The Great White North? Exploring Whiteness, Privilege and Identity in Education* (2007).

Paul R. Carr (right) is Assistant Professor in the Beeghly College of Education at Youngstown State University in Ohio. Originally from Toronto, he continues to conduct research on antiracism, equity, identity, and policymaking in education in, and on, Canada as well as in an international context. For 17 years Carr was a senior policy advisor in the Ontario government, primarily in the Ministry of Education, where he worked on a range of equity in education policies, programs, and initiatives. He completed his doctorate in the sociology of education at the Ontario Institute for Studies in Education at the University of Toronto, with a thesis focusing on antiracism and transformational change in education. With Darren E. Lund, Carr recently co-edited a book entitled *The Great White North? Exploring Whiteness, Privilege and Identity in Education* (2007). He is presently involved in collaborative research on democracy in education and environmental education.

Studies in the Postmodern Theory of Education

General Editors
Joe L. Kincheloe & Shirley R. Steinberg

Counterpoints publishes the most compelling and imaginative books being written in education today. Grounded on the theoretical advances in criticalism, feminism, and postmodernism in the last two decades of the twentieth century, Counterpoints engages the meaning of these innovations in various forms of educational expression. Committed to the proposition that theoretical literature should be accessible to a variety of audiences, the series insists that its authors avoid esoteric and jargonistic languages that transform educational scholarship into an elite discourse for the initiated. Scholarly work matters only to the degree it affects consciousness and practice at multiple sites. Counterpoints' editorial policy is based on these principles and the ability of scholars to break new ground, to open new conversations, to go where educators have never gone before.

For additional information about this series or for the submission of manuscripts, please contact:

Joe L. Kincheloe & Shirley R. Steinberg
c/o Peter Lang Publishing, Inc.
29 Broadway, 18th floor
New York, New York 10006

To order other books in this series, please contact our Customer Service Department:

(800) 770-LANG (within the U.S.)
(212) 647-7706 (outside the U.S.)
(212) 647-7707 FAX

Or browse online by series:
www.peterlang.com